Pro ASP.NET 2.0 E-Commerce in C# 2005

Paul Sarknas

Pro ASP.NET 2.0 E-Commerce in C# 2005

Copyright © 2006 by Paul Sarknas

ISBN-13 (pbk): 978-1-59059-724-8

ISBN-10 (pbk): 1-59059-724-9

Printed and bound in the United States of America 9 8 7 6 5 4 3 2 1

Trademarked names may appear in this book. Rather than use a trademark symbol with every occurrence of a trademarked name, we use the names only in an editorial fashion and to the benefit of the trademark owner, with no intention of infringement of the trademark.

Lead Editor: Ewan Buckingham
Technical Reviewer: Fabio Claudio Ferracchiati
Editorial Board: Steve Anglin, Ewan Buckingham, Gary Cornell, Jason Gilmore, Jonathan Gennick,
    Jonathan Hassell, James Huddleston, Chris Mills, Matthew Moodie, Dominic Shakeshaft, Jim Sumser,
    Keir Thomas, Matt Wade
Project Manager: Kylie Johnston
Copy Edit Manager: Nicole Flores
Copy Editor: Kim Wimpsett
Assistant Production Director: Kari Brooks-Copony
Production Editor: Kelly Winquist
Compositor/Artist: Kinetic Publishing Services, LLC
Proofreader: Lori Bring
Indexer: Brenda Miller
Cover Designer: Kurt Krames
Manufacturing Director: Tom Debolski

Distributed to the book trade worldwide by Springer-Verlag New York, Inc., 233 Spring Street, 6th Floor, New York, NY 10013. Phone 1-800-SPRINGER, fax 201-348-4505, e-mail `orders-ny@springer-sbm.com`, or visit `http://www.springeronline.com`.

For information on translations, please contact Apress directly at 2560 Ninth Street, Suite 219, Berkeley, CA 94710. Phone 510-549-5930, fax 510-549-5939, e-mail `info@apress.com`, or visit `http://www.apress.com`.

The information in this book is distributed on an "as is" basis, without warranty. Although every precaution has been taken in the preparation of this work, neither the author(s) nor Apress shall have any liability to any person or entity with respect to any loss or damage caused or alleged to be caused directly or indirectly by the information contained in this work.

The source code for this book is available to readers at `http://www.apress.com` in the Source Code/Download section.

Contents at a Glance

PART 5 ▪▪▪ Core Development

PART 6 ▪▪▪ Order Fulfillment and Promotion

PART 7 ▪▪▪ Deployment

PART 8 ▪▪▪ Aftercare

Contents

PART 1 ■ ■ ■ The Basics

PART 2 ■■■ The Business Aspects

PART 3 ■ ■ ■ The Project Plan and Design

PART 4 ■ ■ ■ Architecture

PART 5 ■■■ Core Development

PART 6 ■ ■ ■ Order Fulfillment and Promotion

PART 7 ■ ■ ■ Deployment

PART 8 ■ ■ ■ Aftercare

About the Author

PAUL SARKNAS currently is the president of his own consulting company, Sarknasoft Solutions LLC, which provides enterprise solutions to a wide array of companies utilizing the .NET platform. He specializes in C#, ASP.NET, and SQL Server. Paul works intimately with all aspects of developing software including planning, requirements gathering, designing, developing, testing, and deploying.

Paul has worked with Microsoft technologies for almost a decade and has used .NET since its inception.

In addition to authoring and technical reviewing for Apress, Paul was the coauthor of *ASP to ASP.NET Migration Handbook: Concepts and Strategies for Successful Migration* (Wrox Press, 2003).

Paul is available on a consulting basis for any of your technology needs, including building an application, offering guidance for an existing project, and helping resolve a difficult scenario or business logic question.

You can contact Paul via his consulting company's website at www.sarknasoft.com or via his personal site at www.paulsarknas.com. He welcomes questions and feedback of any kind.

About the Technical Reviewer

FABIO CLAUDIO FERRACCHIATI is a senior consultant and a senior analyst/developer using Microsoft technologies. He works for Brain Force (www.brainforce.com) in its Italian branch (www.brainforce.it). He is a Microsoft Certified Solution Developer for .NET, a Microsoft Certified Application Developer for .NET, and a Microsoft Certified Professional, and he is a prolific author and technical reviewer. Over the past ten years he has written articles for Italian and international magazines and coauthored more than ten books on a variety of computer topics.

Introduction

In this book, I will use a real-world example to demonstrate how to construct a multitiered ASP.NET application that allows a business to sell its merchandise online. Using this real-world, case-study approach, the discussion will start with gathering the requirements. Then I'll go into designing and modeling the database, building the architecture, completing the code base, and finally compiling and deploying the production environment.

By following the case study in this book, you will be able to use the skills you've learned to expand a company's customer base and sell products online, thus increasing the company's profitability.

Who This Book Is For

The audience for this book includes developers who have experience building ASP.NET applications. Although that experience will help with the overall understanding of the information provided, it is also beneficial if you have some experience working with object-oriented principles and multitiered architectures.

How This Book Is Structured

This book is structured in a unique way compared to many of the other books you'll find on the shelves. Specifically, it covers the business-related issues of e-commerce in addition to covering the technological aspects.

The discussion will begin with an introduction of the fictitious company used for the case study; then I'll cover gathering the requirements, modeling the application, designing the database, establishing the architecture, coding the functionality, and finally deploying to the production environment.

Prerequisites

To follow along with the book's case study, you should have a few years experience working with object-oriented programming languages and an understanding of multitiered software applications.

In addition, you will need Microsoft Visual Studio 2005 or Microsoft Visual Web Developer Express and Microsoft SQL Server 2005 or SQL Server Express.

Downloading the Code

You can download the complete source code and database scripts used in this book from the Source Code/Download section of the Apress website (http://www.apress.com) and from the case study's sample website (www.littleitalyvineyards.com).

Contacting the Author

You can contact the author via psarknas@sarknasoft.com or via www.sarknasoft.com or www.paulsarknas.com.

PART 1

■ ■ ■

The Basics

The first three chapters of this book will introduce commerce systems, focusing on electronic commerce systems. After explaining commerce, I'll discuss the tools you'll use and the case study you'll examine throughout the remainder of the book.

■ ■ ■

CHAPTER 1

Introducing E-commerce Systems

Welcome to *Professional ASP.NET 2.0 E-Commerce with C# 2005*! Undoubtedly, this book has attracted you because you have built some e-commerce systems and have an intermediate to professional level of programming and development experience with Microsoft ASP.NET and C#. You probably want to take your development and programming skills to the next level. Well, this book will help you do just that.

Although many books on the market cover similar topics, this book will go beyond the competition; specifically, I will not only provide a great deal of engineering and development information but will also focus on the business aspects of creating, implementing, and maintaining an e-commerce system for your business. This focus will give you the information you need to build a successful e-commerce business.

In the process, this book will present a case study so you can examine the progression of how a retail store can enable its business with e-commerce to enhance its bottom line. After completing the book, you will be able to apply the concepts you have learned across many different industries within the marketplace.

I would like to thank you for your interest in this topic; I am confident you will find the information presented to be helpful in all your professional e-commerce endeavors. Without further ado, you'll start on your quest to build the best possible e-commerce system.

Defining Commerce

What exactly is commerce? It is a term used quite a bit in the English language today, and it happens to have different meanings in different contexts. Before I get ahead of myself, you should examine the actual definition of the word *commerce* from Dictionary.com:

> *Commerce: The buying and selling of goods, especially on a large scale, as between cities or nations.*

—Dictionary.com

As mentioned, the term has several meanings in different contexts. For this book's purposes, I will be focusing on commerce that pertains to the buying and selling of goods and services. Even though the previous definition refers to that action on a large scale, that doesn't necessarily have to be the situation.

Let's take the definition just one step further; I have discussed what only the term *commerce* means. However, I will be focusing on commerce that is conducted electronically, or what is commonly referred to as *e-commerce*, in this book. In other words, the commerce will be conducted over the Internet and through web-based software applications. You still need human interaction at some point in the transaction, such as when fulfilling and delivering the order, but much of the activity will be automated.

Studying the Benefits of E-commerce

Now that you have explored what commerce and electronic commerce are, what can you do with it? How can your business benefit from it? Imagine a small retail store that sells a small amount of products; these products consist mostly of handmade crafts that people would use to decorate their homes. This retail store is in a rural area and for the most part is known only to the locals of the area in which it is located. As a result of this retail store being known to only a small segment of people, the potential sales are limited. The reason is quite clear: customers who can drive to the physical location of the store within a reasonable amount of time will have the most likelihood of being repeat customers. Anyone who does not live within a relatively short distance will most likely take their business elsewhere. So, how can this particular retail store maximize potential sales?

If this local retail craft store can electronically enable its commerce activities, that effort will result in the greatest probability of maximizing sales and profits for the company. Why will this endeavor benefit the store? Well, this will be beneficial for a number of reasons. Probably the most advantageous reason to implement e-commerce is so the retail store can reach potential customers far beyond its current local limit. The store could even attract customers from countries around the world. In addition, no retail store hours will limit the sales as with the physical location of the store. The store hours of the e-commerce application (or *virtual store*) will have no restrictions; the doors will be open twenty-four hours a day, seven days a week.

The following are the primary advantages of having an e-commerce system:

- You can reach customers around the globe instead of a limited geographic location.

- You have the ability to be open twenty-four hours a day, seven days a week.

- You can automate the process of taking and fulfilling orders.

- In addition to automating the order taking, you can receive many more orders at one time than you can with one salesperson working at the physical store location.

While I'm mentioning all the positive aspects of enabling a business with e-commerce, I need to mention that these advantages are accurate *in theory*. It is important to keep in mind that you may encounter many challenges when it comes to e-commerce. In the next section, I will outline some of the common obstacles.

Examining the Barriers to Entry

After learning about all of these benefits, why wouldn't you want to enable your business with e-commerce? In most situations, having an e-commerce system will be beneficial. Then why do many businesses still not take advantage of the great technological advancements of the Internet and of e-commerce? The reasons are known in marketing or economical terms as the *barriers to entry*; these are issues preventing or discouraging people from entering into a new area of operating a business.

Some businesses can encounter the following barriers to entry when it comes to e-commerce:

- Aversion to change

- Intimidation or ignorance of technology

- Up-front investment and cost

- Inability for maintenance

- Improper coordination with shipping companies

- Inability to ensure the customer receives the merchandise

These are some of the reasons that prevent or discourage some individuals from entering into e-commerce. Aversion to change is probably the most common issue that prevents individuals from embracing such advancements. In fact, many individuals will simply be content with what they are accustomed to doing. For example, a small business owner who has been relatively successful for a number of years may not want to move to an e-commerce system because of the notion that the business has been doing fine for quite some time; basically, they just might not want to deal with such an enhancement. This kind of thinking is usually directly related to the second item listed—that many individuals today are still intimidated by technology and are not well versed in technological aspects of business. Therefore, this fear of technology (or of learning new aspects of technology) is a major barrier in the e-commerce marketplace. In addition, e-commerce will always require an up-front investment to establish such a system. Many companies will not view this cost as an investment but instead as an additional cost that cannot be justified at the given time. Other companies simply do not have the budget for such activities. Also, an advanced e-commerce system will have to be maintained over time, and that will discourage some.

Although these are all major factors that have the potential to prevent people from entering the e-commerce arena, another barrier to entry probably cannot be overcome for many companies in specific industries. This barrier is for companies that sell oversized items, such as companies that sell musical instruments, farming equipment, or perhaps heavy machinery. All the products these companies sell are traditionally very large. Customers will not want to pay extremely expensive shipping costs for these items (except in a few unique circumstances). For this reason, these types of companies are usually not in a hurry to enable their businesses with e-commerce capabilities. However, these companies could tweak their Internet presence strategies so that their websites become online brochures, or they could offer customers the option to pay online but then pick up the merchandise at the store location.

Although the topic of barriers to entry is large enough to fill several chapters, the goal of this section was to outline some of the main challenges you might encounter. You'll need to examine every situation on an individual basis and draft a strategy to overcome any such barriers.

Looking Forward

As mentioned, this book will not only give thorough engineering advice on how to build a solid e-commerce infrastructure but will also give information about the actual business aspects of the system. The engineering side will deal with thoroughly planning the system along with designing the database and modeling objects. I will also introduce project management so you can keep your client informed about the progress of the project and so you can efficiently manage your resources. You will use the best tools available for managing this project and building the system.

Summary

Well, you have arrived at the end of the first chapter, which defined e-commerce and how it can help maximize the potential sales of a business. Many more chapters are to come. In the next chapter, I'll discuss the main tools you will use in this book to build, manage, and complete a solid and scalable e-commerce system.

■ ■ ■

CHAPTER 2

Introducing the Microsoft Tools

When planning to build and design any kind of project or structure, whether it is a house or a software system, it is imperative that you obtain the right tools.

The tools you'll be using in this book are arguably the best available from Microsoft for building and managing software applications. You can break down all the tools into different environments: the development environment and the production environment. Each tool will have its own purpose within one of the environments or both.

This chapter will be fairly brief and primarily outline the following topics so that you can progress toward building the case study application of the book:

- The individual tools and software applications

- The development environment

- The production environment

Introducing the Individual Tools

The range of the tools you'll use consists of engineering and management tools. The following sections will briefly describe each and outline some of their major features that are relevant to this book and to building e-commerce solutions.

Visual Studio 2005

Visual Studio 2005 is a comprehensive integrated development environment (IDE). This is Microsoft's de facto development tool for building and designing .NET software and applications. You can use it to quickly develop a variety of multitiered applications such as Windows or client-server applications, web applications, and even mobile applications for devices such as cellular phones and personal digital assistants (PDAs).

Unique features of Visual Studio 2005 include debugging tools, IntelliSense, and other built-in features such as controls. These features will greatly aid your development effort when writing the code and when starting the maintenance and debugging process.

Finally, at the end of the development, Visual Studio 2005 lets you compile and deploy the code with only a few clicks.

Microsoft .NET Framework 2.0

The Microsoft .NET Framework 2.0 is the latest development environment that allows developers to take advantage of specific libraries. Having such a setup is referred to as *managed code*.

C# 2.0

C# (pronounced "see sharp") is one of many .NET-compliant languages from Microsoft that is an object-oriented programming language. Version 2.0 is the number of the overall programming language and is the latest version available.

Microsoft Visio or Visual Studio 2005 Class Designer

Microsoft Visio is a complete diagramming and modeling software tool. This will come in handy when modeling the system and architecture utilizing Unified Modeling Language (UML) and even when modeling and diagramming the database design. You can use Visio in more advanced ways by reverse engineering databases and generating code from class diagrams. For the purposes of this book, you will use Visio primarily for its UML and diagramming features.

If you do not own Microsoft Visio, you can certainly use the new Class Designer tool that is included with Visual Studio 2005.

SQL Server 2005

SQL Server 2005 is the latest database engine from Microsoft that provides enterprise data management along with business intelligence tools. This data storage mechanism provides a secure and scalable data management platform that you can use for a variety of applications when you need to manage a great amount of data.

A new feature included with SQL Server 2005 is compatibility with the common language runtime (CLR); in other words, it gives you the ability to write C# code within stored procedures in addition to Transact-SQL (T-SQL).

Internet Information Services

Internet Information Services (IIS) is the web server included in Microsoft Windows Server 2003. This will serve the requested web pages that are eventually built and displayed to the user.

SSL Certificate

A Secure Sockets Language (SSL) certificate is a standard used for web applications or e-commerce applications when sensitive data is transmitted from the client to the server. You can purchase a certificate from various sources, and it is integrated within the web server, which in this case is IIS. The cost of SSL certificates has declined considerably over the past couple of years. In Chapter 27, I will give extensive instructions for how to obtain and configure such a certificate.

Introducing the Development Environment

The development environment consists of everything you need to perform the preliminary work of developing, testing, and preparing to deploy the finalized application.

The following are included within the development environment:

- Visual Studio 2005

- SQL Server 2005

- Microsoft Visio or Visual Studio Class Designer

- IIS and SSL certificate

All these tools will be necessary to plan, develop, and eventually test the entire application, which you will ultimately deploy to the production environment (discussed next). In addition, all these tools will work in conjunction to produce the end result.

The size of the team that will be working on the project and application will determine how extensive the development environment will be. It is possible that only one person will be working on the entire project, which would mean the development environment would be confined to a single computer. On the other hand, several developers could be working on this project, and the environment could expand across an entire network or even allow for remote access.

Introducing the Production Environment

Discussing the production environment at this point of the book seems to be getting ahead of myself. However, it is extremely important to start thinking about it and start making some decisions now. This is because you must consider several factors, such as whether you'll host the application in-house or outsource the hosting to a company that specializes in such services. Several advantages and disadvantages are associated with either decision. You'll first look at purchasing the equipment and hosting the application in-house.

Going with In-House Hosting

As mentioned, hosting the e-commerce application in-house has advantages and disadvantages. You also need to consider other factors. For instance, who is your client? Is the client a large company or corporation? Is your client a small company with few employees? This is important because many larger corporations and companies will already have established data/server centers within their current infrastructure and will have enough employees to manage them. With this being said, I'll highlight the advantages and disadvantages of hosting the application in-house in the next two sections.

Advantages

The main advantages are the following:

- Nonfixed cost, usually on a monthly or annual basis

- Total ownership of equipment

Although these advantages are apparent, they of course come at a significant cost. In other words, for you to gain these advantages, you need a specific infrastructure or foundation in place. This comes in the form of having redundant power supplies and Internet feeds or connections. A small company with a cable or DSL Internet connection would not be able to host such an application and thus gain the associated benefits. You would need additional requirements of backup power generators and redundant Internet connections. As such, the following section explains the numerous disadvantages of hosting the application in-house.

Disadvantages

The following are several disadvantages:

- Extensive infrastructure required (including many servers, database servers, redundant networks, and power connections)

- Software licensing required

- Expensive to maintain

- Employees with specific skills and knowledge required

- Regularly scheduled upgrades and security maintenance

- Potential of many hours spent to maintain

By simply comparing the advantages and disadvantages, it is quite evident that hosting an application in-house is not in everyone's best interest. However, you cannot arrive at this decision by simply looking at these issues. Every company and client you deal with will be different in size and ability; therefore, you will need to analyze every situation for its own unique capabilities.

Larger clients and corporations will often already have an infrastructure set up that the e-commerce application can fit into nicely. However, for this book, you will be dealing with a small company (you'll find out details about the company in the next chapter), which will not have such an extensive infrastructure. Given this information, outsourcing the hosting is the best decision; I will discuss this in more detail in the next section.

Outsourcing the Hosting

Currently, many companies specialize in hosting web applications of all sizes. As a result of the increased number of companies offering such services, the competition is quite extensive, and competitive rates are passed onto the consumer. Therefore, you will find in many scenarios that outsourcing the hosting is the best choice. However, it is still a good idea to compare and contrast the advantages and disadvantages in the same manner as you did for in-house hosting.

Advantages

In many situations, the advantages will outweigh the disadvantages when outsourcing the hosting of an e-commerce application:

- They offer a competitive monthly cost.

- Specialists available for support on a 24/7 basis.

- Software licensing fees are leveraged through the hosting company.

- Upgrades and security patches are included.

- Regular backups take place.

- You can leverage the hosting company's redundant power supplies, redundant Internet connections, and security infrastructure.

To sum, the advantages of outsourcing the application hosting include having a monthly expenditure that is cost effective because you are leveraging the hosting company's expertise, support personnel, software licensing, and backup and redundant connections within their infrastructure.

Disadvantages

Along with the many advantages, outsourcing the hosting does have some disadvantages. They are the following:

- Monthly or annual fixed cost

- Nonownership of the hardware and equipment

- Limited or no control over the infrastructure or overall setup

It is apparent that the disadvantages are fewer than the advantages listed. The main disadvantage is that some companies or clients will see the monthly (or annual) cost essentially as "renting" the equipment; they may think that purchasing the equipment will be more advantageous and cost effective in the long run. However, as mentioned earlier, you need to consider many other factors when purchasing hardware or equipment. These additional factors are costly and usually can be justified only in larger corporations. Therefore, you can achieve more benefits in the outsourcing model for a much smaller cost with the monthly (or annual) fixed fee. You can think of this as simply a cost of doing business.

Therefore, in this book, the case study will use a hosting company under the outsourcing model.

Summary

In this chapter, I outlined the tools you will use throughout this book. I explained and compared the options available for how the application will be hosted. Although you might not think of this as a specific tool, it is critical to start thinking of the hosting options at this stage. As mentioned, you will use the outsourcing model for hosting in the case study because it involves a small company that does not have (or cannot afford) an extensive data/server center within the physical constraints of its office. This will become clearer in the next chapter, where I introduce the company of the case study. Let's move forward and learn about your client.

■ ■ ■

CHAPTER 3

Exploring the Company Background for the Case Study

In this book, to relate the building of an e-commerce system to real-world development scenarios as much as possible, you will follow along with a case study of a fictitious company. This chapter will outline all the details of the company, along with its industry, and show how building an e-commerce application will help the company. I will not only give the name of the company and where they are located but also give a brief history about who they are.

In addition, I will briefly describe how the company will have the ability and potential to expand its current customer base to all parts of the world as opposed to selling to primarily the local residents of the community only.

Lastly, I will explain why it is beneficial to utilize the case study approach as opposed to merely laying out the strict engineering aspects and being completely technical in a book of this nature.

Note In this book, I will use a fictitious company and name. All names of companies, products, and individuals are strictly fictitious, and any occurrences of real names are merely coincidences.

Getting Some Company Background

As mentioned, I will give you some history of the company used in this book's case study. The name of the company is Little Italy Vineyards, and as you have probably already guessed, it is in the wine business. Little Italy Vineyards has been a family-owned business since the early 1950s. It was founded by the current owner's parents, who were born in Italy and owned a vineyard there but wanted to move to America to raise their family. As a result, they moved to America after selling their vineyard in Italy and eventually started a new vineyard, Little Italy Vineyards, in California. Sales have been steady since the opening many years ago. However, the vineyard has to deal with a high level of competition. More specifically, they are located in Sonoma Valley, which is a well-known wine-making area and home to many vineyards. Many companies provide wine-tasting tours through the area, which produces many of the customers and potential sales. Although the wine-tasting tours bring in a lot of people to the area, many vineyards are competing for the same customers.

Throughout the following sections, I will outline the current situation of the company, how it currently operates, and who the competition is.

The Current Situation

Currently, Little Italy Vineyards has a steady flow of sales and many repeat customers. This has been the case with its volume of sales and customers since the company started. As a result of the company being family owned, its has been able to keep the overhead of staff and employees to a minimum by having many of the family members help in the day-to-day operations of the vineyard.

The vineyard can continue doing business as it has been for many years, but now the children of the family are going to be taking over the day-to-day operations when their parents retire. Therefore, the family has decided, after some careful thought, to expand the business and sales into the world of technology. More specifically, the family wants to sell its wine products online through a newly created website.

As it stands now, Little Italy Vineyards is old-fashioned in the sense that it does not use any modern technology in its current business operations. In fact, the vineyard still uses a great deal of paper and manual record-keeping methods. Currently, the vineyard accepts only cash and checks and would like to accept credit card payments. Sometimes, checks that are accepted for payment from customers are ultimately returned from that bank for nonsufficient funds, and the vineyard is unable to collect on these returned checks because the payment is ultimately never fulfilled.

As mentioned, the vineyard faces a great deal of competition. In the next section, I will outline the competition in more detail.

The Competition

In Sonoma Valley where the vineyard is located, several other vineyards are similar in size and also family owned. With this situation, a steady level of competition always has been present for Little Italy Vineyards. Many of the wines in the region are similar, and many customers develop a relationship with maybe one or two individual vineyards, which results in a potential lower amount of repeat customers to other vineyards.

It is this situation that has caused Little Italy Vineyards to step outside its normal business model and attempt to differentiate itself from the competition. By selling products online in addition to continuing to sell on the property, this will give the vineyard a competitive advantage—most of the local competition has not yet used technology to expand and sell wine online.

Moving Forward and Increasing Sales

Since Little Italy Vineyards has decided to enter the e-commerce business, this will obviously present a challenge and require a different type of thinking than in the past. The primary reason for this is because once Little Italy Vineyards is able to sell online and promote its products to a worldwide audience, its overall customer base will have the ability to expand immediately. This larger customer base will be the most beneficial aspect of expanding the business to an e-commerce platform. The natural question is, how will this expanded business take place specifically?

As mentioned, Little Italy Vineyards will experience the potential of a mass increase of sales as a result of selling its wine online. Why will this be the case? Well, let's take its original business model of selling wine only from the small store located on the vineyard grounds. When Little Italy Vineyards is selling its wine only on the premises, the potential volume of sales is not being maximized. Essentially all the customers are local residents, except for a few tourists who come in via a wine-tasting tour. Regardless how great the wine is, if individuals live far from the vineyard, most likely they are not going to visit the vineyard frequently.

Therefore, the family has decided to maximize the vineyard's sales potential by entering into e-commerce and selling the wine over the Internet. The results of expanding the vineyard's operations into e-commerce will maximize the potential of sales and eliminate the locals-only client base.

When the vineyard's business is enhanced and the online e-commerce application is complete, Little Italy Vineyards will have a potential customer base that has the ability to reach anyone in the world. The key word here is *potential* because the ability for anyone in the world to place orders through the Internet exists, but that does not necessarily mean that, say, customers in Japan or Australia will be purchasing the wine from the vineyard. Again, the key is that they would be able to do so if they wanted.

As stated, expanding sales and the customer base means customers who live far away from the vineyard can become customers for the first time. For example, customer A lives a short distance from the vineyard and likes the wine very much. Well, customer A has relatives in New York. During the holidays, customer A takes some Little Italy Vineyards wine to relatives in New York. Over the holiday dinner, the wine is consumed by not only the relatives who live in New York but also by some other relatives in town from Philadelphia and Pittsburgh. Everyone drinking the wine loves it and wonders how they can get more in the future. Customer A explains that the wine is from a small family-owned vineyard in California. Customer A also explains that the vineyard has a website. The other relatives enjoyed the wine so much that they visit the website in the next few days and purchase some additional bottles. Instantly, the relatives of customer A just became customer B, C, D, and so on, and so forth.

■Note If Little Italy Vineyards were not selling online, it would be up to customer A to buy the wine and send it to their relatives; this could certainly happen, but the likelihood of the relatives buying from the website themselves is much greater. In fact, this word of mouth can even expand to other customers.

Selling online will give Little Italy Vineyards a competitive advantage in the already highly competitive wine industry over their nearby competition.

Why a Case Study?

Using a case study when writing about technology—and more specifically in this case, building an e-commerce application—has many advantages. In this section, you'll examine why I decided to use the case study approach and how it will ultimately benefit you when taking on a project to build and implement an e-commerce application.

Everyone involved in this book wanted it to have a unique feel and approach. Many similar books on the market, for the most part, only give step-by-step instructions on how to engineer or build a software application. When that is the case, a great deal is left open to interpretation.

Using the case study model, the main focus is to eliminate most of this interpretation and present the instruction in the best possible real-world setting. For example, in the previous section, you were able to imagine a current customer taking some wine to their relatives during the holidays, resulting in Little Italy Vineyards gaining customers who live on the other side of the country. These examples are just the start of the benefits of using a case study, as opposed to merely showing the engineering aspects and loading the book full of code examples. In addition, a case study highlights the business aspects of e-commerce solutions, which you also need to consider.

Regardless of how great of an e-commerce application is, you'll encounter up-front investments and some ongoing maintenance costs. That is why paying attention to the business aspects of how it will expand the current sales is important to the overall process. Having a case study will show exactly how a company can benefit from selling online, and comparing how the company operated prior to expanding will demonstrate all the benefits.

■**Note** For the hard-core engineers who want details on code development and design, rest assured—this book will focus plenty of attention on that type of detail as well.

Summary

Now that I have introduced the company in the case study and have given information about its background along with its competition, you have reached the end of Part 1. You will now move on to the next part, which will deal with the business aspects of setting up and developing the e-commerce system for Little Italy Vineyards. Hard-core programmers (something I certainly consider myself) should not despair; you are not far away from rolling up your sleeves, digging into the design of the database, and actually coding the application within the architecture.

PART 2

■■■

The Business Aspects

The second part of this book will focus on the business aspects of building an e-commerce system, with particular regard to the case study. At the end of the day, whatever type of system you are building, it will have to generate revenue so it can be maintained and so it can justify the client's business model. The next three chapters will address the most important business aspects to consider when you commence building the actual e-commerce system.

CHAPTER 4

■ ■ ■

Gathering the Requirements

In a perfect world when you start building a structure such as a house, all the parties involved communicate all the details of the project in a detailed fashion. However, as you probably know, we do not live in a perfect world. You will certainly find that this is the case when developing software systems and applications. Typically, the client is not sure of what they want the system or project to do; or, they are aware of what they want it to do, but only conceptually. Regardless of what the client knows or can communicate, one factor seems to be a constant—the client wants the project completed as soon as possible. The phrase "I want it finished yesterday" seems to be common in the software world. This pressure from the client can often result in the developer or development team overlooking the requirements phase of the project and proceeding prematurely to the actual coding and development phases with only a slim idea about what they need to build.

In this chapter, you will explore the ins and outs of gathering the requirements from the client for your project. You will also examine the pressure to bypass this phase that clients and management teams often place upon the development teams. Specifically, I will answer the following questions in this chapter:

- What exactly is requirement gathering?

- Why is it beneficial?

- What is the Microsoft Solution Framework?

- How do you gather requirements?

- What are the official case study requirements?

What Is Requirement Gathering?

You may be asking, why is the author explaining to me what a requirement is? To answer this question, many development teams and companies overlook this phase and jump straight to the development phase as a result of wanting to get the project finished as soon as they can. A common quote attributed to Yogi Berra is, "If you don't know where you are going, how will you know when you get there?" This is applicable within this discussion because some developers and development teams indeed start building software applications without knowing what they're building. But how will you know for sure when the project is finished for your customer or client? The simple answer is, you never really will, and you can find yourself in quite the predicament.

This oversight in my experience has often led to the project duration being longer and more work being performed than necessary, thus creating more of an expense for the client.

After reading the previous paragraph, you are probably thinking that this is an overstatement. Perhaps it is; however, many projects today in the real world will be managed in this fashion, without requirements gathering, because of the pressure to produce a system as quickly as possible for the client. Many undesired results can arise from proceeding in this way. That is why it is much more beneficial to inform your client that taking the extra time in the beginning to discuss, gather, and document the specific requirements will almost always save a great amount of time at the end and produce a system that will function in the way it has been expected to function.

Now, I will briefly explain what a requirement is and then what the entire process entails. A *requirement* is a sometimes detailed—and sometimes not detailed—instruction that a system or finished product must include or perform. When in the context of software, a requirement is typically referring to a feature that the overall system needs to perform. For example, a requirement of an e-commerce system might be that the system will implement a customized shopping cart as opposed to a premade, third-party shopping cart.

Every system or structure needs to have an initial plan so that those constructing it know what they need to build. Therefore, when setting out to build a software application or an e-commerce application, you need to establish some type of blueprint, prior to taking the first step, that contains all the requirements.

You might be thinking that gathering requirements seems pretty simple to do. In reality, though, it will require a lot of work. In the following sections, I'll explain how to gather requirements.

THE MICROSOFT SOLUTION FRAMEWORK

The Microsoft Solution Framework (MSF) is a set of guidelines, principles, concepts, and proven practices for designing and engineering software applications with Microsoft technologies. These best practices allow all developers to take advantage of Microsoft technologies because following such guidelines will provide for the best possibility that your projects will be delivered on schedule, will be under budget, and will avoid the common obstacles that accompany every software project. The guidelines established within the MSF have been tested and used across many different projects in many different industries and therefore gives anyone following the guidelines an advantage from this past experience and expertise.

As with many topics in this book, the MSF is broad enough to have entire books dedicated to the topic. However, while you're learning about planning the project and gathering the requirements, it will be helpful to read the basics of the MSF provided by Microsoft.

To read about more about MSF, visit the MSF home page at `http://msdn.microsoft.com/msf/`.

How to Gather Requirements

Now that you know you have to pay proper attention to gathering requirements, let's discuss how exactly to go about collecting and documenting requirements.

The main method in which to gather and document the requirements for an application is to interview the client and discuss the functionality with the client and any other employees or managers. These individuals are the ones who have knowledge of the business functionality; in other words, they understand how their business in their industry operates while you as the engineer or developer might have little knowledge with this regard. You will need to ask extensive questions in these meetings to gain the fullest understanding of what the client expects and ultimately how the system needs to function. As a result of these numerous meetings and interactions, you can expend a great deal of time before you write even the first line of code. As mentioned earlier, this is the reason why many projects will bypass this phase of gathering thorough requirements. However, as mentioned, I have found that spending time gathering requirements saves time in the development phase.

In the following sections, I will assume you are not going to bypass this phase and that you will give the necessary time and attention to gathering and documenting the requirements.

Interviews

As mentioned, the primary and most effective method of gathering and defining the requirements for a project is to interview the clients, managers, employees, and anyone else in your client's company who will eventually be using the system you are building. These individuals should provide information regarding the specifics of their industry. Take, for instance, the client in the case study, Little Italy Vineyards; the company, of course, sells wine. You or the other engineers and developers might not know anything about wine or about selling wine. This is why having interviews and in-depth discussions about the business and what the clients expect will provide the knowledge necessary to complete the task.

Another reason why interviews and discussions are important to the success of the project is that the client might know only conceptually what they want as far as the system is concerned. They have hired you to build and implement the system because they do not have the expertise to do so. The discussions might have to follow a pattern where you present individual scenarios to the client to get their feedback. Regardless, it will require give and take on both ends for an exchange of information, because you'll be educating the client about technology and the client will be educating you and the development team about their business practices.

Documentation

After the interview process, you will undoubtedly accumulate many notes from meeting with several individuals. Most instances, these notes will be handwritten on some type of notepad. It is now time to formalize these notes into an official document and then pass it along to the client for approval. This document will also become a checklist for what functionality needs to be included in the system that is going to be built.

In addition to functioning as a checklist, the document will also act as an aid for what the client will expect from you as a consultant. This will help prevent against what is commonly referred to as *scope creep*. Scope creep describes a system that was originally intended to perform one set of functionality, but in the course of the development, additional features are requested. This can turn into a vicious circle and push the focus away from the initial foundation of the product or system. By creating an official requirements document and then presenting it to the client for approval, you can communicate that additions to the original requirements will entail additional time, resources, and costs.

The Official Requirements

I have discussed why it is beneficial to gather the requirements for a project, why oftentimes a development team will not give sufficient time for this phase of the project, and how to go about gathering and organizing the requirements. For the project with Little Italy Vineyards, you'll take the necessary time to not only gather the requirements but also to formally document them and present them to the management of Little Italy Vineyards.

In the following sections, I will outline what the requirements will be for the e-commerce application for Little Italy Vineyards. To incorporate the previous section within this process, I will give you some insight into the interviews that have been conducted with the managers and employees of the vineyard along with some of the notes and other information gathered during the process. This information will provide a template that you can build upon and even use in future case studies and projects.

Product Catalog

The product catalog will give the user the ability to browse the bottles of wine the vineyard is offering. Searching functionality will also be available to the user. Each product in the catalog will have an explanation of the individual wine. From the product catalog, the user will have the ability to add any of the individual products to the shopping cart, which will be explained in more detail in the next section. Lastly, the product catalog will have the ability to be maintained from the administrator control panel or from their content management system, which will be explained in more detail in the "Content Management System" section.

This information has been conveyed to you as a result of interviewing not only the manager of the vineyard but also some of the other employees who have worked there for many years and know how the business operates on a day-to-day basis. The manager expressed in the interview that it will be important for all the wines to be classified into different categories. In addition to the categories, the manager expressed a great concern that when a user or customer searches for a product, the search functionality should be flexible enough to provide as many results as possible for the user to explore and possibly purchase.

Shopping Cart

The system will have a customized shopping cart that will handle the products that are purchased; in addition, it will add the applicable sales tax and information about the user such as their shipping address. The user will have to either log in to their existing account or create a new account when finally checking out of the shopping cart and making the final purchase.

Through the interview process, the manager did not have any extensive concerns about how the shopping cart would function; it just needs to be user-friendly and not utilize another website to process the transactions. In other words, the shopping cart will be built into the Little Italy Vineyards site so the user won't leave the vineyard website to process their payment securely (which tends to portray a disconnection to the overall application and user experience).

PayPal Credit Card Handling

All transactions and purchases from the e-commerce system will be processed by using the PayPal software development kit (SDK). This will provide a merchant account for the winery along with the application programming interfaces (APIs) or web services necessary to communicate from the e-commerce application to the PayPal credit card transaction center. This will all be conducted over a secure channel utilizing a Secure Socket Layer (SSL) certificate.

The concerns of the managers at the vineyard are that they are not sure what costs will be associated with accepting credit cards because they have accepted only cash and personal checks to this point within their business. Because there are many options in which a company can accept credit card payments, the competition has increased over the past several years, thus yielding more competitive processing rates in the overall marketplace.

Therefore, PayPal will be a perfect match for the vineyard because the processing fees are kept at a minimum, and the vineyard will have easy access to the money processed from all transactions.

Tracking Information

The customer will be informed about when their order has been shipped so they can see the estimated time that the order will be delivered. Currently, a few companies provide these shipping services and even offer web services you can implement. In fact, if Little Italy Vineyards partners with only one shipping company, then it can incorporate that shipping company's technology into its website and allow the user to query this tracking information directly.

As a result of your interview with the manager of the vineyard, he has expressed he wants the e-commerce application to be able to supply the customers with as close to real-time shipping information as possible. His initial fear was that new customers might be leery of ordering from a small vineyard and wonder whether they would ever receive their goods that were ordered. Having real-time data and the tracking information from the carrier will most likely ease any of this hesitation.

Lastly, for the purposes of this case study and the development, the user will have the ability to view the tracking information that the administrator adds to the orders.

Content Management System

The contact management system will be extensive and consist of a number of components. More specifically, these components will provide the ability for an administrator to access a back end of the website and add, edit, and manipulate the content that the user will view. This will include managing customer orders, managing information on the site regarding the company, and managing the individual products being sold.

During the interview, the manager expressed he wanted to have the application be a "one-stop shop." In other words, the system needs to be inclusive in that not only can the customers make orders and track their information, but it needs also to be equally as simple for all the administrators and employees of the vineyard to access and fulfill the orders and respond to any questions or comments. Lastly, the products for sale will change on a regular basis, and it needs to be easy to add and alter products in the database to keep the workflow from slowing down. You will accomplish this by having the administrator control panel, or what is commonly referred to as a *content management system*.

About Us

The About Us section of the website and application will be quite simple in that it will give an overview and perhaps a history of the company. This area could be a static section, but to stay with the dynamics of the site, you will incorporate it as a section in which the administrator can add or alter the content from the content management system.

Including a thorough About Us section in the website will allow for the customer to understand the vineyard and its history. Creating an atmosphere of a family-owned-and-operated business is a key aspect of the business, according to the manager.

Contact Form

The contact form will be a generalized section that will allow a user to enter their name, e-mail address, and any comments or questions they might have. When the user has finished with the input, the information is then submitted to the company.

The manager of the vineyard expressed that he would like to see an easy way for the customer or potential customer to submit a question or comment from the website with little effort on the customer's part. As a result of having a brief contact form, any user will have the ability to send a question, comment, or feedback to the vineyard; and within only a few minutes time, they should receive a confirmation message saying that the message was successfully received by the vineyard and a response is not far away.

User Account Login

All users will be required to create a free account prior to making any purchases. On the site, the user will also be able to subscribe to a newsletter. In addition, the user will be able to view their account in a historical fashion. All history, purchases, and payment activity will be readily available. The account will be password protected and offer a mechanism for the user to have their password e-mailed to them if they happened to forget it.

Lastly, to ensure that sales are not being made to minors, the customers will need to agree to a disclaimer when registering for the account and ultimately making a wine purchase.

As mentioned earlier, the manager wanted to give the customer a feeling of comfort when purchasing from the vineyard, and allowing the customer to have the ability to log into their account at anytime and see the status of their order will extend this feeling of comfort.

Wine of the Month Club

A user can purchase a membership in the Wine of the Month Club and will be charged a monthly or annual fee to join the club. The benefits of the membership will be that the user will receive two bottles of wine per month that are determined by management.

This not only allows the subscribed users to try a different product each month but also acts as an advertising arm to promote the product and offer the potential for the customer to purchase additional quantities.

The concept of having a club with a monthly subscription was an important aspect that the manager expressed in his interview about the system. He thinks that it will help promote additional sales but also that it will give the customer a feeling that they are part of a special segment of customers and thus get special benefits and discounts that those who are not members of the club do not get.

Age Verification

Since the product that is being sold is regulated by the government and has age restrictions associated with it, you will need to implement a verification process that will ensure that those making purchases are at least a certain age.

As a result of the vineyard being located in the United States where the legal drinking age is 21 years of age, the manager expressed a great concern of the possibility that customers who are underage and have a credit card will be able to buy wine. This could result in legal implications and expensive fines if this were to happen; in fact, the vineyard would be held accountable by the government. Because of this concern and potential liability, the system needs to have a disclaimer so the customer can agree to the terms indicating that they are of age. The manager is adamant about having this kind of functionality since the vineyard will not be able to afford any type of legal action or expensive fines. All sales will need to verify that the customer making the purchase meets this age requirement. Sales in different countries will have different restrictions that you also need to consider.

■**Note** This case study and book is not meant to act as a legal counsel, which is certainly beyond the scope of this publication. However, we will provide a disclaimer that will act as a form of a contract that the user or customer will agree to prior to making a purchase.

Summary

Throughout this chapter, I discussed a great deal about gathering and documenting the business requirements in order to build a complex e-commerce application. I mentioned several times in this chapter that although the phase of gathering the requirements is important, people often overlook it because of time constraints. When a time constraint is presented and the temptation is there to not pay adequate attention to this phase, remember that skipping this phase could result in a greater expenditure of time and money toward the end of the project.

■ ■ ■

CHAPTER 5

Turning Sales into Profits

Regardless of what type of business is being conducted, one fact is quite obvious: the business has to generate enough revenue to exceed its overall expenses. If this is not true, the company will ultimately lose money and cease doing business.

In this chapter, I will discuss all the business aspects of maximizing sales by developing a new e-commerce website and of attaining the ultimate goal—profits. Specifically, I will discuss the following in detail:

- Selling the main product or products

- Selling and recommending affiliate products

- Partnering with similar businesses

- Creating a membership with monthly dues

- Selling advertising space

Throughout the chapter, I will show how all these business topics relate to the case study of Little Italy Vineyards.

Selling the Main Product

The most obvious way to turn sales into profits is for a company to sell its own products and services. However, even as obvious as it seems, it is worth discussing this topic. The main advantage of selling your own product online is that *you* have the most control over your product, including how much to sell it for and ultimately what your profit will be. Selling your own product will undoubtedly create the largest profit margin for the company. This is because of several reasons. First, your product is exactly that—your product. No one knows the product better than you, and no one knows what your product consists of or how much cost is involved when creating your product. From this, you can determine your exact costs and then add the appropriate markup to the product when you sell it to your customers. How much this markup will be is up to you. Lastly, since the product is yours, when your customers embrace the product—regardless of whatever it is—they will associate you and your company with the product.

Selling Affiliate Products

The next aspect of turning sales into profits might not be quite as obvious as the previous. However, it is equally as important as selling your own products. You can turn sales into profits not only by selling your own products but also by selling affiliate products. *Affiliate products* are all the products or services that have a strong relation to your own product. These aren't items you produce or create yourself; they are items that are provided from a supplier but are sold with a markup. You sell the other company's product for a possible percentage or some type of commission.

For example, in the case study, the primary product is the wine from the vineyard; however, several products are closely related to wine and can be sold. These include wine glasses, wine racks or shelves, wine toppers, wine openers, corkscrews, and maybe even a guide or manual explaining wine and explaining what foods go best with the different types of wines. You can sell all of these additional products to customers since they are closely related. These sales will probably account for the second most sales and profits next to selling the company's main products. For example, when a customer is purchasing wine, if you can show them some affordable wine glasses, the customer might just add the wine glasses to their shopping cart and thus increase the overall sale.

■**Note** When a customer is purchasing a product on your site and you offer them some related product, this is known as *upselling*. You can upsell an affiliate's products or even your own products.

Within the case study of Little Italy Vineyards, the affiliate products that will be sold are wine glasses, wine racks, and a guide about wine and what foods best accompany the wines.

Partnering with Similar Businesses

When a business is just starting or has limited cash flow, one of the best ways to increase sales and gain more customers is by creating various partnerships with other companies that are in a similar business or industry. This kind of formal networking can have a profound effect on increasing your visibility with potential customers. In addition to partnering with companies that are similar, another advantage is to partner with a company that is involved in a related business.

For example, Little Italy Vineyards wants to sell wine glasses. To do this in the most efficient manner, by partnering with a household appliance store or a glassware company, Little Italy Vineyards can offer its customers additional products. This is a more formal relationship than just being affiliates.

The main benefit of aligning your business with other businesses is to leverage each other's advertising and market exposure. Lastly, there is essentially no risk to either company involved and typically no up-front cost. Until a sale of a product is made, the other company involved will not be paid anything; in addition, both companies have it in their best interests to sell as much as possible.

Creating a User Membership

An effective program to incorporate into your e-commerce business is to establish some sort of membership for your users and customers. By offering this type of service with benefits, the users will gain a feeling of acceptance from the company. In other words, they will feel like they are in a special group of customers beyond the regular, everyday customer.

This also helps overall sales for the company primarily because it is a fixed fee for a specified amount of time, usually a year. If a customer enjoys the membership's benefits, they will probably continue to renew their membership, establishing recurring revenue for the company.

For example, Little Italy Vineyards is going to offer a Wine of the Month Club based on an annual fee. The customer will pay a fixed fee to join and subsequently will be sent two select bottles of wine per month. The members will receive regular shipments of wine, and the company hopes the customer will purchase additional bottles of that particular wine.

As you can probably see, this can be a strong technique for advertising as well. In addition to the customer or member receiving the two bottles of wine a month, by paying for a membership they will also have access to other features such as information about wine and all the different types available at Little Italy Vineyards.

Selling Advertising Space

Last in the discussion of how to turn sales into profits, but certainly not least, is using your website or e-commerce application to sell advertising space. This can be a solid revenue stream for any type of business. Although this can be beneficial, it will probably have to wait until the e-commerce application has been established for a while. In other words, in order to sell advertising space, you have to have a significant amount of traffic coming to your site, which will take some time to establish. As opposed to the previous methods where they were the main focal points of revenue streams, selling advertising space will most likely yield a lower amount of profit. It is usually supplemental revenue, but at the same time it is an aspect you should consider. After all, the more revenue coming in, the bigger the company's profits.

To expand in more detail about selling advertising on your website, most sites sell small banner ads that appear somewhere on the site. For example, perhaps your company will sell advertising space to a glass company that sells only wine glasses or maybe a company that sells wine racks and shelves.

Summary

Within this short chapter, I discussed how to make profits for your company from your e-commerce application. You already know that a company has to attain profits at some point to keep it in business. By creating an e-commerce application, you can make profits from not only your main product but also from other companies' products and from advertising.

These different techniques have shown over the years to be quite beneficial to an e-commerce business. They give your e-commerce business a high probability of maximizing its overall sales. However, you have no guarantee of making profits when you embark on an e-commerce project; risk will still be present. In the next chapter, you'll examine in more detail the associated risks of e-commerce and how to be best prepared.

CHAPTER 6

▪▪▪

Examining the Risks

In the previous chapter, I discussed some strategies for turning sales into profits for your company and selling your product and others online. However, up until this chapter, I have not discussed in depth the associated risks of opening your business to e-commerce and selling online.

When moving into e-commerce, often the owners and managers of the business will have many concerns and wonder how they will safeguard against the risks. Your job as a consultant is to inform them of the risks and how you will design and implement prevention mechanisms to minimize all the risks and put their minds at ease.

Therefore, in this chapter, you will examine the associated risks of e-commerce, along with the proper safeguards to implement. This discussion is not meant to discourage any business from conducting business online but merely intends to bring up the major issues before you start designing or building any part of the e-commerce system.

Specifically, this chapter will cover the major risks associated with having and maintaining an e-commerce system along with accepting and transacting payments from customers. I will discuss the following concepts along with the best practices of how to minimize the risk as much as possible:

- Supply for the demand

- System downtime

- Payment processing

- Physical and logical attacks

- Sensitive information and data

These items are some of the most common in e-commerce and are likely to lead to questions from your client. Let's waste no time and continue to the first item of discussion.

Supply for the Demand

To begin the discussion of the risks associated with e-commerce systems, I will discuss something that you probably don't think of as a risk but that can ultimately pose a great threat to the company overall: not having enough supply for the demand. What does this mean exactly? Well, this refers to the company not being able to produce or manufacture enough of its product to meet the potential demand that an e-commerce system will yield. I use the phrase *potential demand* because in theory opening your business up to e-commerce will expand your geographical region to the entire world. But you may not see your sales and orders grow exponentially overnight once your system is implemented; still, if the proper marketing and advertising is in place, over a short time it is possible that the business will have many more orders than in the past. And that can cause supply-and-demand problems.

Let's again refer to the case study. Before Little Italy Vineyards begins selling its wine online, the sales are primarily limited to the local community and any visiting tourists. When the company starts selling the wine online, the customer base really has no boundaries. What does this mean? The vineyard could be bombarded with orders, possibly too many for the small business to accommodate. What is the maximum amount of wine the vineyard can produce for a given time, such as over a three-month span? If the vineyard cannot handle or produce sufficient quantities, this might turn away customers who then go to another vineyard that has the wine in stock and ready to ship. Therefore, when you don't have enough supply to meet the demand, the potential for lost sales can be high. This could be damaging to the business overall and can counteract the act of selling online. So, what can you do to prevent or prepare for such an event? Answering this question will be of the utmost benefit to the company and your client.

The best preventative medicine for this is to, in the beginning of the planning phase, determine the maximum quantity of products that can be produced in a given amount of time. This will give the company the threshold they can withstand regarding demand. Having this knowledge will keep the company prepared when demand exceeds the supply. When this is the case (although it is a good problem to have), the company can take a number of actions to protect itself. For example, you can tell the customers from the beginning how many products the company has for sale. In other words, when the quantity or inventory begins to dwindle, you can display a message to the customer informing them that supplies are limited or that the order might take additional time to be fulfilled. Being up front with the customer will help ensure you have a happy customer, and usually a happy customer is a repeat customer. If this is not implemented and the customer simply places the order assuming the product will be delivered shortly after the sale is completed, your company will run the risk of keeping the customer waiting. Most customers do not have a great deal of patience; however, keeping them informed will help prevent customers from taking their money to your competitor.

System Downtime

The nature of selling your products online is that the products are available 24/7. If your e-commerce system should happen to crash or be unavailable for any number of reasons, your company can lose a great deal of sales. Not only will customers simply not be able to place an order, but also this will hurt the reputation of your company for future sales because the customer might take their business elsewhere.

A system can go down for many reasons: too much traffic for the web server to handle at one time, a power outage, a hardware failure . . . just to name a few. The best way to minimize downtime is to use a reputable server-hosting company. These companies have an infrastructure that would be expensive to duplicate. They have backup power supplies and generators, backup Internet connections, and monitoring equipment. Since there is a great deal of competition between hosting companies, you can find competitive and affordable pricing.

Processing Payments

Accepting payments when selling your products online will undoubtedly need to be in an electronic form. In other words, you will need to accept credit cards and possibly even electronic checks. This has become the standard practice of paying for merchandise when buying online. Your customers will expect to use this payment method. However, people may have a certain fear of accepting credit card payments, and most important, you will need to assure your customers that your system is taking all the necessary prevention methods to protect their data when ordering from your company online.

To protect your customers' credit card information, you need to transmit all sensitive data over a secure connection. You can implement this secure connection with a security certificate, more commonly referred to as a Secure Sockets Layer (SSL) certificate. With this certificate installed on the web server, all information passed through the secure channel will be encrypted and therefore will prevent someone from intercepting the transmission from the client to the server.

Another option to consider is to not use and implement your own SSL certificate and instead leverage that of the processing company. For instance, when using PayPal as the credit card–processing company, you have many options. The ability is available to process your own transactions in the sense of implementing your own SSL certificate, or you can leverage a premade shopping cart and use the associated security that the processing company ultimately provides. The decision will usually become clear after the system or application that is being built is defined. In either case, it is good to always be aware of the options available.

Lastly, the best practice to use when and if it is necessary to store any sensitive data within the system is to encrypt the data, making it difficult for an intruder to access and interpret this data. You should implement this regardless of how you will actually process the credit card transactions.

Physical and Logical Attacks

Having any system available to anyone on the Internet poses the risk of it being attacked by an intruder. This form of attack can be malicious and be by someone purposely looking for sensitive data such as Social Security numbers, credit card data, or checking account information. Another kind of attack could be to simply disrupt your system from running properly by infecting it with a virus or just slowing down the system. Let's look at these different types of attacks in more detail.

Physical Attack

A *physical* attack is an attack that is focused on the system's hardware or infrastructure. This happens when a hacker is not necessarily looking for sensitive data but perhaps just wants to disrupt a system. The intruder could infect the system with a virus that looks for e-mail addresses and uses its own Simple Mail Transfer Protocol (SMTP) server to spam the recipients it finds. This might turn out to cause less damage to the company than if sensitive data were stolen; however, this kind of attack can certainly result in a great deal of downtime. It also opens the door to other attacks, namely, a logical attack, which I will discuss next.

Logical Attack

A *logical* attack is an attack that is focused on the system or the software. This happens when a hacker targets the code and the software looking for a flaw or vulnerability that will allow them unauthorized access. From this targeted attack, the hacker will most likely want to be looking for any sensitive data that is stored in the system.

A likely scenario is using a password cracker to force its way into a user's account. This attack usually will have the intent of gaining access to sensitive information and data while gaining access to the account. If this attack is successful, it can do a great deal of damage not only to your system but also to your customer and ultimately the company's reputation.

Now that I have discussed different types of attacks, I'll discuss how you can take proactive and preventative measures against these possible attacks.

Prevention

The possibility of attacks to your e-commerce system will always exist. The important aspect to be educated on is how to use the best practices available to ward off, prevent, and be prepared for any type of attack to your system.

Prevention will come in several varieties. I'll now talk about preventative measures for physical attacks. Since physical attacks are geared toward the hardware and infrastructure, the best prevention for this is to have your e-commerce system hosted in an environment that has a sophisticated security infrastructure in place. That is why it is best to turn to hosting companies that specialize in maintaining and protecting server infrastructures. Leverage their expertise and their around-the-clock monitoring of the infrastructure. In the event of a successful attack, by hosting your system with a reputable hosting company that has extensive monitoring, you can quickly quarantine the attack and therefore prevent the damage that can result.

When dealing with logical attacks, the hosting company will help to some degree. However, since they are targeted more to the software and code, it will be up to the development practices that are implemented to give the best prevention. You should use encryption for all sensitive data, and you should use stored procedures and no inline SQL to avoid SQL injection attacks and password protection.

Sensitive Information and Data

Regardless of what you or your client intends on selling online, you will be dealing with the user or customer's personal data, oftentimes referred to as *sensitive data*. The most common form of this type of sensitive data is credit card information. All sales within an e-commerce system will be paid for via a credit card from the consumer. When this sensitive data—in other words, the credit card number, expiration date, and many times the security code located on the back of the card—ends up in the hands of an unauthorized user, it can obviously create numerous problems. This data usually presents a potential risk in two distinct areas. The first issue is the transmission of the actual credit card data from the client or customer to the system, and the second issue is the storing of the credit card information within the system database. To safeguard the system as best as possible, you will need to consider your options regarding the processing of credit card transactions.

With that said, many different options are available when choosing a credit card–processing company. This is a result of a great deal of competition and the payment-processing companies all attempting to gain the business of e-commerce businesses. Since there is a lot of competition, it is best to shop around and gather as much detail as possible before committing to a specific processing company.

It is also important to consider and research the options that are available from the local banking establishments because the client you are perhaps implementing an e-commerce system for might already have a longstanding relationship with a bank. The systems available from banks, just as the other processing companies, often have the ability to easily integrate within your code base.

So, credit card processing is an absolute must when selling online. When selling online, the customer expects to pay via a credit card. Therefore, obviously there is no workaround to this particular item or risk. Many consumers are comfortable, or are becoming comfortable, purchasing merchandise online by using a credit card. So to keep up with the competition, your company will obviously have to accept credit cards to pay for the merchandise it sells. However, you don't necessarily have to store or save a user's credit card information within the database of the system. The benefit of storing the information is that when the customer returns to your site as a repeat customer, they do not have to reenter their payment or credit card data. But storing this sensitive information in a database, while being convenient for the customer, presents a potential security risk. How is this sensitive information stored? It is stored as plain text in the database? No, this plain text could be easily read by the naked eye if someone were to intrude the system and extract the credit card information. Can you store the data in a safe method? The answer is yes; a best practice is that if you are going to store any sensitive information within your database, then you must encrypt the sensitive data. If the sensitive information is encrypted, then if an intruder is able to see the information, they will not be able to interpret or use that information so readily.

Sometimes you need to store and recall a user's credit card information, such as when you charge a recurring fee for a service or product, perhaps on a monthly or quarterly basis. A good example is the monthly subscription or even the Wine of the Month Club mentioned earlier. To alleviate any concern for your customers, encrypt the data, and then assure the customers you are encrypting this sensitive data and that no one will have ready access to it. This will be important to convey since there is an abundance of credit card and identity theft these days on the Internet.

Summary

In this chapter, you examined the major risk factors of entering into e-commerce. Along with noting the risks, I offered solutions and workarounds so you can be as prepared as possible and incorporate all the appropriate security. If you are a die-hard programmer or member of a development team that builds e-commerce systems, you're in luck—the next chapter will focus on the architecture and on building the system.

PART 3

■ ■ ■

The Project Plan and Design

The third part in this book will focus on the phase immediately before actually coding and developing the system. This phase includes designing the objects that will be utilized, designing the database schema, and setting up and organizing the Visual Studio 2005 solution.

CHAPTER 7

■ ■ ■

Modeling Objects with UML

Modeling a software system is a phase that almost always needs to be performed before actually coding the system. Undoubtedly, some type of modeling will take place for most systems. This can be some simple diagrams sketched on paper or can be the best scenario—using a formal modeling structure, namely, Unified Modeling Language (UML).

UML is a language that represents how a system or application will behave, how it will interact with the user and other components within the system, and how it will process data. To complete this chapter, you do not have to be a UML expert; however, you will need some fundamental knowledge of UML. Since including a complete reference or tutorial on UML is outside the scope of this publication, you can read more about the basics of UML at the Object Management Group site (`http://www.uml.org`). This nonprofit consortium produces and maintains the standards for UML, and its website contains UML documentation and tutorials.

This chapter will outline all the details necessary to thoroughly model the project for the Little Italy Vineyards case study. You will be utilizing UML with Microsoft Visio to create the different modeling designs and diagrams. I'll cover the following with regard to the case study:

- Activity diagrams

- Use cases

- Class diagrams

Prior to modeling the case study system, you'll look into the basics of why it is beneficial to take the time in a project to implement this formal type of modeling and designing.

Benefits of Object Modeling

Formally modeling your software system prior to performing any coding has many benefits. The main benefit is that you'll gain a thorough understanding of what exactly the system will need to perform. Having this thorough understanding of the system will allow for the utmost scalability and the best performance possible. This is because while modeling the system at a macro level, along with the individual micro levels, you'll create a blueprint for how information will flow through the system. At the onset of developing a software system, the individuals involved might assume they know everything that the system is required to do or perform. But it's only by thoroughly modeling the system that you'll truly know how the system should behave, how it should interact with the user and other components within the system, and how it should process data.

Activity Diagrams

A common diagram used within UML is an *activity diagram*, which represents the flow of the business logic of your system. The activity diagram will detail a specific task, or *scenario*, and how the system will accommodate the individual scenario. It will give a high-level view of the operation and is like a common flowchart. Although a single activity diagram might outline and model the system at the highest level, several other activity diagrams will show the functionality of the many individual scenarios that comprise the entire system. For example, a common scenario for an application is when a user logs into their account. At the level of the user, they will see the web page that will allow them to enter their username and password; however, as you are aware, several functions are executing behind the scenes. To model this scenario, you would create an activity diagram using UML to show the business flow of a user logging in to the system and how the business flow is handled.

Modeling these different scenarios that occur within your software system will help you understand how to develop and code this functionality. The activity diagrams will eliminate many of the surprises that would be otherwise present if this phase of modeling were not performed.

Within the following sections, I will discuss the high-level functionality that the Little Italy Vineyards e-commerce system is going to include. In other words, I'll define the scenarios that make up the high-level activity diagrams. Prior to learning how to design the activity diagrams, refer to Table 7-1, which identifies the symbols that I'll use in the activity diagrams.

Table 7-1. *Activity Diagram Symbols and Objects*

Symbol/Object	Description
Solid black circle	Demonstrates the initial state of the activity
Arrow	Shows the flow of action between different activities
Oval/rectangular	Presents a specific action state
Diamond	Represents a decision that proceeds in one way or another
Black circle/clear edge	Demonstrates the final state of the diagram

Searching

The first activity diagram will outline the searching functionality within the e-commerce system. The user will have the ability to enter criteria for searching; regarding the case study, this will usually be a name of a specific wine or type of wine. Since this is a high-level view, the diagram will outline two occurrences. First, if the search functionality finds results in the database, the results will be displayed to the user so they can browse in further detail. Second, if the search functionality doesn't find any results matching the criteria, the user will be informed and provided with the opportunity to return to the search page to search again. Figure 7-1 shows the Search Activity diagram.

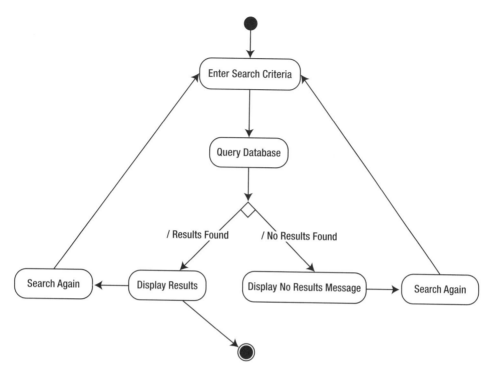

Figure 7-1. *Search Activity diagram*

As shown in Figure 7-1, after the initial state, the user will enter their search criteria. Specifically for the case study, the individual criteria will be the name of the wine, the type of the wine such as red or white, the range in price, and finally the age of the wine.

Adding Items to the Shopping Cart

After users search for their items, they will browse through the results listed. Upon finding an item or product they want to buy, they will click the button to add the product to their shopping cart. Figure 7-2 shows the Shopping Cart activity diagram.

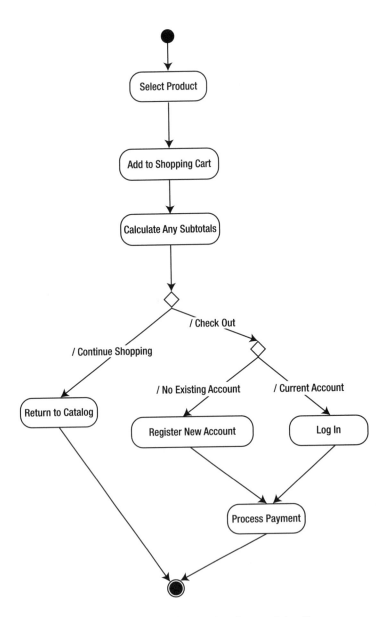

Figure 7-2. *Adding items to the Shopping Cart activity diagram*

As mentioned, the customer will add various items to the shopping cart during their shopping experience on the site. Once they add the items to the shopping cart, the subtotals and any associated fees will be added and summarized for the user. At this point, the user can then continue shopping or decide that their order is complete and therefore check out and pay for the merchandise. As shown in Figure 7-2, when the user decides to finalize the transaction, they will have the ability to log in to the current system if they have an existing account. If they do not have an existing account, they will need to register their information and establish a new account. Later in the "Account Registration" section, I will show an activity diagram reserved for this process. However, in this instance, when a new account is completed, the user will not have to register again; instead, when returning, they will need to merely enter their newly created account credentials. Finally, after the user logs in with already established credentials, the final step will be for the user to enter the payment or credit card information.

Checking Out

When the user has finished shopping and wants to check out, pay, and finalize their order, several steps will need to occur for processing this task. The next activity diagram, Checking Out, will illustrate this very process. Figure 7-3 shows that after the decision has been made to finalize the order, the user needs to enter the payment information (most likely the credit card number) with the shipping address, which may or may not be the same as that of the billing address of the credit card. The payment is processed by sending the payment information to the credit card processing gateway, and then a response is returned. This response is one of two possible items. Either the transaction is accepted and the payment has been processed or the payment has not been accepted. The payment may not be accepted for any number of reasons, and typically a code will explain why.

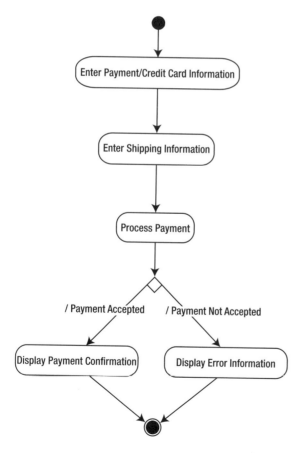

Figure 7-3. *Checking Out activity diagram*

Examine the diagram in Figure 7-3, and walk through the ordering process. As mentioned, the user will enter the billing information along with the billing address and finally the shipping address. After entering this information, the user sees a summary displaying all the information they have entered so that they can verify the entry. If they are satisfied with the entry and accept the verification, they can then confirm the order, which will submit the payment to the payment gateway. Once the payment information is submitted to the payment gateway, the system will be looking for a return response.

This response will contain significant information. The most important information within the response will be a notification or identifier about whether the payment was processed successfully. If the payment was transacted successfully, the response will contain a confirmation code. When this is the case, as shown in the diagram, this information will be displayed to the user on the next web page. On the other hand, if the payment is not successful and the money has not changed hands from the customer to the company, an indicator will explain why the payment was not accepted. It could be that the credit card information was not found, an expiration date was not correct, or there was not a sufficient amount of credit available on the customer's credit card. These are a few of the many possible reasons. Regardless of the reason, the system will take the user to a web page informing them of the reason why the payment was not completed. From this point, the user can reenter their payment information or close the application (and possibly return later to buy the product). Perhaps they will need to get in contact with their credit card company or wait until their next payday to buy some Little Italy Vineyards wine.

Processing Abandoned Shopping Carts

Each time a customer adds items to the shopping cart, the information is stored in the database. I'll explain this in more detail in future chapters; however, at this time I'll explain the concept from a high level via an activity diagram. As you probably have already guessed at this point, when a user adds an item to the shopping cart, they may not always continue to the end of the process by checking out and completing the transaction. So, what happens to the items that are added to the shopping cart that is never finalized? The answer is that the ShoppingCart table will begin to have many abandoned or orphaned shopping cart items. To prevent the database from storing a great deal of this information, at some point the abandoned shopping carts will need to be deleted or cleaned. Figure 7-4 shows the Processing Abandoned Shopping Carts activity diagram that illustrates this procedure.

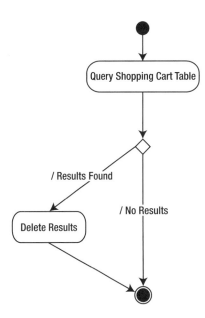

Figure 7-4. *Processing Abandoned Shopping Carts activity diagram*

Again, later in the book I will explain in detail how you can set up this process. For now, a high-level discussion is sufficient. Therefore, this process will be a scheduled process as a job within the SQL Server database. A specific time will be established as to when this process should be executed. When this process is executed, as shown in the diagram, the stored procedure will query the database for the abandoned shopping carts. Abandoned shopping carts will be defined by the date on which they are created. Therefore, when the process is executed, if the current time is greater than the time limit specified, perhaps 24 hours, then those results will be deleted. If no results are found, then the process simply does nothing except ends the execution and waits until the next scheduled execution.

Account Registration

When a user or customer is searching the website and finding items they are interested in, they are free to do so without registering an account. They can even add as many products to the shopping cart as they want without registering. However, when they want to begin the process of checking the items out of the shopping cart and offering the payment details, they will be prompted for their current username or password, or if they are not a current member, they will need to establish a user account. When establishing this user account, the system will need to record specific information. If the customer is a return customer and has an established username and password, they will have the ability to log in and bypass the registration process. This is a standard practice with most of today's e-commerce systems when making purchases online. Figure 7-5 shows the Account Registration activity diagram.

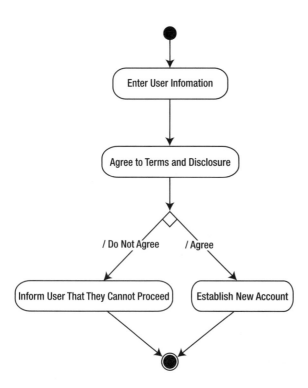

Figure 7-5. *Account Registration activity diagram*

When the user finds out they need to register a new account, they will see a standard form-field web page for entering all the necessary user contact information. Within this particular information, the system will ask the user to agree to the terms of service. In addition, since the wine business is unique, you will ask the user to agree to have their age verified by a third-party verification service. An important aspect for a new user registering an account will be that they agree to this verification. Basically, if a customer does not agree to have their age information verified—or if they agree but then the verification fails—they will not be able to proceed with registering an account with the vineyard.

The Account Registration activity diagram has brought you to the end of the activity diagrams. You'll now get a macro view of the system by studying and developing some use cases.

Use Cases

The use cases you will be designing and using for the purposes in this chapter will be slightly different from the activity diagrams. More specifically, the use cases will show a macro-level view of the system and how users will interact with it. Before getting ahead of myself, I'll first discuss some basics of what exactly use cases are and how you'll use them for the Little Italy Vineyards case study.

Use cases are typically diagrams that outline the usage requirements for the system. They are helpful in that they show a high-level view in which different elements of the system interact. Contained within a use case are several elements:

Actors: Represent a person, organization, entity, or external component of the system and are drawn as stick figures

Associations: Represent situations that are present when an actor is involved with a use case

System boundaries: Provide a specific scope of the use case

Packages: Aid in organizing the use cases into specific groups

Figure 7-6 shows the use cases for the Little Italy Vineyards case study.

Figure 7-6. *Use cases for Little Italy Vineyards*

Within these use cases, you can see that the system contains a few actors. The obvious actors are the customer, the verification service, and the credit card processing company or gateway. Each of the actors interacts with each other differently. You can see that the customer has the most use cases. However, when the customer happens to be a new user and needs to register for a new account, they will share a use case with the verification service to identify whether the customer is eligible to make purchases from the vineyard.

Class Diagrams

In this section, you'll model the common objects used with the e-commerce system. These are, of course, individual classes and are certainly not going to be the only classes that the finalized system will contain. They will be the most common objects or classes that the system will use or be based upon.

As a result of first identifying and then modeling these common objects, you will have your first blueprint of the database; you'll use this blueprint to design from in the following chapter. Table 7-2 lists the common classes.

Table 7-2. *Common Objects*

Common Class	Description
EndUser	Describes all users within the system
EndUserType	Describes the classification of the users and their associations
Product	Describes what is being sold
ProductCategory	Describes the categories in which products can be classified
Orders	Contains the information about what the customer purchase
OrderDetails	Contains the details about an individual order
Address	Contains address information for any other related object
ContactInformation	Contains contact information for any other related object
ShoppingCart	Contains the information about the products the customer chooses to purchase
CreditCard	Contains the information for payment

From each of these common classes, I will provide a class diagram that will depict each of the attributes and properties within the class. These classes will not have any methods or functions because they are simply objects that will contain detailed information about the overall system objects. Let's now explore the classes.

EndUser

The EndUser class will contain all the information for any type of user who interacts with the e-commerce system. This user could be a customer or even an administrator. The distinction between the roles of the different users will be identified with the EndUserTypeID property, which will be explained in more detail in the "EndUserType" section. Lastly, the EndUser class will contain the first name, last name, address ID, and contact information ID from the

ContactInformationID class, which will also be discussed later in this chapter. Figure 7-7 shows the class diagram of the EndUser class.

Figure 7-7. *EndUser class diagram*

EndUserType

The EndUserType class will be fairly brief. It will contain only two separate properties within the class. This class will serve as a lookup class for identifying and associating different types of users and their respective roles or classifications. The EndUserTypeID property will have a unique ID, which is then subsequently associated with a unique name for that ID. This will be located under the Name property, as shown in Figure 7-8.

Figure 7-8. *EndUserType class diagram*

Product

The Product class will be a major class that is going to be used throughout the e-commerce system. This is the case because, after all, the goal of the system is to enhance and automate more sales for the vineyard. The company wants to sell its products, which of course are wine and any related items. Therefore, the Product class will outline all the individual details of each product. Each product will have a unique ID, a name, a description, and a price. Figure 7-9 shows the Product class diagram.

Figure 7-9. *Product class diagram*

ProductCategory

The ProductCategory class will be similar to the EndUserType class in that it will serve as a lookup table for adding descriptions for each product. Figure 7-10 shows the ProductCategory class diagram.

Figure 7-10. *ProductCategory class diagram*

Orders

The Orders class will also play a major role in the overall system in that it will contain all the information about each order that is being processed by the customer when they choose to check out of the shopping cart and finalize their purchase. The Orders class will have one or possibly a multitude of products associated with the OrderDetails class, which I will discuss next. Figure 7-11 shows the Orders class diagram.

Figure 7-11. *Orders class diagram*

OrderDetails

As mentioned in the Orders section, a single order will have the ability to have one or many individual associated products. Within the OrderDetails class, this will be where the association is conducted. The OrderDetails class will have the link for the individual product or products that will be added to the finalized order. Figure 7-12 shows the OrderDetails class diagram.

Figure 7-12. *OrderDetails class diagram*

Address

The Address class will be an overall general class that will contain only address information. Having the structure set up in this manner will allow the address class to be associated with any other class that needs address data, and from the address class perspective, it does not care who is using this data. This is a technique that will further normalize the data. Figure 7-13 shows the Address class diagram.

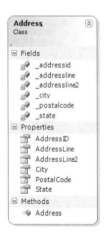

Figure 7-13. *Address class diagram*

ContactInformation

The ContactInformation class will be similar to the previous Address class in that it will contain only contact information for an individual, company, or user. Figure 7-14 shows the ContactInformation class diagram.

Figure 7-14. *ContactInformation class diagram*

ShoppingCart

The ShoppingCart class will be for the shopping cart within the application. This class will outline the items that are added to the shopping cart while customers are shopping at the vineyard's online store. Figure 7-15 shows the ShoppingCart class diagram.

Figure 7-15. *ShoppingCart class diagram*

CreditCard

When processing a payment for merchandise, the customer will submit their credit card for payment. As you can see in the class diagram shown in Figure 7-16, the individual information of the specific credit card will be contained within the CreditCard class. You will not be storing any credit card information on the server or database, but the class will be used to pass the information along within the application.

Figure 7-16. *CreditCard class diagram*

Summary

You have finished modeling the data for the e-commerce system. As mentioned, this provides a blueprint for the system in its early stages so you can move on to creating and designing your database. This is not to say that the modeling is set in stone and cannot be altered later within the development process. It is merely a preliminary design to establish the foundation, which can be expanded or tweaked as necessary later.

CHAPTER 8

■ ■ ■

Designing the Database with SQL Server 2005

You are finally moving along with the case study and beginning to deal with the engineering aspects of Little Italy Vineyards as opposed to the business side. This chapter will focus on building the database; this will be based on the model of the database and its objects that you developed in the previous chapter. In this chapter, I will discuss in detail how exactly you model and create the database; I'll provide step-by-step exercises along with a thorough explanation of the reasons for the modeling. I will also give some insight into why it is important to take the time in this early phase to pay special attention to designing the database with all its constraints and relationships.

This chapter will assume you have a moderate amount of experience with relational databases, specifically SQL Server 2005. Therefore, I will not explain what tables and stored procedures are and how they work, but I will explain what ones you will create and the reasons why you're creating them. If you find yourself needing to reference any fundamental information about SQL Server 2005, browse through the help files (more commonly known as Books Online), which have a wealth of information for you to digest.

The application for the Little Italy Vineyards case study will have several tables that you will create. This chapter will demonstrate how to create new tables, create new fields within the tables, and assign data types to the columns. Many of the tables when you are finished will have significant relationships to one another. Therefore, I'll also cover creating and managing the relationships in this chapter.

Please note that I'll show how to create the database, tables, and relationships through the SQL Server Management Studio interface. However, I will also supply the actual scripts to create these elements, so if you're more advanced, you can execute the scripts to create the database objects instead of using SQL Server Management Studio. Also, with this book's downloadable source code, the complete database script is available for your convenience. (See the introduction for more information about the code download.)

Creating the Database

The first order of business is to create the new database within SQL Server 2005. The tool in which you manage all the activity in SQL Server 2005 is called SQL Server Management Studio.

■**Note** Although the examples in this chapter use SQL Server 2005, it is also possible to use SQL Server 2005 Express, which is free and does not require any licensing. Although SQL Server 2005 Express has its limitations, it might prove to be a better alternative for some projects.

The following exercise will walk you through creating the database for the Little Italy Vineyards case study.

Exercise: Creating the Database

In the exercise, you'll create a new database within SQL Server 2005 from which you will build the associated tables and stored procedures:

1. Launch SQL Server Management Studio, and log in to the database engine that you will be utilizing for development within this project. After logging in to the database, you will see a tree from which you can expand the details of the database engine within Object Explorer, as shown in Figure 8-1. You can see that within my development environment, I have several databases that I have already created.

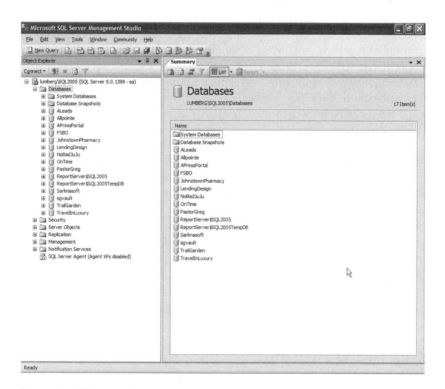

Figure 8-1. *Object Explorer*

2. Right-click the Databases directory listed directly below the main root in Object Explorer, and choose New Database, as shown in Figure 8-2.

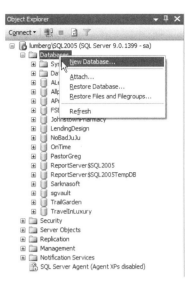

Figure 8-2. *Creating a new database*

3. After right-clicking this menu item, you will see the dialog box shown in Figure 8-3 where you can specify the details of your new database. Enter the name of the database, **LittleItalyVineyard**, in the Database Name box. After entering this information, you can keep the remaining default features and save your addition by clicking the OK button.

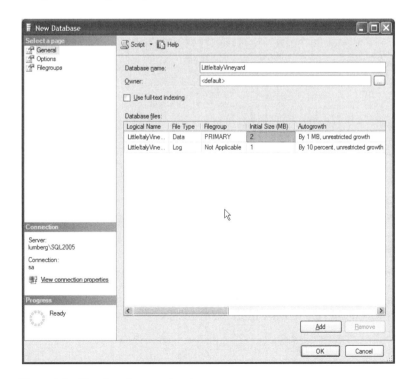

Figure 8-3. *Naming the new database*

If you would rather create the database by executing a script rather than using the graphical interface, you can execute the following script, which will provide you with the same result:

```
CREATE DATABASE LittleItalyVineyard

GO
```

After clicking the OK button or executing the script, you can use the new database to begin constructing the tables and stored procedures. At this point, you will see the new database in Object Explorer, as shown in Figure 8-4.

Figure 8-4. *Exploring the new database*

Once you have expanded the LittleItalyVineyard database, you can view the details of the database, which you'll explore in the following sections.

Since you have now created the database, you will proceed to the main focus of the chapter where you actually design the tables within the database.

Creating the Tables

You'll now focus on adding the tables to the database. You have already modeled the objects within the system in the previous chapter, so you will use that information to create the tables. It is important to remember, however, that what you create and model in this chapter might not necessarily be the final outcome of what is needed.

In the following exercise, you will create the first table in the database. When creating subsequent tables for the database, use this exercise as the model. In the following sections, I'll discuss each of the tables in detail by providing an overall outline of each field in each table along with the data types and whether each field will allow null values. I'll also show a diagram of each table.

Exercise: Creating a Table

As mentioned, you can use this exercise to create the first table and then use it as the base steps to create other tables. Without further ado, create the first table by following these steps:

1. After creating the database, expand the LittleItalyVineyard database within Object Explorer, right-click the Tables directory, and select New Table, as shown in Figure 8-5.

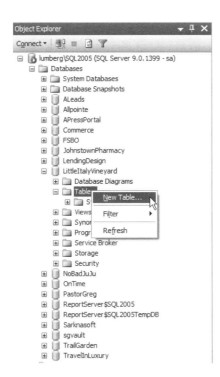

Figure 8-5. *Adding a new table*

After selecting this menu item, you will see the blank database shown in Figure 8-6 where you can enter the individual details. From this point within the exercise, you can begin constructing the individual fields.

Figure 8-6. *Adding new fields*

2. Begin entering the field names and the data types listed in Table 8-1 (in the next section), and indicate whether the field will allow null values. Figure 8-7 shows the final result of the table.

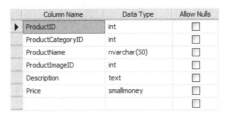

Figure 8-7. *The new fields*

3. After you have entered all the field names, defined the data types, and indicated whether each field will allow null values, you will set the primary key and any additional properties. Specifically, right-click the ProductID field, and select Set Primary Key, as shown in Figure 8-8.

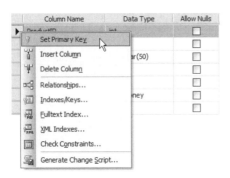

Figure 8-8. *Setting the primary key*

4. Now give the ProductID field a property of an autoincrement by clicking the option (Is Identity) and choosing Yes, as shown in Figure 8-9.

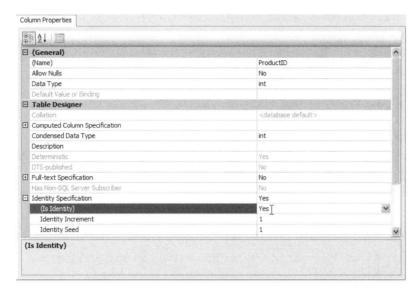

Figure 8-9. *Setting the identity property*

5. Now you'll save the table for which you just entered the information. Specifically, click the Save icon, as shown in Figure 8-10.

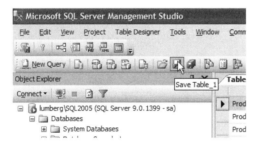

Figure 8-10. *Saving the new table*

6. When executing this action, you will be prompted to enter the name of the table. Enter **Products**, as shown in Figure 8-11.

Figure 8-11. *Naming the new table*

7. Click the OK button to save and execute the actions.

If you want to create the table manually, you can execute the following script:

```
CREATE TABLE [Products]
(
            [ProductID] [int] IDENTITY(1,1) NOT NULL,
            [ProductCategoryID] [int] NOT NULL,
            [ProductName] [nvarchar](50)  NOT NULL,
            [ProductImageID] [int] NOT NULL,
            [Description] [text]  NOT NULL,
            [Price] [smallmoney] NOT NULL,
CONSTRAINT [PK_Products] PRIMARY KEY CLUSTERED
(
            [ProductID] ASC
)
)
```

You have created the first table within your database. As mentioned, follow this model when creating all the subsequent tables for your database.

Products

The Products table was the first table you created because the system will focus on displaying and selling the individual products from the Little Italy Vineyards company. Table 8-1 shows the individual fields within the table.

Table 8-1. *Products Table*

Autoincrement?	Primary Key?	Field Name	Data Type	Allow Null?
Yes	Yes	ProductID	int	No
		ProductCategoryID	int	No
		ProductName	nvarchar(50)	No
		ProductImageID	int	No
		Description	text	No
		Price	smallmoney	No

You'll notice in Table 8-1 that the first field, ProductID, has some properties that specify the field will be a primary key and will be an identity, or *autoincrement*, field. This means each time a new product is inserted into the table, the ProductID field will automatically give itself a value that is one greater than the previous entry in the table.

Now I'll discuss the individual fields and explain what their roles will be in the overall database, along with why you are choosing the specific data types. Figure 8-12 shows the fields.

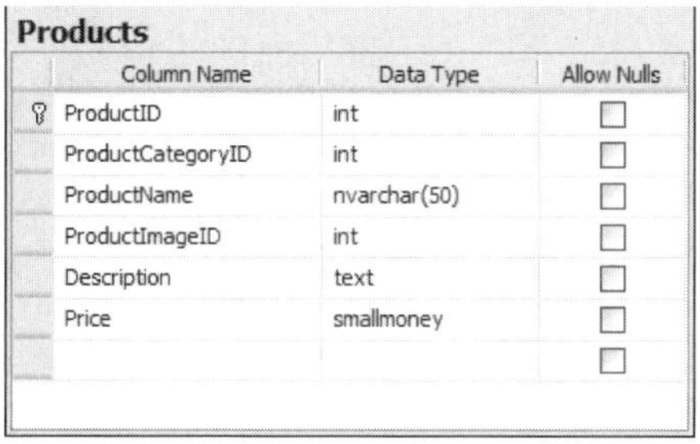

Products

Column Name	Data Type	Allow Nulls
ProductID	int	☐
ProductCategoryID	int	☐
ProductName	nvarchar(50)	☐
ProductImageID	int	☐
Description	text	☐
Price	smallmoney	☐
		☐

Figure 8-12. *Products table*

ProductID

The ProductID field provides the unique identifying number for a specific product being sold. This field is the primary key and has an autoincrement property; in addition, as a result of being a numeric value, its data type is an int, and the field will not allow any null values.

ProductCategoryID

The ProductCategoryID field is a foreign key to the ProductCategory table. This will create a relationship from the Products table to the ProductCategory table (discussed in the "ProductCategory" section) in that each product will be associated to a specific category. As a result, the data type is an int, and the field will not allow any null values.

ProductName

This is probably the most intuitive field in the table. The ProductName field simply holds the plain-text name of each product in the table. The data type is nvarchar(50), and this field will not allow any null values. If you find that your products have the tendency to have long names, you can increase the size of the nvarchar data type field; however, for the purposes of the case study, the names of the products will be on the shorter side.

ProductImageID

The ProductImageID field is a foreign key to the ProductImages table. I will explain more about the ProductImages table later in the "ProductImages" section; however, for now just know that all products will have an associated image to display. The images within the system will be stored in the database, as opposed to having them in the file system and providing the path to the images. This field will create the association to the image from the ProductImages table. As a result, it is an int data type and will not allow null values.

Description

Another quite obvious field in the Products table is the Description field. This, as the name implies, provides the description of the product. These descriptions can be quite lengthy at times, so to allow for this, this field will use the text data type and not allow null values.

Price

The Price field holds the monetary value of the cost of each product in the table. Since it will be a currency value, the data type will be a smallmoney type, and the field not allow null values.

At this point, you might be asking yourself, why not have a field for shipping cost and sales tax when charging sales tax for the products sold? You will be dealing with these values; however, they are considered to be aggregate values, and it is a good practice to not store aggregate values within your database schema. Instead, these values will be automatically calculated.

ProductCategory

Continuing along with products, the next table you'll create should be the ProductCategory table. This table will be a fairly simple table with only a few fields because this table will be what is known as a *lookup table*. In other words, it will give specific category names to all the products while associating them to the Products table with a unique ID. Table 8-2 shows the specifics of the ProductCategory table.

Table 8-2. *ProductCategory Table*

Autoincrement?	Primary Key?	Field Name	Data Type	Allow Null?
Yes	Yes	ProductCategoryID	int	No
		ProductCategoryName	text	No

In the following sections, I'll discuss the individual fields of the ProductCategory table. Figure 8-13 shows the fields.

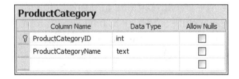

Figure 8-13. *ProductCategory table*

ProductCategoryID

The ProductCategoryID field is the unique identifier in the table along with being the primary key. As a result, it will have a data type of int and not allow any null values.

ProductCategoryName

The ProductCategoryName field simply gives the text description of what the category is. This field can be lengthy, or it can be relatively brief. To allow for maximum scalability, you will use the data type of text and not allow null values.

Table Script

The following script will create a new table named ProductCategory:

```
CREATE TABLE [ProductCategory]
(
          [ProductCategoryID] [int] IDENTITY(1,1) NOT NULL,
          [ProductCategoryName] [text] NOT NULL,
            CONSTRAINT [PK_ProductCategory] PRIMARY KEY CLUSTERED
            (
               [ProductCategoryID] ASC
            )
)
```

ProductImages

The ProductImages table is also brief and contains only a few fields. This table will primarily contain binary data for the images that are associated with the products. The natural question to ask is, why not simply have an image field with the Products table itself? Well, having a separate table for the image data will provide greater performance when querying the data from a dedicated table containing the binary images. Table 8-3 shows the specifics of the ProductImages table.

Table 8-3. *ProductImages Table*

Autoincrement?	Primary Key?	Field Name	Data Type	Allow Null?
Yes	Yes	ProductImageID	int	No
		ProductImage	image	No

In the following sections, I'll discuss the individual fields of the ProductImages table. Figure 8-14 shows the fields.

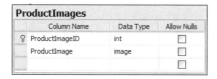

Figure 8-14. *ProductImages table*

ProductImageID

The ProductImageID field is the primary key of the table and has an autoincrement property. Therefore, keeping with the consistency of the other tables, the data type will be an int, and no null values will be allowed.

ProductImage

The ProductImage field is the only other field in the table; however, it has some unique characteristics compared to some of the others to this point. This field will contain the binary information for the image that is associated with the product. As a result of the information being in its binary form, the data type will be image, and no null values will be allowed.

Table Script

The following script will create the ProductImages table:

```
CREATE TABLE [ProductImages]
(
            [ProductImageID] [int] IDENTITY(1,1) NOT NULL,
            [ProductImage] [image] NOT NULL,
                CONSTRAINT [PK_ProductImages] PRIMARY KEY CLUSTERED
                (
                [ProductImageID] ASC
                )
)
```

Orders

The Orders table will be a major portion of the overall database. This table contains all the information about the items a customer intends to purchase. Table 8-4 shows the specifics of the Orders table.

Table 8-4. *Orders Table*

Autoincrement?	Primary Key?	Field Name	Data Type	Allow Null?
Yes	Yes	OrderID	int	No
		TransactionID	nvarchar(50)	No
		EndUserID	int	No
		OrderStatusID	int	No
		OrderDate	smalldatetime	No
		ShipDate	smalldatetime	Yes
		TrackingNumber	nvarchar(50)	Yes

In the following sections, I'll discuss the individual fields of the Orders table. Figure 8-15 shows the fields.

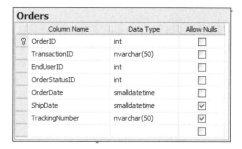

Figure 8-15. *Orders table*

OrderID

The OrderID field is the same as the other primary key fields in the other tables thus far. It will also have an autoincrement property along with a data type of int, and no null values will be permitted.

TransactionID

The TransactionID field is a string of characters that is returned from PayPal when processing the payment. This unique ID allows you to refer to the transaction that has been processed with PayPal and even issue a refund if necessary.

EndUserID

The EndUserID field simply provides a foreign key of the unique identification of the customer who has registered an account with the company and provided their contact information. This ID will reside in the EndUser table, which will be discussed later in the "EndUser" section. Lastly, the EndUserID field will have a data type of int and not allow any null values.

OrderStatusID

The OrderStatusID field refers to the OrderStatus table and corresponds to the appropriate status type of the order. The default value for this column is 1, which can be added to the column properties by entering a value of 1 for the Default Value or Binding property.

OrderDate

The OrderDate field simply contains the date when the order is created. To provide additional simplicity, this field has a default value that is equal to the current date. Therefore, when a new order is inserted into the table, the code or stored procedure will not have to specify that OrderDate field, and as a result, the current date will be taken from what's found on the server on which SQL Server 2005 is running. You can do this by specifying the GetDate() function in the Default Value or Binding column property. As a result, the data type used will be a small-datetime and not allow null values.

ShipDate

The ShipDate field holds the date of when the order is shipped to the customer. It primarily is for historic purposes when either the administrator or the customer needs to find out when their order has been shipped so they can anticipate when it will actually be delivered. This field actually allows null values because you will not know when the order will ship at the time the order is created. When this information is prepared, the table will need to be updated for this date.

TrackingNumber

The TrackingNumber field contains the identifying field that is provided by the shipping company. This will usually be a long number that also includes alpha characters, so to provide for this, the data type is an nvarchar(50), and the field will also allow null values. This is because you will not know the tracking number until the shipping company has arranged to pick up the order and has provided the company with this information. At that time, the tracking number will be updated in the table.

Table Script

The following script will create the Orders table:

```
CREATE TABLE [Orders]
(
        [OrderID] [int] IDENTITY(1,1) NOT NULL,
        [TransactionID] [nvarchar](50) NOT NULL,
        [EndUserID] [int] NOT NULL,
        [OrderStatusID] [int] NOT NULL DEFAULT ((1)),
        [OrderDate] [smalldatetime] NOT NULL DEFAULT (getdate()),
        [ShipDate] [smalldatetime] NULL,
        [TrackingNumber] [nvarchar](50) NULL,
            CONSTRAINT [PK_Orders] PRIMARY KEY CLUSTERED
            (
                [OrderID] ASC
            )
)
```

OrderDetails

The OrderDetails table provides all the information regarding the details of a specific order. Each order that a customer enters has the ability to have as many individual items as they want. In other words, the customer can purchase one product or can order 25 different products—it makes no difference. Table 8-5 shows the specifics of the OrderDetails table.

Table 8-5. *OrderDetails Table*

Autoincrement?	Primary Key?	Field Name	Data Type	Allow Null?
Yes	Yes	OrderDetailID	int	No
		OrderID	int	No
		ProductID	int	No
		Quantity	int	No

Figure 8-16 shows the fields of the OrderDetails table.

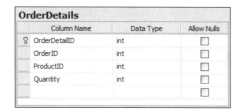

Figure 8-16. *OrderDetails table*

OrderDetailID

The OrderDetailID field is the primary key and is an autoincrement that will be the unique identifier for the associated record within the OrderDetails table.

OrderID

The OrderID field is the foreign key that relates to the Orders table and associates the individual order detail to the overall order. This field will have a data type of int and will not allow null values.

ProductID

The ProductID field is the foreign key that relates to the Products table to specify what product is being added to be eventually purchased. The data type will be int, and the field will not allow null values.

Quantity

The Quantity field is exactly what its name indicates. It indicates how many products are being requested for the purchase. It will have a data type of int and not allow any null values, because at least one product will need to be indicated for the order.

Table Script

The following script will create the OrderDetails table:

```
CREATE TABLE [OrderDetails]
(
        [OrderDetailID] [int] IDENTITY(1,1) NOT NULL,
        [OrderID] [int] NOT NULL,
        [ProductID] [int] NOT NULL,
        [Quantity] [int] NOT NULL,
            CONSTRAINT [PK_OrderDetails] PRIMARY KEY CLUSTERED
            (
                [OrderDetailID] ASC
            )
)
```

OrderStatus

The OrderStatus table provides the associated status names for any order that is placed within the system. It will have two separate columns: one for the associated ID and the other for the name of the status. Table 8-6 shows the specifics of the OrderStatus table.

Table 8-6. *OrderStatus Table*

Autoincrement?	Primary Key?	Field Name	Data Type	Allow Null?
Yes	Yes	OrderStatusID	int	No
		OrderStatusName	nvarchar(50)	No

Figure 8-17 shows the fields of the OrderStatus table.

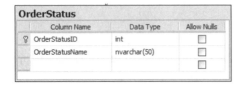

Figure 8-17. *OrderStatus table*

OrderStatusID

The OrderStatusID field serves as the primary key field and has an autoincrement property. This ID will relate any order's status to other tables within the database.

OrderStatusName

The OrderStatusName field is the associated text or string name to that of the foreign key field, OrderStatusID, that will relate to the Orders table. Setting the structure up in this way will allow for maximum scalability of the different status names. Lastly, the data type is an nvarchar(50), and no null values will be allowed.

Table Script

The following script will create the OrderStatus table:

```
CREATE TABLE [OrderStatus]
(
    [OrderStatusID] [int] IDENTITY(1,1) NOT NULL,
    [OrderStatusName] [nvarchar](50) NOT NULL,
        CONSTRAINT [PK_OrderStatus] PRIMARY KEY CLUSTERED
        (
            [OrderStatusID] ASC
        )
)
```

EndUser

The EndUser table contains all the information regarding the users who will be interacting within the system. The users will range from administrators to customers, but regardless, to keep the database and its information normalized, all this information will be contained in a single table. Table 8-7 shows the specifics of the EndUser table.

Table 8-7. *EndUser Table*

Autoincrement?	Primary Key?	Field Name	Data Type	Allow Null?
Yes	Yes	EndUserID	int	No
		EndUserTypeID	int	No
		FirstName	nvarchar(50)	No
		LastName	nvarchar(50)	No
		AddressID	int	No
		ContactInformationID	int	No
		Password	nvarchar(50)	No
		IsSubscribed	bit	No

I'll discuss the fields of the EndUser table in the following sections; Figure 8-18 shows them.

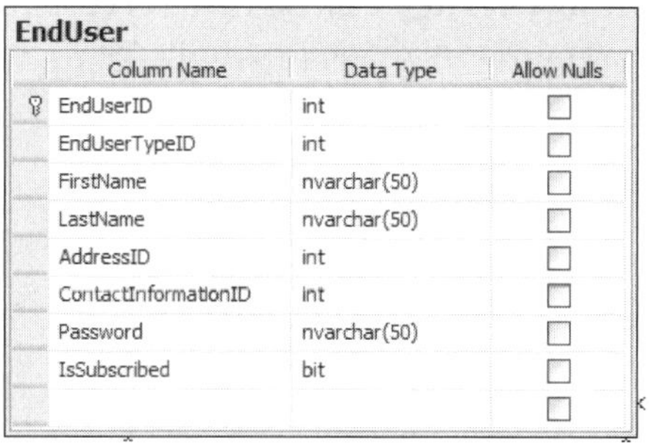

Figure 8-18. *EndUser table*

EndUserID

The EndUserID field serves as the primary key field and has an autoincrement property. This ID will relate any user to other tables within the database.

EndUserTypeID

The EndUserTypeID field is a foreign key field that will relate to the EndUserType table, which will specify what type of user the specific user is. Having the structure set up in this way will allow for maximum scalability of the different types of users. Lastly, the data type is an int, and no null values will be allowed.

FirstName

The FirstName field is exactly what its name indicates. It will contain the information of the user's first name. Therefore, the data type will be an nvarchar(50), and no null values will be permitted.

LastName

The LastName field is exactly what its name indicates. It will contain the information of the user's last name. Therefore, the data type will be an nvarchar(50), and no null values will be permitted.

AddressID

The AddressID field will contain the foreign key related to the Address table in the database. I will discuss the Address table in the "Address" section. The data type is an int, and no null values will be allowed.

ContactInformationID

The ContactInformationID field contains the foreign key related to the ContactInformation table within the database. I'll discuss the ContactInformation table in the "ContactInformation" section. Therefore, the data type will be an int, and no null values will be allowed.

Password

The Password field contains the password that the user supplies to get access to their account. Their password will be encrypted within the database to provide additional security. As a result, the data type used will be an nvarchar(50) and will not allow null values.

IsSubscribed

The IsSubscribed field provides for the value that is either a 0 or a 1. This value will be set when a customer or user registers for a new account; they can elect to subscribe to the newsletter.

Table Script

The following script will create the EndUser table:

```
CREATE TABLE [EndUser]
(
    [EndUserID] [int] IDENTITY(1,1) NOT NULL,
    [EndUserTypeID] [int] NOT NULL,
    [FirstName] [nvarchar](50)  NOT NULL,
    [LastName] [nvarchar](50)  NOT NULL,
    [AddressID] [int] NOT NULL,
    [ContactInformationID] [int] NOT NULL,
    [Password] [nvarchar](50)  NOT NULL,
    [IsSubscribed] [bit] NOT NULL,
        CONSTRAINT [PK_EndUser] PRIMARY KEY CLUSTERED
        (
            [EndUserID] ASC
        )
)
```

EndUserType

The EndUserType table will be a brief lookup table to specify the different roles a user can have and to provide different categorizations. Table 8-8 shows the specifics of the EndUserType table.

Table 8-8. *EndUserType Table*

Autoincrement?	Primary Key?	Field Name	Data Type	Allow Null?
Yes	Yes	EndUserTypeID	int	No
		TypeName	nvarchar(50)	No

I'll discuss the fields of the EndUserType table in the following sections; Figure 8-19 shows them.

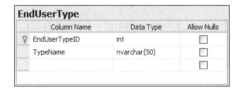

Figure 8-19. *EndUserType table*

EndUserTypeID

The EndUserTypeID field serves as the primary key field and has an autoincrement property. Its data type will be an int, and the field will not allow null values.

TypeName

The TypeName field provides the text description of what the EndUserTypeID will be. This descriptive field will usually have the name Administrator, Customer, or perhaps Vendor.

Table Script

The following script will create the EndUserType table:

```
CREATE TABLE [EndUserType]
(
    [EndUserTypeID] [int] IDENTITY(1,1) NOT NULL,
    [TypeName] [nvarchar](50) NOT NULL,
        CONSTRAINT [PK_EndUserType] PRIMARY KEY CLUSTERED
        (
            [EndUserTypeID] ASC
        )
)
```

Address

The Address table contains all the address information. It will contain address information only and can be used for users or any other part of the system or database that needs to include address information. For the purposes of the case study, it will mostly be used for the EndUser table. This structure is a technique used to further normalize the data within the schema of the database. Table 8-9 shows the specifics of the Address table.

Table 8-9. *Address Table*

Autoincrement?	Primary Key?	Field Name	Data Type	Allow Null?
Yes	Yes	AddressID	int	No
		AddressLine	nvarchar(50)	No
		AddressLine2	nvarchar(50)	Yes
		City	nvarchar(50)	No
		State	nvarchar(50)	No
		PostalCode	nvarchar(50)	No

I'll discuss the fields of the Address table in the following sections; Figure 8-20 shows them.

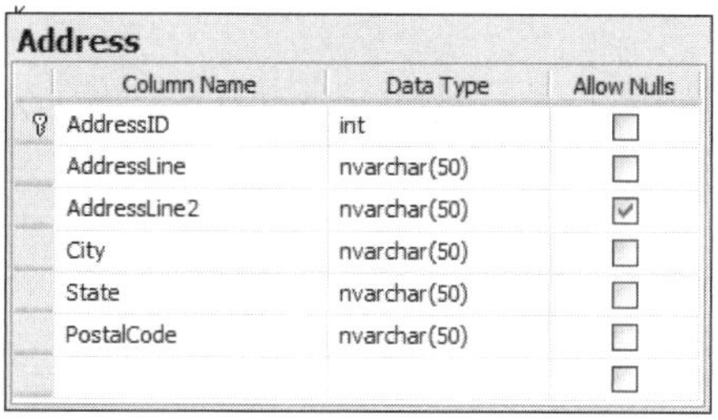

Address

Column Name	Data Type	Allow Nulls
AddressID	int	☐
AddressLine	nvarchar(50)	☐
AddressLine2	nvarchar(50)	☑
City	nvarchar(50)	☐
State	nvarchar(50)	☐
PostalCode	nvarchar(50)	☐
		☐

Figure 8-20. *Address table*

AddressID

The AddressID field is the primary key and has an autoincrement property. Therefore, the data type will be int, and the field will not allow null values.

AddressLine

The AddressLine field contains the information for the street number and the street name of an entity's address. For instance, "105 Main St." could be a value that is found in the table. Therefore, the data type is an nvarchar(50) and does not allow null values.

AddressLine2

The AddressLine2 field contains the information for addresses that sometimes have additional information. For instance, an address might be "100 South Main Blvd." but might also need to specify a suite or maybe even an apartment number. Therefore, information found in this field can often resemble that of "Suite 200" or "Apartment Number 4D." As a result, the data type is an nvarchar(50), and since only some addresses will have this additional information, null values will be allowed.

City

The City field specifies the name of the city within the full address. This will contain the full text, such as "Pittsburgh" or "Tampa Bay." As a result, the data type will be an nvarchar(50), and the field will not allow null values.

State

The State field specifies the name of the state within the full address. This will contain the full text, such as "Pennsylvania" or "Florida." As a result, the data type will be an nvarchar(50), and the field will not allow null values.

PostalCode

The PostalCode field specifies the value of the postal code (or the ZIP code) for the full address. An example is 15222 or 15282; therefore, this field will have a data type of nvarchar(50) and not allow null values.

Table Script

The following script will create the Address table:

```
CREATE TABLE [Address]
(
    [AddressID] [int] IDENTITY(1,1) NOT NULL,
    [AddressLine] [nvarchar](50)  NOT NULL,
    [AddressLine2] [nvarchar](50)   NULL,
    [City] [nvarchar](50) NOT NULL,
    [State] [nvarchar](50)  NOT NULL,
    [PostalCode] [nvarchar](50) NOT NULL,
        CONSTRAINT [PK_Address] PRIMARY KEY CLUSTERED
        (
            [AddressID] ASC
        )
)
```

ContactInformation

The ContactInformation table is similar to that of the Address table in the database. However, instead of containing address information for a specific entity, it specifies contact information for an entity to keep with the normalization technique mentioned within the Address table description. By utilizing this technique, all contact information can be in one table and be associated with any type of entity. For the purposes of the case study, the users are the only entities that have related contact information. Table 8-10 shows the specifics of the ContactInformation table.

Table 8-10. *ContactInformation Table*

Autoincrement?	Primary Key?	Field Name	Data Type	Allow Null?
Yes	Yes	ContactInformationID	int	No
		Phone	nvarchar(50)	Yes
		Phone2	nvarchar(50)	Yes
		Fax	nvarchar(50)	Yes
		Email	nvarchar(50)	No

I'll discuss the fields of the ContactInformation table in the following sections; Figure 8-21 shows them.

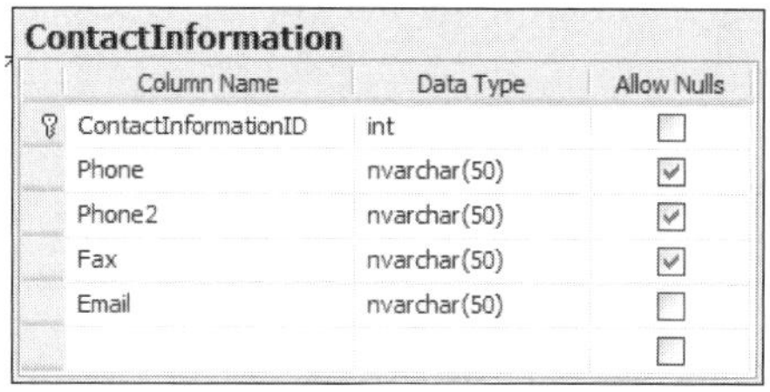

Figure 8-21. *ContactInformation table*

ContactInformationID

The ContactInformationID field serves as the primary key and has the autoincrement property. Therefore, it will have a data type of int and not allow null values.

Phone

The Phone field contains the raw numbers of the primary phone number of the overall contact information entity. There will be no formatting of the phone number because any formatting will be performed on the presentation layer side of the system. It will have a data type of nvarchar(50) and allow null values.

Phone2

The Phone2 field contains the raw numbers of a secondary phone number of the overall contact information entity. Perhaps this is a cellular or mobile phone number. However, not all entities will have a secondary number; therefore, it will allow null values and have a data type of nvarchar(50).

Fax

The Fax field specifies the raw numbers of an entity's fax. Not every entity will have an associated fax; therefore, this field will allow null values and have a data type of nvarchar(50).

Email

The Email field contains the e-mail address of the entity's contact information. It will show the e-mail address in plain text; therefore, the data type will be an nvarchar(50), and no null values will be permitted.

Table Script

The following script will create the ContactInformation table:

```
CREATE TABLE [ContactInformation]
(
    [ContactInformationID] [int] IDENTITY(1,1) NOT NULL,
    [Phone] [nvarchar](50)  NULL,
```

```
        [Phone2] [nvarchar](50)  NULL,
        [Fax] [nvarchar](50)  NULL,
        [Email] [nvarchar](50)  NOT NULL,
            CONSTRAINT [PK_ContactInformation] PRIMARY KEY CLUSTERED
            (
               [ContactInformationID] ASC
            )
)
```

ShoppingCart

The ShoppingCart table contains all the information from when customers are browsing through the product catalog and then adding a specific item to the shopping cart to eventually purchase. Table 8-11 shows the specifics of the ShoppingCart table.

Table 8-11. *ShoppingCart Table*

Autoincrement?	Primary Key?	Field Name	Data Type	Allow Null?
Yes	Yes	ShoppingCartID	int	No
		CartGUID	Nvarhcar(50)	No
		Quantity	int	No
		ProductID	int	No
		DateCreated	smalldatetime	No

I'll discuss the fields of the ShoppingCart table in the following sections; Figure 8-22 shows them.

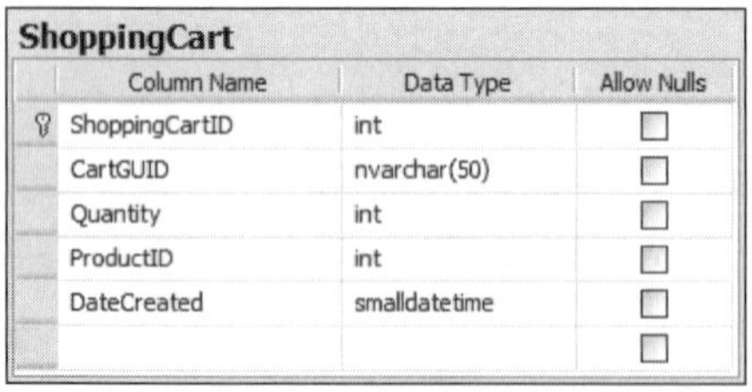

Figure 8-22. *ShoppingCart table*

ShoppingCartID

The ShoppingCartID field is the primary key of the table and has an autoincrement property. Therefore, the data type will be an int, and no null values will be allowed.

CartGuid

The CartGuid field is a global unique identifier (GUID) that is created from the ASP.NET code and then passed along to be inserted into the database. This identifier will allow for a customer to have all the items that they have placed within the shopping cart be identified as theirs.

Quantity

The Quantity field holds the value of how many of the individual products the customer would like when adding them to the shopping cart. As a result of the values being a single number, the data type will be an int, and the field not allow null values, because at least a value of 1 must be entered.

ProductID

The ProductID field is a foreign key to the Products table to specify and relate a specific product item to the cart. This will have a data type of an int and not allow null values.

DateCreated

The DateCreated field provides a date stamp of when the user creates the shopping cart by adding products. The value of the date will be generated by the GetDate() function placed within the Default Value property. This will have a data type of smalldatetime and will have a default value of using the current date, which will be extracted from the server's date on which SQL Server 2005 is installed and running. This field will be important when processing abandoned shopping carts, which will be explained in greater detail in Chapter 17.

Table Script

The following script will create the ShoppingCart table:

```
CREATE TABLE [ShoppingCart]
(
    [ShoppingCartID] [int] IDENTITY(1,1) NOT NULL,
    [CartGUID] [nvarchar](50)  NOT NULL,
    [Quantity] [int] NOT NULL,
    [ProductID] [int] NOT NULL,
    [DateCreated] [smalldatetime] NOT NULL DEFAULT (getdate()),
        CONSTRAINT [PK_ShoppingCart] PRIMARY KEY CLUSTERED
        (
          [ShoppingCartID] ASC
        )
)
```

Creating the Relationships

As mentioned earlier within the chapter, several of the tables will have distinct relationships with each other. At this point, you have created each of the necessary tables along with their respective data types and associated properties. Similar to the methodology earlier explained when creating the tables, you will follow a single exercise to create a single relationship between two tables. You can then use this as a model to follow when creating the other relationships.

Exercise: Creating a Relationship

This exercise will outline how to create a relationship between two tables. A table might have a single relationship or multiple relationships. In either case, utilize this exercise to model all the relationships for the tables within the database:

1. Within Object Explorer, expand the Tables node, and choose the table from which you want to create a relationship. For this exercise, you will be dealing with the OrderDetails table. Therefore, right-click the OrderDetails table, and choose Modify, as shown in Figure 8-23.

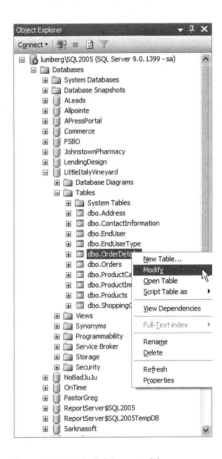

Figure 8-23. *Modifying a table*

After choosing Modify, you will see the table details, as shown in Figure 8-24.

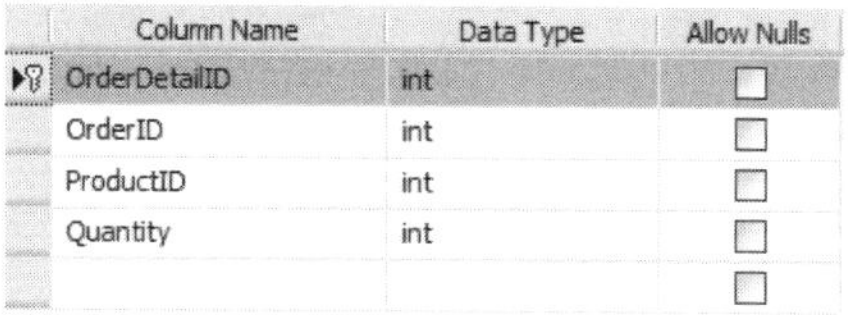

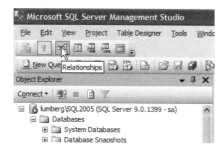

Figure 8-24. *The table columns*

2. From here, click the Relationships icon to view the current relationships, as shown in Figure 8-25.

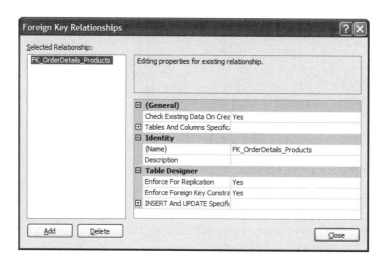

Figure 8-25. *The relationships*

3. After clicking the Relationships icon, you will see the dialog box shown in Figure 8-26 where you can click the Add button.

Figure 8-26. *Foreign key relationships*

4. In the Foreign Key Relationship dialog box, expand the Tables and Columns Specification property, as shown in Figure 8-27.

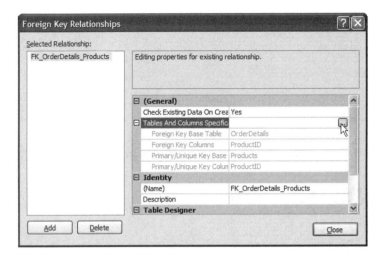

Figure 8-27. *Adding a relationship*

5. After clicking the ellipsis, you will be presented with the Tables and Columns dialog box, as shown in Figure 8-28.

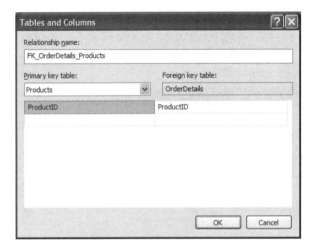

Figure 8-28. *Setting the relationship*

6. From the drop-down list on the left, choose the Products table, and then select the ProductID field from within the OrderDetails table, as shown in Figure 8-29.

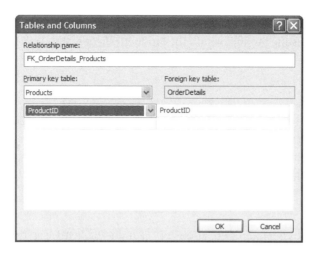

Figure 8-29. *Saving the relationship*

7. Upon ensuring that both the ProductID selections are made in both the columns, click the OK button to execute the changes. You have created the first relationship.

As an alternative to creating the relationship using the graphical user interface, you can run the following script to create the relationship:

```
ALTER TABLE [OrderDetails]  WITH CHECK ADD  CONSTRAINT
[FK_OrderDetails_Products] FOREIGN KEY([ProductID])
REFERENCES [Products] ([ProductID])
```

Follow this model for creating all the subsequent relationships for the other tables within the database that I'll outline in the remainder of the chapter.

OrderDetails

The OrderDetails table has two relationships. These relationships are with OrderID and ProductID from the Orders and Products tables, respectively. Table 8-12 shows the specifics of the OrderDetails relationships.

Table 8-12. *OrderDetails Relationships*

Constraint Name	Foreign Key	Reference Table	Reference Field
FK_OrderDetails_Orders	OrderID	Orders	OrderID
FK_OrderDetails_Products	ProductID	Products	ProductID

FK_OrderDetails_Orders

The first constraint allows only an existing OrderID from the Orders table within the OrderID field of the OrderDetails table.

FK_OrderDetails_Products

This constraint allows only an existing product within the ProductID field of the OrderDetails table.

Relationship Script

The following script will add the constraint:

```
ALTER TABLE [OrderDetails]  WITH CHECK ADD  CONSTRAINT [FK_OrderDetails_Orders]
FOREIGN KEY([OrderID])
REFERENCES [Orders] ([OrderID])
```

Orders

The Orders table has only a single constraint or relationship. Examine Table 8-13; an explanation follows.

Table 8-13. *Orders Relationships*

Constraint Name	Foreign Key	Reference Table	Reference Field
FK_Orders_OrderStatus	OrderStatusID	OrderStatus	OrderStatusID

FK_Orders_OrderStatus

This constraint allows for a status type within the Orders table to be that of an existing status ID only.

Relationship Script

The following script will create the constraint:

```
ALTER TABLE [Orders]  WITH CHECK ADD  CONSTRAINT [FK_Orders_OrderStatus]
FOREIGN KEY([OrderStatusID])
REFERENCES [OrderStatus] ([OrderStatusID])
```

EndUser

The EndUser table has three separate constraints and relationships, as described in Table 8-14.

Table 8-14. *EndUser Relationships*

Constraint Name	Foreign Key	Reference Table	Reference Field
FK_EndUser_Address	AddressID	Address	AddressID
FK_EndUser_ContactInformation	ContactInformationID	ContactInformation	ContactInformationID
FK_EndUser_EndUserType	EndUserTypeID	EndUserType	EndUserTypeID

FK_EndUser_Address

This relationship ensures that the AddressID field will be that of an existing value within the Address table.

FK_EndUser_ContactInformation

This relationship ensures that the ContactInformationID field will be that of an existing value within the ContactInformation table.

FK_EndUser_EndUserType

This relationship ensures that the EndUserTypeID field will be that of an existing value within the EndUserType table.

Relationship Script

The following script will create the constraints:

```
ALTER TABLE [EndUser]  WITH CHECK ADD  CONSTRAINT [FK_EndUser_Address]
FOREIGN KEY([AddressID])
REFERENCES [Address] ([AddressID])

GO

ALTER TABLE [EndUser]  WITH CHECK ADD  CONSTRAINT [FK_EndUser_ContactInformation]
FOREIGN KEY([ContactInformationID])
REFERENCES [ContactInformation] ([ContactInformationID])

GO

ALTER TABLE [EndUser]  WITH CHECK ADD  CONSTRAINT [FK_EndUser_EndUserType]
FOREIGN KEY([EndUserTypeID])
REFERENCES [EndUserType] ([EndUserTypeID])
```

Products

The Products table has two individual relationships, as described in Table 8-15.

Table 8-15. *Products Relationships*

Constraint Name	Foreign Key	Reference Table	Reference Field
FK_Products_ProductCategory	ProductCategoryID	ProductCategory	ProductCategoryID
FK_Products_ProductImages	ProductImageID	ProductImages	ProductImageID

FK_Products_ProductCategory

This relationship ensures that the ProductCategoryID field will be that of an existing value within the ProductCategory table.

FK_Products_ProductImages

This relationship ensures that the ProductImageID field will be that of an existing value within the ProductImages table.

Relationship Script

The following script will create the constraints:

```
ALTER TABLE [Products]  WITH CHECK ADD  CONSTRAINT [FK_Products_ProductCategory]
FOREIGN KEY([ProductCategoryID])
REFERENCES [ProductCategory] ([ProductCategoryID])

GO

ALTER TABLE [Products]  WITH CHECK ADD  CONSTRAINT [FK_Products_ProductImages]
FOREIGN KEY([ProductImageID])
REFERENCES [ProductImages] ([ProductImageID])
```

ShoppingCart

The ShoppingCart table has a single relationship, as described in Table 8-16.

Table 8-16. *ShoppingCart Relationships*

Constraint Name	Foreign Key	Reference Table	Reference Field
FK_ShoppingCart_Products	ProductID	Products	ProductID

FK_ShoppingCart_Products

This relationship ensures that the ProductID field will be that of an existing value within the Products table.

Relationship Script

The following script will create the constraint:

```
ALTER TABLE [ShoppingCart]  WITH CHECK ADD CONSTRAINT [FK_ShoppingCart_Products]
FOREIGN KEY([ProductID])
REFERENCES [Products] ([ProductID])
```

Writing the Type Inserts

The *type inserts* for the database are a series of insert statements that will populate specific tables with values that will be required. For instance, you'll have a series of product categories along with different types with which a user will be associated.

The following sections show the insert statements that you'll need to execute against the database.

EndUserType

The following script will create two records within the EndUserType table:

```
INSERT INTO EndUserType (TypeName) VALUES ('Customer')
INSERT INTO EndUserType (TypeName) VALUES ('Administrator')
```

OrderStatus

The following script will create the records within the OrderStatus table:

```
INSERT INTO OrderStatus (OrderStatusName) VALUES ('Pending')
INSERT INTO OrderStatus (OrderStatusName) VALUES ('Shipped')
```

ProductCategory

The following script will create the records within the ProductCategory table:

```
INSERT INTO ProductCategory (ProductCategoryName) VALUES('Appetizer Wine')
INSERT INTO ProductCategory (ProductCategoryName) VALUES('White Wine')
INSERT INTO ProductCategory (ProductCategoryName) VALUES('Red Wine')
INSERT INTO ProductCategory (ProductCategoryName) VALUES('Desert Wine')
INSERT INTO ProductCategory (ProductCategoryName) VALUES('Glasses')
INSERT INTO ProductCategory (ProductCategoryName) VALUES('Accessories')
INSERT INTO ProductCategory (ProductCategoryName) VALUES('Membership')
```

Examining the Complete Database

You have completed the database setup and design for the LittleItalyVineyard database, its tables, and all the necessary relationships between those tables. At this point, it is helpful to look at the entire picture from a macro viewpoint. In other words, examine Figure 8-30, which shows all the tables along with the constraints.

■**Note** As a result of the number of tables, you may not be able to see all of the details in Figure 8-30. However, within the book's downloadable code and accompanying files, you'll find a Portable Document Format (PDF) file of this database diagram.

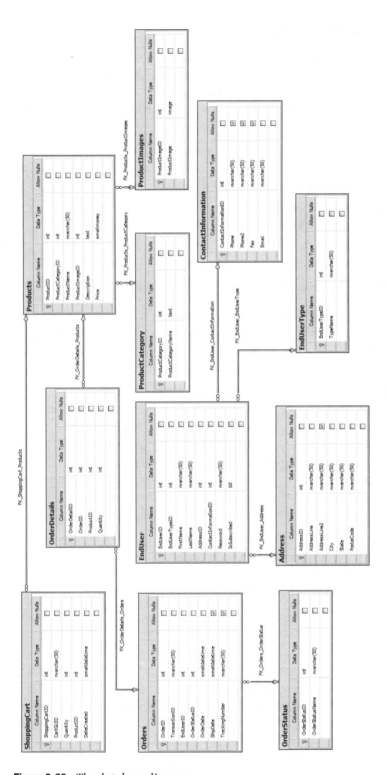

Figure 8-30. *The database diagram*

Summary

This chapter showed you how to create the LittleItalyVineyard database along with the individual tables within the database. Then you established the relationships between certain tables.

One important aspect to remember is that although you have completed most of the work for the database, you might alter the database later in the development phase, based on details you flesh out during the development process. This practice is totally acceptable; however, you have established the main schema of the database, so any changes will be minor—more like tweaking than reconstructing the major facets of the database foundation.

CHAPTER 9

Using Visual Studio 2005

Continuing with the engineering side of the case study, in this chapter I'll introduce the main tool you'll use to develop the web application. This tool, as you might have already guessed, is Microsoft Visual Studio 2005. It is the de facto Microsoft tool to use when developing .NET applications.

In this chapter, you'll focus on setting up your environment within Visual Studio 2005. You'll follow a formalized approach to organize the web pages and all the other files within the Visual Studio solution and project. As in the previous chapter, I'll assume you have previous experience using Visual Studio 2005 to develop web applications. Although I'll demonstrate specific instructions, this chapter is not meant to be a beginner's guide to Visual Studio 2005.

I'll first discuss the reasoning for taking a structured approach to the solution.

Understanding the Case Study's Approach

Prior to walking you through the individual techniques for organizing your source code, I'll explain why the Visual Studio 2005 solution and projects will be laid out in the fashion discussed in this chapter. It is true that you can build a web application, without any complications or flaws, without following the methodology in this book. However, you should keep two issues in mind as you work on your individual projects.

The first reason for having such a structured approach to setting up your solution and project files is continuity. As your application progresses, you'll need to manage a great deal of code, either by yourself or with a team of developers. Establishing the methodology at the beginning of the process means other developers who come to the project later can maintain the application and implement enhancements.

The second main reason behind the proposed structure is the inevitable fact that you will spend a significant amount of time debugging your application throughout its lifetime. As a result, having an organized layout will minimize the time expended when looking for the specific area or section of code you need to troubleshoot. The overall organization will allow for a lot less time expended when the troubleshooting begins. Any developer or engineer will be able to make an educated guess as to where the bug might be occurring or simply where the activity can be trapped to gain further information.

Understanding the Case Study's Solution

The first piece to the puzzle is the solution file. The *solution* is the overall container for all the projects, files, and other items that make up the web application as a whole. Usually when creating a new website within Visual Studio 2005, you will create a solution file. However, you can set whether you want this to be included.

For the purposes of the case study, you'll organize your structure a little differently by not having only a single project with all the code. Therefore, in the following exercise, you'll see exactly how to create the solution.

Exercise: Creating the Solution

In this exercise, you'll create the solution within Visual Studio 2005 that will contain the remaining items. Follow these steps:

1. The first order of business is to open a new instance of Visual Studio 2005. Once Visual Studio 2005 is open, you can see the Start Page screen and any recent projects you have created, as shown in Figure 9-1.

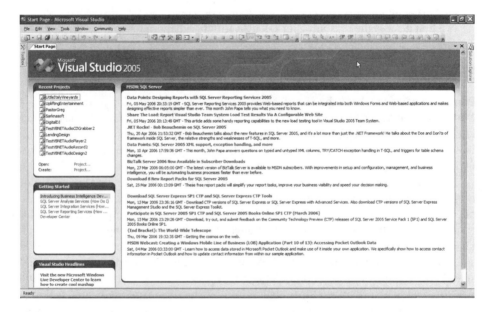

Figure 9-1. *Opening Visual Studio 2005*

2. Select File ➤ New ➤ Project, as shown in Figure 9-2.

Figure 9-2. *Creating a new project*

3. After selecting Project, you will see the New Project dialog box.

4. Navigate to the Other Project Types list within the Project Types tree, and choose Visual Studio Solutions. Select Blank Solution from the Templates section located on the right side of the dialog box, as shown in Figure 9-3.

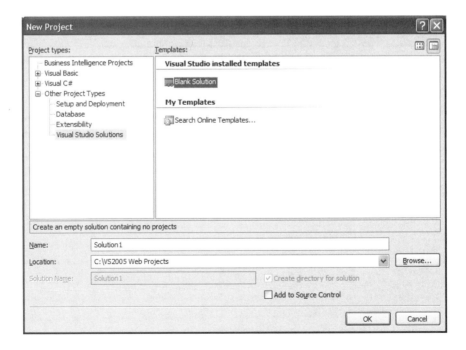

Figure 9-3. *New Project dialog box*

5. Now you need to enter two pieces of information. The first piece of information is the name of the solution; enter **LittleItalyVineyards**. For the second piece of information, browse to the location on your hard drive where you want to set up your solution file and the subsequent source code. Finally, notice that the option Create Directory for Solution is checked. This is the desired option. The New Project dialog box will now look like Figure 9-4.

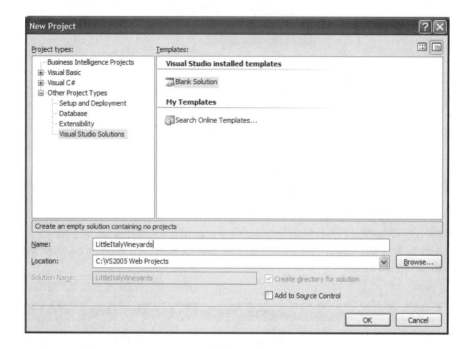

Figure 9-4. *Finalized New Project dialog box*

6. Click the OK button to execute and save the new solution file.

7. You can now view the new solution within Solution Explorer in Visual Studio 2005, as shown in Figure 9-5.

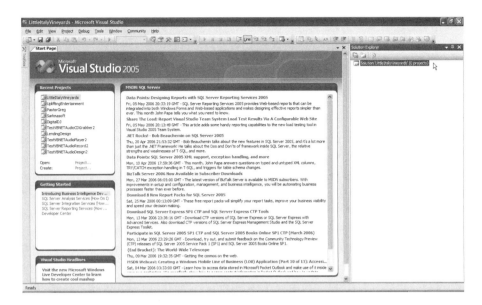

Figure 9-5. *The new solution*

At this point, you have set up your solution; however, it doesn't contain any projects at this time. But at least you have the foundation of the container that will hold all your source code for the application.

Creating the Web Project

Since the solution is now set up, you can add the next vital piece to the overall puzzle; in the following exercise, you'll create the web portion, or *presentation layer*, of the solution that contains the actual website project. The web project will contain all the web pages and web forms, a directory for images, all the scripts, and all the style sheets.

Exercise: Adding the Web Project to the Solution

In this exercise, you will resume working with the solution file within Visual Studio 2005. Specifically, you'll add the Web directory to the solution to continue setting up your project. Follow these steps:

1. Return to the Visual Studio 2005 solution you created in the previous exercise. Continue to Solution Explorer, and right-click the solution. Then select Add ➤ New Solution Folder, as shown in Figure 9-6.

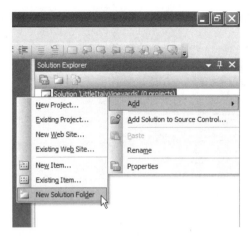

Figure 9-6. *Adding a new solution folder*

2. The new folder will appear below the main solution file within Solution Explorer. Rename the new folder to **Web**, as shown in Figure 9-7.

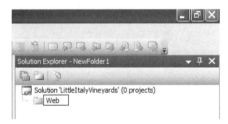

Figure 9-7. *Renaming the new solution folder*

■**Note** Adding a new solution folder does not create a directory or folder within the file system. It creates only a virtual directory within the Visual Studio 2005 solution infrastructure as noted by the faded dotted-line representation of the solution folder.

3. Right-click the newly added web folder, and then select Add ➤ New Web Site, as shown in Figure 9-8.

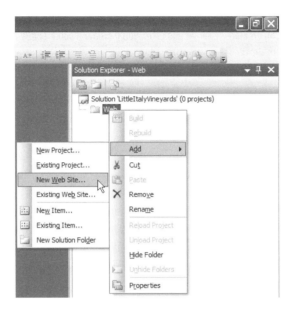

Figure 9-8. *Adding a new website*

4. Now you need to enter some additional setup information in the Add New Web Site dialog box. Specifically, in the Add New Web Site dialog box, select ASP.NET Web Site located in the Visual Studio Installed
   Templates list, and then select the File System option for the location and Visual C# for the language,
   as shown in Figure 9-9.

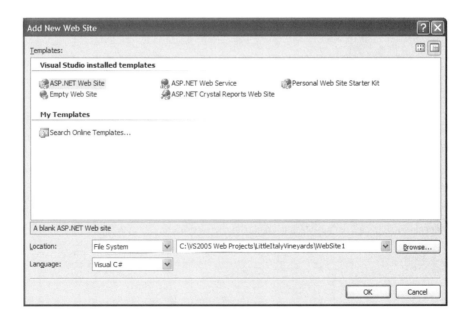

Figure 9-9. *Add New Web Site dialog box*

5. Next, you'll select the location for the website. Specifically, click the Browse button, and choose the main directory, LittleItalyVineyards, you created earlier. At this point, you'll create a subdirectory named Web. Append this in the Folder box, as shown in Figure 9-10.

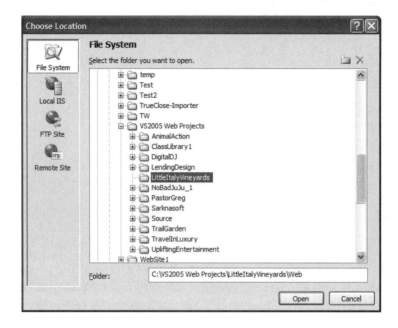

Figure 9-10. *Choosing a new location*

6. Click the Open button, and you will be prompted with the message shown in Figure 9-11.

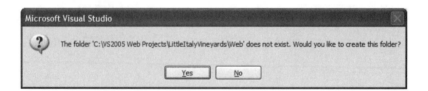

Figure 9-11. *Creating the subdirectory*

7. When prompted to create the new folder, click the Yes button. The new subdirectory will be created, and you will be returned to the Add New Web Site dialog box, which will show the newly selected subdirectory and the full path in which to create the new website, as shown in Figure 9-12.

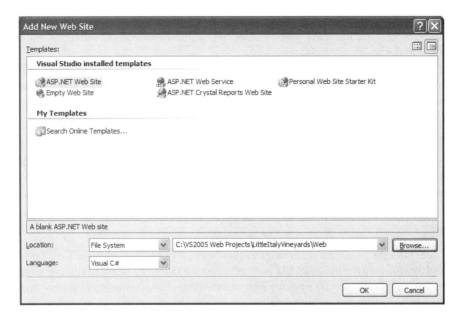

Figure 9-12. *Finalizing the new website*

8. Now that you have entered all the information, click the OK button. The new website will be created with the information you have specified. You can now see the new site located in the Web folder in Solution Explorer, as shown in Figure 9-13.

Figure 9-13. *The new website*

The exercise is now complete, and you have successfully added the web project portion of the Visual Studio 2005 solution.

Expanding the Web Project

Now that you have created the first project within the solution, you cannot stop there; obviously, you will need to expand upon what you have created so far. In this chapter, I will not discuss or demonstrate the exact web forms needed for the case study project. I will discuss this in detail in the soon-to-follow chapters. However, in this chapter, you need to create additional directories and complete some organization so that you are fully prepared when the time comes to add the necessary web forms.

As mentioned, you will be expanding the web project in the solution with additional directories. In the following sections, you will get a brief overview of each of these directories, and then I'll present another exercise so you can expand the web project.

Images

The Images directory will contain all the images incorporated in the Hypertext Markup Language (HTML) design of the application. The Images directory can also contain additional subdirectories to further organize specific images or image groups.

Scripts

The Scripts directory will contain JavaScript files (the *.js files). These files will contain all the necessary JavaScript functions that will be used within the web application. Common examples of JavaScript functions include opening new windows or pop-up windows, closing windows, and prompting a user to delete an item from the application. Any web page that needs to incorporate JavaScript will be able to link to the JavaScript files and subsequently reference the functions.

CSS

The name of the CSS directory is an abbreviation for *cascading style sheet*. This directory contains any style sheet files (the *.css files). In these files, you'll enter all the styles that are subsequently used to style the HTML within the application. Each web page will be able to link to the style sheets located in the CSS directory.

Admin

The Admin directory will contain all the web pages that comprise the administrative section of the web application. I will discuss this section of the application in more detail later in the book, but for the current purposes, it is important to understand what you will eventually put in this directory. The administrative section will be password protected and will allow only designated personnel access to alter information within the website. This information will come in the form of adding products, altering information such as pricing, and ultimately managing the orders and purchases made by the customers.

The following exercise will demonstrate how to add separate folders to the web project.

Exercise: Expanding the Web Project

In this exercise, you will expand the web project in the solution you created previously. Upon completion, you will be prepared to add your code and HTML to the project, which you'll do later in the book. Follow these steps:

1. Proceed to the web project you created within the LittleItalyVineyards solution. In Solution Explorer, right-click the web project, and select New Folder, as shown in Figure 9-14.

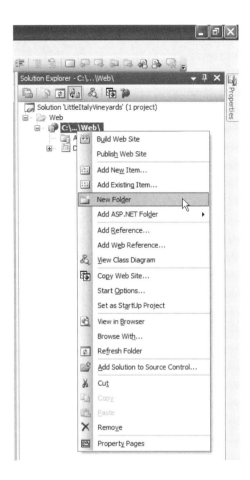

Figure 9-14. *New Folder menu item*

2. This creates a new folder within the web project under the solution; it has a default name of NewFolder 1. Change the name of this new folder to **Images**, as shown in Figure 9-15.

Figure 9-15. *The Images folder*

3. Repeat this process to add new folders to the web project named **Scripts**, **CSS**, and **Admin**, as shown in Figure 9-16, Figure 9-17, and Figure 9-18.

Figure 9-16. *The Scripts folder*

Figure 9-17. *The CSS folder*

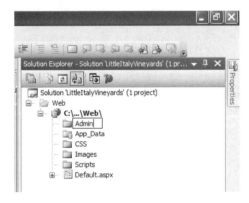

Figure 9-18. *The Admin folder*

After adding all the new folders, the web project will resemble Figure 9-19.

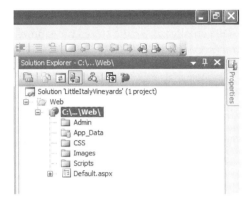

Figure 9-19. *The folder structure*

The web project within the solution is now organized and ready to be added to, which you'll do later in this book when you begin writing the code and integrating the HTML for the application. Lastly, note that the folders you created are in fact physical folders as opposed to the virtual folders created earlier.

Adding the Class Libraries

So far, you have set up the web project within your solution so that it will be prepared when you begin coding. One piece to the puzzle remains: the class library section within the solution for Visual Studio 2005.

A *class library* with regard to setting up a Visual Studio solution is a specific type of project where the ultimate output is an assembly with a .dll file extension. These class libraries process the data, business logic, or operational tasks such as sending an e-mail or entering items in a message queue. They do not deal with displaying information or images in the browser; instead, they deal with the processes that occur behind the scenes and that ultimately deliver this information to the presentation layer or browser. The flow of information can also occur in the reverse order; in other words, it can take information from the browser or user input and deliver it to the database, use it in data processing, or use it to execute a business logic rule.

In the following sections of the chapter, you will add the individual class library projects to the Visual Studio solution and organize the file structure in a similar fashion as the web project. The individual class libraries you will add are called Common, DataAccess, Operational, and BusinessLogic. I'll give you an overview of each of these, followed by an exercise demonstrating the exact procedures involved.

Common

The Common class library will contain all the main objects within the system as classes, which is why it's called *Common*. With regard to the case study project, some examples of the classes will be Products, Users, Orders, Address, and ShoppingCart. These classes will be modeled directly from the previous class diagrams you created in Chapter 7.

DataAccess

The DataAccess class library will contain the section that processes all the data and transactions to the database. This will be in the form of selecting data, inserting data, deleting data, and updating data. The code contained here will actually invoke the stored procedures within the SQL Server database to perform all the data processing.

Operational

The Operational class library will contain all the functionality that executes operations that do not directly involve the database within the system. Examples of this type of operability include sending e-mail messages, processing a report, performing system input/output (IO), and connecting to and communicating with any web services that the application utilizes.

BusinessLogic

The BusinessLogic class library will contain the functionality that processes individual business rules that are specific to the system as a whole. This will serve as a bridge from the presentation layer or web project section that will maintain the flow of the data to all the back-end processing and will ultimately return information to the user.

The following exercise will be the beginning of building the *n*-tier architecture of your application because you'll create the individual class library projects and individual class.

Exercise: Creating the Class Libraries

In this exercise, you'll add the class library projects to your existing Visual Studio 2005 solution that you have been organizing thus far. Follow these steps:

1. Return to the Visual Studio 2005 solution, and right-click the solution to add a new solution folder. Name the new folder **Class Libraries,** as shown in Figure 9-20.

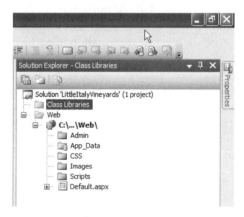

Figure 9-20. *The Class Libraries solution folder*

2. Navigate in Windows Explorer to the root directory where you saved all the Visual Studio files, and add a new directory named **Class Libraries**. This is where you will be saving all the subsequent class libraries. Then right-click the newly added Class Libraries solution folder within the Visual Studio solution, and choose Add ➤ New Project, as shown in Figure 9-21.

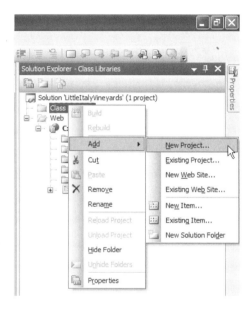

Figure 9-21. *Adding a new project*

3. You will now see the Add New Project dialog box. In this dialog box, you will need to specify additional information. First select Visual C# from the Project Types tree on the left side, and then select the Class Library template from the Visual Studio Installed Templates section. Change the name of the project being added to **LittleItalyVineyard.Common**, and finally browse to the location of the subdirectory you created previously named Class Libraries. After entering this information, the Add New Project dialog box will resemble Figure 9-22.

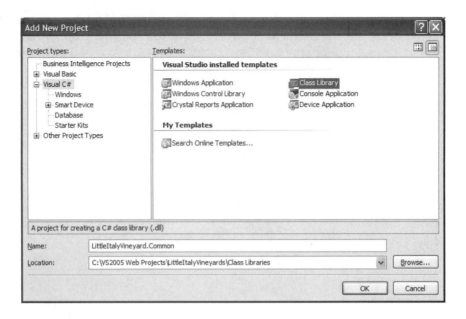

Figure 9-22. *Configuring the new project information*

4. Finally, click the OK button to create the new class library. Upon the new class library being created, you will be able to view the newly added item, as shown in Figure 9-23.

Figure 9-23. *The Common class library*

Notice that the new class library automatically created a new class named Class1. You can keep this class for the time being; however, in a future chapter, you will either delete or rename this class.

5. Continue adding the remaining class libraries that were discussed prior to this exercise, namely, the DataAccess, Operational, and BusinessLogic class libraries, keeping the same naming convention used with the Common class library. Figure 9-24, Figure 9-25, and Figure 9-26 show these libraries.

Figure 9-24. *The DataAccess class library*

Figure 9-25. *The Operational class library*

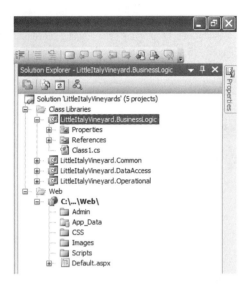

Figure 9-26. *The BusinessLogic class library*

The Visual Studio 2005 project and solution is now prepared for you to use later within the case study in this book.

Summary

You have finished setting up and organizing the Visual Studio 2005 solution for your application. You are now prepared to establish the overall system's architecture and how each layer of the architecture will be implemented in the Visual Studio solution.

PART 4

■ ■ ■

Architecture

The fourth part of this book is where you'll implement the architecture in order to establish the foundation of your complete system. In the following chapters, I'll explain each layer in detail. I'll also show diagrams to demonstrate how data will travel through the entire system.

CHAPTER 10

■■■

Building the Complete System Architecture

Any type of complex system needs to have a strong foundation so that the system will be able to support its contents and occupants. This is certainly the case when engineering software. Many software systems today, whether developed professionally or not, do not have a solid foundation. Although these systems often still function, inevitably at some point they need to be expanded, and when that time comes, it is difficult to achieve any type of scalability because the architecture lacks cohesiveness.

When building the e-commerce system for the Little Italy Vineyards case study, you will avoid these pitfalls and spend adequate time establishing and documenting a solid architecture for the system. This chapter will take a macro approach and examine the entire architecture as a whole. Then, the next five chapters will go into more detail on each part of the architecture introduced in this chapter.

In this chapter, I will assume you have prior experience with multitiered architecture and systems. This chapter will not be an introductory guide to architecting a system but rather give you insight about why the case study project is being constructed in this fashion. Specifically, I'll focus on the architecture of the Little Italy Vineyards application.

Introducing Multitier Architecture

Multitier architecture, often referred to as *n-tier* architecture, is a software system that is segregated into separate sections referred to as *tiers*, or *layers*. The standard number of layers is usually three. Software applications are constructed with this methodology for many reasons. The main reason is to provide the optimal amount of scalability to the system and allow any of the tiers to be upgraded, replaced, or interchanged independently. Inevitably, your software system will face change at some point during its lifetime. This change can come in the form of a functionality change, a functionality enhancement, a completely new module, or even a hardware infrastructure enhancement. In any case, these changes can occur during the initial development or after the first version is complete. Having the architecture of the system designed from the beginning as multitiered will help minimize the impact on the system when implementing any of these changes.

As a result of having the source code organized into multiple tiers, debugging and maintaining your application as a whole will be easier. The organization will allow for you as a developer (or any other developers you might be working with) to easily locate specific sections where an exception is occurring or where a change needs to be implemented.

If the system does not implement a well-structured architecture, your application will be prone to defects and bugs; this will also make any type of upgrades or enhancements difficult and time-consuming to execute. The system will not be very scalable, which will result in a poor application.

Introducing the LittleItalyVineyards Architecture

All software applications have a common architecture to some degree, but at the same time the slight variations will resemble the style of the individual architect or team of architects. I've created the architecture you'll use within this book as a result of examining many different best practices provided by Microsoft and having years of experience building the architectures of many software systems. Over the years, I have collaborated with an experienced and talented software engineer and architect named Joe Merlino. Joe and I have worked together many times while building architectures for software systems in different industries.

Based on my experiences working with Joe, I have taken many of the aspects of architectures we have built and modeled them for the case study you will be using throughout this book. With that said, the e-commerce system being developed for the case study will resemble Figure 10-1.

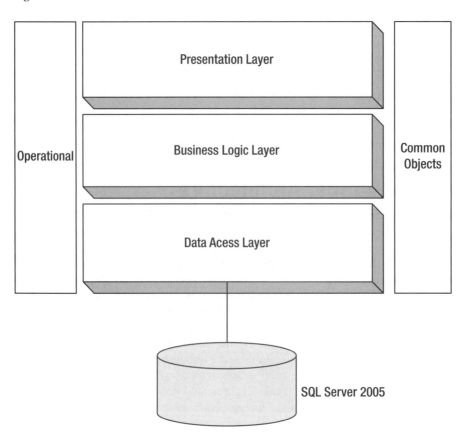

Figure 10-1. *The complete architecture*

You can easily see that the architecture will follow the multitiered fashion I have mentioned. The presentation layer is followed by the business logic layer and then finally the data access layer. Notice that two additional items appear in the diagram that I have not discussed yet. More specifically, the common objects and the operational shapes within the diagram will not act as separate layers or tiers in the architecture; however, they will interact with the different tiers within the architecture. I'll discuss these more in the coming chapters.

Introducing the Presentation Layer

The *presentation layer* of the web application, or any other software application, is ultimately what all the users will view on the surface. Since this chapter is taking a macro approach, I'll give the equivalent overview of the presentation layer. I'll provide a much more in-depth overview and guidelines on how and what to implement in Chapter 15, which is dedicated to the presentation layer.

The presentation layer should be a thin layer within the architecture with the main purpose of showing the user the best visual experience. After all, this layer is what the user will witness, and user-friendliness will play a major role in the user's opinion of the application.

In the presentation layer, the majority of the content will be Hypertext Markup Language (HTML) and server controls. Validation will also occur at this level but will mostly be relatively simple tasks such as ensuring the user is entering the required data or ensuring the data entered matches a specific format.

Introducing the Data Access Layer

For the most part, essentially all software systems, whether they are client-server applications or web applications, need to process some sort of data. This processing will most likely be in the form of selecting, querying, inserting, updating, or deleting information to and from the database. Other processing includes utilizing Extensible Markup Language (XML) data, but this will ultimately vary based upon your specific system and its business requirements.

The project for the case study will have extensive interaction with the database. The *data access layer* will process all this data by receiving requests that originate from the user within the presentation layer and will then process the data and return either a notification or some type of data or objects to the presentation layer.

Also included in the data access layer will be a component provided by Microsoft. This data component is a Microsoft Data Access Blocks component that is part of the Microsoft Enterprise Library Application Blocks for .NET. You can download these free components, and their source code, and distribute them royalty free within your applications. Incorporating these into the architecture saves you time on the overall development and maintains a cohesive data execution point. In other words, the application will have a single point where DataSets, SQLDataReaders, and other objects can directly interact with the database.

In Chapter 12, I will provide a much more detailed explanation of how to use and implement the data access block.

Introducing the Business Logic Layer

The *business logic layer* is the remaining tier; it provides a dedicated portion of the system that processes the business rules set forth from the earlier gathered requirements. This tier, in addition to doing the actual processing, will act as a bridge from the presentation to the data access tier, and vice versa. Although the system will have many fairly simple data-processing needs, it will also have many instances where transactions of data will need to be processed. The business logic layer acts as the orchestrator of processing the transactions and remains in that capacity until each process is complete.

Summary

This chapter opened Part 4 of the book by discussing architecture pertaining to software systems; it also examined the high-level view of the architecture you'll establish for the case study. Other chapters in this part will be dedicated to the individual parts of the case study architecture; specifically, they will provide detailed information about how exactly to implement the architecture within the e-commerce system.

CHAPTER 11

Creating the Common Objects

This chapter will not cover a specific tier within the architecture of the Little Italy Vineyards case study but will play an important role within the overall system. This chapter will cover all the common objects, or *classes*, that the system will contain. These objects will make passing data much simpler because the objects will be able to contain data and provide a uniform method of encapsulation for this information. As a result of this modeling, it will be easier for all the engineers involved to understand what the system contains. In other words, having individual classes that resemble the real-world objects will provide a better understanding of the overall system.

In this chapter, you'll examine all the aspects of the common objects. In the coming chapters, you'll learn exactly how the common objects will be used and implemented throughout the entire system and architecture. In summary, this chapter will cover the following topics:

- Understanding why you're using common objects

- Introducing the individual objects and classes

- Creating the classes within Visual Studio 2005

Why Use Common Objects?

At this point in the project and the book, some engineers reading this chapter might ask the question, why do you need to use common objects and classes? The main answer stems from the decision to use the object-oriented programming principles of C# and ASP.NET. Basically, having common objects will allow you to model the overall system and provide an additional layer of abstraction to the design and architecture. Common objects will also provide a direct mapping from the database tables you created earlier to the classes within your code. This is not to say every common object will be a table within the database. Many will, but sometimes you'll need a container of information that needs to be passed throughout the application, and this will come in the form of a common object.

Object-oriented programming at its core takes advantage of modeling the system after real-life objects. The properties you add to the individual classes will provide the description of the individual classes. In other words, these classes will encapsulate all the necessary information, which will allow for better organization and for a better flow of data.

Revisiting the Classes

In the following sections, you'll revisit the common objects you'll implement and use within the application. In Chapter 7, you modeled the system with Uniform Modeling Language (UML), including creating the activity diagrams, use cases, and class diagrams. In this chapter, you'll revisit some of this content.

EndUser

Table 11-1 shows the EndUser class.

Table 11-1. *EndUser Class*

Data Type	Field Name	Property Name
Int	_enduserid	EndUserID
Int	_endusertypeid	EndUserTypeID
String	_firstname	FirstName
String	_lastname	LastName
Int	_addressid	AddressID
Address	_address	Address
Int	_contactinformtationid	ContactInformationID
ContactInformation	_contactinformation	ContactInformation
String	_password	Password
Bool	_issubscribed	IsSubscribed

EndUserType

Table 11-2 shows the EndUserType class.

Table 11-2. *EndUserType Class*

Data Type	Field Name	Property Name
Int	_endusertypeid	EndUserTypeID
String	_endusername	EndUserName

Product

Table 11-3 shows the Product class.

Table 11-3. *Product Class*

Data Type	Field Name	Property Name
Int	_productid	ProductID
Int	_productcategoryid	ProductCategoryID
ProductCategory	_productcategory	ProductCategory

Data Type	Field Name	Property Name
String	_name	Name
Int	_imageid	ImageID
Byte Array	_imagedata	ImageData
String	_description	Description
Int	_quantity	Quantity
Decimal	_price	Price

ProductCategory

Table 11-4 shows the ProductCategory class.

Table 11-4. *ProductCategory Class*

Data Type	Field Name	Property Name
Int	_productcategoryid	ProductCategoryID
String	_productcategoryname	ProductCategoryName

Orders

Table 11-5 shows the Orders class.

Table 11-5. *Orders Class*

Data Type	Field Name	Property Name
Int	_orderid	OrderID
Int	_enduserid	EndUserID
EndUser	_enduser	EndUser
String	_transactionid	TransactionID
DateTime	_orderdate	OrderDate
Address	_shippingaddress	ShippingAddress
Int	_orderstatusid	OrderStatusID
Decimal	_shippingtotal	ShippingTotal
OrderDetails	_orderdetails	OrderDetails
Decimal	_subtotal	SubTotal
Decimal	_ordertotal	OrderTotal
Decimal	_tax	Tax
CreditCard	_creditcard	CreditCard
DateTime	_shipdate	ShipDate
String	_trackingnumber	TrackingNumber

OrderDetail

Table 11-6 shows the OrderDetail class.

Table 11-6. *OrderDetail Class*

Data Type	Field Name	Property Name
Int	_orderdetailid	OrderDetailID
Int	_orderid	OrderID
Int	_productid	ProductID
Products	_products	Products
Int	_quantity	Quantity

Address

Table 11-7 shows the Address class.

Table 11-7. *Address Class*

Data Type	Field Name	Property Name
Int	_addressid	AddressID
String	_addressline	AddressLine
String	_addressline2	AddressLine2
String	_city	City
String	_state	State
String	_postalcode	PostalCode

ContactInformation

Table 11-8 shows the ContactInformation class.

Table 11-8. *ContactInformation Class*

Data Type	Field Name	Property Name
Int	_contactinformationid	ContactInformationID
String	_phone	Phone
String	_phone2	Phone2
String	_fax	Fax
String	_email	Email

ShoppingCart

Table 11-9 shows the ShoppingCart class.

Table 11-9. *ShoppingCart Class*

Data Type	Field Name	Property Name
Int	_shoppingcartid	ShoppingCartID
String	_cartguid	CartGUID
Int	_quantity	Quantity
Int	_productid	ProductID
DateTime	_datecreated	DateCreated

CreditCard

Table 11-10 shows the CreditCard class.

Table 11-10. *CreditCard Class*

Data Type	Field Name	Property Name
Address	_address	Address
String	_cardtype	CardType
Int	_expmonth	ExpMonth
Int	_expyear	ExpYear
String	_number	Number
String	_securitycode	SecurityCode

Implementing the Common Classes

In this section, I will give you detailed instructions for adding the common classes to your overall source code within the Visual Studio 2005 solution file and projects. Keep the following in mind: the common classes will not provide any functionality or methodology. The classes will merely contain a series of properties, which will encapsulate the most common objects you will be able to utilize throughout the system.

The following exercise shows how to add the common classes to your existing source code that you previously organized within the Visual Studio 2005 solution.

Exercise: Creating a Common Class

In this exercise, you will create one of the many common classes you will need for your application. Follow these steps:

1. Revisit the Visual Studio 2005 solution you set up in the previous chapter. Relaunch the project, and once the entire Visual Studio solution has successfully loaded, you will be see the screen shown in Figure 11-1.

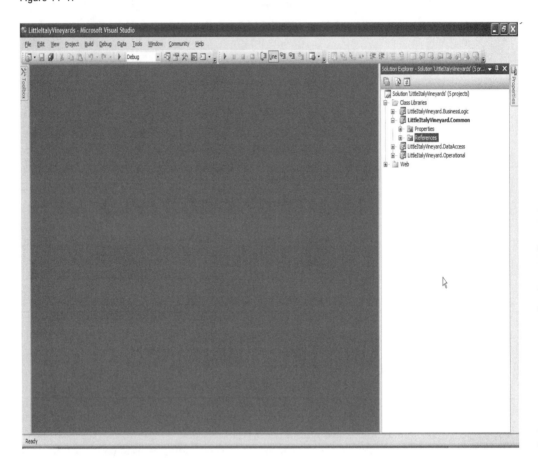

Figure 11-1. *Revisiting Visual Studio 2005*

2. Next, choose the common object class library project named LittleItalyVineyard.Common. Right-click the project, and then choose Add ➤ Class, as shown in Figure 11-2.

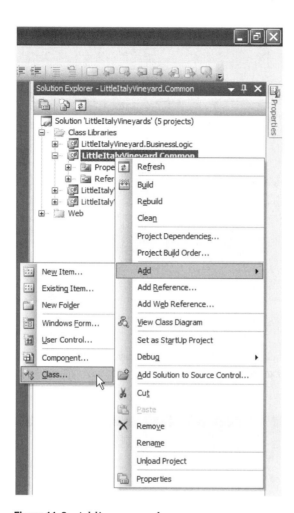

Figure 11-2. *Adding a new class*

3. After choosing to add a new class to the class library project, you will see the dialog box shown in Figure 11-3 where you can enter the name of your new class, **EndUser**.

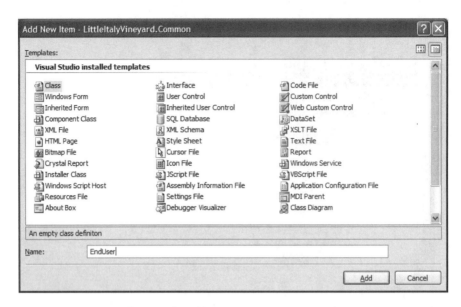

Figure 11-3. *Naming the new class file*

4. As shown in Figure 11-3, in this exercise you'll create only one of the classes of the common objects. This first class will be the EndUser common object; after clicking the Add button, you'll see the class, which looks like Figure 11-4.

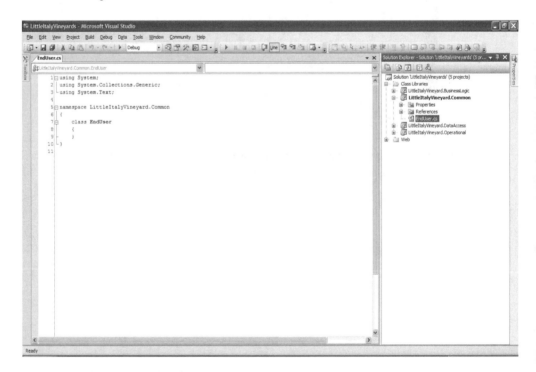

Figure 11-4. *The EndUser class file*

5. You are able to view the new class that was created; however, you still need to do some additional work within the class file. At the moment, the class simply shows the name of class. Change the code within the class to resemble the following:

```
using System;
using System.Collections.Generic;
using System.Text;

namespace LittleItalyVineyard.Common
{
    public class EndUser
    {
        public EndUser()
        {

        }
    }
}
```

You have changed the class to that of a public class, and you have added the subsequent constructor. Now you are ready to move along with the implementation of the properties contained in the EndUser class.

6. The constructor you created in the previous step will allow you to add the field variables along with the individual properties. So, you can create the first of the series of fields and properties, which will be the EndUserID property, as shown here:

```
using System;
using System.Collections.Generic;
using System.Text;

namespace LittleItalyVineyard.Common
{
    public class EndUser
    {
        private int _enduserid;

        public EndUser()
        {

        }

        public int EndUserID
        {
            get { return _enduserid; }
            set { _enduserid = value; }
        }
    }
}
```

You added a new field, _enduserid, just above the constructor and then added its respective property, EndUserID. Although in this example you're creating this new information manually, later in the chapter you will use a shortcut in Visual Studio that will make the task of creating this information a whole lot easier and less time-consuming.

7. To complete the remaining properties within the class, repeat the same procedure as in the previous step by creating the private field name along with its associated property that is specified in Table 11-1. When complete, the class will resemble the following code:

```csharp
using System;
using System.Collections.Generic;
using System.Text;

namespace LittleItalyVineyard.Common
{
    public class EndUser
    {
        private int _enduserid;
        private int _endusertypeid;
        private string _firstname;
        private string _lastname;
        private Address _address;
        private int _addressid;
        private ContactInformation _contactinformation;
        private int _contactinformtationid;
        private string _password;
        private bool _issubscribed;

        public EndUser()
        {

        }

        public int EndUserID
        {
            get { return _enduserid; }
            set { _enduserid = value; }
        }

        public int EndUserTypeID
        {
            get { return _endusertypeid; }
            set { _endusertypeid = value; }
        }

        public string FirstName
        {
            get { return _firstname; }
```

```csharp
            set { _firstname = value; }
        }

        public string LastName
        {
            get { return _lastname; }
            set { _lastname = value; }
        }

        public Address Address
        {
            get { return _address; }
            set { _address = value; }
        }

        public int AddressID
        {
            get { return _addressid; }
            set { _addressid = value; }
        }

        public ContactInformation ContactInformation
        {
            get { return _contactinformation; }
            set { _contactinformation = value; }
        }

        public int ContactInformtationID
        {
            get { return _contactinformtationid; }
            set { _contactinformtationid = value; }
        }

        public string Password
        {
            get { return _password; }
            set { _password = value; }
        }

        public bool IsSubscribed
        {
            get { return _issubscribed; }
            set { _issubscribed = value; }
        }
    }
}
```

You have now referenced the remaining properties within the EndUser class and added them in a similar fashion as you did with the EndUserID property. After completing this portion of the EndUser class, you could now create the remaining common objects and classes. However, the following section will show you how to do this easily in Visual Studio 2005.

You have now completed not only the exercise but also the first common object and class that will be used within your application. As a result of there being several common classes, I won't present a separate exercise for each of the objects. After completing this exercise, it should be relatively simple to model the remaining classes discussed earlier in this chapter. The important point is that within this specific portion of the architecture, these common classes will only represent objects and not provide any functionality themselves. Again, you'll use them throughout the entire system and architecture but as part of the functionality.

You created the first common class manually, but Visual Studio 2005 offers a shortcut you can use to build the remaining classes quite easily. The next section of the chapter will show how you can minimize your time while building the remaining common classes and be as efficient as possible.

Refactoring Within Visual Studio 2005

In the previous exercise, you created a new class file, added a field name, and then with the field name created a public property. In doing so, you created the property manually—in other words, you simply typed all the code by hand. This can become quite tedious, especially when the class files contain many properties.

You are in luck; Visual Studio 2005 has a new feature within the refactoring that will allow you to specify the field name and then create the subsequent property with only a couple of clicks. To demonstrate this functionality, the following exercise walks you through creating the next common object class, the EndUserType class.

Exercise: Using the Refactoring Functionality in Visual Studio 2005

The next class within the common objects will be a relatively small class with only two properties. However, this exercise will show how to use Visual Studio 2005 and its refactoring features to speed up the creation process. Follow these steps:

1. Relaunch the LittleItalyVineyards Visual Studio solution. After the solution loads successfully, as demonstrated in the previous exercise, add a new class named EndUserType to the LittleItalyVineyard.Common class library project, as shown in Figure 11-5.

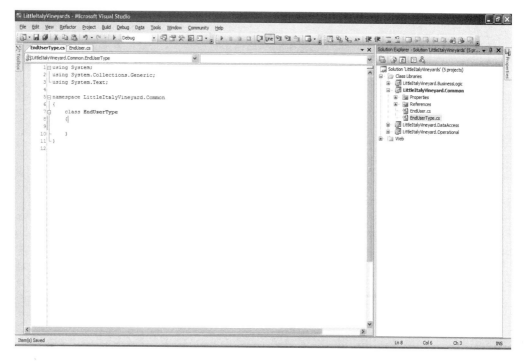

Figure 11-5. *The EndUserType class file*

2. In a similar fashion as you did in the previous exercise when creating the EndUser class, add the public identifier to the class name along with a constructor that will yield the following code:

```
using System;
using System.Collections.Generic;
using System.Text;

namespace LittleItalyVineyard.Common
{
    public class EndUserType
    {
        public EndUserType()
        {

        }
    }
}
```

3. Now that you have the basic setup of the class, you'll proceed to add the first field name, _endusertypeid, as shown here:

```
using System;
using System.Collections.Generic;
using System.Text;
```

```
namespace LittleItalyVineyard.Common
{
    public class EndUserType
    {
        private int _endusertypeid;

        public EndUserType()
        {

        }
    }
}
```

4. In this step, use the refactoring functionality to create the property as opposed to manually coding it. To do so, right-click the newly added field name, _endusertypeid, and choose Refactor ➤ Encapsulate Field, as shown in Figure 11-6. If you happen to be using the Express version for development, the refactoring tools will not be available, and unfortunately you'll need to create the properties manually.

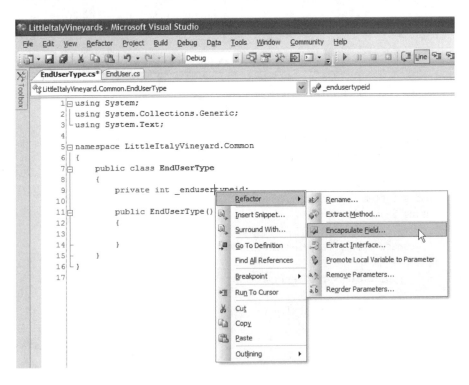

Figure 11-6. *Selecting the Refactor ➤ Encapsulate Field menu*

5. After selecting this item, you will see the dialog box shown in Figure 11-7 where you will add the name of the property to be added to the class.

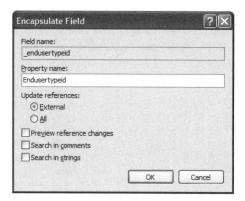

Figure 11-7. *Encapsulate Field dialog box*

6. In the Encapsulate Field dialog box, you can see that the field name that was selected was the
   _endusertypeid field and the next item to address is the actual property name. At this point,
   change the name of the property to EndUserTypeID to reflect camel-casing naming conventions.
   Notice the other options in the Encapsulate Field dialog box. You won't use any of the other
   options, but they give you the ability to search within the comments and within any string values
   you might have created in the code. Lastly, another option offers the ability to preview all your
   changes before the code is committed. When finished, click the OK button, and you will see the
   following code:

```
using System;
using System.Collections.Generic;
using System.Text;

namespace LittleItalyVineyard.Common
{
    public class EndUserType
    {
        private int _endusertypeid;

        public int EndUserTypeID
        {
            get { return _endusertypeid; }
            set { _endusertypeid = value; }
        }

        public EndUserType()
        {

        }
    }
}
```

7. You can see that the EndUserTypeID property was automatically created for you with only a few clicks as opposed to manually hand-coding the get and set items for the property. Continue to the remaining property of the EndUserType class—the EndUserName property with its respective field, _endusername. The completed class will resemble the following code:

```csharp
using System;
using System.Collections.Generic;
using System.Text;

namespace LittleItalyVineyard.Common
{
    public class EndUserType
    {
        private int _endusertypeid;
        private string _endusername;

        public EndUserType()
        {

        }

        public int EndUserTypeID
        {
            get { return _endusertypeid; }
            set { _endusertypeid = value; }
        }

        public string EndUsername
        {
            get { return _endusername; }
            set { _endusername = value; }
        }
    }
}
```

Notice that the code was rearranged slightly to be consistent with the class design in that the field names are listed followed by the constructor and finally the individual properties. Continue using the refactoring functionality to create the remaining common object class files for the project that were specified in the previous tables. It will be quite apparent that this will save you time in your development.

Summary

In this chapter, you explored the ins and outs of not only why you are incorporating common objects within your system but also how to create them effectively with a new technique in Visual Studio 2005. However, I didn't discuss how you'll use the common objects throughout the system's architecture. I'll cover this in the next chapters, which will discuss in more detail how to use the common objects.

■ ■ ■

CHAPTER 12

Creating the Data Access Layer

This chapter will deal with a main layer of the Little Italy Vineyards' application architecture. The layer in question is the data access layer, which will play a vital role in the entire application from start to finish. It is apparent that any enterprise application will have extensive interaction and connectivity with its database and all the data that is associated with it. With advances in technology and, more specifically, the new version of the .NET Framework 2.0, it is significantly easier to maintain such functionality. However, even though this makes some of the work easier than in the past, you still need to maintain cohesion and organization.

This cohesion and organization will come in the form of the data access layer as well as in the advancements of the new version of the framework. Having this structure will give the case study application several benefits.

This chapter will focus on the following topics to give you a solid understanding of the data access layer of the architecture:

- Understanding why you should use a data access layer

- Using the Microsoft Data Access Application Block

- Implementing the data access layer into the project

Why a Data Access Layer?

Thus far I briefly touched upon why you would want to have a specific section within your system and architecture dedicated to the data access functional points. Basically, you will have many reasons for dedicating a specific segment, or tier, to the data access of your system. One of the key reasons for having a multitiered architecture is to have separate layers that can be updated or changed independently of one another. Well, in the case of the data access layer, this is certainly true, as I'll illustrate with a specific example related to databases. (You can refer to Chapter 10, which was about architecture as a whole, for more benefits.)

Say an application is designed initially for one specific database, such as Oracle. Then sometime in the lifetime of the application, your client or boss informs you that the company is going to switch the database it uses for storing data. In this case, the new database will be Microsoft SQL Server. After being informed of this, you realize you will have to migrate your application, which was originally targeted to use Oracle, so that it conforms to a SQL Server database. That sounds like fun, right? Unfortunately, this scenario happens frequently in today's marketplace, so it is best to be prepared for a migration such as this.

If you didn't have a specific data access layer, accommodating such a change would be a monumental task. You would probably find code throughout the application that dealt with connecting and communicating to the database. Repetitive code would most likely be a common theme. If this were the situation, to convert everything to use a new database, the development team would have to look at essentially every line of code and replace all the code that dealt with accessing and processing the data to some new form of functionality that would be compatible with the new database being implemented. Undoubtedly, this would be a long process and could be somewhat compared to almost starting at "square one."

On the other hand, from the outset of a project, say you know that some changes will be inevitable; preparing for situations such as this and implementing a data access layer will behoove all involved. As a result of having a predefined data access layer from the beginning of the project, any application, whether it's a web or Windows desktop or a client-server application, will have the ability to adapt to a major shift in which database it is using.

With a defined data access layer, changing databases will still not be simplistic, but at least you will have a single section within the application on which you can focus. You won't need to scavenge throughout the entire code base because you will know that only a specific section will be affected by the change. In fact, this section, the data access layer, can be essentially extracted and worked upon independently so the migration has a minimal effect on other sections of the code and the overall application. Although this will not trivialize the overall task, it will significantly shorten the timeframe to achieve the task.

Although this example, as mentioned earlier, can certainly be a common scenario, it is not the only reason to design a data access layer. You get many more benefits from having this dedicated tier within the architecture. To name only a few, having one dedicated area where connections will be opened and closed in a methodical fashion will promote enhanced performance. In addition, storing the information and credentials will allow for a successful connection to the database and just improve the overall processing of the data. For instance, where will the application use DataSets, SqlDataReaders, and Extensible Markup Language (XML)? Having a centralized location to encapsulate this activity will provide the most efficient maintenance and scalability.

Using the Microsoft Data Access Application Block

Prior to discussing the actual implementation for the data access layer in the source code and Visual Studio 2005, I'll discuss a companion component that you'll use with the data access layer. This companion project will be a class file that you add to the LittleItalyVineyard.DataAccess class library project within the solution. I'm referring to the Microsoft Data Access Application Block, which is a free component from Microsoft with a royalty-free distribution.

■**Note** At the time of this writing, you can download the Microsoft Data Access Application Block from the Microsoft Download Center (http://www.microsoft.com/downloads/search.aspx).

The Microsoft Data Access Application Block is an extremely useful component that will work in conjunction with your own LittleItalyVineyard.DataAccess class library project. This component will encapsulate the actual code that will execute against the database. It will automatically manage the connections, the parameters, and the name of the stored procedure as a result of this information being passed into the class. The class that has this capability is named SQLHelper, and it has many methods that are overloaded to handle these tasks.

Discussing the application blocks in great detail is beyond the scope of this book; however, I will discuss how you will implement it in the overall solution. The following exercise shows how to implement it in your architecture.

Exercise: Implementing the Microsoft Data Access Application Block

In this exercise, you will add the application block class, SQLHelper, to the LittleItalyVineyard.DataAccess class library project. Follow these steps:

1. First download the application block from the link provided earlier, or install it from the source code provided with this book. Once installed, you can proceed to the LittleItalyVineyard.DataAccess project, and right-click the project. Choose Add ➤ Existing Item, as shown in Figure 12-1.

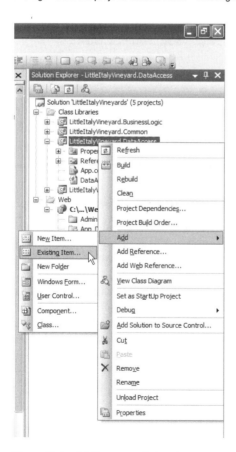

Figure 12-1. *Adding an existing item*

2. After choosing to add an existing item, you will see a dialog box to navigate to the file you want to add. If you chose the default location when you installed the application block, then you can navigate to C:\Program Files\Microsoft Application Blocks For .Net\Data Access v2\Code\CS\ Microsoft.ApplicationBlocks.Data and select the SQLHelper.cs file, as shown in Figure 12-2.

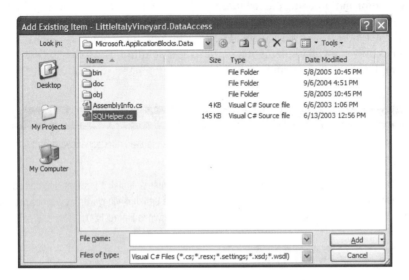

Figure 12-2. *Add Existing Item dialog box*

3. Finally, click the Add button, which will add the SQLHelper class file to the project.

The data access project can now take advantage of the Microsoft Data Access Application Block component. In the next section of the chapter, I will discuss how you can take advantage of using the application blocks.

Implementing the Classes

You'll now examine two aspects of this individual tier of the architecture. However, before discussing the details, I'll discuss the specifics of how and exactly what you will need to implement in your source code baseline to begin constructing the data access layer for your project in the case study.

For the purposes of this chapter, you will implement the main structure of the data access layer, which will prepare you for the subsequent chapters and examples on how data will be processed throughout this tier of the architecture. In the following chapters, I'll provide many more examples to show how the overall system will interact with the data access layer and thus demonstrate its benefits. Therefore, you'll now learn about the first item to implement, which is the base class within the data access layer.

The DataAccessBase Class

The first step of implementing the data access layer within the overall project will be a single class from which all other classes within the data access layer will inherit. This class will be the base class of the tier and will be appropriately named DataAccessBase. This class, for the case study purposes, will primarily have only a few functions to perform. However, as your application scales, the class will have the ability to be expanded upon depending on the individual needs.

As mentioned, this class will have limited functionality for the purposes of the case study. More specifically, it will have two separate properties: one for the name of the stored procedure being used and the other for returning the connection string for the database. At the moment, I have not specified what the connection string is or where it will be contained. I'll provide this information in the section "The Connection String." The following exercise demonstrates how to implement the base class within the data access layer.

Exercise: Implementing the DataAccessBase Class

This exercise will show how to add the necessary class files and finally all the associated code in Visual Studio 2005. Follow these steps:

1. Proceed to Visual Studio 2005. Navigate to the Class Libraries solution folder and then to the LittleItalyVineyard.DataAccess class library project. Then right-click the project. From the menu, select Add ➤ Class, as shown in Figure 12-3.

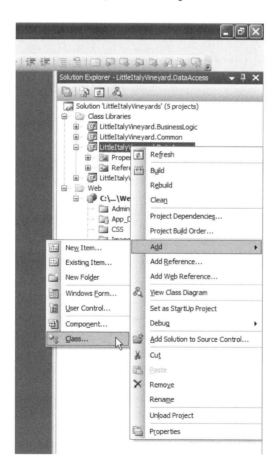

Figure 12-3. *Adding the DataAccessBase class*

2. When presented with the Add New Item dialog box, you will notice that the Class template is selected. Enter the name of the class file being added, **DataAccessBase**, as shown in Figure 12-4, and click the Add button when complete.

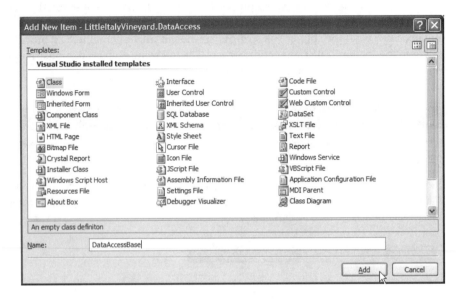

Figure 12-4. *Naming the class*

Upon adding the class successfully, you will see the shell code of a new class, as shown here:

```
using System;
using System.Collections.Generic;
using System.Text;

namespace LittleItalyVineyard.DataAccess
{
    class DataAccessBase
    {
    }
}
```

3. You can now enter the properties that this base class will contain. The first item to add is a public identifier for the class followed by a private string field, _storedprocedurename, and finally the associated property, StoredProcedureName. When complete, the code will resemble the following:

```
using System;
using System.Collections.Generic;
using System.Text;

namespace LittleItalyVineyard.DataAccess
{
    public class DataAccessBase
```

```
        {
            private string _storedprocedureName;

            protected string StoredProcedureName
            {
                get { return _storedprocedureName; }
                set { _storedprocedureName = value; }
            }
        }
    }
```

4. The base class is almost complete. However, before you add the final property to obtain the connection string, you need to add a reference to the class library project. The reference you need is the
   System.Configuration class from the framework library. To add this reference, right-click the References folder within the project, and select the Add Reference menu item, as shown in Figure 12-5.

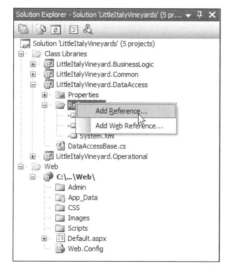

Figure 12-5. *Adding a reference*

5. After selecting the Add Reference option, within a few seconds you will see the Add Reference dialog
   box. Select the System.Configuration reference located on the .NET tab, as shown in Figure 12-6, and
   then click the OK button.

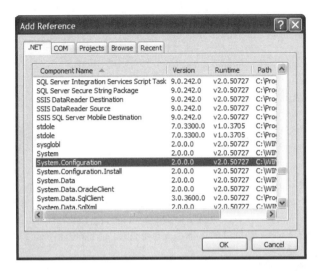

Figure 12-6. *Add Reference dialog box*

6. This adds the reference to System.Configuration to the data access class library project, which will not be visible in the References folder. You can now complete the base class by adding the ConnectionString property. First you have to declare the new namespace being used at the top of the code:

```
using System.Configuration;
```

This will give you the following declarations:

```
using System;
using System.Collections.Generic;
using System.Text;
using System.Configuration;
```

7. Now you can add the ConnectionString property, which will return the connection string that you will provide later in this chapter. This property will be a read-only property because it has only a get and not a set within the property. The property will not need to have an associated field as the other properties have had because it will use the ConfigurationManager class and the ConnectionStrings function to return the connection string for the database:

```
protected string ConnectionString
{
    get
    {
        return ConfigurationManager. ➥
            ConnectionStrings[ "SQLCONN" ].ToString();
    }
}
```

As mentioned, you have created a read-only property that will return the connection string with the name SQLCONN, which will be within the Web.config file. The base class code as a whole will now resemble the following:

```
using System;
using System.Collections.Generic;
using System.Text;
using System.Configuration;

namespace LittleItalyVineyard.DataAccess
{
    public class DataAccessBase
    {
        private string _storedprocedureName;

        protected string StoredProcedureName
        {
            get { return _storedprocedureName; }
            set { _storedprocedureName = value; }
        }

        protected string ConnectionString
        {
          get
          {
           return ConfigurationManager. ➥
             ConnectionStrings[ "SQLCONN" ].ToString();
          }
        }
    }
}
```

You have completed the base class for the data access layer of the case study project. You should remember one important issue: even though you have the ability to retrieve the connection string to the database, I have not discussed how to implement the connection string or where it will reside within the overall application. If you were to execute the code as it is now, you would not get an error or exception but simply an empty string. Don't despair—the next section will provide all the details for not only the connection string but also where you'll place it and why.

The Connection String

As mentioned previously, the project is missing the actual connection string. Prior to diving directly into where the connection string will be located, I'll briefly discuss the concept behind having only one connection string in case it's not already obvious.

Every application that will utilize a database will need to have information that supplies the credentials for the database. This is what is referred to as the *connection string* and will need to be utilized each time you want the code to interact with the database. With this being said, you should specify the connection string only once within the application so that if and when it needs to change, you can change it in that single place.

For the application and architecture, the single place where the connection string will be located is within the web project in the Web.config file.

The main reason for having the connection string located in the Web.config file is to simply have it in a single location. The following exercise shows how to implement the connection string.

Exercise: Implementing the Connection String

In this exercise, you will add the Web.config file to the web project and add the connection string. Follow these steps:

1. Return to Visual Studio 2005. Right-click the web project, and choose Add ➤ New Item. You will see the Add New Item dialog box once again.

2. In this dialog box, select the Web Configuration File item, which will provide a default name of Web.config, as shown in Figure 12-7. You don't need to rename this, so click the Add button.

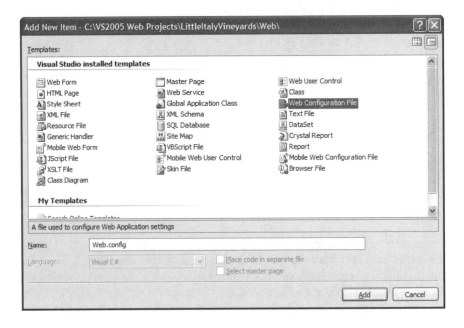

Figure 12-7. *Add New Item dialog box*

After adding the Web.config file to the project, the shell of the file will resemble the following:

```
<?xml version="1.0"?>
<!--
    Note: As an alternative to hand editing this file you can use the
    web admin tool to configure settings for your application. Use
    the Website->Asp.Net Configuration option in Visual Studio.
    A full list of settings and comments can be found in
    machine.config.comments usually located in
    \Windows\Microsoft.Net\Framework\v2.x\Config
-->
<configuration>
```

```
    <appSettings/>
    <connectionStrings/>
    <system.web>
        <!--
            Set compilation debug="true" to insert debugging
            symbols into the compiled page. Because this
            affects performance, set this value to true only
            during development.
        -->
        <compilation debug="false" />
        <!--
            The <authentication> section enables configuration
            of the security authentication mode used by
            ASP.NET to identify an incoming user.
        -->
        <authentication mode="Windows" />
        <!--
            The <customErrors> section enables configuration
            of what to do if/when an unhandled error occurs
            during the execution of a request. Specifically,
            it enables developers to configure html error pages
            to be displayed in place of a error stack trace.

    <customErrors mode="RemoteOnly"
            defaultRedirect="GenericErrorPage.htm">
            <error statusCode="403" redirect="NoAccess.htm" />
            <error statusCode="404" redirect="FileNotFound.htm" />
    </customErrors>
        -->
    </system.web>
</configuration>
```

3. Within the configuration settings of the Web.config file, you will need to alter the ConnectionStrings tags as follows:

```
<?xml version="1.0"?>
<!--
    Note: As an alternative to hand editing this file you can use the
    web admin tool to configure settings for your application. Use
    the Website->Asp.Net Configuration option in Visual Studio.
    A full list of settings and comments can be found in
    machine.config.comments usually located in
    \Windows\Microsoft.Net\Framework\v2.x\Config
-->
<configuration>
    <appSettings/>
    <connectionStrings>
```

```
        </connectionStrings>
        <system.web>
            <!--
                Set compilation debug="true" to insert debugging
                symbols into the compiled page. Because this
                affects performance, set this value to true only
                during development.
            -->
            <compilation debug="false" />
            <!--
                The <authentication> section enables configuration
                of the security authentication mode used by
                ASP.NET to identify an incoming user.
            -->
            <authentication mode="Windows" />
            <!--
                The <customErrors> section enables configuration
                of what to do if/when an unhandled error occurs
                during the execution of a request. Specifically,
                it enables developers to configure html error pages
                to be displayed in place of a error stack trace.

            <customErrors mode="RemoteOnly"
                defaultRedirect="GenericErrorPage.htm">
                <error statusCode="403" redirect="NoAccess.htm" />
                <error statusCode="404" redirect="FileNotFound.htm" />
            </customErrors>
            -->
        </system.web>
    </configuration>
```

4. The remaining step is to add the actual connection string, as shown here:

```
<connectionStrings>
<add
name="SQLCONN" connectionString="server=Lumberg\SQL2005; ➥
 uid=sa;pwd=*****;database=LittleItalyVineyard"/>
</connectionStrings>
```

You now have successfully implemented the Web.config file with the connection string for database connectivity. I have shown the specifics for my development database server, so you will need to modify your connection string to represent your individual settings and credentials according to the credentials you have set up in your own database.

The StoredProcedure Class

Continuing with the implementation phase of the data access layer in the architecture, you will specify the name of each stored procedure used in the application. This class is named

StoredProcedure and will contain only a single enumeration that will list all the stored procedure names. You might be wondering why you will have a dedicated section for this. Well, you could simply add a string value throughout the application, which would represent the name of each stored procedure. However, when designing this application, you want to achieve the most scalability possible. Therefore, having a single location, via an enumeration, will allow you to change one place when you need to change the name of a stored procedure or, more likely, when you need to add stored procedures. This will provide a much cleaner maintenance process and will reduce the time you have to expend when dealing with these operations. The following exercise shows how to create the StoredProcedure class.

Exercise: Creating the StoredProcedure Class

This exercise will continue with the overall implementation of the data access layer. You will add the stored procedure class file and create the enumeration that will list all the names of the stored procedures that will be used throughout the entire application. Follow these steps:

1. The first task is similar to the prior exercises. Proceed to the LittleItalyVineyard.DataAccess class library project, and right-click. Choose Add ➤ Class. Finally, rename the class to **StoredProcedure**, and click the Add button. You will use the shell code, as shown here:

```
using System;
using System.Collections.Generic;
using System.Text;

namespace LittleItalyVineyard.DataAccess
{
    class StoredProcedure
    {
    }
}
```

2. In the code, add a public identifier, and then add the enumeration called Name:

```
using System;
using System.Collections.Generic;
using System.Text;

namespace LittleItalyVineyard.DataAccess
{
    public class StoredProcedure
    {
        public enum Name
        {

        }
    }
}
```

3. Everything is now set up for the stored procedure enumeration. All you need to do is list the individual names of the stored procedures within the Name enum. Since you have not created any stored procedures yet, I will list three sample names of stored procedures to demonstrate how the listing will be implemented:

```
using System;
using System.Collections.Generic;
using System.Text;

namespace LittleItalyVineyard.DataAccess
{
    public class StoredProcedure
    {
        public enum Name
        {
            STOREDPROCEDURE_A ,
            STOREDPROCEDURE_B ,
            STOREDPROCEDURE_C
        }
    }
}
```

Later in the book when you implement code for specific functionality, you will need to create stored procedures for the given functionality, and when doing so, you will add each name to this enumeration within the StoredProcedure class.

The DataBaseHelper Class

The last class you need to add to the data access layer and project will be the class that utilizes the Microsoft Data Access Application Block class. It is the DataBaseHelper class, and it will contain a number of overloaded methods and functions that will essentially wrap the SQLHelper class functionality. These methods and functions will return DataSets, SqlDataReaders, and any necessary transactions. In addition, one property will contain the array of parameters that will be needed to pass along the individual data processes. The following exercise shows you how to implement the DataBaseHelper class.

Exercise: Implementing the DataBaseHelper Class

This exercise shows how to create the new DataBaseHelper class file and add the associated code. Follow these steps:

1. The first step is to add the actual class file. As you have done several times in previous exercises, right-click the LittleItalyVineyard.DataAccess class library project, and select Add ➤ Class. You will then see the Add New Item dialog box. Name the class **DataBaseHelper**, as shown in Figure 12-8, and click Add.

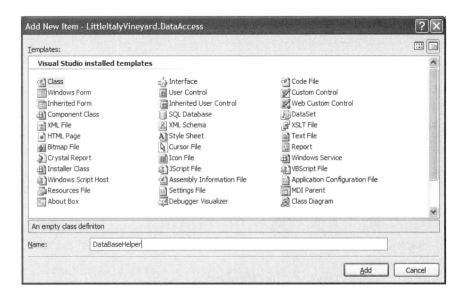

Figure 12-8. *Adding the DataBaseHelper class file*

2. After adding the new class, you will see the standard shell code for a new class. For the DataBaseHelper class, have it inherit from the DataAccessBase, and add the public identifier for the class, as shown here:

```
using System;
using System.Collections.Generic;
using System.Text;

namespace LittleItalyVineyard.DataAccess
{
    public class DataBaseHelper : DataAccessBase
    {

    }
}
```

3. Next, add some declarations to the namespaces at the top of the code. The namespaces will be System.Data, System.Data.SqlClient, and finally Microsoft.ApplicationBlocks.Data, as shown here:

```
using System;
using System.Collections.Generic;
using System.Text;
using System.Data;
using System.Data.SqlClient;

using Microsoft.ApplicationBlocks.Data;

namespace LittleItalyVineyard.DataAccess
{
```

```
        public class DataBaseHelper : DataAccessBase
        {

        }
    }
```

4. You are now ready to add the individual functions and properties to the class. To begin, first add a field for an array of SqlParameters along with its associated property, Parameters:

```
using System;
using System.Collections.Generic;
using System.Text;
using System.Data;
using System.Data.SqlClient;

using Microsoft.ApplicationBlocks.Data;

namespace LittleItalyVineyard.DataAccess
{
    public class DataBaseHelper : DataAccessBase
    {
        private SqlParameter[ ] _parameters;


        private SqlParameter[ ] Parameters
        {
            get { return _parameters; }
            set { _parameters = value; }
        }
    }
}
```

In the following chapters, I will provide additional details about what this property will be used for; at this point, it is sufficient to understand that this property will supply the parameters for the stored procedures in the code.

5. The final step of the exercise is to add five overloaded methods named Run. This will allow you to take advantage of the SqlHelper class and use DataSets, SqlDataReaders, and even associated transactions. The following code is for the complete DataBaseHelper class:

```
using System;
using System.Collections.Generic;
using System.Text;
using System.Data;
using System.Data.SqlClient;

using Microsoft.ApplicationBlocks.Data;
```

```csharp
namespace LittleItalyVineyard.DataAccess
{
    public class DataBaseHelper : DataAccessBase
    {
        private SqlParameter[ ] _parameters;

        public DataBaseHelper( string storedprocedurename )
        {
            StoredProcedureName = storedprocedurename;
        }

        public void Run( SqlTransaction transaction )
        {
            SqlHelper.ExecuteNonQuery( transaction ,
                        CommandType.StoredProcedure ,
                        StoredProcedureName , Parameters );
        }

        public void Run( SqlTransaction transaction ,
                            SqlParameter[] parameters )
        {
            SqlHelper.ExecuteNonQuery( transaction ,
                        CommandType.StoredProcedure ,
                        StoredProcedureName , parameters );
        }
    }

    public DataSet Run( string connectionstring ,
                            SqlParameter[ ] parameters )
    {
        DataSet ds;
        ds = SqlHelper.ExecuteDataset( connectionstring ,
                            StoredProcedureName ,  parameters );
        return ds;
    }

    public object RunScalar( string connectionstring ,
                                SqlParameter[ ] parameters )
    {
        object obj;
        obj = SqlHelper.ExecuteScalar( connectionstring ,
                    StoredProcedureName , parameters );
        return obj;
    }

    public object RunScalar( SqlTransaction transaction ,
                                SqlParameter[] parameters )
```

```csharp
        {
            object obj;
            obj = SqlHelper.ExecuteScalar( transaction ,
                                           StoredProcedureName ,
                                                     parameters );
            return obj;
        }

        public DataSet Run( string connectionstring )
        {
            DataSet ds;
            ds = SqlHelper.ExecuteDataset➥
                ( connectionstring ,
                  CommandType.StoredProcedure ,
                StoredProcedureName );
            return ds;
        }

        public void Run()
        {
            SqlHelper.ExecuteNonQuery➥
            ( base.ConnectionString ,
              CommandType.StoredProcedure ,
                          StoredProcedureName , Parameters );
        }

        public SqlDataReader Run( SqlParameter[ ] parameters )
        {
            SqlDataReader dr;
            dr = SqlHelper.ExecuteReader➥
                ( base.ConnectionString ,
                  CommandType.StoredProcedure ,
    StoredProcedureName , parameters );
            return dr;
        }

        public SqlParameter[ ] Parameters
        {
            get { return _parameters; }
            set { _parameters = value; }
        }
    }
}
```

How It Works

You have certainly added quite a lot of code to this class. Let's examine some of the individual items for some clarification. The first item to discuss is within the constructor. The constructor takes a parameter of the stored procedure name that is going to be used and then sets the StoredProcedureName property from the base class equal to that of the parameter:

```
public DataBaseHelper( string storedprocedurename )
{
    StoredProcedureName = storedprocedurename;
}
```

After the constructor, a series of methods and functions are overloaded that will perform the data access task by taking advantage of the SQLHelper class and the Microsoft Data Application Block components. For instance, when a DataSet is needed to return information from the database, you will utilize a function that returns a DataSet object such as the following:

```
public DataSet Run( string connectionstring )
{
    DataSet ds;
    ds = SqlHelper.ExecuteDataset( connectionstring ,
        CommandType.StoredProcedure , StoredProcedureName );
    return ds;
}
```

In this function, the connection string is passed as a parameter, and then finally the SqlHelper.ExecuteDataset function is called specifying that a stored procedure will be used, specifying the name of the stored procedure, and specifying the connection string. The DataSet object is then returned to the calling code.

The class is now complete for the time being. When you proceed to coding the individual functionality to complete the application, you might have to adjust or add to this class. That is perfectly OK because at this point you have a solid foundation for the overall data access layer.

Summary

You have arrived at the end of the chapter dedicated to the data access tier of the overall architecture. In this chapter, I discussed the common objects, and of course this chapter dealt with the data access portion of the system. The data access tier is one of the most important sections of the architecture because the case study application will be processing, storing, and retrieving data from a database frequently. You have a solid data access layer at this point in the code; however, as mentioned previously, as you continue to code the individual functionality, you may have to revisit the structure and possibly tweak it or add some updates. In the next chapter, I'll discuss the business logic layer of the architecture.

CHAPTER 13

■ ■ ■

Creating the Business Logic Layer

Moving along to the next part of the system's architecture brings you to the business logic layer. Each software application has its own set of logic and functionality that needs to be implemented. Up to this point in the book, I have discussed where and how the data will be processed, and I have discussed the common objects, which are the entities contained in the system; however, I have not discussed where the individual processing of the required business-specific rules will take place. Therefore, this chapter covers the business logic layer of the architecture. The *business logic layer* of the architecture will act as a bridge from the presentation to the data access so that the information can be processed in some cases and, in other cases, can simply be the conduit to ensure the smooth flow of information.

Throughout the chapter, I'll discuss several topics related to the business logic layer:

- How the business logic layer works

- How the common objects will be integrated

- How to implement the business logic layer

- How everything will work together

Introducing the Business Logic Layer

As mentioned in previous chapters, having a business logic layer within your architecture offers you many benefits. The business logic layer is standard within a common *n*-tier, or multitier, system architecture. In short, the business logic layer allows for the explicit separation of the data access and presentation layers. Although the data access tier performs all the functionality related to processing the data, it does not enforce any rules or logic that might be required for the business. In fact, the data access tier has no knowledge of any logic that needs to be performed. It simply will perform the data processing or retrieve any data it is asked to perform. In addition, this section of the architecture does not have any knowledge about Hypertext Markup Language (HTML) and does not directly output it. It does not know about ADO.NET or SQL and instead will connect the sections of the architecture that are responsible for knowing the other items.

This section of the architecture is the overall brain of the application. In other words, it will have the most information about the activity and the processing that needs to take place. For example, say your application needs to process a list of rules prior to allowing the user to proceed to their account. For example, when a user enters their credentials while logging in, the information that the user enters needs to be compared to the credentials within the database when the account was originally created. This is the type of checklist or comparison that would occur at this level.

The common classes will be heavily integrated throughout the business logic layer. Remember that the common classes are simply that—common entities that are found throughout the system, some being tangible and some being intangible. While providing a model of what the system contains, they also provide a mapping from the code to the database structure or overall schema, which will make it easier for the application to process and manage data.

For example, when a user logs in to their account, this will originate at the presentation layer, with a text box for the username and password that will eventually be verified against the same information stored within the database. After the user enters their username and password and clicks a button to execute the process, a common object will be used. That common object will be the EndUser class. It will be instantiated, and then the respective properties will be populated with the username and password that will be subsequently passed from the business logic layer to the data access layer to retrieve the information stored in the database. Once retrieved from the database, the passwords will be compared, and if there is a match, the remaining properties from the EndUser class will be populated and then saved in memory while the user successfully logs in to the system. To review, an instantiated EndUser class is populated only with the username and password, and upon a successful match from the information in the database, the remaining information is populated so the EndUser object can exist in memory while the user is interacting with the application.

Implementing the Business Logic Layer

You should now understand what the business logic layer is and why it is important to have such a structure within the application architecture. The next step is to implement this piece of the structure into the existing source code base and Visual Studio 2005 solution. The following exercise will walk you through the process of adding the first item needed in the business logic layer and subsequent class library project within Visual Studio 2005. This first item is the IBusinessLogic interface from which all classes will be implemented.

An *interface* is a reference type that contains only abstract members. The members contained in it can be only methods, indexers, properties, and events. It cannot contain any constants, constructors, static members, or data fields. The interface contains only the declaration of these members, and the implementation must be initiated from any of the classes that implement the interface. All declarations within an interface will be public and thus accessible from the classes that implement the interface. Although this is quite the textbook explanation, you can think of interfaces as being contracts that specify to any class that implements them that they need to have specific methods or implementations to fulfill the contract.

For example, refer to the following simple interface, which will require a method and property:

```
interface IExample
{
    bool GetName();

    string Name
    {
        get;
        set;
    }
}
```

This interface is named IExample, which is the standard naming convention for interfaces. In other words, an interface usually has the letter *I* as a prefix to the main word describing the interface. A method returns a boolean data type named GetName() along with a property named Name. Therefore, any class that implements the IExample interface will be required to have a GetName() method as well as a Name property.

Now, let's create a simple class that will implement the IExample interface:

```
public class ExampleClass : IExample
{
    public ExampleClass()
    {

    }
}
```

The previous class named ExampleClass implements the IExample interface by specifying it in the following line:

```
public class ExampleClass : IExample
```

However, at this point in the class, there is only a constructor, and it does not meet the contract requirements of the interface and does not allow for the code to be compiled in the state it is in at the moment. You need an implementation of the GetName() method along with the Name property, as shown here:

```
public class ExampleClass : IExample
{
    private string _name;

    public ExampleClass()
    {

    }
```

```
    public bool GetName()
    {
        bool complete = false;

        // Code to complete the method and return a boolean.

        return complete;
    }

    public string Name
    {
        get { return _name; }
        set { _name = value; }
    }
}
```

The class is now in contractual agreement with the IExample interface as a result of containing all the required methods and properties; in other words, ExampleClass successfully implements the IExample interface.

In the following exercise, you'll add the interface that all classes within the business logic layer will implement. This interface will be appropriately named IBusinessLogic and will have a method named Invoke(), which will be the method from which all classes initiate the contact with the data access layer to process its task and information.

Exercise: Implementing the Business Logic Layer into Visual Studio 2005

In this exercise, you'll implement the business logic layer in your existing architecture by utilizing the business logic class library project that you created when you originally set up the Visual Studio 2005 solution. Follow these steps:

1. Open the Visual Studio 2005 solution if you closed it, and navigate to the Class Libraries solution folder and then to the LittleItalyVineyard.BusinessLogic class library project. Right-click the project, and select Add ➤ New Item, as shown in Figure 13-1.

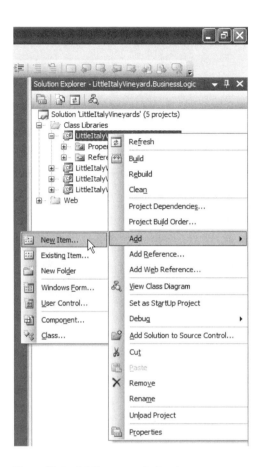

Figure 13-1. *Adding an existing item*

2. You will see the Add New Item dialog box; however, instead of adding a new class or configuration item, select the Interface item, and name it **IBusinessLogic**, as shown in Figure 13-2.

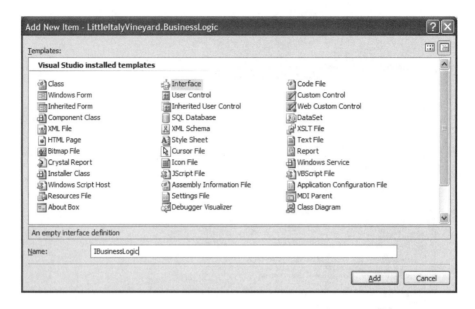

Figure 13-2. *Adding the IBusinessLogic interface*

3. Click the Add button, which will add the IBusinessLogic interface to the LittleItalyVineyard.
   BusinessLogic class library. You will see the following code:

```
using System;
using System.Collections.Generic;
using System.Text;

namespace LittleItalyVineyard.BusinessLogic
{
    interface IBusinessLogic
    {
    }
}
```

4. The next step is to add any necessary methods or properties. For these purposes, you'll add only one
   method named Invoke(), which will look like the following:

```
using System;
using System.Collections.Generic;
using System.Text;

namespace LittleItalyVineyard.BusinessLogic
{
    interface IBusinessLogic
    {
        void Invoke();
    }
}
```

5. Now that you have a completed interface, you'll add the first class in the business logic layer that will implement this interface. You will leave this class in its preliminary, or shell, condition but will implement the IBusinessLogic interface. Right-click the LittleItalyVineyard.BuinessLogic class library, and add a new class named **ProcessGetProducts**, as shown in Figure 13-3.

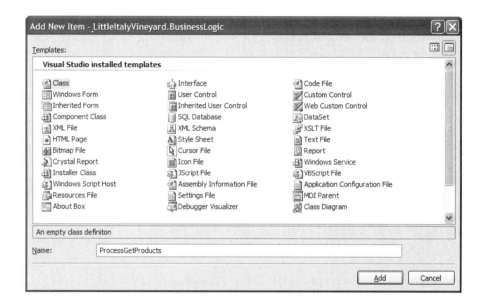

Figure 13-3. *Adding the ProcessGetProducts class*

When finished entering the name of the class and clicking the Add button, you will see the following code:

```
using System;
using System.Collections.Generic;
using System.Text;

namespace LittleItalyVineyard.BusinessLogic
{
    class ProcessGetProducts
    {
    }
}
```

6. Now that you have the basic shell of the ProcessGetProducts class, you have to add the implementation of the IBusinessLogic interface as well as add a public class identifier, as described here:

```
using System;
using System.Collections.Generic;
using System.Text;

namespace LittleItalyVineyard.BusinessLogic
{
    public class ProcessGetProducts : IBusinessLogic
```

```
        {
        }
    }
```

7. You have now indicated that the ProcessGetProducts class will implement the IBusinessLogic interface, but now you have to add the actual implementation. After you finish typing the name of the interface, the Visual Studio 2005 integrated development environment (IDE) will give you a shortcut where you can complete the implementation. Figure 13-4 shows the indicator just below the letter *I* in the word IBusinessLogic.

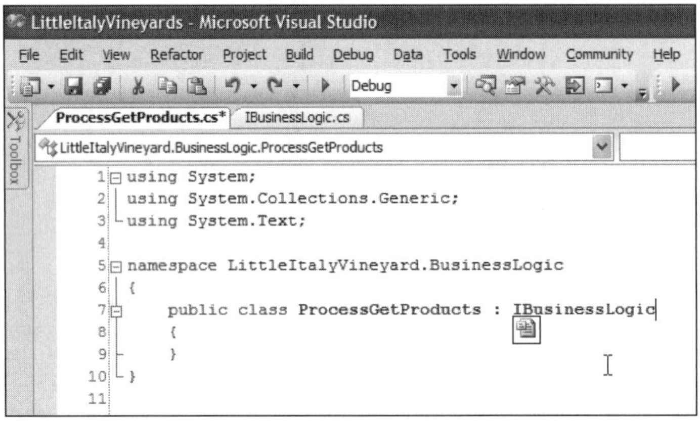

Figure 13-4. *The interface indicator*

8. Move your cursor over the indicator, and click the down arrow to display the options shown in Figure 13-5.

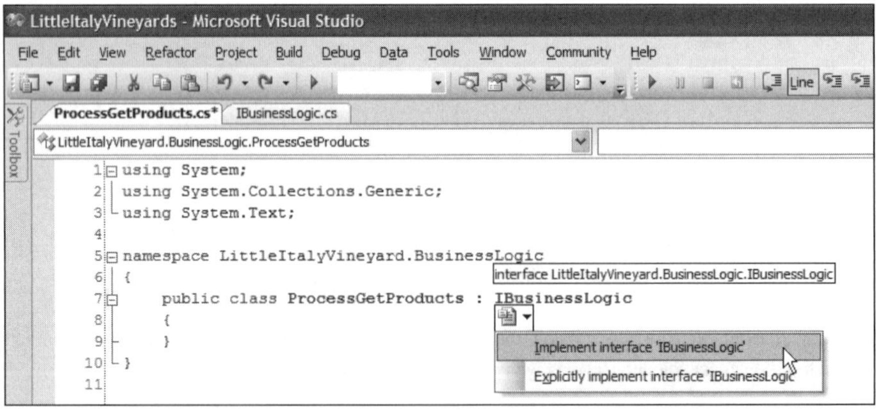

Figure 13-5. *Choosing the implementation*

9. You will see two options, Implement Interface IBusinessLogic and Explicitly Implement Interface IBusinessLogic. Click the first option, and you will then see that the implementation is complete for the class, as shown in Figure 13-6.

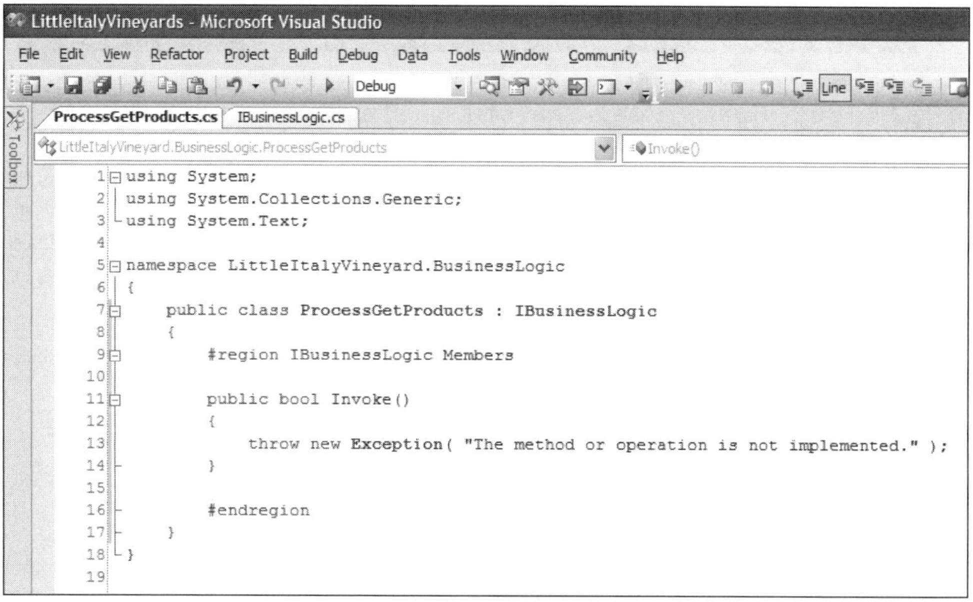

Figure 13-6. *The complete implementation from the IDE*

You can see that the Invoke() method has been added to the ProcessGetProducts class for you. To have the code compile at this point, you need to have the Invoke() method return a true or false value. In the next exercise, I will explain in detail how to implement whether the value being returned is true or false.

Finally, Visual Studio has added some filler code that you can keep or discard. This includes the region section added named IBusinessLogic Members and an exception within the method that throws a new exception saying there is nothing implemented yet. It is up to you whether you keep the region, but you will eventually be implementing the Invoke() method for the class, so you'll delete the exception later.

You have learned how the business logic layer will work for the overall architecture and system. All the classes within the business logic layer will implement the IBusinessLogic interface, and thus the class will be required to implement the Invoke method to initiate the communication from this section of the architecture to the data access layer and eventually return the information to the presentation layer. In the next section of the chapter, I will take everything a step further and demonstrate how the business logic layer will communicate with the data access layer along with the common objects so you can gain a better understanding of how all the pieces will work together.

Getting Everything Working Together

Now that you have completed the initial piece of the business logic layer with the IBusinessLogic interface, I will demonstrate how a class from the business logic layer will interact with the data access portion of the architecture. You first need to revisit the data access layer and class library project to add the necessary classes to process your requested data. Therefore, in the following exercise, you'll implement the business logic layer with the data access layer.

Exercise: Implementing the Business Logic Layer with the Data Access Layer

In this exercise, you will take a step back and look at the data access layer so you can fully understand just how the business logic layer will be able to interact with it. Follow these steps:

1. Return to the Visual Studio 2005 solution and then to the LittleItalyVineyard.DataAccess class library project. You'll first add another folder to the project by selecting Add ➤ New Folder, as shown in Figure 13-7. Name it **Select**. This directory will provide an additional namespace where all the classes will reside that select data. After adding a new folder, you can then add the data access class that will select the data for the exercise.

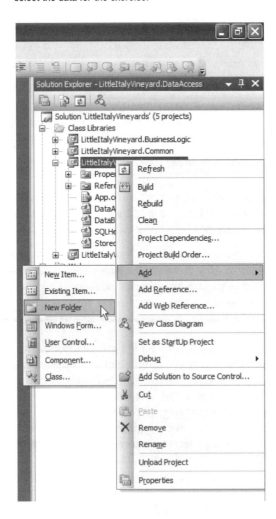

Figure 13-7. *Adding a new folder*

2. You now have a new folder or directory within the data access project named Select. Right-click this new folder, and choose Add ➤ Class, as shown in Figure 13-8.

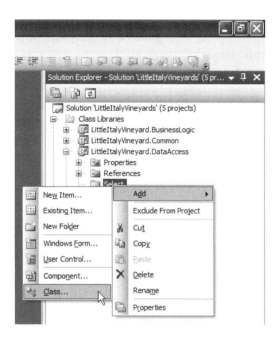

Figure 13-8. *Adding a new class*

3. After choosing to add a new class, you will see the ever-so-common Add New Item dialog box where you need to name your new class; name it **ProductSelectByIDData**, as shown in Figure 13-9.

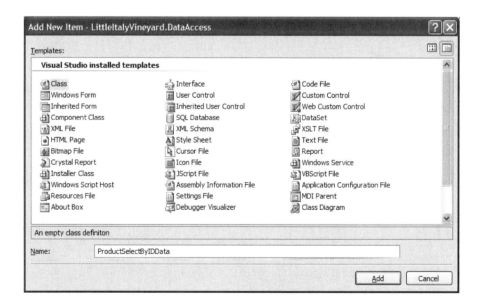

Figure 13-9. *Naming the new class*

4. You now have your first class within the Select folder (or namespace) that you need to integrate with the common objects. To accomplish this task, you will need to add a reference to the LittleItalyVineyard.Common class library project. To do so, right-click the References directory in the data access class library, and choose Add Reference, as shown in Figure 13-10.

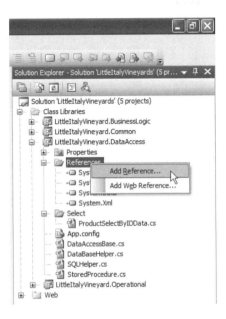

Figure 13-10. *Adding a reference*

5. You will see the Add Reference dialog box. Proceed to the Projects tab, select the LittleItalyVineyard.Common class library project, and finally click the OK button, as shown in Figure 13-11.

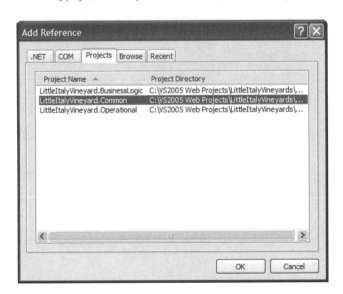

Figure 13-11. *Selecting the LittleItalyVineyard.Common project reference*

6. The data access project now has a reference to the common object via the project within the Visual Studio 2005 solution. You can now declare, within the code, the common object's namespace to the ProductSelectByIDData class, as shown in the following code:

```
using System;
using System.Collections.Generic;
using System.Text;

using LittleItalyVineyard.Common;

namespace LittleItalyVineyard.DataAccess.Select
{
    public class ProductSelectByIDData
    {

    }
}
```

7. You can now add some code that will contain the common object of the Product class, which will be represented with a property and associated field:

```
using System;
using System.Collections.Generic;
using System.Text;

using LittleItalyVineyard.Common;

namespace LittleItalyVineyard.DataAccess.Select
{
    public class ProductSelectByIDData : DataAccessBase
    {
        private Product _product;

        public ProductSelectByIDData()
        {

        }

        public Product Product
        {
            get { return _product; }
            set { _product = value; }
        }
    }
}
```

How It Works

Within the class, you have added the reference to the common objects and then added a field, _product, along with its associated property, Product.

8. You have not implemented the property for the Product class so that the class can be instantiated elsewhere in the architecture, be passed into the ProductSelectByIDData class by the Product property, and subsequently be used to query the database. To actually query the information from the database, you need to add some code. This code will utilize the SQLHelper class from the Microsoft Data Access Application Block, but first you need to add its namespace, as shown in the following code, along with an additional method named Get, which will return a DataSet:

```csharp
using System;
using System.Collections.Generic;
using System.Text;
using System.Data;

using LittleItalyVineyard.Common;

namespace LittleItalyVineyard.DataAccess.Select
{
    public class ProductSelectByIDData : DataAccessBase
    {
        private Product _product;

        public ProductSelectByIDData()
        {

        }

        public DataSet Get()
        {

        }

        public Product Product
        {
            get { return _product; }
            set { _product = value; }
        }
    }
}
```

How It Works

You have added the Get() method that will return a DataSet of the information and records that will be queried from the database.

9. To further enhance and build upon the class, you need to first specify the name of the stored procedure that will be used to query the database for a product with a specific ID. To accomplish this, proceed to the StoredProcedure class that is also located within the data access project, and add the name of the stored procedure to the Name enumeration, as follows:

```
using System;
using System.Collections.Generic;
using System.Text;

namespace LittleItalyVineyard.DataAccess
{
    public class StoredProcedure
    {
        public enum Name
        {
            ProductByID_Select
        }
    }
}
```

After adding the name of the stored procedure, SelectProductByID, return to the ProductSelectByIDData class.

10. Now that you have the name of the stored procedure that will be used, you need to specify that name in the constructor, as shown here:

```
public ProductSelectByIDData()
{
    StoredProcedureName =➡
        StoredProcedure.Name.ProductByID_Select.ToString();
}
```

You can see that you are using the StoredProcedureName property from the DataAccessBase class to be equal to that of the SelectProductByID enumeration that is finally cast to a string data type by means of the ToString() method. Using the ToString() method will allow you to use the string representation of the enumeration as opposed to the numeric value.

11. You are now ready to complete the Get() method, which will utilize the SQLHelper class from the Microsoft Data Application Blocks and take into account any parameters that will need to be specified for the stored procedure. In this case, you have a single stored procedure that specifies the product ID. To accomplish this, add a new class within the ProductSelectByIDData class file named ProductSelectByIDDataParameters, as shown here:

```
using System;
using System.Collections.Generic;
using System.Text;
using System.Data;
using System.Data.SqlClient;

using LittleItalyVineyard.Common;
```

```csharp
namespace LittleItalyVineyard.DataAccess.Select
{
    public class ProductSelectByIDData : DataAccessBase
    {
        private Product _product;


        public ProductSelectByIDData()
        {

        }

        public DataSet Get()
        {

        }

        public Product Product
        {
            get { return _product; }
            set { _product = value; }
        }
    }

    public class ProductSelectByIDDataParameters
    {
        private Product _product;
        private SqlParameter[ ] _parameters;

        public ProductSelectByIDDataParameters(Product product )
        {
            Product = product;
            Build();
        }

        private void Build()
        {
            SqlParameter[ ] parameters =
            {
                new SqlParameter( "@ProductID" , Product.ProductID )
            };

            Parameters = parameters;
        }

        public Product Product
        {
```

```
                get { return _product; }
                set { _product = value; }
        }

        public SqlParameter[ ] Parameters
        {
                get { return _parameters; }
                set { _parameters = value; }
        }
    }
}
```

You can see that within the new parameter class you have added a collection of SQL parameters contained in the Build() method that is called in the constructor. Finally, the parameter values are obtained from the common object class; in this case, the Product class is passed along to the constructor and subsequently added to the Product class in the form of a property.

12. The final step within the ProductSelectByIDData class is to add the code that will actually use the DataBaseHelper class you created in the previous chapter to return a DataSet of the product specified by the ID. To accomplish this, add the following code to the Get() method:

```
public DataSet Get()
{
    DataSet ds;

    ProductSelectByIDDataParameters _productselectbyiddataparameters➥
             = new ProductSelectByIDDataParameters( Product );
     DataBaseHelper dbhelper = new DataBaseHelper➥
            ( StoredProcedureName );
     ds = dbhelper.Run( base.ConnectionString ,
            _productselectbyiddataparameters.Parameters );

    return ds;
}
```

How It Works

Within the Get() method, a new DataSet object is declared and then subsequently used with the DataBaseHelper class. The ProductSelectByIDDataParameters class will be instantiated, and its Parameters property will be passed into the dbhelper class.

This will now give you the entire code within the class to accomplish everything you need to query the database for a specific product. Prior to moving on to the business logic class to utilize what you have just implemented, let's look at the code in its entirety:

```
using System;
using System.Collections.Generic;
using System.Text;
using System.Data;
using System.Data.SqlClient;
```

```csharp
using LittleItalyVineyard.Common;

namespace LittleItalyVineyard.DataAccess.Select
{
    public class ProductSelectByIDData : DataAccessBase
    {
        private Product _product;

        public ProductSelectByIDData()
        {

        }

        public DataSet Get()
        {
            DataSet ds;

            ProductSelectByIDDataParameters
                _productselectbyiddataparameters =➡
                    new ProductSelectByIDDataParameters( Product );
            DataBaseHelper dbhelper = new DataBaseHelper➡
                    ( StoredProcedureName );
            ds = dbhelper.Run( base.ConnectionString ,
                productselectbyiddataparameters.Parameters );

            return ds;
        }


        public Product Product
        {
            get { return _product; }
            set { _product = value; }
        }
    }

    public class ProductSelectByIDDataParameters
    {
        private Product _product;
        private SqlParameter[ ] _parameters;
```

```
public ProductSelectByIDDataParameters(Product product )
{
    Product = product;
    Build();
}

private void Build()
{
    SqlParameter[ ] parameters =
    {
        new SqlParameter( "@ProductID" , Product.ProductID )
    };

    Parameters = parameters;
}

public Product Product
{
    get { return _product; }
    set { _product = value; }
}

public SqlParameter[ ] Parameters
{
    get { return _parameters; }
    set { _parameters = value; }
}
    }
}
```

How It Works

To summarize the complete functionality that you have included, you added the ProductSelectByIDData class and then the ProductSelectByIDDataParameters class to handle all the parameters needed. The Product common class is implemented, and then the ProductID is passed into the ProductSelectByIDDataParameters class by the Product class to specify the parameter needed.

13. To finalize the exercise, return to the business logic project library. Because you added a reference to the common objects in the data access project, you need to add a reference to not only the common project (see Figure 13-12) but also to the data access project (see Figure 13-13) within the business logic class library project.

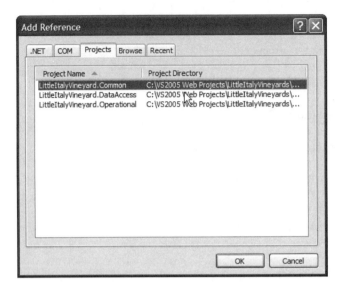

Figure 13-12. *Selecting the LittleItalyVineyard.Common project reference*

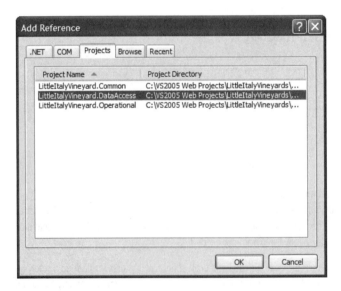

Figure 13-13. *Selecting the LittleItalyVineyard.DataAccess project reference*

14. Now that you have the necessary references, add a new class named ProcessGetProductByID. After successfully adding the new class, you need to make some modifications to the class, such as adding the references and implementing the interface, as shown here:

```csharp
using System;
using System.Collections.Generic;
using System.Text;
using System.Data;

using LittleItalyVineyard.Common;
using LittleItalyVineyard.DataAccess.Select;

namespace LittleItalyVineyard.BusinessLogic
{
        public class ProcessGetProductByID : IBusinessLogic
        {
                private Product _product;
                private DataSet _resultset;

                public ProcessGetProductByID()
                {

                }

                 public void Invoke()
                {
                        ProductSelectByIDData selectproduct➥
                            = new ProductSelectByIDData();
                        selectproduct.Product = Product;
                        ResultSet = selectproduct.Get();

                        Product.Name = ResultSet. ➥
Tables[0 ].Rows[0]["ProductName"].ToString();
                            Product.Description = ResultSet. ➥
Tables[0].Rows[0]["Description"].ToString();
                            Product.Price = Convert. ➥
ToDecimal( ResultSet.Tables[0].Rows[0]["Price"].ToString() );
                            Product.ImageID = int. ➥
Parse( ResultSet.Tables[0].Rows[0]["ProductImageID"].ToString() );
                            Product.ProductCategory. ➥
```

```
            ProductCategoryName = ResultSet. ➡
            Tables[0].Rows[0]["ProductCategoryName"].ToString();
                        }


                public Product Product
                {
                        get { return _product; }
                        set { _product = value; }
                }

                public DataSet ResultSet
                {
                        get { return _resultset; }
                        set { _resultset = value; }
                }
            }
        }
```

You have added quite a bit of code in this class. To review, you implemented the IBusinessLogic interface along with its required Invoke() method that will call the ProductSelectByIDData class located in the data access layer. In Chapter 16, the Product class will be instantiated within the presentation layer and populated with the product ID. This will be subsequently passed to the business logic class and then executed against the database via the Invoke() method calling the data access class. Finally, a DataSet will be returned from the data access class that is then in turn passed back by the ResultSet property to the presentation layer, which will ultimately be bound to another object for display purposes.

This exercise was quite lengthy. However, it did present a great deal of material that is necessary to establish the pattern of the overall application and architecture. You can repeat these steps for each process that is requesting data, updating, adding, or deleting data.

Summary

You have arrived at the end of the business logic tier of the architecture. In this chapter, you examined how the common objects will be utilized within the data access and business logic tiers of the application architecture. It is important to have a thorough understanding of how these tiers of the architecture work in unison before you move to the final architecture tier to be discussed—the presentation layer.

■■■

CHAPTER 14

Exploring Your Integration Options

This chapter will cover an integral part of the system and overall architecture. Although this chapter is not about a dedicated layer of the complete architecture, the functionality discussed in this chapter is closely related to the architecture and is similar to how the common objects and classes are integrated throughout the system. As the name of the chapter suggests, this chapter will cover functionality for integration or specific operations. What does this really mean? This refers to when an application needs to perform an action or task repeatedly. For instance, virtually every software system at some point will have to send an e-mail, log an exception or other information, interact with a message queue, or, perhaps one of the most popular tasks, consume and expose web services.

This chapter will deal with how to organize and manage these portions of the application. I'll refer to the segment that encapsulates the different integrations as the *operational manager*.

Throughout the chapter, you will focus primarily on establishing a solid infrastructure that will allow you to revisit this segment of the architecture later to fully implement its functionality. In brief, this chapter will cover the following topics:

- Introducing the operational manager

- Implementing it into the solution

- Integrating web services

- Handling exceptions

Introducing the Operational Manager

As mentioned, essentially all software applications need to perform redundant tasks throughout the life of the system. When you have this repetitive code or functionality, your first thought might be to create functions that execute the code and that can be called from anywhere needed within the source code base. Within the case study system, you will be implementing this concept; you'll also take it a step further. The additional step is that you'll organize and manage these functions in separate classes all within its own namespace and class library, thus resulting in a separate DLL.

Why take this extra step of organization? In short, this additional organization will enhance scalability, make debugging easier, improve maintenance, and even give you the ability to reuse the code in other projects:

Scalability: When you have an operational manager implemented within your software application, the functionality it performs is encapsulated and organized in only one section of the system. When the unavoidable time arises that it needs to be changed or updated, your changes will have to be implemented in only one section of the system and architecture. If the change required is more of an enhancement to the existing functionality, you can alter the existing class as desired—without having to redo your entire system.

Make debugging easier: This will become evident when implementing interaction with outside services or, namely, web services. During the course of the overall implementation, you'll have to debug a great deal of code via stepping through the code, and having this organized in the operational manager will ensure that this task is as manageable as possible.

Easy maintenance: You'll get easy maintenance for adding or removing any functionality.

Code reuse: Designing the code so it can be reused will undoubtedly save time in many future development efforts. For example, you will not have to retest the functionality since this has already been performed when it was first developed.

In the next section, you'll learn about how to implement the operational manager into the system.

Implementing the Operational Manager

Now that you understand why having an operational segment or manager is beneficial to your system, you need to know how to implement it. As mentioned, I will be introducing this segment as a separate class library similar to that of the common objects, which too had their own class library.

In the next exercise, you will be taking functionality from the .NET Framework by using specific classes and libraries. From these classes, you will present a wrapper; more simply put, you'll write your own code around the functionality of the .NET classes to provide a better method of managing the functionality within your application. Specifically, you'll implement an e-mail manager as one part of the operational manager. Upon completion, you will have a fully functional segment of the application that will be able to send e-mail messages.

Exercise: Implementing the E-mail Manager

In this exercise, you'll add the e-mail manager to the operational manager. Upon completion, the e-mail manager will be able to send e-mail messages from within the application. Follow these steps:

1. Return to the Visual Studio 2005 solution and to the LittleItalyVineyard.Operational class library. Right-click the project, and choose Add ➤ Class, as shown in Figure 14-1.

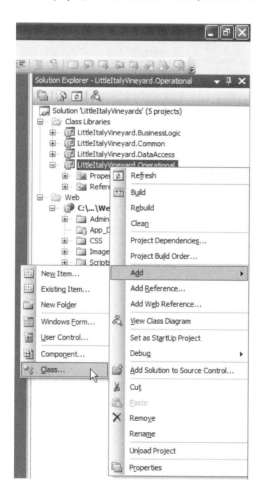

Figure 14-1. *Adding a new class*

2. You'll then see the Add New Item dialog box. Enter the name of the new class, **EmailManager**, as shown In Figure 14-2, and click the Add button.

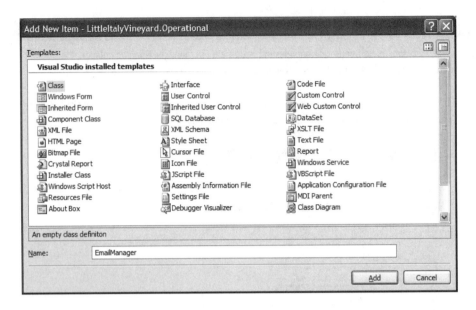

Figure 14-2. *Add New Item dialog box*

3. You will now see the shell code of the new class. Since you are implementing functionality to send e-mail messages from the application, you need to add two namespaces to the code. The namespaces you need to add are System.Net.Mail and System.Configuration. The class code resembles the following:

```
using System;
using System.Collections.Generic;
using System.Text;
using System.Net.Mail;
using System.Configuration;

namespace LittleItalyVineyard.Operational
{
    public class EmailManager
    {

    }
}
```

4. You now have the namespace added to the class, which you will utilize to successfully send e-mail messages. Next you need to add a structured way in which you can pass the information into the EmailManager class. You will accomplish this by adding a struct within the same class file named EmailContents. The code will resemble the following:

```
using System;
using System.Collections.Generic;
using System.Text;
using System.Net.Mail;
using System.Configuration;
```

```
namespace LittleItalyVineyard.Operational
{
    public class EmailManager
    {

    }

    public struct EmailContents
    {
        public string To;
        public string FromName;
        public string FromEmailAddress;
        public string Subject;
        public string Body;
    }
}
```

5. Now that the struct is in place, you can add the heart of the class that will actually send the e-mail messages. To do so, add a function to the EmailManager class named Send, which will have a parameter of the struct EmailContents and will return a boolean value. The code will now resemble the following:

```
using System;
using System.Collections.Generic;
using System.Text;
using System.Net.Mail;
using System.Configuration;

namespace LittleItalyVineyard.Operational
{
    public class EmailManager
    {
        public EmailManager()
        {

        }

        public void Send( EmailContents emailcontents )
        {

        }
    }

    public struct EmailContents
    {
        public string To;
        public string FromName;
        public string FromEmailAddress;
```

```
        public string Subject;
        public string Body;
    }
}
```

6. The basic function named Send is in place; now you need to add the actual code from the System.Net.Mail library that will send the e-mail messages. More specifically, you will use the MailMessage class along with the SmtpClient class, as demonstrated here:

```csharp
using System;
using System.Collections.Generic;
using System.Text;
using System.Net.Mail;
using System.Configuration;

namespace LittleItalyVineyard.Operational
{
    public class EmailManager
    {
        public EmailManager()
        {

        }

        public void Send( EmailContents emailcontents )
        {
            SmtpClient client = new SmtpClient( SMTPServerName );
            client.UseDefaultCredentials = true;
            MailAddress from = new MailAddress➥
          ( emailcontents.FromEmailAddress , emailcontents.FromName );
            MailAddress to = new MailAddress( ToAddress );

            MailMessage message = new MailMessage( from , to );

            message.Subject = emailcontents.Subject;
            message.Body = Utilities.FormatText➥
              ( emailcontents.Body , true );
            message.IsBodyHtml = true;

            try
            {
                client.Send( message );
                IsSent = true;
            }
            catch ( Exception ex )
            {
                throw ex;
            }
```

```csharp
    }

    public bool IsSent
    {
        get { return _issent; }
        set { _issent = value; }
    }

    private string SMTPServerName
    {
        get { return ConfigurationManager. ➥
        AppSettings[ "SMTPServer" ]; }
    }

    private string ToAddress
    {
        get { return ConfigurationManager. ➥
        AppSettings[ "ToAddress" ]; }
    }

}

public struct EmailContents
{
    public string To;
    public string FromName;
    public string FromEmailAddress;
    public string Subject;
    public string Body;
}
}
```

How It Works

You have added a good amount of code to provide the functionality to send e-mail messages. Basically, the first section instantiates an SmtpClient class and specifies the name of the mail server that will be used. The name of the mail server, SMTPServerName, is a read-only property that returns a string configured within the appSettings tag of the Web.config file. For security and credential purposes, the UseDefaultCredentials property is set to true. By using this property, the default credentials of the user who is logged in will be used with the SMTP server sending the message. Next, the MailAddress class is instantiated two times to set the e-mail address and name that the message will display that it is originating from as well as the e-mail address to which the message is being sent. The e-mail address that the message is being sent to is retrieved from another property, ToAddress, which is a read-only property that retrieves a value from AppSettings as well from the Web.config file. The function is completed by populating the subject and body from the struct and finally sent by using the Send method of the SmtpClient class. Upon successful completion, the IsSent boolean property will be set to true so that the calling code can reference this property to determine the success.

7. You will notice within the MailMessage's Body property that you use a class named Utilities along with a static method named FormatText. You have not yet implemented this class, but you will do so now. Within the operational project, add a new class named Utilities, and add the following code:

```
using System;
using System.Collections.Generic;
using System.Text;
using System.Web;
using System.IO;

namespace LittleItalyVineyard.Operational
{
    public class Utilities
    {
        public static string FormatText( string text , bool allow )
        {
            string formatted = "";

            StringBuilder sb = new StringBuilder( text );
            sb.Replace( "  " , "  " );
            if ( !allow )
            {
                sb.Replace( "<br>" , Environment.NewLine );
                sb.Replace( " " , " " );
                formatted = sb.ToString();
            }
            else
            {
                StringReader sr = new StringReader( sb.ToString() );
                StringWriter sw = new StringWriter();
                while ( sr.Peek() > -1 )
                {
                    string temp = sr.ReadLine();
                    sw.Write( temp + "<br>" );
                }

                formatted = sw.GetStringBuilder().ToString();
            }
            return formatted;
        }
    }
}
```

The purpose of this function is to parse the spaces and returns that are included in a message. In other words, when a user enters text in a text box and then presses the Enter key, this will not be represented in HTML format correctly. It will be represented in a straight line and will not maintain any of the breaks or paragraph formats. Therefore, with this function, the text will be parsed, and the proper HTML tags will be added so that the original formatting will be maintained.

8. As demonstrated, you now have the code in place for sending e-mail messages with information that will be populated with the EmailContent struct. However, the last piece to implement is the name of the Simple Mail Transfer Protocol (SMTP) server and the address to which the e-mail messages will be delivered. To accomplish this, proceed to the Web.config file, and add two keys within the appSettings tag, as demonstrated here:

```
<configuration>
    <appSettings>
        <add key="SMTPServerName" value="localhost"/>
        <add key="ToAddress" value="info@littleitalyvineyards.com"/>
    </appSettings>
    ...
```

The code is now complete, so you have a fully functional piece of the operational manager segment that will send an e-mail message from anywhere within the application. Even though you have a fully functional piece of the operational manager, at this time in the book, the EmailManager class will be sufficient. However, later you will in all likelihood make some minor changes to the EmailManager class.

Implementing Web Services

This section will address how to integrate web services into the overall architecture and more specifically into the operational manager. Although this book will be utilizing web services, the section is not meant to be a thorough reference on web services; the topic warrants an entire book. For example, see the upcoming *Beginning ASP.NET 2.0 Web Services in C#* from Apress. However, I'll discuss how to implement and use web services throughout the case study system and application.

To fully demonstrate how to integrate a web service into your application, the following exercise explains how to connect to the PayPal payment-processing system. This exercise will demonstrate the initial steps of how to set up the basic infrastructure for the PayPal web service. Chapter 18 gives more information about how to set up a PayPal account, how to write the code that will utilize the web service, and finally how to transact a credit card payment.

Exercise: Using the PayPal Web Service

This exercise demonstrates how to implement a web service into the operational manager segment of the architecture. You'll add a new class that will be dedicated to the PayPal implementation and add the web reference to the project. In this exercise, you will need a live Internet connection to connect to the web service provided by PayPal. Follow these steps:

1. Add a new class to the project by right-clicking the LittleItalyVineyard.Operational class library and choosing Add ➤ Class, as shown in Figure 14-3.

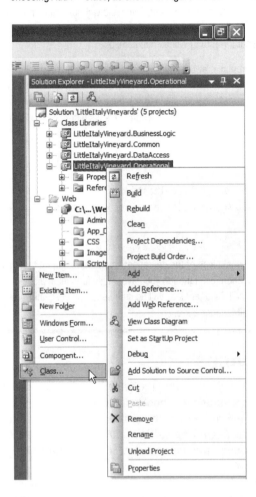

Figure 14-3. *Adding the new class*

2. You will see the Add New Item dialog box where you need to enter the name the new class, **PayPalManager**, as shown in Figure 14-4.

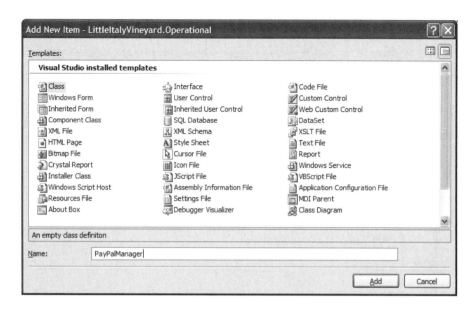

Figure 14-4. *Naming the PayPalManager class*

3. You have now added the PayPalManager class to the LittleItalyVineyard.Operational project. You now need to add the web reference to the project for the test account within PayPal. This test account is called the *sandbox*, and it will allow you to use the PayPal application programming interface (API) and test all the functionality without actually processing a real credit card. To add the web reference, right-click the References directory, and choose the Add Web Reference menu item, as shown in Figure 14-5.

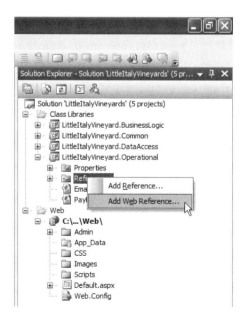

Figure 14-5. *Adding the web reference*

You will see the Add Web Reference dialog box, as shown in Figure 14-6.

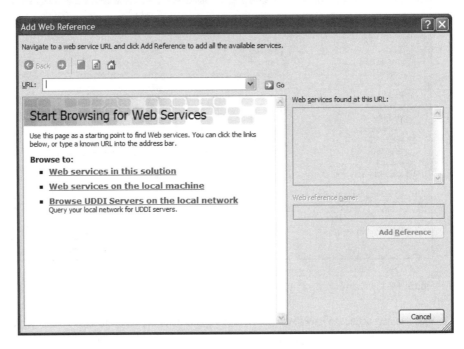

Figure 14-6. *Add Web Reference dialog box*

4. As shown in Figure 14-6, you now have the ability to browse for web services within the current solution, on the local machine, on the Universal Description, Discovery, and Integration (UDDI) servers (if installed), or finally via a uniform resource locator (URL) that you can manually specify. As mentioned, you are will connect only to the sandbox PayPal account for the time being. The URL for the PayPal sandbox is as follows: `http://www.sandbox.paypal.com/wsdl/PayPalSvc.wsdl`. Enter this URL in the text box provided, and click the Go button to connect to the service. This will connect you to the Web Services Description Language (WSDL) file provided by PayPal, as shown in Figure 14-7. The content of the WSDL file is quite extensive.

5. Now that you are able to browse the PayPal service as well as view the WSDL content, you need to give it a name that you will use to refer to it within your code. To do so, in the Web Reference Name text box, enter **PayPalAPI.Sandbox**, as shown in Figure 14-8, and click the Add Reference button.

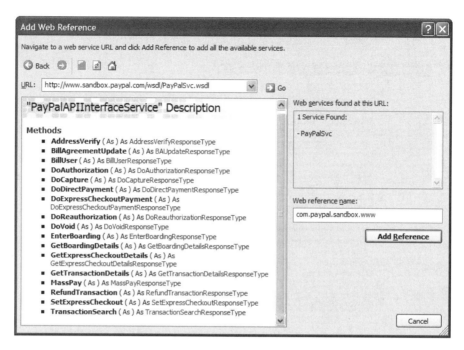

Figure 14-7. *Browsing PayPalAPIInterfaceService*

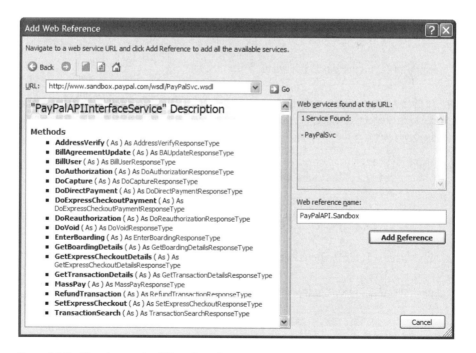

Figure 14-8. *Naming and adding the reference*

6. After adding the PayPal web reference, you are able to view that a number of other references are added to the LittleItalyVineyard.Operational class library project, as shown in Figure 14-9.

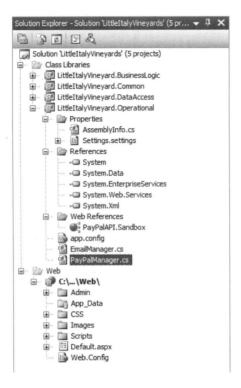

Figure 14-9. *Viewing the references*

7. All the necessary references are in place to use the service; therefore, return to the PayPalManager class you previously created. You will need to add the newly created PayPal namespace you created; the code resembles the following:

```csharp
using System;
using System.Collections.Generic;
using System.Text;

using LittleItalyVineyard.Operational.PayPalAPI.Sandbox;

namespace LittleItalyVineyard.Operational
{
    public class PayPalManager
    {
        public PayPalManager()
        {

        }
    }
}
```

You now have a functional class within your operational manager segment of the architecture. You have not implemented any of the functionality that will communicate with the PayPal servers and transact a credit card payment, but you have the shell upon which you can build.

Performing Some Exception Handling

Regardless of what type of software application you decide to build, it is inevitable that at some point it will run into unexpected errors or exceptions during normal processing. During the development, however, you should make every attempt to keep this occurrence to a minimum. With that being said, you need to be prepared to gracefully handle any errors and exceptions and track the errors by logging them in some way.

This discussion is, of course, referring to *exception handling* within a software application. Within the case study, you'll implement exception handling by using the Global.asax file and the Application_Error event. Along with this, you will specify a default error page within the Web.config file that will be displayed anytime an exception occurs during the user experience. This will accomplish the tasks of gracefully handling an exception and showing the user that an error occurred; in addition, a more pleasant web page than the default ASP.NET exception page will be displayed.

The following exercise in this chapter demonstrates the tasks necessary to implement the overall exception handling.

Exercise: Implementing the Exception Handling

In this exercise, you will add the Global.asax file and default error web page and handle any exceptions as gracefully as possible. Follow these steps:

1. Proceed to the web project, and add the Global.asax file by right-clicking the project, choosing to add a new item, and then choosing the Global Application Class item. Then click the Add button; you'll see the following code within the file:

```
<%@ Application Language="C#" %>

<script runat="server">

    void Application_Start(object sender, EventArgs e)
    {
        // Code that runs on application startup

    }

    void Application_End(object sender, EventArgs e)
    {
        //  Code that runs on application shutdown

    }

    void Application_Error(object sender, EventArgs e)
```

```
    {
        // Code that runs when an unhandled error occurs

    }

    void Session_Start(object sender, EventArgs e)
    {
        // Code that runs when a new session is started

    }

    void Session_End(object sender, EventArgs e)
    {
        // Code that runs when a session ends.
        // Note: The Session_End event is raised only
        // when the sessionstate mode
        // is set to InProc in the Web.config file.
        // If session mode is set to StateServer
        // or SQLServer, the event is not raised.

    }

</script>
```

Notice that the Global.asax page does not have an associated code file or .cs file. Each of the methods included has associated comments about its individual functionality.

2. You'll focus on the Application_Error event for your exception-handling purposes. The first line of code to implement is to capture the last exception that occurred on the server side. You will accomplish this by adding the following code:

```
void Application_Error(object sender, EventArgs e)
{
    // Code that runs when an unhandled error occurs
    Exception ex = Server.GetLastError();

}
```

How It Works

This line of code is quite simple. An exception class is declared as the variable ex, which is then set equal to the GetLastError() function of the Server class. The GetLastError() function returns an exception class containing the last exception that occurred on the server.

3. You have now implemented the code that will capture the exception information. However, now you'll add the functionality that will gracefully handle the exception within the user experience. To do so, redirect your attention to the Web.config file within the web project. Look specifically at the System.Web tags, and add the following:

```
<system.web>

    <customErrors mode="On"  defaultRedirect="ErrorPage.aspx">
    </customErrors>

</system.web>
```

How It Works

Within the System.Web tags, focus your attention on the customErrors tags. I will address two elements within the customErrors tag. The first is the mode element you set to On, which specifies the application will use custom errors. The second is defaultRedirect, which you set to ErrorPage.aspx. This web page is now designated to display when an exception occurs, which you will add to the web project in the next chapter. The user will now know whether an exception occurs and will not see the default ASP.NET exception web page, which can be quite unattractive.

4. The next task to implement for the exception handling is to log or record the information that is contained within the exception that occurred. You can log the information in many different ways. These different methods include entering the information to the database, sending an e-mail message, or logging to a file. For these purposes, you will be simply logging the information to a text file that you will be able to refer to at any time. So, return to the Utilities class found in the LittleItalyVineyard.Operational namespace and project. Add the following method to the class:

```
public static void LogException( Exception ex )
{
    using ( StreamWriter sw = new StreamWriter➥
        ( HttpContext.Current.Server.MapPath➥
        ( "~/ExceptionLog/LogFile.txt" ) , true ) )
    {
        sw.WriteLine( DateTime.Now.ToShortDateString() +
        Environment.NewLine +
            ex.InnerException.ToString() +
          Environment.NewLine +
          Environment.NewLine );
    }
}
```

How It Works

The LogException method is a static method, meaning you do not need a new instantiation, and it has a parameter of an Exception class. A using statement is implemented with the StreamWriter class to append text to a specified text file with the path. By having the using declaration, all resources will be disposed of regarding the StreamWriter after the code is executed; thus, you don't need to close or explicitly dispose of the StreamWriter. Then, the full file path is determined by using the current HTTPContext and then the Server.MapPath method. This will return the physical file path of the specified directory and the filename, ~/ExceptionLog/LogFile.txt. You have not yet added the

ExceptionLog directory or the LogFile.txt file, but you will do so in the next step. Finally, the WriteLine method of the StreamWriter will take the current date and then append the string to the InnerException of the exception class that was passed into the class as a parameter. Then for some formatting, the NewLine function adds some spacing to the log file for better readability.

5. For the final task of the exercise, you need to add the new folder to the web project named ExceptionLog and, within the newly created directory, add a text file named LogFile.txt. After completing this, you are all set for writing the exceptions to the log file. Return to the Global.asax file where you captured the server's last exception. Add the following code:

```
void Application_Error(object sender, EventArgs e)
{
        // Code that runs when an unhandled error occurs
        Exception ex = Server.GetLastError();
        LittleItalyVineyard.Operational.Utilities.LogException( ex );
}
```

The line of code added to the Application_Error event declares the LogException class and passes the server's last exception class as the parameter.

You have arrived at the end of the exercise, and the case study application now has exception handling incorporated. As you add more and more code to your application, you will notice that try/catch statements are used in the data access layer code. However, in the presentation layer, you will not use try/catch statements. Thus, if an exception occurs, it will be unhandled, and the information will be logged and gracefully handled for the user. If the exception occurs below the presentation layer, the exception will be thrown up the stack.

Summary

This chapter covered your integration options. Although this topic is not a specific tier of the architecture, it is a close counterpart of the architecture and is similar to how the common objects and classes are integrated throughout the system.

As mentioned a number of times in the chapter, especially with the PayPal web service, this chapter was intended to merely introduce the concepts and build the foundation of the operational manager within the system architecture. Chapter 18 will be dedicated to establishing a PayPal account and test account and will include step-by-step directions on how to implement it into the system to ensure secure credit card transactions, which will ultimately result in selling your products online.

CHAPTER 15

■ ■ ■

Creating the Presentation Layer

At long last, you have arrived at the final tier of the architecture of your application. I am, of course, talking about the presentation layer, which serves an important purpose for your overall application. Each tier of the architecture is equally important, but the presentation layer is the only tier that is readily visible to the users. The data access layer and business logic layers work completely in the background, and although they are important to what the user will ultimately view on the browser, only the developers will see those tiers. However, the presentation layer contains the Hypertext Markup Language (HTML) along with the graphics and associated styles. It will set the standard for how user-friendly the navigation is and the overall look and feel of the application, which are vital aspects of any system.

In this chapter, you will examine and implement the presentation layer, providing the application with the best possible look and feel and with a clean, consistent, and concise navigation.

Specifically, I'll discuss the following in this chapter:

- The overall design of the HTML layout

- The master pages

- The individual web pages

Looking at the Overall Design

The key to any successful software application, especially web applications, is to have an aesthetically pleasing user interface. The reason for this, in short, is that the user interface, along with the associated graphics, is what the end user will see. And as they say, you have only one time to make a first impression. This is the case when presenting your online storefront to potential customers. On average, if users see a pleasant design and they experience easy navigation, thus allowing them to find what they are looking for, they will most likely stay at your site and make purchases.

For the application for the Little Italy Vineyards winery, you will start with an already completed HTML design including wine- and vineyard-related graphics. The extremely talented graphic designers and software engineers Eric Starkowicz and Jeff Reese, who I have worked with on several projects over the years, created this design. They will provide the overall layout and design as well as the associated styles and the HTML code. Figure 15-1 shows the initial design of the Little Italy Vineyard web application. You will use this design as a starting point so you are ready when it is time to add server controls to the web forms.

Figure 15-1. *The initial Little Italy Vineyards design*

As you can see, the design has an exceptionally clean and professional-looking layout. The design includes an image of a vineyard with long rows of grapes going into the horizon. At the top of the design, the empty area is where the logo of the vineyard will appear. Below that, four links to the other web pages in the site will appear. You'll define the names of these specific links later in the chapter. Lastly, toward the bottom of the design is a bottle of wine, a wine glass, and some cheese followed by some grapes on the right side.

Overall, this initial design will provide an excellent layout for the vineyard and provide easy navigation along with a professional, clean-looking interface. The remaining work to be completed is as follows: you'll establish the links and the logo in a master page in which all the associated web pages will be incorporated. In the next section, I will begin outlining how to implement the master page with the associated HTML.

■**Note** You can find all the images in the Images folder and the style sheet in the CSS folder. Review these items in the sample code that accompanies this book.

Implementing the Master Page

Now that you have the initial design, you need to finalize the design by implementing a master page. This master page will include the links for the individual pages of the website, as well as the images and HTML that will be included on all the pages. Prior to jumping directly into implementing the master page, I'll explain what exactly a master page is and why you should use such a technique.

A *master page* is a new concept introduced in ASP.NET 2.0; it allows a common base file to provide a consistent design for all the web pages in your web application. The content can consist of HTML as well as .NET-compliant source code. After you have determined what common features the web pages will be using, you add these elements to the master page. Finally, for the section that has unique content on web forms that use the master page, you place a control, called a ContentPlaceHolder, in the master page. For subsequent web pages you add, you can specify that they utilize the master page, so all their content will be inherited from that master page.

To create the design for the vineyard web application shown in Figure 15-1, you'll include the links and the logo. You'll include all the content, except for what will appear in the middle section of the design, in the master page. The middle section is where you'll use the ContentPlaceHolder and subsequently where the content from the other web pages will appear when you implement it throughout the remainder of this book.

Exercise: Implementing the Master Page

In this exercise, you will implement the master page in the Visual Studio 2005 solution and add the associated HTML code and design. Follow these steps:

1. Return to the Visual Studio 2005 solution, navigate to the web project, and right-click. Choose the Add New Item menu item, as shown in Figure 15-2.

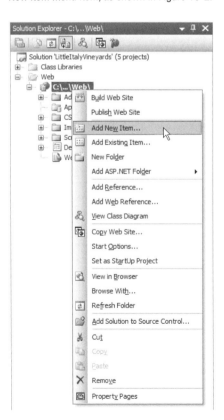

Figure 15-2. *Adding a new item to the web project*

2. You will then see the Add New Item dialog box. Choose Master Page from the items available, and then name the master page **Main**, as shown in Figure 15-3. Click the Add button.

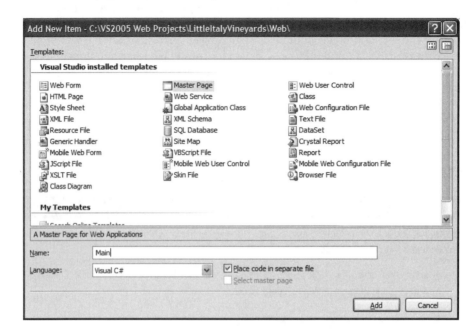

Figure 15-3. *Adding and naming the master page*

3. You now have a master page added to your presentation layer. Upon the master page being added, you will see the following HTML code generated from the master page:

```
<%@ Master Language="C#" AutoEventWireup="true"
CodeFile="Main.master.cs"
Inherits="Main" %>

<!DOCTYPE html
PUBLIC "-//W3C//DTD XHTML 1.0
Transitional//EN"
"http://www.w3.org/TR/xhtml1/DTD
/xhtml1-transitional.dtd">

<html xmlns="http://www.w3.org/1999/xhtml" >
<head runat="server">
<title>Untitled Page</title>
</head>
<body>
<form id="form1" runat="server">
<div>
<asp:contentplaceholder id="ContentPlaceHolder1" runat="server">
</asp:contentplaceholder>
```

```
</div>
</form>
</body>
</html>
```

4. You can see the basic HTML layout with the ContentPlaceHolder control. Rename the ContentPlaceHolder control to **contentplaceholderMain**, as shown here:

```
<asp:contentplaceholder id="contentplaceholderMain" runat="server">
</asp:contentplaceholder>
```

5. The master page now has a basic shell. You next need to add the HTML that has been designed specifically for the vineyard application, including the links, logo, and all the other elements in the base design. The following is the HTML followed by the master page:

```
<%@ Master Language="C#" AutoEventWireup="true"
CodeFile="Main.master.cs"
Inherits="Main" %>

<html>
<head runat="server">
    <title></title>
    <meta http-equiv="Content-Style-Type" content="text/css" />
    <link href="Css/style.css" type="text/css" rel="stylesheet" />
    <script language="javascript" src="Scripts/scriptLibrary.js"></script>
</head>
<body>
    <form id="form1" runat="server">
<table width="100%" height="100%" border="0" cellpadding="0"
cellspacing="0"
style="background-image:
url(images/til_1.jpg);">
    <tr>
    <td> </td>
    <td width="490" align="left" valign="top">
      <table width="490" border="0" cellspacing="0"
cellpadding="0">
        <tr>
      <td width="10"> </td>
      <td width="470" align="left" valign="top">
<table width="470" height="100%" border="0"
cellpadding="0" cellspacing="0">
      <tr>
<td height="164" align="left" valign="top"
background="images/top_1.jpg">
<div style="padding-left: 156px; padding-top: 69px">
<a href="Default.aspx"><img src="images/logo.jpg"
```

```
width="159" height="36" border="0"></a></div>
        </td>
        </tr>
        <tr>
<td height="43" align="left" valign="top">
<table width="100%" border="0" cellspacing="0"
cellpadding="0">
        <tr>
<td><img src="images/left.jpg" width="10"
height="43">
      </td>
<td><a href="default.aspx">
<img src="images/about.jpg" width="114"
height="43" border="0">
    </a></td>
<td><a href="winery.aspx">
<img src="images/vineyard.jpg" width="112"
 height="43" border="0">
</a></td>
<td><a href="Faq.aspx">
<img src="images/faq.jpg" width="112"
height="43" border="0">
</a></td>
<td><a href="contactus.aspx">
<img src="images/contact.jpg" width="112"
 height="43" border="0">
</a></td>
<td><img src="images/right.jpg" width="10"
 height="43"></td>
        </tr>
        </table>
        </td>
        </tr>
        <tr>
<td height="172" align="right" valign="top"
background="images/back_1.jpg">
<div style="padding-left: 0px; padding-top: 14px;
padding-right: 23px; padding-bottom: 0px">
<a href="login.aspx">
<img src="images/login.jpg" border="0"></a>
      </div>
       </td>
       </tr>
       <tr>
<td height="100%" align="left" valign="top">
<table width="100%" height="100%"
border="0" cellpadding="0"
```

```
cellspacing="0" background="images/rep_3.jpg">
            <tr align="left" valign="top">
<td background="images/rep_left.jpg" style="width: 10px">
<img src="images/rep_left.jpg" width="10" height="1"></td>
<td height="100%">
<table width="450" height="100%" border="0"
cellpadding="0" cellspacing="0">
<tr align="left" valign="top">
<td background="images/rep_line.jpg"
bgcolor="#F3E9BF"
style="background-repeat: repeat-y;
background-position: top left;">
<asp:ContentPlaceHolder ID="contentplaceholderMain"
runat="server"></asp:ContentPlaceHolder>
        </td>
        </tr>
        </table>
      </td>
<td width="10" background="images/rep_right.jpg">
<img src="images/rep_right.jpg" width="10" height="1">
</td>
        </tr>
         <tr>
        <td colspan="3" valign="top" align="center">
<img src="images/bottom_1.jpg" width="470" height="23">
</td>
      </tr>
      </table>
      </td>
      </tr>
      </table>
      </td>
      <td></td>
      </tr>
      </table>
       </td>
       <td> </td>
       </tr>
       <tr>
       <td></td>
       <td height="100%">
<table cellpadding="0" cellspacing="0" border="0"
width="100%" height="100%">
        <tr>
<td style="height: 100%; background-image:
url(images/rep_bot.jpg); background-repeat: repeat-y;
background-position: center;"></td>
      </tr>
```

```
        </table>
      </td>
      <td></td>
    </tr>
      </table>
  </form>
</body>
</html>
```

Figure 15-4 shows the master page in design view.

Figure 15-4. *Master page, design view*

The master page is complete. You are now ready to address the remaining web pages in the presentation layer and associate all of them to the master page you just created.

Creating the Individual Web Pages

Now that you have established the master page, you can implement the remaining web pages that will be visible to all users.

About Us

The About Us web page will be a basic page that is actually the default page, or *home page*, when the users first come to the site. This page will describe the history of the vineyard along with all the different types of wines and accessories that are available. That being said, it will probably be the web page with the most simplistic contents.

Exercise: Adding the About Us Web Page

In this exercise, you'll add the About Us web page, which will actually be named Default.aspx; you will use the master page you created and implemented in the prior exercise. Please note that when creating a new web project, Visual Studio will create a web form named Default.aspx. You have two options here. You can keep this web form, or you can delete it and add another web form with the same name, which will be easier to associate with the respective master page. Follow these steps:

1. Proceed to the web project, right-click, and choose the Add New Item menu item, as shown in Figure 15-5.

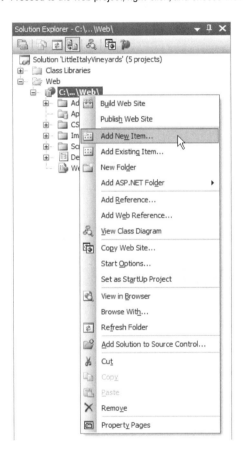

Figure 15-5. *Adding a new item to the web project*

2. You will see the Add New Item dialog box. In this dialog box, choose Web Form from the available items, and name the web form **Default.aspx**. Then select the Select Master Page box, as shown in Figure 15-6.

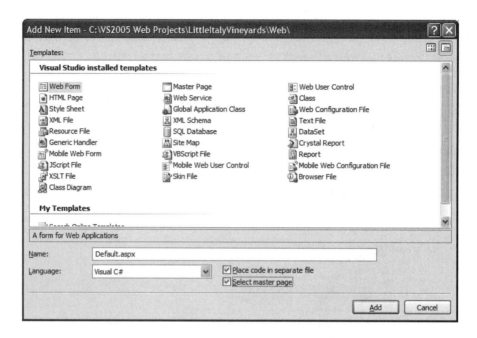

Figure 15-6. *Adding the About Us web form*

3. After naming the new web form, click the Add button. You will see the Select a Master Page dialog box, as shown in Figure 15-7.

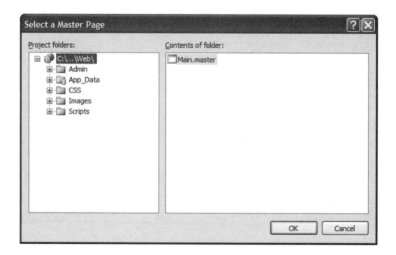

Figure 15-7. *Selecting a master page*

4. Select the Main.master master page from the Contents of folder pane on the right. Finally, click the OK button, which will add the Default.aspx web form:

```
<%@ Page Language="C#" MasterPageFile="~/Main.master"
AutoEventWireup="true" CodeFile="Default.aspx.cs"
Inherits="_Default" Title="Untitled Page" %>

<asp:Content ID="Content1" ContentPlaceHolderID="contentplaceholderMain"
Runat="Server">
</asp:Content>
```

5. Now that the infrastructure is in place, you can add the following HTML code to the Default.aspx file:

```
<%@ Page Language="C#" MasterPageFile="~/Main.master"
AutoEventWireup="true"
CodeFile="Default.aspx.cs"
Inherits="_Default" Title="Welcome to Little Italy Vineyard" %>

<asp:Content ID="Content1"
ContentPlaceHolderID="contentplaceholderMain"
runat="Server">
    <table cellpadding="10" cellspacing="0" border="0">
        <tr>
        <td>
         <b>Welcome to Little Italy Vineyards</b><br />
         <br>
         Little Italy Vineyards has been a family-owned business since
         the early 1950s. It was founded and started by the
         current owner's parents who were born in Italy and owned a
         vineyard there but wanted to move to America
         to raise their family.
         <br />
         <br />
         As a result, they moved to America after selling their vineyard
         in Italy and eventually started a new vineyard,
         Little Italy Vineyards, in California.
          <br />
         <br />
         Many tours are available on a daily basis.  Please browse
         throughout our vineyard to find some of the fines
         wines available.
         <br />
           <img src="images/spacer.gif" width="1" height="11" />
           </td>
        </tr>
    </table>
</asp:Content>
```

6. Switch to design view in Visual Studio 2005 to preview how the newly added HTML code is integrated in the master page, as shown in Figure 15-8.

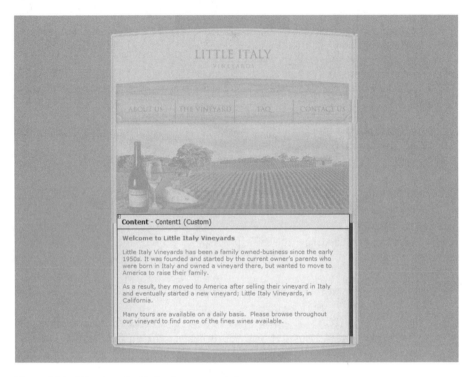

Figure 15-8. *Viewing the Default.aspx web form*

You have successfully added the first web page to the presentation layer that will be associated with the master page. You'll now move along to similar exercises to implement the remaining web pages and associate them to the master page.

Winery

The Winery web page will be the area in which the products for sale are listed. Users will have the ability to browse through the individual products for sale and to search for specific products by name or by category.

Exercise: Adding the Winery Web Page

This exercise will outline how to add the Winery web form and associate it with the master page. Follow these steps:

1. Proceed to the web project, right-click, and choose the Add New Item menu item, as shown in Figure 15-9.

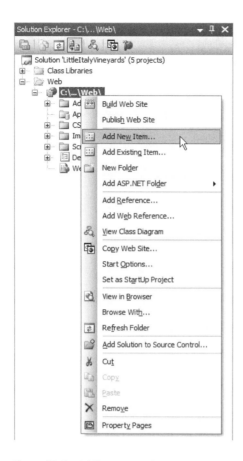

Figure 15-9. *Adding a new item*

2. You will see the Add New Item dialog box. In this dialog box, choose Web Form from the available items, and name it **Winery**. Then select the Select Master Page box, as shown in Figure 15-10.

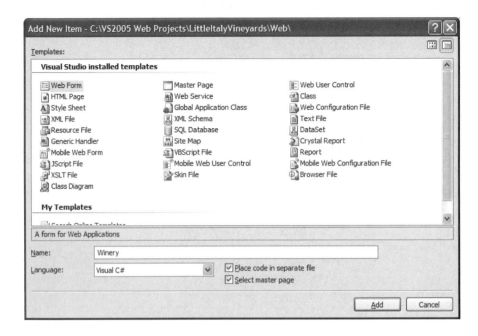

Figure 15-10. *Adding the Winery web form*

3. After naming the new web form, click the Add button. You will see the Select a Master Page dialog box, as shown in Figure 15-11.

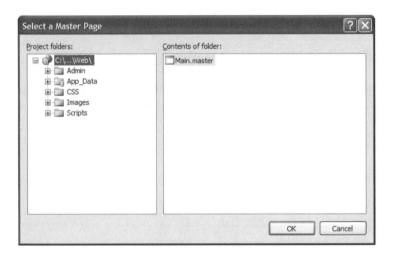

Figure 15-11. *Selecting a master page*

4. Select the Main.master master page from the Contents of folder pane on the right. Then click the OK button, which will add the Winery.aspx web form:

```
<%@ Page Language="C#" MasterPageFile="~/Main.master"
AutoEventWireup="true" CodeFile="Winery.aspx.cs"
```

```
Inherits="Winery"
Title=" Little Italy Vineyard | The Vineyard " %>

<asp:Content ID="Content1"
ContentPlaceHolderID="contentplaceholderMain"
Runat="Server">
</asp:Content>
```

5. Now that the infrastructure is in place, you can add the following HTML code to the Winery.aspx file:

```
<%@ Page Language="C#" MasterPageFile="~/Main.master"
AutoEventWireup="true" CodeFile="Winery.aspx.cs"
Inherits="Winery"
Title="Little Italy Vineyard | The Vineyard" %>

<asp:Content ID="Content1" ContentPlaceHolderID="contentplaceholderMain"
Runat="Server">
    <img src="images/spacer.gif" width="1" height="5" border="0" /><br/>
    <img src="images/spacer.gif" width="5" height="1"
        border="0" /><br />
                 

</asp:Content>
```

6. Switch to design view in Visual Studio 2005 to preview how the newly added HTML code is integrated in the master page, as shown in Figure 15-12.

Figure 15-12. *Viewing the Winery.aspx web form*

The Winery.aspx web form is now prepared for you to add the product catalog in upcoming chapters.

FAQ

The FAQ (or frequently asked questions) page will list common questions that a customer might want to ask. You want to provide answers for these types of questions; therefore, you will have a web page that lists these answers for the customers.

Exercise: Adding the FAQ Web Page

This exercise will outline how to add the FAQ web form and associate it with the respective master page. Follow these steps:

1. Proceed to the web project, right-click, and choose the Add New Item menu item, as shown in Figure 15-13.

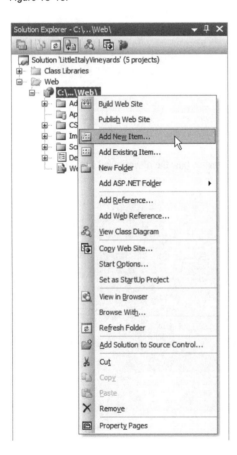

Figure 15-13. *Adding a new item*

2. You will see the Add New Item dialog box. In this dialog box, choose Web Form from the available items, and name it **FAQ**. Then select the Select Master Page box, as shown in Figure 15-14.

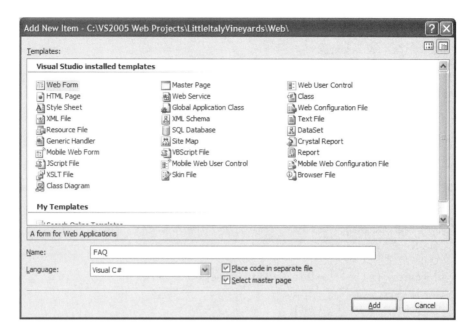

Figure 15-14. *Adding the FAQ.aspx web form*

3. After naming the new web form, click the Add button, and you will see the Select a Master Page dialog box, as shown in Figure 15-15.

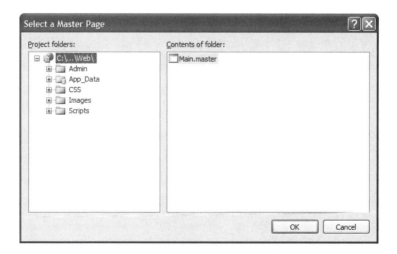

Figure 15-15. *Selecting a master page*

4. Select the Main.master master page from the Contents of folder pane on the right. Finally, click the OK button, which will add the FAQ.aspx web form:

```
<%@ Page Language="C#" MasterPageFile="~/Main.master"
AutoEventWireup="true"
CodeFile="FAQ.aspx.cs"
Inherits="FAQ" Title="Untitled Page" %>


<asp:Content ID="Content1"
ContentPlaceHolderID="contentplaceholderMain"
Runat="Server">
</asp:Content>
```

5. Now that the infrastructure is in place, you can add the following HTML code to the FAQ.aspx web form that will display some frequently asked questions and the answers:

```
<%@ Page Language="C#" MasterPageFile="~/Main.master"
AutoEventWireup="true"
CodeFile="FAQ.aspx.cs"
Inherits="FAQ" Title="Little Italy Vineyard | FAQ" %>

<asp:Content ID="Content1"
ContentPlaceHolderID="contentplaceholderMain"
Runat="Server">
    <table border="0" cellpadding="10" cellspacing="0" width="100%">
        <tr>
         <td>
      <table border="0" cellpadding="0"
             cellspacing="0" width="100%">
        <tr>
        <td>
<strong>
What are the locations that you ship your products?
</strong>
</td>
    </tr>
<tr><td><img src="images/spacer.gif" width="1" height="2"
border="0" />
</td></tr>
      <tr>
      <td>
Little Italy Vineyards ships to anywhere within the USA.
</td>
    </tr>
    <tr><td>
<img src="images/spacer.gif" width="1" height="15"
border="0" />
</td>
```

```
</tr>
        <tr>
<td align="center" >
<table cellpadding="0" cellspacing="0" border="0"
width="50%">
<tr>
<td width="100%" class="separatorBG">
<img src="images/spacer.gif"
width="1" height="1"
 border="0" />
</td>
<td><img src="images/textSeparatorRight.gif" />
</td>
</tr>
        </table>
        </td>
        </tr>
 <tr><td><img src="images/spacer.gif" width="1" height="15"
border="0" />
</td></tr>
<tr>
   <td>
<strong>
How old do I have to be to purchase wine from your vineyard?
</strong>
</td>
        </tr>
<tr><td><img src="images/spacer.gif" width="1" height="2"
border="0" />
</td></tr>
<tr>
<td>
You must be at least 21 years of age to make a purchase.
</td>
      </tr>
<tr><td><img src="images/spacer.gif" width="1" height="15"
border="0" />
</td></tr>
<tr>
<td align="center" >
<table cellpadding="0" cellspacing="0" border="0"
width="50%">
        <tr>
<td width="100%" class="separatorBG">
<img src="images/spacer.gif"
width="1" height="1" border="0" />
</td>
<td><img src="images/textSeparatorRight.gif" />
```

```
        </td>
            </tr>
              </table>
              </td>
              </tr>
<tr><td>
<img src="images/spacer.gif" width="1"
height="15" border="0" />
</td></tr>
<tr>
      <td>
 <strong>
What types of wine does your vineyard offer?
</strong></td>
        </tr>
        <tr>
        <td>
We offer many different types of wine. 
Please browse throughout our winery
online.</td>
</tr>
<tr><td><img src="images/spacer.gif" width="1"
height="15" border="0" />
</td></tr>
            <tr>
            <td align="center" >
 <table cellpadding="0" cellspacing="0" border="0"
width="50%">
        <tr>
<td width="100%" class="separatorBG">
<img src="images/spacer.gif" width="1"
height="1" border="0" />
</td>
<td><img src="images/textSeparatorRight.gif" />
      </td>
      </tr>
      </table>
      </td>
      </tr>
<tr><td><img src="images/spacer.gif" width="1"
height="15"
border="0" />
</td></tr>
      <tr>
      <td>
<strong>
Do you offer any monthly clubs or wines of the month?
</strong>
```

```
    </td>
    </tr>
<tr><td><img src="images/spacer.gif" width="1" height="2"
border="0" />
    </td></tr>
    <tr>
    <td>
Yes, we offer a Wine of the Month Club. 
Please refer to our product catalog.</td>
    </tr>
<tr><td><img src="images/spacer.gif" width="1" height="15"
border="0" />
</td></tr>
</table>
</td>
</tr>
    </table>
</asp:Content>
```

6. Switch to design view in Visual Studio 2005 to preview how the newly added HTML code is integrated into the master page, as shown in Figure 15-16.

Figure 15-16. *The FAQ.aspx in design view*

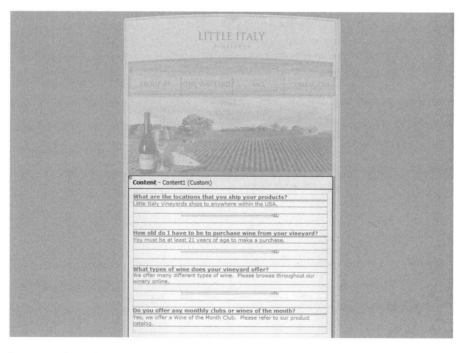

You now have a complete web page that lists some of the frequently asked questions asked by the customers and the answers to those questions.

Contact Us

The Contact Us web page will have all the necessary contact information regarding the vineyard and company. It will list the address and phone numbers along with an e-mail contact form that will allow a user to submit questions or feedback to the vineyard.

This exercise will outline how to add the Contact Us web form and associate it with the master page. Follow these steps:

1. Proceed to the web project, right-click, and choose the Add New Item menu item, as shown in Figure 15-17.

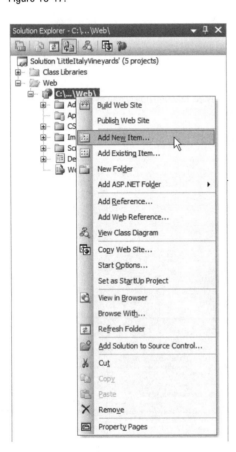

Figure 15-17. *Adding a new item*

2. You will see the Add New Item dialog box. In this dialog box, choose Web Form from the available items, and name it **ContactUs**. Then select the Select Master Page box, as shown in Figure 15-18.

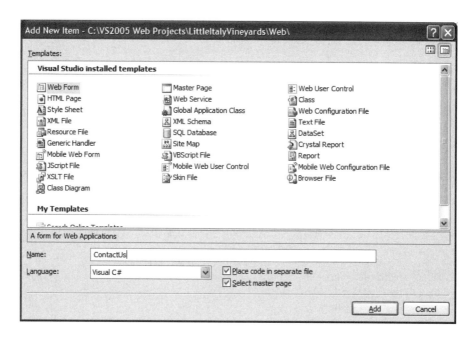

Figure 15-18. *Adding the ContactUs.aspx web form*

3. After naming the new web form, click the Add button, and you will see the Select a Master Page dialog box, as shown in Figure 15-19.

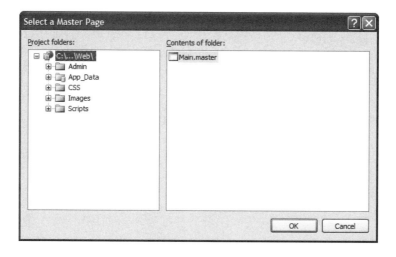

Figure 15-19. *Selecting a master page*

4. Select the Main.master master page from the Contents of Folder pane on the right. Finally, click the OK button, which will add the ContactUs.aspx web form:

```
<%@ Page Language="C#" MasterPageFile="~/Main.master"
AutoEventWireup="true"
CodeFile="ContactUs.aspx.cs"
Inherits="ContactUs"
Title="Untitled Page" %>


<asp:Content ID="Content1"
ContentPlaceHolderID="contentplaceholderMain"
Runat="Server">
</asp:Content>
```

5. Now that the infrastructure is in place, you can add the following HTML code to the ContactUs.aspx file:

```
<%@ Page Language="C#" MasterPageFile="~/Main.master"
AutoEventWireup="true"
CodeFile="ContactUs.aspx.cs"
Inherits="ContactUs"
Title="Little Italy Vineyard | Contact Us" %>


<asp:Content ID="Content1"
ContentPlaceHolderID="contentplaceholderMain"
runat="Server">
    <table width="100%" height="100%" border="0" cellpadding="0"
cellspacing="0"
background="images/rep_3.jpg">
        <tr align="left" valign="top">
            <td height="100%">
<table width="450" border="0" cellpadding="0"
cellspacing="0"
background="images/back_4.jpg"
    style="background-position: top right; background-repeat:
no-repeat">
        <tr>
<td align="left" valign="top" style="background-repeat:
no-repeat;
background-position:
top left;
height: 103px;">
<div style="padding-left: 16px;">
<img src="images/tradit_3.jpg" width="73"
height="11"></div>
<div style="padding-left: 15px; padding-top: 12px;
padding-right: 45px;
padding-bottom: 24px;
line-height: 12px">
<img src="images/pic_4.jpg" width="114"
```

```
height="78" align="left"
style="margin-right: 19px">
<table
width="260" border="0" cellspacing="0"
cellpadding="0">
<tr align="left" valign="top"
style="line-height: 12px">
<td class="light" style="width: 221px">
<div style="padding-left: 0px;
padding-top: 3px">
Little Italy Vineyards, Inc.<br>
9863 Merlot Dr. <br>
Sonoma Valley, CA 90211</div>
<div style="padding-left: 0px;
padding-top: 10px">
<table cellpadding="0"
cellspacing="0" border="0">
<tr>
<td class="light">Tel:
</td>
<td><img src="images/spacer.gif"
width="10" height="1" /></td>
<td class="light">
555-555-5555</td>
</tr>
<tr>
<td class="light">Fax:
</td>
<td><img src="images/spacer.gif"
width="10" height="1" /></td>
<td class="light">
555-555-5522</td>
</tr>
</table>
</div>
</td>
<td class="light">
<div style="padding-left: 0px;
padding-top: 3px">
 </div>
</td>
</tr>
            </table>
          </div>
            </td>
            </tr>
        <tr>
```

```
<td height="100%" align="left" valign="top"
background="images/rep_line.jpg"
bgcolor="#F3E9BF"
style="background-repeat: repeat-y;
background-position: top left">
<table width="100%" height="100%"
border="0" cellpadding="0"
cellspacing="0"
background="images/rep_5.jpg"
style="background-repeat: repeat-x;
background-position: top">
<tr><td>
<img src="images/spacer.gif" width="1"
height="15" /></td></tr>
<tr align="left" valign="top">
        <td height="100%">
    <div  align="Center">
       <table width="375" border="0"
cellspacing="0"
cellpadding="0">
            <tr>
             <td height="28" align="left"
valign="top" style="width: 191px">
Name:
<asp:RequiredFieldValidator ID="requiredName"
runat="server" ControlToValidate="textName"
Display="Dynamic" EnableClientScript="False"
ErrorMessage="<br />Please enter your name.">
</asp:RequiredFieldValidator><br />
<asp:TextBox ID="textName" runat="server"
CssClass="textField"></asp:TextBox>
<td height="28" align="right" valign="top"
style="text-align: left">
Email:
<asp:RequiredFieldValidator ID="requiredEmail"
runat="server" ControlToValidate="textEmail"
Display="Dynamic" EnableClientScript="False"
ErrorMessage="<br />Please enter your email.">
</asp:RequiredFieldValidator>
<asp:RegularExpressionValidator ID="regularexpEmail"
runat="server" ControlToValidate="textEmail"
```

```
Display="Dynamic" EnableClientScript="False"
ErrorMessage="<br />Please enter a valid email."
ValidationExpression="\w+([-+.']\w+)*@\w+([-.]\w+)*\.\w+([-.]\w+)*">
</asp:RegularExpressionValidator><br />
<asp:TextBox ID="textEmail" runat="server"
CssClass="textField"></asp:TextBox>
      </tr>
<tr><td><img src="images/spacer.gif" width="1" height="10" />
      </td></tr>
      <tr>
<td colspan="2" align="left" valign="top">
Comments:<br />
<asp:TextBox ID="textComment" TextMode="MultiLine"
 runat="server" CssClass="textField" Height="75px">
</asp:TextBox></td>
      </tr>
<tr><td><img src="images/spacer.gif" width="1"
 height="5" /></td></tr>
<tr align="right">
<td colspan="2" valign="bottom" style="height: 17px">
<asp:Button ID="commandReset" runat="server"
Text="Reset" CausesValidation="False"
OnClick="commandReset_Click" CssClass="button" /> 
<asp:Button ID="commandSubmit" runat="server"
OnClick="commandSubmit_Click"
Text="Submit" CssClass="button" /> </td>
        </tr>
         </table>
         </div>
         </td>
         </tr>
<tr><td><img src="images/spacer.gif" width="1"
height="15" /></td></tr>
   </table>
     </td>
        </tr>
        </table>
         </td>
         </tr>
     </table>
</asp:Content>
```

6. Switch to design view in Visual Studio 2005 to preview how the newly added HTML code is integrated into the master page, as shown in Figure 15-20.

Figure 15-20. *Viewing the ContactUs.aspx web form*

7. The presentation section of the ContactUs.aspx page is in place, so you now need to implement the code that will take the input that the customer enters and submit it in an e-mail message to the vineyard. To do this, proceed to the C# code section of the ContactUs.aspx web form, and implement a reference to the operational project as well as the page load event, as demonstrated here:

```
using System;
using System.Data;
using System.Configuration;
using System.Collections;
using System.Web;
using System.Web.Security;
using System.Web.UI;
using System.Web.UI.WebControls;
using System.Web.UI.WebControls.WebParts;
using System.Web.UI.HtmlControls;

using LittleItalyVineyard.Operational;

public partial class ContactUs : System.Web.UI.Page
{
    protected void Page_Load( object sender , EventArgs e )
    {
```

```
        if ( !IsPostBack )
        {
            textName.Focus();
        }
    }

  private void SendMessage()
  {
    if ( IsValid )
    {
        EmailContents contents = new EmailContents();
        contents.FromName = textName.Text;
        contents.FromEmailAddress = textEmail.Text;
        contents.Body =  textComment.Text;
        contents.Subject = "Website Feedback";

        EmailManager emailmngr = new EmailManager();
        emailmngr.Send( contents );

        if ( emailmngr.IsSent )
        {
          Response.Redirect( "ContactUsConfirm.asp" );
        }
      }
    }

    protected void commandSubmit_Click( object sender , EventArgs e )
    {
        SendMessage();
    }

    protected void commandReset_Click( object sender , EventArgs e )
    {
        textName.Text = "";
        textEmail.Text = "";
        textComment.Text = "";
        textName.Focus();
    }
}
```

How It Works

The previous code implements first the EmailContents struct and then the EmailManager class. The EmailContents struct populates the necessary information from the user's input that will subsequently be passed along in the Send method of the EmailManager class. If the message has been sent successfully, the IsSent property will be true, and then you can then redirect the user to the ContactUsConfirm.aspx web form, which you will implement in the next exercise step.

8. The final step in this exercise is to implement the web form that will confirm to the customer that the feedback message was sent successfully. To do so, you will add another web form named ContactUsConfirm.aspx and associate it with the respective master page. This web form will be essentially the same as the ContactUs.aspx web form except that where the text boxes were, you will simply add a message to inform the user that the message was sent and someone will be contacting them as soon as possible.

This brings you to the end of yet another exercise; you have implemented the ability for a user to submit feedback to the site by way of an e-mail submission form. By having this type of contact form, you can stay in touch with customers, and even with potential customers, by answering their questions.

Default Error Page

I'll now address the error web form you specified in the previous chapter when you implemented the exception handling for the application. Add a new web form to the web project named ErrorPage.aspx, which you declared in the prior chapter as the default error page. When adding this page, associate it with the master page. Regarding this error page, you will want to inform the user that an error has occurred. Figure 15-21 shows the message that is displayed to the user.

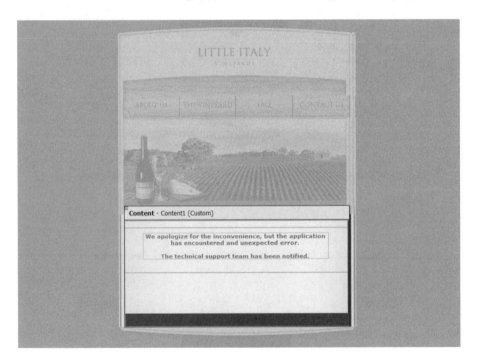

Figure 15-21. *Viewing the ErrorPage.aspx web form*

Summary

You have arrived at the end of the chapter dedicated to the presentation layer of the architecture, taking you to the end of the in-depth discussions regarding the application's architecture. Now that a solid architecture is in place, you can move forward with building upon the architecture and implement the various functionality that was decided upon earlier in the book from gathering the requirements.

PART 5

■ ■ ■

Core Development

Welcome hardcore developers and programmers—you have finally arrived at the part of the book where you will program the main functionality of the e-commerce application for the case study. The following chapters will contain extensive exercises that show how to implement the product catalog, the searching functionality, the shopping cart, the credit card–processing functionality, and the customer accounts. After these chapters, your e-commerce application will just about be ready for the production environment.

■ ■ ■

CHAPTER 16

Developing the Product Catalog

You have arrived at last where you can roll up your sleeves and focus on some heavy-duty programming in C#. I don't mean to downplay all the earlier setup work you have implemented, but many individuals in this industry truly love coding applications. I consider myself one of these individuals, but at the same time, I have gained an affinity for all aspects of building e-commerce applications.

This chapter is the lengthiest so far, and it contains a fair amount of code that you need to write. I will cover the following aspects, which will result in a fully functional product catalog:

- Implementing the product catalog

- Displaying the product images

- Viewing the product details

- Searching the product catalog

Creating the Product Catalog

The product catalog in many ways is the most important piece of the overall system since ultimately the amount of sales over a period of time will dictate the success of the business and of the e-commerce application. Therefore, you need to have a clear, concise, and easy-to-navigate product catalog. So, let's get to work!

Creating the Stored Procedure

The first order of business for implementing the product catalog is to create a stored procedure that will return the products stored in the database. Customers will be able to view these products in order to get more information about them. Before creating the stored procedure, you'll review the database tables from which you'll create the stored procedure.

Figure 16-1 shows the Products table, which contains the fields for the basic attributes of the individual products. Figure 16-2 shows the ProductCategory table, which contains the category names and IDs. Figure 16-3 shows the ProductImages table, which contains the product image IDs along with the binary data of the images.

Products

Column Name	Data Type	Allow Nulls
ProductID	int	☐
ProductCategoryID	int	☐
ProductName	nvarchar(50)	☐
ProductImageID	int	☐
Description	text	☐
Price	smallmoney	☐
		☐

Figure 16-1. *The Products table*

ProductCategory

Column Name	Data Type	Allow Nulls
ProductCategoryID	int	☐
ProductCategoryName	text	☐
		☐

Figure 16-2. *The ProductCategory table*

ProductImages

Column Name	Data Type	Allow Nulls
ProductImageID	int	☐
ProductImage	image	☐
		☐

Figure 16-3. *The ProductImages table*

Each of these tables has specific relationships. Figure 16-4 shows the macro view of the three tables and their relationships.

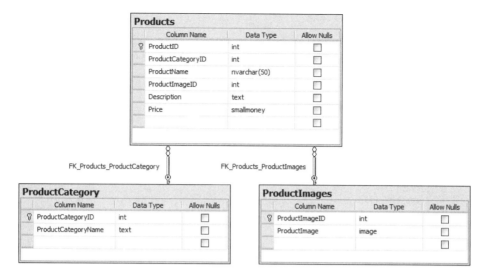

Figure 16-4. *The tables and relationships*

These relationships ensure that every product in the Products table has an associated product category and product image with a defined set of values. For instance, each wine for sale will fit into a certain category, such as Red Wine, White Wine, or Appetizer Wine. All these different categories will appear in the ProductCategory table, which is then referenced from the Products table by a unique ID number. Each product will also have an associated image that is stored in the ProductImages table as a binary value with a unique ID number. The ID number will also be referenced from the Products table.

Now that you are familiar with the tables you'll use for the stored procedure, the following exercise shows how to create the Products_Select stored procedure.

Exercise: Creating the Products_Select Stored Procedure

This exercise shows you how to create the stored procedure that you will name Products_Select. This stored procedure will query the database for all the products that are for sale. The exercises in this chapter show how to use Microsoft SQL Server Management Studio; however, you can use an alternative tool, and the actual scripts will work equally as well. Follow these steps:

1. Launch SQL Server Management Studio.

2. Next, log in to your development database in which you created the tables. Navigate to the LittleItalyVineyard database in Object Explorer, uncollapse the objects, and proceed to Programmability, as shown in Figure 16-5.

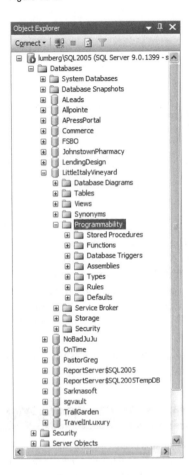

Figure 16-5. *The LittleItayVineyard database*

3. Right-click the Stored Procedures object, and choose New Stored Procedure, as shown in Figure 16-6.

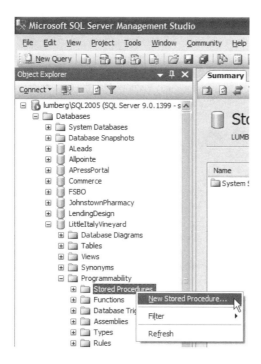

Figure 16-6. *Adding a stored procedure*

4. You will see the default script template. For these purposes, you can delete the default script template so there is no entry in the query window. The next step is to create the basic script for creating a new stored procedure, as shown here:

```
CREATE PROCEDURE Products_Select

AS
```

5. You now need to add the SQL to query the individual tables for the products. To accomplish this, you need to join the ProductCategory table to the Products table so only one result set is returned from the query that displays the matching product category name. Add the following body to the stored procedure:

```
SELECT
ProductID,
ProductName,
ProductCategoryName,
ProductImageID,
SUBSTRING(Description, 1, 150) + '...' AS Description,
Price
FROM Products
INNER JOIN ProductCategory ON
ProductCategory.ProductCategoryID = Products.ProductCategoryID
```

Notice for the Description field that the SUBSTRING function is querying only the first 150 characters of the full text of the description. Since you will have a details page for each product and the description for the individual products can be quite lengthy, when displaying all the products, the description will be brief—brief enough to give the customer a bit of a teaser to entice them to explore the details in depth and (you hope) purchase the product.

6. Now that you have the complete script for the stored procedure, it is time to create it by executing the script against the database. To do so, with the script in the query window, click the Execute button located on the toolbar in SQL Server Management Studio, as shown in Figure 16-7.

Figure 16-7. *The Execute command*

7. Upon successful execution of the script against the database, you will see the confirmation message "Command(s) completed successfully," as shown in Figure 16-8.

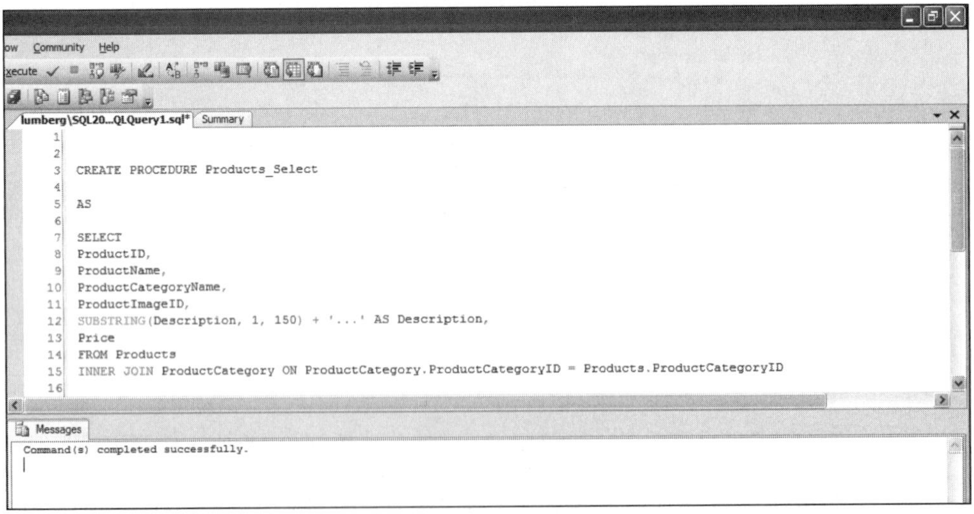

Figure 16-8. *Successfully executing the stored procedure script*

Now that you have created the stored procedure for querying the result set for all the products in the database, you need to add the code that will execute this functionality and finally display the results for the user in the presentation layer.

Writing the Code and Classes

You have just completed the database portion of querying the products from the database by creating the stored procedure. Now you need to implement the code in the architecture to fulfill the requests of showing the products on the web form after it progresses through the architecture to actually query the database and return the result set. Accomplishing this will take your journey through a few different exercises, starting at the data access layer followed by the associated business logic tier and finally the presentation layer.

This exercise shows how to implement the code in the data access layer class library project to incorporate all the necessary functionality to query the database for the products using the newly stored procedure. Follow these steps:

1. Return to the Visual Studio 2005 solution, go to the Class Libraries solution folder, and then go to the LittleItalyVineyard.DataAccess class library project. From the class library project, open the StoredProcedure class. You'll see an enumeration created in a previous chapter containing all the names of the stored procedures in the system. Add the name of your new stored procedure, **Products_Select**, as shown in the following code:

```
using System;
using System.Collections.Generic;
using System.Text;

namespace LittleItalyVineyard.DataAccess
{
    public class StoredProcedure
    {
        public enum Name
        {
            ProductByID_Select ,
            Products_Select
        }
    }
}
```

2. You now have the name of the stored procedure that will be used. Next, add the actual data access class that will use the enumeration to query the database for the products and return the results. To do so, while still in the LittleItalyVineyard.DataAccess class library, proceed to the Select folder, right-click, and choose Add ➤ Class, as shown in Figure 16-9.

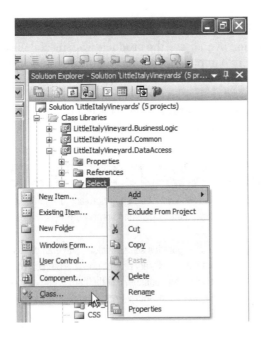

Figure 16-9. *Adding a new class*

3. Now you will see the Add New Item dialog box. In this dialog box, add the name of the new class, **ProductSelectData**, as shown in Figure 16-10.

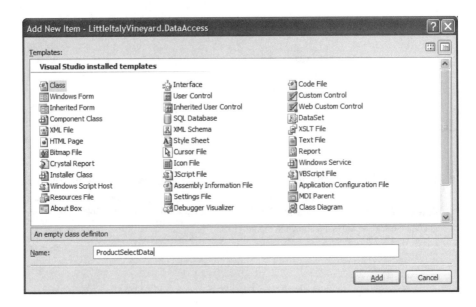

Figure 16-10. *Naming the new class*

4. When finished entering the new name of the class, click the Add button, and you will see your new class. The following template, or shell code, will be in the newly added class:

```
using System;
using System.Collections.Generic;
using System.Text;

namespace LittleItalyVineyard.DataAccess.Select
{
    class ProductSelectData
    {
    }
}
```

5. You need to alter the template code from the class, so add the System.Data namespace, as shown here:

```
using System.Data;
```

6. After adding the new namespaces, specify the name of the stored procedure that you will use in the constructor of the ProductSelectData class you just created. The following is the code sample:

```
using System;
using System.Collections.Generic;
using System.Text;
using System.Data;

namespace LittleItalyVineyard.DataAccess.Select
{
    public class ProductSelectData : DataAccessBase
    {
        public ProductSelectData()
        {
          StoredProcedureName = StoredProcedure.Name.Products_Select.➥
                ToString();
        }
    }
}
```

7. The final step to complete the ProductSelectData class is to add the Get function that will return the DataSet from which the stored procedure will query the result set for you. Add the following code:

```
using System;
using System.Collections.Generic;
using System.Text;
using System.Data;


namespace LittleItalyVineyard.DataAccess.Select
{
    public class ProductSelectData : DataAccessBase
```

```
        {
            public ProductSelectData()
            {
                StoredProcedureName = StoredProcedure.Name.Products_Select.➥
                    ToString();
            }

            public DataSet Get()
            {
                DataSet ds;

                DataBaseHelper dbhelper = new DataBaseHelper➥
                    ( StoredProcedureName );
                ds = dbhelper.Run( ConnectionString );

                return ds;
            }
        }
    }
}
```

With the use of the DataBaseHelper class, you will use the overloaded Run function to return a DataSet with the results from the stored procedure that it queries.

The integration of the code to query the product catalog and display it to the users is almost complete. You have created the stored procedure and added the necessary code in the data access layer, so now you need to add the necessary code in the business logic layer that will utilize the class just created in the data access layer. To accomplish this, the next exercise shows how to add the class and code for the business logic layer.

Exercise: Implementing the Code for the Business Logic Layer

This exercise shows how to add the code to the business logic layer that will ultimately be called from the presentation layer and then connect to the data access layer to query the product catalog. Follow these steps:

1. Proceed to the Visual Studio 2005 solution and then to the LittleItalyVineyard.BusinessLogic class library project. Earlier you created a class named ProcessGetProducts. Open this class; you'll see the following code:

```
using System;
using System.Collections.Generic;
using System.Text;

namespace LittleItalyVineyard.BusinessLogic
{
    public class ProcessGetProducts : IBusinessLogic
    {
        public void Invoke()
```

```
            {

            }
        }
}
```

As you can see, the ProcessGetProducts class implements the IBusinessLogic interface, which ensures that you implement or add the Invoke function that returns a boolean value.

2. The Invoke function is where you need to focus your attention for this exercise. However, first you need to add the data access namespace along with the data namespace:

```
using System;
using System.Collections.Generic;
using System.Text;
using System.Data;

using LittleItalyVineyard.DataAccess.Select;
```

3. Add a property that will return a DataSet that will be queried from within the Invoke method. This property will ultimately be the property that the data control will be data bound to in the presentation layer:

```
using System;
using System.Collections.Generic;
using System.Text;
using System.Data;

using LittleItalyVineyard.DataAccess.Select;

namespace LittleItalyVineyard.BusinessLogic
{
    public class ProcessGetProducts : IBusinessLogic
    {
        private DataSet _resultset;

        public ProcessGetProducts()
        {

        }

        public void Invoke()
        {

        }

        public DataSet ResultSet
        {
            get { return _resultset; }
            set { _resultset = value; }
```

```
            }
        }
    }
```

4. Now, you can focus your attention on the Invoke function that will yield the population of the ResultSet property. To do so, instantiate the ProductSelectData class from the data access classes and then call the Get function, setting the return value to that of the ResultSet property, as shown in the following code:

```csharp
using System;
using System.Collections.Generic;
using System.Text;
using System.Data;

using LittleItalyVineyard.DataAccess.Select;

namespace LittleItalyVineyard.BusinessLogic
{
    public class ProcessGetProducts : IBusinessLogic
    {
        private DataSet _resultset;

        public ProcessGetProducts()
        {

        }

        public void Invoke()
        {
            ProductSelectData productdata = new ProductSelectData();
            ResultSet = productdata.Get();
        }

        public DataSet ResultSet
        {
            get { return _resultset; }
            set { _resultset = value; }
        }
    }
}
```

The code is now complete for the business logic layer in the classes to be the conduit for the results of the products stored in the database. The final step is to add the code for the section that will actually display the products with Hypertext Markup Language (HTML).

The final section of the implementation is the presentation layer of the architecture.

Exercise: Implementing the Code for the Presentation Layer

This exercise shows how to implement the proper code in the web page that will initiate calling the business logic and ultimately the data access layers of the application to query the product catalog from the database. Follow these steps:

1. Return to the Visual Studio 2005 solution and to the web project. In Chapter 15, you added a web page named Winery.aspx. Open that page in design view in Visual Studio, and place a DataView control so that the HTML of the page resembles the following:

```
<%@ Page Language="C#" MasterPageFile="~/Main.master"
AutoEventWireup="true" CodeFile="Winery.aspx.cs"
Inherits="Winery" Title="Little Italy Vineyard | The Vineyard" %>

<asp:Content ID="Content1" ContentPlaceHolderID="contentplaceholderMain"
 Runat="Server">

<asp:DataList id="DataList1" runat="server">
</asp:DataList>

</asp:Content>
```

2. You can see that the DataList HTML code is in the ContentPlaceHolder control of the master page. To proceed, you need to modify the DataList control starting with the ID. You also need to specify how the columns of the data will be displayed. The runat tag will specify this control as a server control, and the RepeatColumns property will enforce that only a single column of data will be displayed vertically. The HTML should now resemble the following.

```
<%@ Page Language="C#" MasterPageFile="~/Main.master"
AutoEventWireup="true" CodeFile="Winery.aspx.cs"
Inherits="Winery" Title="Little Italy Vineyard | The Vineyard" %>

<asp:Content ID="Content1" ContentPlaceHolderID="contentplaceholderMain"
  Runat="Server">

<asp:DataList id="datalistProducts" RepeatColumns="1" runat="server">
</asp:DataList>

</asp:Content>
```

3. As the code is now, the DataList control has the bare minimum of what you need to data bind it to the DataSet that the query from the database will return. Therefore, turn your attention to the code to data bind the DataList control, thus utilizing the classes you created in the previous exercises. To do so, switch to the C# view in Visual Studio of the Winery.aspx web page. In the Page Load method, add the following code to prevent data binding when there is a postback to the server, as shown here:

```
using System;
using System.Data;
using System.Configuration;
```

```csharp
using System.Collections;
using System.Web;
using System.Web.Security;
using System.Web.UI;
using System.Web.UI.WebControls;
using System.Web.UI.WebControls.WebParts;
using System.Web.UI.HtmlControls;

public partial class Winery : System.Web.UI.Page
{
    protected void Page_Load( object sender , EventArgs e )
    {
        if ( ! IsPostBack )
        {

        }
    }
}
```

4. Now add a method that will bind the products to the DataList control. The code will look like the following:

```csharp
using System;
using System.Data;
using System.Configuration;
using System.Collections;
using System.Web;
using System.Web.Security;
using System.Web.UI;
using System.Web.UI.WebControls;
using System.Web.UI.WebControls.WebParts;
using System.Web.UI.HtmlControls;

public partial class Winery : System.Web.UI.Page
{
    protected void Page_Load( object sender , EventArgs e )
    {
        if ( ! IsPostBack )
        {
            LoadProducts();
        }
    }

    private void LoadProducts()
    {

    }
}
```

5. Now you need to add a reference to the LittleItalyVineyard.BusinessLogic project by right-clicking the web project and choosing to add a reference, as shown in Figure 16-11.

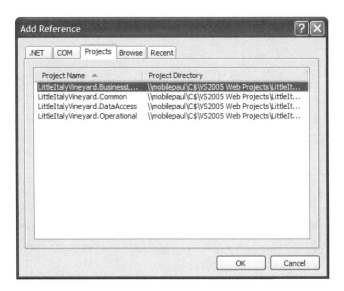

Figure 16-11. *Adding the reference*

6. Select the LittleItalyVineyard.BusinessLogic reference on the Projects tab, and click the OK button. You are now able to add the business logic namespace, as shown here:

```
using System;
using System.Data;
using System.Configuration;
using System.Collections;
using System.Web;
using System.Web.Security;
using System.Web.UI;
using System.Web.UI.WebControls;
using System.Web.UI.WebControls.WebParts;
using System.Web.UI.HtmlControls;

using LittleItalyVineyard.BusinessLogic;
```

7. Everything is now set up to add the code that will connect to the business logic layer and ultimately show the products in the DataList control. To proceed, you will instantiate the business logic class, ProcessGetProducts, followed by the Invoke method. Then you will data bind the DataList to the DataSet, as shown in the following code:

```
private void LoadProducts()
{
    ProcessGetProducts processproducts = new ProcessGetProducts();
```

```
          try
          {
             processproducts.Invoke();
          }
          catch
          {
            Response.Redirect( "ErrorPage.aspx" );
          }

          datalistProducts.DataSource = processproducts.ResultSet;
           datalistProducts.DataBind();
       }
```

8. The code is now complete to handle the request of querying the products from the database and data binding the results to the DataList. However, you need to return to the HTML of the DataList and add some formatting and the individual fields that will be bound to the data. Return to the source view of the Winery.aspx page. From within the DataList tags, you need to add the ItemTemplate tag, as shown here:

```
<%@ Page Language="C#" MasterPageFile="~/Main.master"
AutoEventWireup="true" CodeFile="Winery.aspx.cs"
Inherits="Winery" Title="Little Italy Vineyard | The Vineyard %>

<asp:Content ID="Content1" ContentPlaceHolderID="contentplaceholderMain"
Runat="Server">
<asp:DataList id="datalistProducts" RepeatColumns="1" runat="server">
<ItemTemplate>
</ItemTemplate>
</asp:DataList>
</asp:Content>
```

9. In the ItemTemplate tags, add an HTML table and rows that will create the structure to display the complete product catalog:

```
<%@ Page Language="C#"
MasterPageFile="~/Main.master" AutoEventWireup="true"
CodeFile="Winery.aspx.cs" Inherits="Winery"
Title="Little Italy Vineyard | The Vineyard" %>

<asp:Content ID="Content1" ContentPlaceHolderID="contentplaceholderMain"
Runat="Server">
<asp:DataList ID="datalistProducts" RepeatColumns="1" runat="server"
Width="100%">
        <ItemTemplate>
            <table border="0" cellpadding="1" cellspacing="0" width="100%">
                <tr>
                    <td><img src="images/spacer.gif" width="50" height="1"
                    border="0" /></td>
                    <td valign="top" align="right">
```

```html
        </td>
        <td width="100%" valign="top">
            <table cellpadding="0" cellspacing="0" border="0"
              width="100%">
                <tr>
                    <td width="17"><img src="images/spacer.gif"
                    width="17" height="3" border="0" /></td>
                    <td></td>
                </tr>
                <tr>
                    <td></td>
                </tr>
                <tr><td><img src="images/spacer.gif" width="1"
                 height="5" border="0" /></td></tr>
                <tr>
                    <td colspan="2">
                        <table cellpadding="0" cellspacing="0"
                          border="0" width="75%">
                            <tr><td class="prodUnderlineBG"
                              width="100%"></td></tr>
                            <tr><td><img src="images/spacer.gif"
                             width="1" height="1" border="0" />
                            </td></tr>
                            <tr><td>
<img src="images/prodDecorRight.gif" />
                            </td></tr>
                        </table>
                    </td>
                </tr>
                <tr><td><img src="images/spacer.gif" width="1"
                    height="5" border="0" /></td></tr>
                <tr><td><img src="images/spacer.gif" width="1"
                    height="5" border="0" /></td></tr>
            </table>
        </td>
        <td><img src="images/spacer.gif" width="15" height="1"
            border="0" /></td>
    </tr>
</table>
        </ItemTemplate>
    </asp:DataList>
</asp:Content>
```

10. In the HTML tables and rows, you will data bind the individual values that will ultimately display each of the products in the catalog. The Eval method will be used for data binding, as shown in the following HTML code. The Eval data-binding method will specify the name of the database column that the stored procedure is querying:

```
<%@ Page Language="C#" MasterPageFile="~/Main.master"
AutoEventWireup="true" CodeFile="Winery.aspx.cs"
    Inherits="Winery" Title="Little Italy Vineyard | The Vineyard" %>

<asp:Content ID="Content1" ContentPlaceHolderID="contentplaceholderMain"
    runat="Server">
    <img src="images/spacer.gif" width="1" height="5" border="0" /><br />
    <table cellpadding="0" cellspacing="0" border="0" width="100%">
        <tr><td><img src="images/spacer.gif" width="1" height="5"
            border="0" /></td></tr>
        <tr>
            <td><img src="images/spacer.gif" width="35" height="1"
                border="0" /></td>
        </tr>
        <tr><td><img src="images/spacer.gif" width="1" height="5"
            border="0" /></td></tr>
        <tr>
            <td align="center" colspan="2">
            <table cellpadding="0" cellspacing="0"
                border="0" width="95%">
                    <tr>
                        <td width="100%" class="separatorBG">
                        <img src="images/spacer.gif" width="1" height="1"
                            border="0" /></td>
        <td><img src="images/textSeparatorRight.gif" />
            </td>
                    </tr>
                </table>
            </td>
            <td></td>
        </tr>
    </table>
    <img src="images/spacer.gif" width="1" height="10" border="0" /><br />
    <asp:DataList ID="datalistProducts" RepeatColumns="1" runat="server"
        Width="100%">
        <ItemTemplate>
            <table border="0" cellpadding="1" cellspacing="0" width="100%">
                <tr>
                    <td><img src="images/spacer.gif" width="50" height="1"
                        border="0" /></td>
                    <td valign="top" align="right">
        <a href='ProductDetails.aspx?ProductID=<%# Eval("ProductID") %>'>
          <img src='ImageViewer.ashx?ImageID=<%# Eval("ProductImageID") %>'
                height="85" border="0"
                                class="prodBorder">
                    </a>
                </td>
```

```
<td width="100%" valign="top">
    <table cellpadding="0" cellspacing="0" border="0"
      width="100%">
        <tr>
            <td width="17"><img src="images/spacer.gif"
             width="17" height="3" border="0" /></td>
            <td></td>
        </tr>
        <tr>
            <td></td>
            <td class="ProductListHead">
<a href='ProductDetails.aspx?ProductID=➥
    <%# Eval("ProductID") %>'>
 <b><%# Eval("ProductName") %></b></a></td>
        </tr>
        <tr><td><img src="images/spacer.gif" width="1"
 height="5" border="0" /></td></tr>
        <tr>
            <td colspan="2">
                <table cellpadding="0" cellspacing="0"
                    border="0" width="75%">
        <tr><td class="prodUnderlineBG" width="100%">
        </td></tr>
    <tr><td>
 <img src="images/spacer.gif" width="1"
     height="1"
        border="0" />
        </td></tr>
<tr><td><img src="images/prodDecorRight.gif" /></td></tr>
                </table>
            </td>
        </tr>
        <tr>
            <td></td>
            <td><%# Eval("Description") %></td>
        </tr>
        <tr><td><img src="images/spacer.gif" width="1"
            height="5" border="0" /></td></tr>
        <tr>
            <td></td>
            <td>
 <span class="ProductListItem">
   <b>Price: </b>
                    <%# Eval("Price", "{0:c}") %>
                </span>
            </td>
        </tr>
```

```
                            <tr><td><img src="images/spacer.gif" width="1"
                                height="5" border="0" /></td></tr>
                            <tr>
                                <td></td>
                                <td>
                    <a href='AddToCart.aspx?ProductID=<%# Eval("ProductID") %>'>
                <span class="ProductListItem">
                            <font color="#9D0000"><b>Add To Cart<b>
                    </font></span> </a>
                                        </td>
                                    </tr>
                                </table>
                            </td>
                            <td><img src="images/spacer.gif" width="15" height="1"
                                border="0" /></td>
                        </tr>
                    </table>
                </ItemTemplate>
            </asp:DataList>
            <img src="images/spacer.gif" width="1" height="10" border="0" /><br />
        </asp:Content>
```

It is apparent that you added a good deal of HTML code to the web form. You also added some additional items worthy of explanation. In addition to the data binding, you added links to the details page of the product, to the product image, and to the web form that will add the product to the shopping cart. These web pages have not been added as of yet, but you have the links implemented and will add these web pages later in this exercise.

11. The next order of business is to add the web pages for which you have implemented the links. You'll start by implementing how the images will be displayed for each of the products in the catalog. Each of the product images is stored in the database as binary data. As a result, you need to query the database for the binary image data by specifying the product image ID. To accomplish this feat, you will use an ASHX file, more commonly known as an *HTTP handler*. The reason you will use this type of file opposed to a standard web form is that all that is required is returning a stream of bytes that will represent an image. In a standard ASPX or web form, ASPX pages need to inherit the System.Web.UI.Page, which will add overhead that is not needed. So, right-click the web project, and choose to add a new item to the project. When prompted with the Add New Item dialog box, choose the GenericHandler item, and name the new file **ImageViewer**, as shown in Figure 16-12.

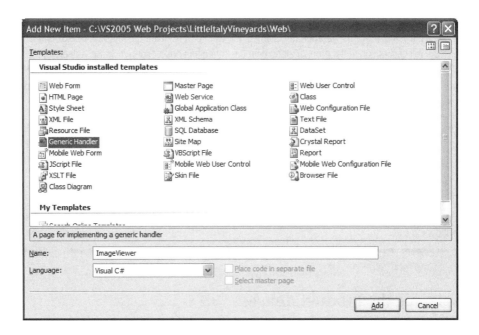

Figure 16-12. *Adding the generic handler, the ASHX file*

12. Upon adding the generic handler to the web project, you will see the following code:

```
<%@ WebHandler Language="C#" Class="ImageViewer" %>

using System;
using System.Web;

public class ImageViewer : IHttpHandler
{

    public void ProcessRequest (HttpContext context) {
        context.Response.ContentType = "text/plain";
        context.Response.Write("Hello World");
    }

    public bool IsReusable {
        get {
            return false;
        }
    }

}
```

As with adding class files to your source code base, you can see some shell code in the generic handler file. You now have the page that will handle displaying the images for the products.

13. One of the other web pages you need to add is the web form that will allow you to show the details of the individual products. Appropriately named, the web form is called ProductDetails.aspx and will show the full description of the product along with the image and price. Right-click the web project, add a new web form, and finally name it **ProductDetails.aspx**. Select the Main.master master page as well. (Similar to implementing the generic handler, you will fully implement the ProductDetails.aspx web form later in the chapter.)

14. The final web form to add in this exercise is the AddToCart.aspx web form. Just as with the other web forms, you will implement the full details of the AddToCart.aspx web form later in the chapter. Right-click the web project, add a new web form, name it AddToCart, and select the Main.master master page.

Well, this has been quite the lengthy exercise to add the product catalog to your application. You still have some work to finish with displaying the images, the product details, and the page to handle requests to add the products to the shopping cart.

Displaying the Product Images

As mentioned in the previous exercise, the images for the products in the database are stored as binary data. Since the data for the images is in a binary format, you cannot simply set a path to the images in a directory on the file system. You need to have the binary data processed and ultimately displayed as an image on the web page. I touched upon this concept in the previous exercise when you added the ASHX file, better known as an *HTTP handler* or *generic handler*. ASHX files implement the IHttpHandler interface and have one main benefit over using a standard web form or ASPX page. Basically, ASHX files have the ability to access the HttpContext while at the same time do not have to inherit from the Page class; thus, they don't require the additional overhead of displaying the images for the product category. More specifically, all the related HTTP information is readily available regarding the request that is received in the page.

ASHX files have two methods, as you saw when you added the ASHX code to the project. These methods are ProcessRequest and IsReusable. Lastly, another great benefit to using these files to display your images is that you will not be required to register the file extension in Internet Information Services (IIS) or in your project's Web.config file. You can simply add them to your project, and everything is good to go. The following exercise will show you the specifics.

Exercise: Displaying the Images

This exercise shows how to implement the product images in the HTTP handler and ASHX page you added to the web project in the previous exercise. Follow these steps:

1. Proceed to the generic handler, the ImageViewer.ashx file, that you added in the previous exercise. You need to modify the template code that was added. As mentioned, you need to keep the two methods; however, you will delete the code from within the ProcessRequest method, and you can keep the IsReusable method as is:

```
<%@ WebHandler Language="C#" Class="ImageViewer" %>

using System;
using System.Web;

public class ImageViewer : IHttpHandler
{
    public void ProcessRequest ( HttpContext context )
    {

    }

    public bool IsReusable
    {
        get { return false; }
    }
}
```

2. For this exercise, you will focus on the ProcessRequest method to eventually display the individual image. The first step in this method is to retrieve the query string for the image ID from the HttpContext being passed into the method, as shown in the following code:

```
<%@ WebHandler Language="C#" Class="ImageViewer" %>

using System;
using System.Web;

using LittleItalyVineyard.Common;

public class ImageViewer : IHttpHandler
{
    public void ProcessRequest ( HttpContext context )
    {
            Product product = new Product();
            product.ImageID = int.Parse➦
                ( context.Request.QueryString[ "ImageID" ] );
    }

    public bool IsReusable
    {
            get { return false; }
    }
}
```

3. You now have an instantiated Product class that will set the ImageID property in the code that will hold the ID for the image you need to query from the database. The next step is to implement functionality to retrieve the binary data from the database according to the image ID. You accomplish this by implementing the necessary code in the architecture to eventually retrieve the binary data of the image. Therefore, let's first add the namespace for the business logic layer to the code:

```
<%@ WebHandler Language="C#" Class="ImageViewer" %>

using System;
using System.Web;

using LittleItalyVineyard.Common;
using LittleItalyVineyard.BusinessLogic;

public class ImageViewer : IHttpHandler
{
    public void ProcessRequest ( HttpContext context )
    {
        Product product = new Product();
        product.ImageID = int.Parse➡
          ( context.Request.QueryString[ "ImageID" ] );
    }

    public bool IsReusable
    {
        get { return false; }
    }
}
```

4. Now, even though you are in the presentation layer, you need to revert to the database and create the stored procedure that will query the database for the image. To do so, proceed to SQL Server Management Studio and to the LittleItalyVineyard database. From there, open the query editor, and create and execute the following stored procedure script:

```
CREATE PROCEDURE ProductImage_Select

@ProductImageID int

AS

SELECT ProductImage FROM ProductImages
WHERE ProductImageID = @ProductImageID
```

5. You now have the stored procedure created to retrieve the image data. The next step is to add the class for the data access layer to use the new stored procedure. Proceed to the LittleItalyVineyard.DataAccess class library project and to the Select solution folder. Finally, add a new class named ProductImageSelectByIDDate, and add the code, as shown here:

```
using System;
using System.Collections.Generic;
using System.Text;
using System.Data.SqlClient;

using LittleItalyVineyard.Common;
```

```
namespace LittleItalyVineyard.DataAccess.Select
{
    public class ProductImageSelectByIDData : DataAccessBase
    {
        private Product _product;

        public ProductImageSelectByIDData()
        {
            StoredProcedureName = StoredProcedure.Name.➡
                ProductImage_Select.ToString();
        }

        public object Get()
        {
            object imagedata;

            ProductImageSelectByIDDataParameters➡
            _productimgselectbyiddataparameters =➡
            new ProductImageSelectByIDDataParameters( Product );
            DataBaseHelper dbhelper = new DataBaseHelper➡
              ( StoredProcedureName );
            imagedata = dbhelper.RunScalar➡
              ( base.ConnectionString ,
              _productimgselectbyiddataparameters.Parameters );

            return imagedata;
        }

        public Product Product
        {
            get { return _product; }
            set { _product = value; }
        }
    }

    public class ProductImageSelectByIDDataParameters
    {
        private Product _product;
        private SqlParameter[ ] _parameters;

        public ProductImageSelectByIDDataParameters(Product product )
        {
            Product = product;
            Build();
        }

        private void Build()
```

```
        {
                SqlParameter[] parameters =
                {
                        new SqlParameter( "@ProductImageID" , Product.ImageID )
                };

                Parameters = parameters;
        }

        public Product Product
        {
                get { return _product; }
                set { _product = value; }
        }

        public SqlParameter[] Parameters
        {
                get { return _parameters; }
                set { _parameters = value; }
        }
    }
}
```

6. In the previous code, notice that you also added the name of the newly created stored procedure to the StoredProcedure class. This parameter class will build the necessary parameters to be passed into the stored procedure. You now have the data access layer code implemented and can implement the business logic layer. Proceed to the LittleItalyVineyard.BusinessLogic class library project, add a new class named ProcessGetProductImage, and add the following code, as shown here:

```
using System;
using System.Collections.Generic;
using System.Text;
using System.IO;

using LittleItalyVineyard.Common;
using LittleItalyVineyard.DataAccess.Select;

namespace LittleItalyVineyard.BusinessLogic
{
    public class ProcessGetProductImage : IBusinessLogic
    {
        private Product _product;
        private Stream _imagestream;

        public ProcessGetProductImage()
        {

        }
```

```csharp
        public void Invoke()
        {
            ProductImageSelectByIDData selectproductimage =➠
              new  ProductImageSelectByIDData();
              selectproductimage.Product = this.Product;
            Product.ImageData = ( byte[ ] ) selectproductimage.Get();
            ImageStream = new MemoryStream➠
                    ( ( byte[] ) Product.ImageData );
        }

        public Stream ImageStream
        {
            get { return _imagestream; }
            set { _imagestream = value; }
        }

        public Product Product
        {
            get { return _product; }
            set { _product = value; }
        }
    }
}
```

7. The code in the business logic layer is now set to be used from the presentation layer, which will return you to the ASHX file that will initiate the request. Add the following code that will query the binary data of the product image and display it:

```csharp
<%@ WebHandler Language="C#" Class="ImageViewer" %>

using System;
using System.Web;
using System.IO;

using LittleItalyVineyard.BusinessLogic;
using LittleItalyVineyard.Common;

public class ImageViewer : IHttpHandler
{
  public void ProcessRequest ( HttpContext context )
    {
        Product product = new Product();
        product.ImageID = int.Parse➠
          ( context.Request.QueryString[ "ImageID" ] );

        ProcessGetProductImage processget = new ProcessGetProductImage();
        processget.Product = product;
```

```
        Stream stream = null;

        processget.Invoke();

        context.Response.ContentType = "image/jpeg";
        context.Response.Cache.SetCacheability( HttpCacheability.Public );
        context.Response.BufferOutput = false;

        int buffersize = 1024 * 16;
        byte[] buffer = new byte[ buffersize ];

        stream = processget.ImageStream;
        int count = stream.Read(buffer, 0, buffersize);

         while ( count > 0 )
         {
             context.Response.OutputStream.Write( buffer , 0 , count );
             count = stream.Read( buffer , 0 , buffersize );
         }
    }

    public bool IsReusable
    {
        get { return false; }
    }
}
```

With the previous finalized code to display the individual product images, the product catalog now has the ability to display the images. However, since you do not have any products in the database at this time, this code will not actually run since no products will be bound to the DataList. You will revisit this code in Chapter 21 when I discuss the administrator control panel of the application; you'll then have the ability to add products to the catalog and edit them.

Creating the Product Details

You have now implemented the complete product catalog where the user will have the ability to browse through the different items. It is now time to implement the functionality that will allow the user to dig into the details of a specific product. You will accomplish this by using a single web page that will display the complete information for an individual product that the user selects.

Certainly you have been to a website such as Amazon.com where you browse through a listing of products and one or several of those products interests you. Naturally, you click the image or the heading of the product, which takes you to a page dedicated to that product. This details page displays the complete description of the product along with other information, such as other suggested products that are similar and even some feedback from other customers who have purchased the product.

Your application will be similar because you will have the same type of details web page. There will be a larger image of the product, the full description of the product, a link to add the item to the shopping cart, and the possibility to scale later to add other suggested items and even user feedback about the product.

The following exercise will walk you through the necessary steps to implement the product details.

Exercise: Implementing the Product Details

This exercise shows how to create all the code in the different architecture layers to display the product details when a user ultimately selects an individual product from the catalog. Follow these steps:

1. Start with your database, and create the stored procedure that will be required to query the database for a single product specified by the ID:

```
CREATE PROCEDURE ProductByID_Select

@ProductID int

AS

SELECT
ProductID,
ProductName,
ProductCategoryName,
ProductImageID,
Description,
Price
FROM Products
INNER JOIN ProductCategory
ON ProductCategory.ProductCategoryID = Products.ProductCategoryID
WHERE ProductID = @ProductID
```

2. You can now move along to the data access layer. In a prior exercise, you already implemented the code in the data access layer to use the stored procedure. Let's revisit that code:

```
using System;
using System.Collections.Generic;
using System.Text;
using System.Data;
using System.Data.SqlClient;

using LittleItalyVincyard.Common;

namespace LittleItalyVineyard.DataAccess.Select
{
    public class ProductSelectByIDData : DataAccessBase
    {
        private Product _product;
```

```csharp
        public ProductSelectByIDData()
        {
            StoredProcedureName = StoredProcedure.Name.➡
              ProductByID_Select.ToString();
        }

        public DataSet Get()
        {
            DataSet ds;

            ProductSelectByIDDataParameters➡
              _productselectbyiddataparameters = new➡
              ProductSelectByIDDataParameters( Product );
            DataBaseHelper dbhelper = new DataBaseHelper➡
              ( StoredProcedureName );
            ds = dbhelper.Run( base.ConnectionString ,
              _productselectbyiddataparameters.Parameters );

            return ds;
        }

        public Product Product
        {
            get { return _product; }
            set { _product = value; }
        }
    }

public class ProductSelectByIDDataParameters
{
    private Product _product;
    private SqlParameter[] _parameters;

    public ProductSelectByIDDataParameters(Product product )
    {
        Product = product;
        Build();
    }

    private void Build()
    {
        SqlParameter[ ] parameters =
        {
            new SqlParameter( "@ProductID" , Product.ProductID )
        };
```

```
                Parameters = parameters;
            }

            public Product Product
            {
                get { return _product; }
                set { _product = value; }
            }

            public SqlParameter[ ] Parameters
            {
                get { return _parameters; }
                set { _parameters = value; }
            }
        }
    }
```

3. The data access code is similar to that of the other exercises. Moving along, proceed to the business logic layer, add a new class named **ProcessGetProductByID**, and focus on the code that will call upon that in the data access layer:

```
using System;
using System.Collections.Generic;
using System.Text;
using System.Data;

using LittleItalyVineyard.Common;
using LittleItalyVineyard.DataAccess.Select;

namespace LittleItalyVineyard.BusinessLogic
{
    public class ProcessGetProductByID : IBusinessLogic
    {
        private Product _product;
        private DataSet _resultset;

        public ProcessGetProductByID()
        {

        }

        public void Invoke()
        {
            ProductSelectByIDData selectproduct = ➥
                new ProductSelectByIDData();
            selectproduct.Product = Product;
            ResultSet = selectproduct.Get();
```

```csharp
            Product.Name = ResultSet.Tables[0 ].Rows[0]➥
                ["ProductName"].ToString();
            Product.Description = ResultSet.Tables[0].Rows[0]➥
                ["Description"].ToString();
            Product.Price = Convert.ToDecimal( ResultSet.Tables[0].➥
                Rows[0]["Price"].ToString()   );
            Product.ImageID = int.Parse(    ResultSet.Tables[0].➥
                Rows[0]["ProductImageID"].ToString() );
            Product.ProductCategory.ProductCategoryName = ➥
    ResultSet.Tables[0].Rows[0]["ProductCategoryName"].ToString();
        }

        public Product Product
        {
            get { return _product; }
            set { _product = value; }
        }

        private DataSet ResultSet
        {
            get { return _resultset; }
            set { _resultset = value; }
        }
    }
}
```

4. The final task is to focus your efforts on the web page in the presentation layer, the ProductDetails.aspx web form. Proceed to the ProductDetails.aspx web form and to the HTML code. You will add to the HTML code a table, an image, and several labels to display the product description, name, and price along with a button that will allow the user to add the product to the shopping cart:

```
<%@ Page Language="C#" MasterPageFile="~/Main.master"
AutoEventWireup="true" CodeFile="ProductDetails.aspx.cs"
Inherits="ProductDetails"
Title="Little Italy Vineyard | Product Details" %>

<asp:Content ID="Content1" ContentPlaceHolderID="contentplaceholderMain"
    Runat="Server">
<table cellSpacing="0" cellPadding="0" width="100%" border="0">
    <tr>
        <td vAlign="top" align="left">
            <table border="0" cellpadding="1" cellspacing="0" width="100%">
                <tr>
                    <td><img src="images/spacer.gif" width="1" height="15"
                    border="0" /></td>
                </tr>
```

```
<tr>
    <td><img src="images/spacer.gif" width="50" height="1"
    border="0" /></td>
    <td valign="top" align="right">
        <asp:Image ID="imageProductDetail" runat="server"
 width="100px" BorderStyle="Double" BorderWidth="3px"
 BorderColor="#92775C" />
    </td>
    <td width="100%" valign="top">
        <table cellpadding="0" cellspacing="0" border="0"
          width="100%">
            <tr>
                <td width="17">
    <img src="images/spacer.gif"
        width="17" height="3" border="0" /></td>
                <td></td>
            </tr>
            <tr>
                <td></td>
                <td class="ProductListHead"><b>
    <asp:label id="labelProductName" runat="server" />
  </b></td>
            </tr>
            <tr><td><img src="images/spacer.gif" width="1"
    height="5" border="0" /></td></tr>
            <tr>
                <td colspan="2">
                    <table cellpadding="0" cellspacing="0"
                      border="0" width="75%">
                        <tr><td class="prodUnderlineBG"
                  width="100%"></td></tr>
            <tr><td>
                <img src="images/spacer.gif"
                    width="1" height="1" border="0" />
                </td></tr>
                    <tr><td>
                <img src="images/prodDecorRight.gif" />
                </td></tr>
                    </table>
                </td>
            </tr>
            <tr>
                <td></td>
                <td><asp:label id="labelDescription"
             runat="server"></asp:label></td>
            </tr>
```

```
<tr><td><img src="images/spacer.gif" width="1"
    height="8" border="0" /></td></tr>
<tr>
    <td></td>
    <td>
<span class="ProductListItem">
    <b>Price: </b>
    <asp:label id="labelPrice" runat="server" />
        </span>
    </td>
</tr>
<tr><td><img src="images/spacer.gif" width="1"
    height="8" border="0" /></td></tr>
<tr>
    <td></td>
<td>Category: <asp:label id="labelCategory"
    runat="server" />
    </td>
</tr>
<tr><td>
<img src="images/spacer.gif" width="1"
    height="12" border="0" /></td></tr>
<tr>
    <td></td>
    <td>

        <b>
<a href="AddToCart.aspx?ProductID=➡
        <%= Request.QueryString[ "ProductID" ] %>"
class="red">Add To Cart</a></b>
            </td>
        </tr>
        <tr><td>
    <img src="images/spacer.gif" width="1"
        height="5" border="0" /></td></tr>
        <tr>
            <td></td>
    <td><asp:hyperlink id="linkContinueShopping"
    runat="server" Text="Continue Shopping"
    NavigateUrl="Winery.aspx">
    </asp:hyperlink></td>
            </tr>
        </table>
    </td>
    <td><img src="images/spacer.gif" width="15" height="1"
    border="0" /></td>
    </tr>
</table>
```

```
        </td>
    </tr>
    <tr>
        <td>
            <img src="images/spacer.gif" width="1"
                height="10" border="0" /></td>
    </tr>
</table>
</asp:Content>
```

5. You now have the layout and HTML to display the individual details for a specific product. If you switch to design view in Visual Studio, you will see that it resembles Figure 16-13.

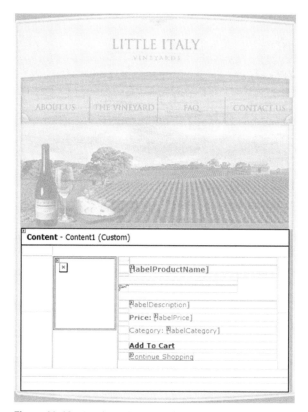

Figure 16-13. *Design view: ProductDetails.aspx*

6. The remaining item to implement is the actual code in the web page to connect the information that is queried from the database. The code will start by getting the value for the query string that is passed into the page and will then call the business logic layer and eventually return the information to set the labels, as shown here:

```
using System;
using System.Data;
using System.Configuration;
using System.Collections;
```

```csharp
using System.Web;
using System.Web.Security;
using System.Web.UI;
using System.Web.UI.WebControls;
using System.Web.UI.WebControls.WebParts;
using System.Web.UI.HtmlControls;

using LittleItalyVineyard.BusinessLogic;
using LittleItalyVineyard.Common;

public partial class ProductDetails : System.Web.UI.Page
{
    protected void Page_Load( object sender , EventArgs e )
    {
        if ( !IsPostBack )
        {
            LoadProduct();
        }
    }

    private void LoadProduct()
    {
        Product prod = new Product();
        prod.ProductID = int.Parse➥
          ( Request.QueryString[ "ProductID" ] );

        ProcessGetProductByID getProduct = new ProcessGetProductByID();
        getProduct.Product = prod;

        try
    {
        getProduct.Invoke();
    }
    catch
    {
        Response.Redirect( "ErrorPage.aspx" );
    }

        labelProductName.Text =getProduct.Product.Name;
        labelDescription.Text = getProduct.Product.Description;
        labelPrice.Text = string.Format("{0:c}", ➥
            getProduct.Product.Price);
        imageProductDetail.ImageUrl ➥
            = "ImageViewer.ashx?ImageID=" + ➥
            getProduct.Product.ImageID.ToString();
        labelCategory.Text = getProduct.Product.➥
            ProductCategory.ProductCategoryName;
```

```
        }
    }
```

This code brings you to the conclusion of yet another exercise; this exercise showed how to display all the details for a specific product when the user selects one from the catalog.

Searching the Catalog

Throughout the chapter, I have discussed in detail how to show all the products in the catalog as well as display the individual details of a single product. You also need to implement the ability to search the catalog and have the search results displayed. The functionality to search for the products is vital to the overall system because many customers will know or have a good idea about what they want to purchase and so can search for it rather than browse the products. Given the competition, if your customer cannot find what they are looking for, they cannot make the purchase; in fact, they may go to another company where they can find their product more easily. Thus, your client would miss out on a sale.

The potential for losing sales as a result of users not being able to find your products could result in the failure of your client's online business. Therefore, to prevent this as much as possible, the following exercise will show how to implement a user-friendly and easy method for your customer to easily find what they want.

Exercise: Implementing the Search Functionality

This exercise shows how to implement the search functionality in the database, data access, business logic, and presentation layers of the architecture. This will result in providing the users with a simple yet effective way of searching the product catalog for what they want. Follow these steps:

1. Similar to the other exercises, you will first focus your attention on the stored procedure that will query the database supplied with the criteria that was specified by the user. Open Microsoft SQL Server Management Studio, and create the following script in the LittleItalyVineyard database:

```
CREATE PROCEDURE Products_SelectSearch

@SearchCriteria nvarchar(255)

AS

SELECT
ProductID,
ProductName,
ProductCategoryName,
ProductImageID,
SUBSTRING(Description, 1, 150) + '...' AS Description,
Price
FROM Products
```

```
INNER JOIN ProductCategory
ON ProductCategory.ProductCategoryID = Products.ProductCategoryID
WHERE
ProductCategoryName LIKE '%' + @SearchCriteria + '%'
OR
ProductName LIKE '%' + @SearchCriteria + '%'
OR
Description LIKE '%' + @SearchCriteria + '%'
```

Notice this is the same procedure you used to select all the products from the database, with the exception of adding a detailed WHERE clause. In the WHERE clause, you have added three pieces of information. Each piece takes the ProductCategoryName, ProductName, and Description and compares it to the @SearchCriteria parameter, which is what the user entered in the search box. Notice you have used the LIKE keyword along with the % symbols prior to the @SearchCriteria parameter and at the end. As a result of using this methodology, the search will look to match a pattern of the criteria and not for an exact match, thus giving more flexibility for returning results to the user. Finally, execute the stored procedure script against the database.

2. You can proceed to the data access layer to add the class and code that will utilize the stored procedure to query the products based on the search criteria. To do so, proceed to the LittleItalyVineyard.DataAccess class library, and add a new class to the Select solution folder named **ProductSelectSearchData**. Add the code similar to that of the other data access classes, as shown here:

```
using System;
using System.Collections.Generic;
using System.Text;
using System.Data;
using System.Data.SqlClient;

namespace LittleItalyVineyard.DataAccess.Select
{
    public class ProductSelectSearchData : DataAccessBase
    {
        private string _searchcriteria;

        public ProductSelectSearchData()
        {
            base.StoredProcedureName = StoredProcedure.Name.➥
         Products_SelectSearch.ToString();
        }

        public DataSet Get()
        {
            DataSet ds;

            ProductSelectSearchDataParameters ➥
                _productselectsearchdataparameters = new ➥C
                    ProductSelectSearchDataParameters( SearchCriteria );
            DataBaseHelper dbhelper = new DataBaseHelper➥
```

```
                          ( StoredProcedureName );
                ds = dbhelper.Run( base.ConnectionString ,
                    _productselectsearchdataparameters.Parameters );

                return ds;
            }

            public string SearchCriteria
            {
                get { return _searchcriteria; }
                set { _searchcriteria = value; }
            }
        }
    }

    public class ProductSelectSearchDataParameters
    {
        private string _searchcriteria;
        private SqlParameter[ ] _parameters;

        public ProductSelectSearchDataParameters( string searchcriteria )
        {
            SearchCriteria = searchcriteria;
            Build();
        }

        private void Build()
        {
            SqlParameter[ ] parameters =
            {
                new SqlParameter( "@SearchCriteria" , SearchCriteria )
            };

            Parameters = parameters;
        }

            public string SearchCriteria
            {
                get { return _searchcriteria; }
                set { _searchcriteria = value; }
            }

            public SqlParameter[ ] Parameters
            {
                get { return _parameters; }
                set { _parameters = value; }
            }
        }
    }
```

3. You now have the complete code in the data access layer that will use the newly created stored procedure that will query the database for all products that match the submitted criteria. You will now need
to proceed to the business logic to implement the necessary class and code. Therefore, add a new
class to the LittleItalyVineyard.BusinessLogic class library project named **ProcessGetProductsSearch**,
and add the following code:

```csharp
using System;
using System.Collections.Generic;
using System.Text;
using System.Data;

using LittleItalyVineyard.DataAccess.Select;

namespace LittleItalyVineyard.BusinessLogic
{
    public class ProcessGetProductsSearch : IBusinessLogic
    {
        private DataSet _resultset;
        private string _searchcriteria;

        public ProcessGetProductsSearch()
        {

        }

        public void Invoke()
        {
            ProductSelectSearchData productdatasearch = ➥
                new ProductSelectSearchData();
            productdatasearch.SearchCriteria = this.SearchCriteria;
            ResultSet = productdatasearch.Get();
        }

        public string SearchCriteria
        {
            get { return _searchcriteria; }
            set { _searchcriteria = value; }
        }

        public DataSet ResultSet
        {
            get { return _resultset; }
            set { _resultset = value; }
        }
    }
}
```

4. Finally, you'll move on to the presentation layer where you will initiate the searching of the products. This will require you to update the existing Winery.aspx web form. Your first task is to add a text box and a command button so the user will be able to enter criteria to search and then execute the search by clicking the button. The revised HTML code will look like the following:

```
<%@ Page Language="C#" MasterPageFile="~/Main.master"
AutoEventWireup="true" CodeFile="Winery.aspx.cs"
    Inherits="Winery" Title="Little Italy Vineyard | The Vineyard" %>

<asp:Content ID="Content1" ContentPlaceHolderID="contentplaceholderMain"
    runat="Server">
    <img src="images/spacer.gif" width="1" height="5" border="0" /><br />
    <table cellpadding="0" cellspacing="0" border="0" width="100%">
        <tr><td><img src="images/spacer.gif" width="1" height="5"
         border="0" /></td></tr>
        <tr>
            <td valign="middle" align="right" width="100%">

<asp:TextBox ID="textSearch" runat="server" CssClass="textField">
</asp:TextBox>
<img src="images/spacer.gif" width="5" height="1" border="0" />
        <asp:Button ID="commandSearch"
                runat="server" Text="Search"
                OnClick="commandSearch_Click"
            CssClass="button" />

            </td>
            <td><img src="images/spacer.gif" width="35" height="1"
border="0" /></td>
        </tr>
        <tr><td><img src="images/spacer.gif" width="1" height="5"
border="0" /></td></tr>
        <tr>
            <td align="center" colspan="2">
            <table cellpadding="0" cellspacing="0"
                border="0" width="95%">
                    <tr>
                        <td width="100%" class="separatorBG">
<img src="images/spacer.gif" width="1" height="1" border="0" /></td>
        <td>
        <img src="images/textSeparatorRight.gif" />
        </td>
                    </tr>
                </table>
            </td>
            <td></td>
        </tr>
    </table>
```

```
<img src="images/spacer.gif" width="1" height="10" border="0" /><br />

<asp:Panel ID="panelResults" runat="Server"
    Visible="false" Height="24px">
    <table border="0" cellpadding="1" cellspacing="0" width="100%">
        <tr>
            <td><img src="images/spacer.gif" width="50" height="1"
border="0" /></td>
            <td valign="top" width="100%" nowrap>No Results Found!</td>
        </tr>
    </table>
</asp:Panel>

<asp:DataList ID="datalistProducts" RepeatColumns="1" runat="server"
Width="100%">
    <ItemTemplate>
        <table border="0" cellpadding="1" cellspacing="0" width="100%">
            <tr>
                <td><img src="images/spacer.gif" width="50" height="1"
        border="0" /></td>
                <td valign="top" align="right">
    <a href='ProductDetails.aspx?ProductID=<%# Eval("ProductID") %>'>
    <img src='ImageViewer.ashx?ImageID=<%# Eval("ProductImageID") %>'
        height="85" border="0" class="prodBorder">
                    </a>
                </td>
                <td width="100%" valign="top">
    <table cellpadding="0" cellspacing="0" border="0"
            width="100%"><tr>
    <td width="17"><img src="images/spacer.gif" width="17"
            height="3" border="0" /></td>
                            <td></td>
                        </tr>
                        <tr>
                            <td></td>
        <td class="ProductListHead">
<a href='ProductDetails.aspx?ProductID=<%# Eval("ProductID") %>'>
    <b><%# Eval("ProductName") %></b></a></td>
                        </tr>
        <tr><td><img src="images/spacer.gif" width="1"
            height="5" border="0" /></td></tr>
                        <tr>
                            <td colspan="2">
    <table cellpadding="0" cellspacing="0" border="0"
width="75%">
        <tr><td class="prodUnderlineBG" width="100%">
    </td></tr>
```

```
    <tr><td><img src="images/spacer.gif" width="1"
height="1" border="0" />
    </td></tr>
      <tr><td><img src="images/prodDecorRight.gif" />
          </td></tr>
                  </table>
                    </td>
                      </tr>
                      <tr>
                        <td></td>
                        <td><%# Eval("Description") %></td>
                      </tr>
                      <tr><td><img src="images/spacer.gif" width="1"
                height="5" border="0" /></td></tr>
                      <tr>
                        <td></td>
                        <td>
              <span class="ProductListItem">
                  <b>Price: </b>
                              <%# Eval("Price", "{0:c}") %>
                          </span>
                        </td>
                      </tr>
                      <tr><td><img src="images/spacer.gif" width="1"
                height="5" border="0" /></td></tr>
                      <tr>
                        <td></td>
                        <td>
        <a href='AddToCart.aspx?ProductID=<%# Eval("ProductID") %>'>
          <span class="ProductListItem">
                              <font color="#9D0000"><b>Add To Cart<b>
          </font></span> </a>
                        </td>
                      </tr>
                  </table>
                </td>
                <td><img src="images/spacer.gif" width="15" height="1"
            border="0" /></td>
              </tr>
            </table>
        </ItemTemplate>
    </asp:DataList>
    <img src="images/spacer.gif" width="1" height="10" border="0" /><br />
</asp:Content>
```

In addition to the command button and the text box, you also added a panel named panelResults that has the visible property set to false. This panel will appear only when the user searches and the search subsequently returns no results; the panel will inform the user that there are no results.

5. Moving along, you now have the text box and command button added to the web page and can add the code that will take the search criteria and return the results. Proceed to the code view of the Winery.aspx page, and add the following code:

```
using System;
using System.Data;
using System.Configuration;
using System.Collections;
using System.Web;
using System.Web.Security;
using System.Web.UI;
using System.Web.UI.WebControls;
using System.Web.UI.WebControls.WebParts;
using System.Web.UI.HtmlControls;

using LittleItalyVineyard.BusinessLogic;

public partial class Winery : System.Web.UI.Page
{
    protected void Page_Load( object sender , EventArgs e )
    {
        if ( ! IsPostBack )
        {
            LoadProducts();
        }

        this.Form.DefaultButton = commandSearch.UniqueID;
        this.textSearch.Focus();
    }

    private void LoadProducts()
    {
        ProcessGetProducts processproducts = new ProcessGetProducts();

        try
        {
          processproducts.Invoke();
        }
        catch
        {
            Response.Redirect( "ErrorPage.aspx" );
        }
```

```
            datalistProducts.DataSource = processproducts.ResultSet;
            datalistProducts.DataBind();
        }

        private void LoadProducts( string searchcriteria )
        {
            ProcessGetProductsSearch processsearch = ➥
                new ProcessGetProductsSearch();
            processsearch.SearchCriteria = searchcriteria;

        try
        {
            processsearch.Invoke();
        }
        catch
        {
            Response.Redirect( "ErrorPage.aspx" );
        }

            if ( processsearch.ResultSet.Tables[0].Rows.Count > 0 )
            {
                panelResults.Visible = false;
                datalistProducts.DataSource = processsearch.ResultSet;
                datalistProducts.DataBind();
            }
            else
            {
                panelResults.Visible = true;
                datalistProducts.DataBind();
            }
        }

        protected void commandSearch_Click(object sender, EventArgs e)
        {
            LoadProducts(textSearch.Text);
        }
    }
```

Simply put, you overloaded the LoadProducts method to include the search criteria, which will then call the previous code you added in the exercise. Finally, you check whether the result set returned and whether there are more than zero items in the set. If there are zero items, you display the panel informing the user that there are no results. You will also notice two other pieces of code in the page load event. This code ensures that the command button is the default button on the page so that when the user presses Enter, they will execute the command button. The other code sets the focus to the text box so the user does not have to click in the text box prior to typing their search criteria.

Summary

You have successfully developed the product catalog for your application. I mentioned that in the exercises, since the database doesn't contain any products at this time, you will not be able to fully test the code you have implemented. That is OK, because you will revisit this topic many times in Chapter 21 when you add the administrator control panel, which is where you will set up the functionality to add and edit all the products for the catalog. Now that you have a working product catalog, you need to add the functionality so the customers can add the products they want to purchase to their shopping cart and ultimately process their payment. With that said, let's waste no time and get started with the next chapter, where you'll learn how to fully implement the shopping cart for your application.

CHAPTER 17

■ ■ ■

Building the Shopping Cart

You have finished your product catalog for your customers to browse through and (you hope) make purchases. So, now that the product catalog is functional, you just need to populate it with the actual products for sale. In this chapter, you'll implement the shopping cart, which identifies the products that a customer wants to purchase and provides a mechanism to allow them to submit a payment for the merchandise.

The application will display the products in the product catalog that the customer can click to add them to their shopping cart. You want to have an easy way for customers to add as many products to their shopping cart as they want, and you want to give them an easy way to update their current shopping cart by changing the quantity of the products or changing their mind and deleting an item altogether. This chapter will show you how to incorporate all this functionality in a concise manner, and it includes extensive exercises that show how to implement the code you need.

Specifically, this chapter will cover how to implement the code for the following functionality:

- Adding an item to the cart

- Displaying the shopping cart

- Updating the shopping cart

- Processing abandoned carts

Adding to the Shopping Cart

The basic functionality of a shopping cart is the user's ability to add a product from the catalog to the shopping cart. You will need to allow the user to easily add any product they view to the shopping cart, and you need to display information about the product they just added. For instance, a customer will browse through the catalog and come across a product they want to purchase, such as a bottle of Merlot, which will fall under the Red Wine category. They then click the Add To Cart button, which will add this information to the database and subsequently display the shopping cart to the customer. You'll need to account for several aspects, such as recording the customer's information and establishing a new customer account, when this action takes place.

The following exercise will walk you through all the steps necessary to achieve this functionality.

Exercise: Inserting a Product in the Shopping Cart

This exercise shows how to insert the proper information in the database when a user adds a product to their shopping cart and then sees the shopping cart with the selected items. Follow these steps:

1. You'll start at the database and create the stored procedure script. This stored procedure is named ShoppingCart_Insert, and it is fairly complex. It will first query the number of items that reside in the shopping cart with the same product ID and the same cart ID. Then, if that number is greater than zero, the product found will be updated. If that number is zero, the product will be inserted in the ShoppingCart table. So, execute the following script against the database:

```
CREATE PROCEDURE ShoppingCart_Insert

@CartGUID nvarchar(50),
@ProductID int,
@Quantity int

AS

DECLARE @ItemCount int

SELECT
@ItemCount = Count(ProductID)
FROM
ShoppingCart
WHERE
ProductID = @ProductID
AND
CartGUID = @CartGUID

IF @ItemCount > 0   /* Update quantity */
    UPDATE
    ShoppingCart
    SET Quantity = (@Quantity + ShoppingCart.Quantity)
    WHERE
    ProductID = @ProductID
    AND
    CartGUID = @CartGUID
ELSE   /* No quantity found - insert */
    INSERT INTO ShoppingCart
    (CartGUID, ProductID, Quantity)
    VALUES
    (@CartGUID, @ProductID, @Quantity)
```

2. You have created the stored procedure in the database to use. Next, proceed to the data access layer and to the LIttleItalyVineyard.DataAccess class library project. In this project, since this is the first time you are inserting an item in the database, you need to create a folder in the project, thus creating another namespace. To do so, right-click the LittleItalyVineyard.DataAccess class library, and choose Add ➤ New Folder, as shown in Figure 17-1. Please note that this will create a physical folder on the file system and not a virtual folder.

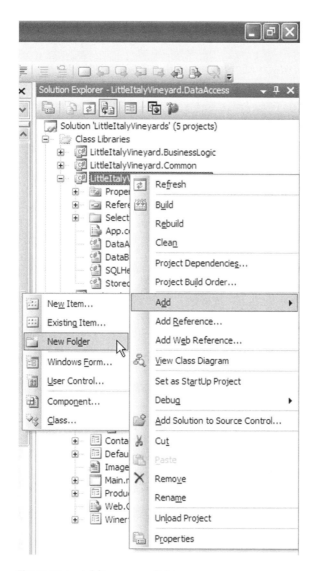

Figure 17-1. *Adding a new folder*

3. This creates a new folder in the class library project. Next, rename the new folder to **Insert**, as shown in Figure 17-2.

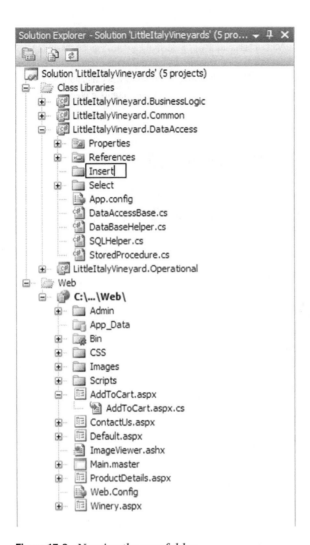

Figure 17-2. *Naming the new folder*

4. You now have a new folder named Insert in the project. As mentioned, this has created a new namespace, LittleItalyVineyard.DataAccess.Insert. The next step is to add a class to this new folder and namespace. To do so, right-click the Insert folder, and choose Add ➤ Class, as shown in Figure 17-3.

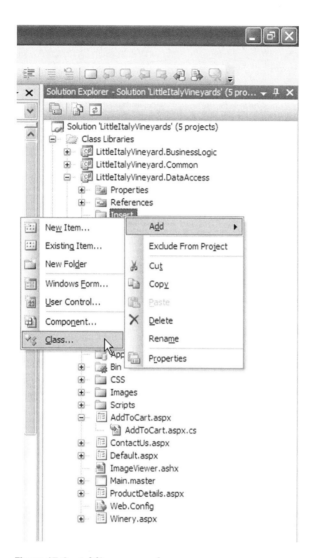

Figure 17-3. *Adding a new class*

5. After adding the new class, you will see the Add New Item dialog box, which you have seen many times before. Name the new class **ShoppingCartInsertData**, as shown in Figure 17-4, and click the Add button.

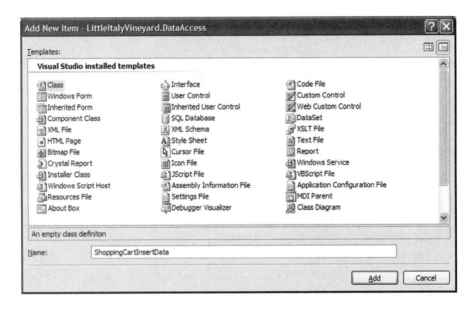

Figure 17-4. *Naming the ShoppingCartInsertData class*

6. This creates the ShoppingCartInsertData class in your project. You will see the standard shell code for a new class. However, before modifying and adding to this new class, you'll proceed to the StoredProcedure class, where the names of the stored procedures are maintained, and add the latest stored procedure to the list as identified, as shown here:

```
using System;
using System.Collections.Generic;
using System.Text;

namespace LittleItalyVineyard.DataAccess
{
    public class StoredProcedure
    {
        public enum Name
        {
            ProductByID_Select ,
            Products_Select ,
            ProductImage_Select ,
            Products_SelectSearch ,
            ShoppingCart_Insert
        }
    }
}
```

7. This adds the ShoppingCart_Insert stored procedure to the enumeration of the StoredProcedure class, so you can return to the ShoppingCartInsertData class for its modification. First add the public identifier to the class, inheriting from the DataAccessBase class. Then add the System.Data, System.Data.SqlClient, and LittleItalyVineyard.Common namespaces, as shown here:

```
using System;
using System.Collections.Generic;
using System.Text;
using System.Data;
using System.Data.SqlClient;

using LittleItalyVineyard.Common;

namespace LittleItalyVineyard.DataAccess.Insert
{
    public class ShoppingCartInsertData : DataAccessBase
    {
    }
}
```

8. Next, add the constructor of the ShoppingCartInsertData class that will, within the constructor, specify the name of the stored procedure that will be used. Then add a common object field and property that will be populated from other tiers of the architecture and will be used within the class. The code is as follows:

```
using System;
using System.Collections.Generic;
using System.Text;
using System.Data;
using System.Data.SqlClient;

using LittleItalyVineyard.Common;

namespace LittleItalyVineyard.DataAccess.Insert
{
    public class ShoppingCartInsertData : DataAccessBase
    {
        private ShoppingCart _shoppingcart;

        public ShoppingCartInsertData()
        {
            StoredProcedureName = StoredProcedure.Name.➥
              ShoppingCart_Insert.ToString();
        }
```

```
        public ShoppingCart ShoppingCart
        {
            get { return _shoppingcart; }
            set { _shoppingcart = value; }
        }
    }
}
```

9. The ShoppingCartInsertData class is beginning to shape up quite well. In the following steps, you'll add the method that will insert the values into the ShoppingCart table, but prior to doing so, you need to add the associated parameters class. This class will be named ShoppingCartInsertDataParameters, and it will also have a common object property of the ShoppingCart and a method to build the parameters that will be necessary for the stored procedure. The code is as follows:

```
using System;
using System.Collections.Generic;
using System.Text;
using System.Data;
using System.Data.SqlClient;

using LittleItalyVineyard.Common;

namespace LittleItalyVineyard.DataAccess.Insert
{
    public class ShoppingCartInsertData : DataAccessBase
    {
        private ShoppingCart _shoppingcart;

        public ShoppingCartInsertData()
        {
            StoredProcedureName = StoredProcedure.Name.➥
                ShoppingCart_Insert.ToString();
        }

        public ShoppingCart ShoppingCart
        {
            get { return _shoppingcart; }
            set { _shoppingcart = value; }
        }
    }

    public class ShoppingCartInsertDataParameters
    {
        private ShoppingCart _shoppingcart;
        private SqlParameter[ ] _parameters;

        public ShoppingCartInsertDataParameters➥
            (ShoppingCart shoppingcart )
```

```
{
    ShoppingCart = shoppingcart;
    Build();
}

private void Build()
{
    SqlParameter[ ] parameters =
    {
        new SqlParameter( "@CartGUID" ,➡
            ShoppingCart.CartGUID ) ,
        new SqlParameter( "@ProductID",➡
            ShoppingCart.ProductID ) ,
        new SqlParameter( "@Quantity",➡
            ShoppingCart.Quantity )
    };

    Parameters = parameters;
}

public ShoppingCart ShoppingCart
{
    get { return _shoppingcart; }
    set { _shoppingcart = value; }
}

public SqlParameter[] Parameters
{
    get { return _parameters; }
    set { _parameters = value; }
}
    }
}
```

10. Now move on to your final method within the ShoppingCartInsertData class, Add(). This method will utilize the parameters class created in the previous step and actually execute the information in the database and more specifically in the ShoppingCart table. The method will consist of instantiating the ShoppingCartInsertDataParameters class and passing in the ShoppingCart common class. After that, the DBHelper class, which will allow for systematic access to executing the stored procedure specified, is again passed in the class followed by setting the parameters equal to the ShoppingCartInsertDataParameters class and then finally the Run() method of the DBHelper class. You can see the complete code here:

```
using System;
using System.Collections.Generic;
using System.Text;
using System.Data;
using System.Data.SqlClient;
```

```
using LittleItalyVineyard.Common;

namespace LittleItalyVineyard.DataAccess.Insert
{
    public class ShoppingCartInsertData : DataAccessBase
    {
        private ShoppingCart _shoppingcart;
        private ShoppingCartInsertDataParameters➥
            _shoppingcartinsertdataparameters;

        public ShoppingCartInsertData()
        {
            StoredProcedureName = StoredProcedure.Name.➥
                ShoppingCart_Insert.ToString();
        }

        public void Add()
        {
            _shoppingcartinsertdataparameters = new➥
                ShoppingCartInsertDataParameters( ShoppingCart );
            DataBaseHelper dbhelper = new DataBaseHelper➥
                ( StoredProcedureName );
            dbhelper.Parameters =➥
             _shoppingcartinsertdataparameters.Parameters;
            dbhelper.Run();
        }

        public ShoppingCart ShoppingCart
        {
            get { return _shoppingcart; }
            set { _shoppingcart = value; }
        }
    }

    public class ShoppingCartInsertDataParameters
    {
        private ShoppingCart _shoppingcart;
        private SqlParameter[ ] _parameters;

        public ShoppingCartInsertDataParameters➥
            ( ShoppingCart shoppingcart )
        {
            ShoppingCart = shoppingcart;
            Build();
        }
```

```
        private void Build()
        {
            SqlParameter[ ] parameters =
            {
                new SqlParameter( "@CartGUID" ,➥
                  ShoppingCart.CartGUID ) ,
                new SqlParameter( "@ProductID",➥
                  ShoppingCart.ProductID ) ,
                new SqlParameter( "@Quantity" ,➥
                  ShoppingCart.Quantity )
            };

            Parameters = parameters;
        }

        public ShoppingCart ShoppingCart
        {
            get { return _shoppingcart; }
            set { _shoppingcart = value; }
        }

        public SqlParameter[] Parameters
        {
            get { return _parameters; }
            set { _parameters = value; }
        }
    }
}
```

11. The data access class is now complete. Next, you'll move on to the business logic layer and imple-
    ment the necessary code that will use the code you just added to the data access tier. So, proceed
    to the LittleItalyVineyard.BusinessLogic class library, and add a new class to the project named
    ProcessAddShoppingCart. Upon adding the class, you will again see the standard template class code.
    Add the LittleItalyVineyard.Common and LittleItalyVineyard.DataAccess.Insert namespaces, the con-
    structor, the IBusinessLogic interface, and finally the public identifier for the class. The code is as follows:

```
using System;
using System.Collections.Generic;
using System.Text;

using LittleItalyVineyard.Common;
using LittleItalyVineyard.DataAccess.Insert;

namespace LittleItalyVineyard.BusinessLogic
{
    public class ProcessAddShoppingCart : IBusinessLogic
    {
        public ProcessAddShoppingCart()
```

```
            {

            }
        }
    }
```

12. Your work is not yet complete. You need to add the necessary implementation that the IBusinessLogic interface requires. To do so, you add the Invoke() function that will later use the data access code you just added:

```
using System;
using System.Collections.Generic;
using System.Text;

using LittleItalyVineyard.Common;
using LittleItalyVineyard.DataAccess.Insert;

namespace LittleItalyVineyard.BusinessLogic
{
    public class ProcessAddShoppingCart : IBusinessLogic
    {
        public ProcessAddShoppingCart()
        {

        }

        public void Invoke()
        {

        }

    }
}
```

13. Now add the common class ShoppingCart to the code with its associated field name, as shown here:

```
using System;
using System.Collections.Generic;
using System.Text;

using LittleItalyVineyard.Common;
using LittleItalyVineyard.DataAccess.Insert;

namespace LittleItalyVineyard.BusinessLogic
{
    public class ProcessAddShoppingCart : IBusinessLogic
    {
        public ProcessAddShoppingCart()
        {
```

```
        }

        public void Invoke()
        {

        }

        public ShoppingCart ShoppingCart
        {
            get { return _shoppingcart; }
            set { _shoppingcart = value; }
        }
    }
}
```

14. The final code to implement in the business logic tier is the code in the Invoke() method that will use the data access class, ShoppingCartInsertData, that you created earlier in this exercise. This class will be instantiated followed by passing the ShoppingCart property of the ProcessAddShoppingCart class to that of the ShoppingCartInsertData class and finally the Add() method. All the code will be wrapped with a try/catch statement, as shown here:

```
using System;
using System.Collections.Generic;
using System.Text;

using LittleItalyVineyard.Common;
using LittleItalyVineyard.DataAccess.Insert;

namespace LittleItalyVineyard.BusinessLogic
{
    public class ProcessAddShoppingCart : IBusinessLogic
    {
        private ShoppingCart _shoppingcart;

        public ProcessAddShoppingCart()
        {

        }

        public void Invoke()
        {
            ShoppingCartInsertData shoppingcartdata = new➡
                ShoppingCartInsertData();
            shoppingcartdata.ShoppingCart = this.ShoppingCart;
            shoppingcartdata.Add();
        }
```

```
        public ShoppingCart ShoppingCart
        {
            get { return _shoppingcart; }
            set { _shoppingcart = value; }
        }
    }
}
```

15. The business logic tier code is complete. You can now proceed to the presentation tier to add the nec-
    essary code that will utilize the code you have implemented thus far. Proceed to the AddToCart.aspx
    web form and to the Hypertext Markup Language (HTML) source. You will see the existing code of
    a content placeholder. You can delete this code and leave only the page declarations, as shown here:

```
<%@ Page Language="C#" MasterPageFile="~/Main.master"
AutoEventWireup="true" CodeFile="AddToCart.aspx.cs"
Inherits="AddToCart" Title="Untitled Page" %>
```

16. It will be evident soon why you do not need any HTML code for this web form. Now, switch to the C#
    code of the web form where you can see the page load event with nothing implemented:

```
using System;
using System.Data;
using System.Configuration;
using System.Collections;
using System.Web;
using System.Web.Security;
using System.Web.UI;
using System.Web.UI.WebControls;
using System.Web.UI.WebControls.WebParts;
using System.Web.UI.HtmlControls;

public partial class AddToCart : System.Web.UI.Page
{
    protected void Page_Load( object sender , EventArgs e )
    {

    }
}
```

17. The first item to add is the namespace to the business logic tier and the common objects of the appli-
    cation, as shown here:

```
using System;
using System.Data;
using System.Configuration;
using System.Collections;
using System.Web;
using System.Web.Security;
using System.Web.UI;
using System.Web.UI.WebControls;
```

```
using System.Web.UI.WebControls.WebParts;
using System.Web.UI.HtmlControls;

using LittleItalyVineyard.Common;
using LittleItalyVineyard.BusinessLogic;

public partial class AddToCart : System.Web.UI.Page
{
    protected void Page_Load( object sender , EventArgs e )
    {


    }
}
```

18. The code for the web form will consist of basically two parts. The first part will use the business logic code, and if a successful addition of the information is added to the shopping cart, the user will be redirected to the shopping cart web page. Second, you will need to retrieve the shopping cart ID, which will be the global unique identifier (GUID) that is stored within a cookie on the user's local machine. If the cookie is not found, it will in most cases mean that the user is adding a product to the shopping cart for the first time; therefore, a cookie with a new GUID will be created. If the user is a return customer or they are adding subsequent items to the shopping cart, the GUID will be retrieved from the local cookie. To retrieve the GUID, you will implement a property that will return the GUID. This property will call upon the static class Utilities in the LittleItalyVineyard.Operational project library and namespace. Add the static function GetCartGUID() to the Utilities class as follows:

```
public static string GetCartGUID()
{
    if ( HttpContext.Current.Request.Cookies➥
            ["LittleItalyVineyard"] != null )
    {
        return HttpContext.Current.Request.Cookies➥
         ["LittleItalyVineyard"]["CartID"].ToString();
    }
    else
    {
        Guid CartGUID = Guid.NewGuid();
        HttpCookie cookie = new HttpCookie( "LittleItalyVineyard" );
        cookie.Values.Add( "CartID" , CartGUID.ToString() );
        cookie.Expires = DateTime.Now.AddDays( 30 );
        HttpContext.Current.Response.AppendCookie( cookie );

        return CartGUID.ToString();
    }
}
```

19. The following is the AddToCart.aspx web form, which will utilize the GetCartGUID function from within the Utilities class by using a read-only property, as demonstrated here:

```
using System;
using System.Data;
using System.Configuration;
using System.Collections;
using System.Web;
using System.Web.Security;
using System.Web.UI;
using System.Web.UI.WebControls;
using System.Web.UI.WebControls.WebParts;
using System.Web.UI.HtmlControls;

using LittleItalyVineyard.Common;
using LittleItalyVineyard.BusinessLogic;
using LittleItalyVineyard.Operational;

public partial class AddToCart : System.Web.UI.Page
{
    protected void Page_Load( object sender , EventArgs e )
    {
        LittleItalyVineyard.Common.ShoppingCart➥
            shoppingcart = new LittleItalyVineyard.Common.➥
                ShoppingCart();
        shoppingcart.ProductID = int.Parse( Request.➥
                QueryString["ProductID"] );
        shoppingcart.CartGUID = CartGUID;
        shoppingcart.Quantity = 1;

        ProcessAddShoppingCart procshoppingcart➥
            = new ProcessAddShoppingCart();
        procshoppingcart.ShoppingCart = shoppingcart;

        try
        {
            procshoppingcart.Invoke();
        }
        catch
        {
            Response.Redirect( "ErrorPage.aspx" );
        }
        Response.Redirect( "ShoppingCart.aspx" );
    }
```

```
        private string CartGUID
        {
            get { return Utilities.GetCartGUID(); }
        }
    }
}
```

With this code added and implemented, you have all the code in place to add a product to the shopping cart in the database. By using a local cookie, as mentioned, you will store the unique cart ID, or cartGuid, field for the user so that when you display the shopping cart, all the items that a user has added will appear.

Finally, since the product catalog in the database currently does not contain any products, you cannot test the code at this time. However, I will soon demonstrate how all the code will execute from start to finish. You'll learn how to add the ShoppingCart web form next.

Displaying the Shopping Cart

In the previous section of the chapter, you successfully added the selected products to the shopping cart, which added the information to the ShoppingCart table within your database. The following exercise will show how to add the functionality so that the user will see what they just added to the shopping cart and be able to view the list of items. This primarily will consist of displaying the subtotal of the individual product cost along with a final total for all the items contained in the shopping cart.

Exercise: Displaying the Shopping Cart Items

You will now learn how to display the products that you added to the shopping cart in the prior exercise. As with the previous exercises, you will start at the database with the necessary stored procedures followed by the data access, business logic, and presentation tiers of the architecture and code. Follow these steps:

1. You'll first create a stored procedure that will query the ShoppingCart table in the database to display the items that have been added according to the cart ID, or more specifically the CartGUID field. Refer to the following script:

```
CREATE PROCEDURE ShoppingCart_Select

@CartGUID nvarchar(50)

AS

SELECT
ShoppingCartID,
Products.ProductName,
Quantity,
Products.Price as UnitPrice,
(Products.Price * Quantity) AS TotalPrice
FROM ShoppingCart
INNER JOIN Products ON Products.ProductID = ShoppingCart.ProductID
WHERE CartGUID = @CartGUID
```

The query is a fairly straightforward select statement that provides you with an aggregate value of the total price of an individual product. This value is calculated by multiplying the individual cost of a product by the quantity of the product.

2. Now proceed to the data access tier code that will use the stored procedure you just created. Add a new class to the LittleItalyVineyard.DataAccess class library within the Select folder. Name the new class **ShoppingCartSelectData**. As usual, you will see the standard template code. Modify this code by adding a public identifier to the class, and have the class inherit from the DataAccessBase class, as shown here:

```
using System;
using System.Collections.Generic;
using System.Text;

namespace LittleItalyVineyard.DataAccess.Select
{
    public class ShoppingCartSelectData : DataAccessBase
    {

    }
}
```

3. Add the namespaces System.Data, System.Data.SqlClient, and LittleItalyVineyard.Common, as shown here:

```
using System;
using System.Collections.Generic;
using System.Text;
using System.Data;
using System.Data.SqlClient;

using LittleItalyVineyard.Common;

namespace LittleItalyVineyard.DataAccess.Select
{
    public class ShoppingCartSelectData : DataAccessBase
    {

    }
}
```

4. Moving along, first add the name of the new stored procedure to the StoredProcedure class. Then add the constructor to the ShoppingCartSelectData class, and within the constructor, specify the name of the new stored procedure that you will be utilizing, as shown here:

```
using System;
using System.Collections.Generic;
using System.Text;
using System.Data;
using System.Data.SqlClient;
```

```
using LittleItalyVineyard.Common;

namespace LittleItalyVineyard.DataAccess.Select
{
    public class ShoppingCartSelectData : DataAccessBase
    {
        public ShoppingCartSelectData()
        {
            StoredProcedureName = StoredProcedure.Name.➥
                ShoppingCart_Select.ToString();
        }
    }
}
```

5. The next step in the code is to add a common object property of the ShoppingCart object. First add the associated field name, and then add the property, as shown in the following code:

```
using System;
using System.Collections.Generic;
using System.Text;
using System.Data;
using System.Data.SqlClient;

using LittleItalyVineyard.Common;

namespace LittleItalyVineyard.DataAccess.Select
{
    public class ShoppingCartSelectData : DataAccessBase
    {
        private ShoppingCart _shoppingcart;

        public ShoppingCartSelectData()
        {
            StoredProcedureName = StoredProcedure.Name.➥
                ShoppingCart_Select.ToString();
        }

        public ShoppingCart ShoppingCart
        {
            get { return _shoppingcart; }
            set { _shoppingcart = value; }
        }
    }
}
```

6. You are almost done with the code. The next step is to add the associated parameters class that will handle implementing the parameters needed for the stored procedure. To do so, you will add a class to the same class file named ShoppingCartSelectDataParameters. This class will have the standard Build() method that will add the required parameter and expose the parameters in a Parameters property. The code is as follows:

```
using System;
using System.Collections.Generic;
using System.Text;
using System.Data;
using System.Data.SqlClient;

using LittleItalyVineyard.Common;

namespace LittleItalyVineyard.DataAccess.Select
{
    public class ShoppingCartSelectData : DataAccessBase
    {
        private ShoppingCart _shoppingcart;

        public ShoppingCartSelectData()
        {
            StoredProcedureName = StoredProcedure.Name.➥
                ShoppingCart_Select.ToString();
        }

        public ShoppingCart ShoppingCart
        {
            get { return _shoppingcart; }
            set { _shoppingcart = value; }
        }
    }

    public class ShoppingCartSelectDataParameters
    {
        private ShoppingCart _shoppingcart;
        private SqlParameter[ ] _parameters;

        public ShoppingCartSelectDataParameters➥
            ( ShoppingCart shoppingcart )
        {
            ShoppingCart = shoppingcart;
            Build();
        }

        private void Build()
        {
            SqlParameter[ ] parameters =
```

```
                {
                        new SqlParameter( "@CartGUID" ,➥
                            ShoppingCart.CartGUID )
                };

                Parameters = parameters;
            }

            public ShoppingCart ShoppingCart
            {
                get { return _shoppingcart; }
                set { _shoppingcart = value; }
            }

            public SqlParameter[ ] Parameters
            {
                get { return _parameters; }
                set { _parameters = value; }
            }
        }
    }
```

7. Now that the parameter class is complete, you can add the final function, Get(), in the ShoppingCartSelectData class. This method will use the parameters class as well as the DBHelper class to return a DataSet from the query within the stored procedure. Here's the code:

```
using System;
using System.Collections.Generic;
using System.Text;
using System.Data;
using System.Data.SqlClient;

using LittleItalyVineyard.Common;

namespace LittleItalyVineyard.DataAccess.Select
{
    public class ShoppingCartSelectData : DataAccessBase
    {
        private ShoppingCart _shoppingcart;

        public ShoppingCartSelectData()
        {
            StoredProcedureName = StoredProcedure.Name.➥
                ShoppingCart_Select.ToString();
        }

        public DataSet Get()
        {
            DataSet ds;
```

```csharp
            ShoppingCartSelectDataParameters➡
                _shoppingcartselectdataparameters =➡
                new ShoppingCartSelectDataParameters( ShoppingCart );
            DataBaseHelper dbhelper = new DataBaseHelper➡
                ( StoredProcedureName );
            ds = dbhelper.Run( base.ConnectionString , ➡
                _shoppingcartselectdataparameters.Parameters );

            return ds;
        }

        public ShoppingCart ShoppingCart
        {
            get { return _shoppingcart; }
            set { _shoppingcart = value; }
        }
    }

    public class ShoppingCartSelectDataParameters
    {
        private ShoppingCart _shoppingcart;
        private SqlParameter[ ] _parameters;

        public ShoppingCartSelectDataParameters➡
            ( ShoppingCart shoppingcart )
        {
            ShoppingCart = shoppingcart;
            Build();
        }

        private void Build()
        {
            SqlParameter[ ] parameters =
            {
                new SqlParameter( "@CartGUID" , ShoppingCart.CartGUID )
            };

            Parameters = parameters;
        }

        public ShoppingCart ShoppingCart
        {
            get { return _shoppingcart; }
            set { _shoppingcart = value; }
        }
```

```
            public SqlParameter[ ] Parameters
            {
                get { return _parameters; }
                set { _parameters = value; }
            }
        }
    }
```

8. The code is now complete within the data access tier, so you can proceed to the business logic tier of the application. To do so, add a new class to the LittleItalyVineyard.BusinessLogic class library named ProcessGetShoppingCart. As with the other newly added classes, you will see the standard class template code. Within this code, modify it to have a public identifier for the class, and implement the IBusinessLogic interface, as shown in the following code sample:

```
using System;
using System.Collections.Generic;
using System.Text;

namespace LittleItalyVineyard.BusinessLogic
{
    public class ProcessGetShoppingCart : IBusinessLogic
    {

    }
}
```

9. Similar to other steps within the exercises, you'll add the necessary namespaces. The namespaces you will need are the System.Data, LittleItalyVineyard.Common, and LittleItalyVineyard.DataAccess.Select namespaces, as shown here:

```
using System;
using System.Collections.Generic;
using System.Text;
using System.Data;

using LittleItalyVineyard.Common;
using LittleItalyVineyard.DataAccess.Select;

namespace LittleItalyVineyard.BusinessLogic
{
    public class ProcessGetShoppingCart : IBusinessLogic
    {

    }
}
```

10. Moving along, you will need to add two separate properties. One property is named ResultSet, which returns a DataSet and a common object property. ShoppingCart is the second property specified. In addition, add the associated field names as follows:

```csharp
using System;
using System.Collections.Generic;
using System.Text;
using System.Data;

using LittleItalyVineyard.Common;
using LittleItalyVineyard.DataAccess.Select;

namespace LittleItalyVineyard.BusinessLogic
{
    public class ProcessGetShoppingCart : IBusinessLogic
    {
        private DataSet _resultset;
        private ShoppingCart _shoppingcart;

        public ProcessGetShoppingCart()
        {

        }

        public ShoppingCart ShoppingCart
        {
            get { return _shoppingcart; }
            set { _shoppingcart = value; }
        }

        public DataSet ResultSet
        {
            get { return _resultset; }
            set { _resultset = value; }
        }
    }
}
```

11. Next add the required Invoke() function that the IBusinessLogic interface requires. This function will implement the data access code to ultimately return a DataSet that represents the query of the shopping cart. Here's the code:

```csharp
using System;
using System.Collections.Generic;
using System.Text;
using System.Data;

using LittleItalyVineyard.Common;
using LittleItalyVineyard.DataAccess.Select;
```

```
namespace LittleItalyVineyard.BusinessLogic
{
    public class ProcessGetShoppingCart : IBusinessLogic
    {
        private DataSet _resultset;
        private ShoppingCart _shoppingcart;

        public ProcessGetShoppingCart()
        {

        }

        public void Invoke()
        {
                ShoppingCartSelectData shoppingcartdata =➡
                   new ShoppingCartSelectData();
                shoppingcartdata.ShoppingCart = ShoppingCart;
                ResultSet = shoppingcartdata.Get();
        }

        public ShoppingCart ShoppingCart
        {
           get { return _shoppingcart; }
           set { _shoppingcart = value; }
        }

        public DataSet ResultSet
        {
           get { return _resultset; }
           set { _resultset = value; }
        }
    }
}
```

12. You will now specify the information for the shopping cart to be queried and thus ultimately view the current shopping cart. First add a web form to the web project named ShoppingCart.aspx, and have it use the Main.master master page. Upon adding this web form, proceed to the HTML code of the source. You will see the following HTML:

```
<%@ Page Language="C#" MasterPageFile="~/Main.master"
AutoEventWireup="true" CodeFile="ShoppingCart.aspx.cs"
Inherits="ShoppingCart" Title="Untitled Page" %>

<asp:Content ID="Content1" ContentPlaceHolderID="contentplaceholderMain"
Runat="Server">
</asp:Content>
```

13. To move forward, you need to add the necessary HTML code that will display the shopping cart. This will consist of a GridView control that has four columns that will be data bound: the name of the product, the quantity of the product within a text box, the unit cost of the product, and finally the subtotal of the product, which will be a calculation of the quantity multiplied by the unit cost. Lastly, add a table with a Label control that will display the total items in the shopping cart. Here's the HTML code:

```
<%@ Page Language="C#" MasterPageFile="~/Main.master"
AutoEventWireup="true" CodeFile="ShoppingCart.aspx.cs"
Inherits="ShoppingCart"
Title="Little Italy Vineyard | Shopping Cart" %>

<asp:Content ID="Content1" ContentPlaceHolderID="contentplaceholderMain"
    Runat="Server">
    <table cellpadding="0" cellspacing="0" border="0" width="100%">
        <tr>
            <td><img src="images/spacer.gif" width="10" height="15" /></td>
            <td width="100%"></td>
            <td><img src="images/spacer.gif" width="10" height="1" /></td>
        </tr>
        <tr>
            <td></td>
            <td>
                <table cellpadding="0" cellspacing="0"
                  border="0" width="100%">
                    <tr>
                        <td width="16%" align="center"><b>Remove</b></td>
                        <td width="30%"><b>Product</b></td>
                        <td width="17%" align="center"><b>Quantity</b></td>
                        <td width="18%" align="center"><b>Unit Cost</b></td>
                        <td width="19%" align="center"><b>Subtotal</b></td>
                    </tr>
                </table>
            </td>
            <td></td>
        </tr>
        <tr>
            <td></td>
            <td class="prodUnderlineBG" width="100%">
<img src="images/spacer.gif" width="1" height="4" /></td>
            <td></td>
        </tr>
        <tr><td><img src="images/spacer.gif" width="1"
             height="3" /></td></tr>
        <tr>
            <td></td>
            <td>
                <asp:GridView ID="gridviewShoppingCart" runat="server"
AutoGenerateColumns="false"
```

```
OnRowDataBound="gridviewShoppingCart_RowDataBound"
Width="100%" BorderWidth="0px" CellPadding="2"
ShowHeader="false">
                <Columns>
                <asp:TemplateField ItemStyle-Width="16%"
ItemStyle-HorizontalAlign="center">
                    <ItemTemplate>
                        <asp:CheckBox ID="checkboxDelete" runat="server" />
                    </ItemTemplate>
                </asp:TemplateField>
                <asp:TemplateField ItemStyle-Width="30%">
                    <ItemTemplate>
                        <%# Eval("ProductName") %>
                    </ItemTemplate>
                </asp:TemplateField>
                <asp:TemplateField ItemStyle-Width="17%"
ItemStyle-HorizontalAlign="center">
                    <ItemTemplate>
                        <asp:TextBox id="textQuantity" runat="server"
Columns="4" MaxLength="3" Text='<%# Eval("Quantity") %>'
width="30px" CssClass="textfield" />
                    </ItemTemplate>
                </asp:TemplateField>
                <asp:TemplateField ItemStyle-Width="18%"
ItemStyle-HorizontalAlign="center">
                    <ItemTemplate>
                        <%# Eval( "UnitPrice" , "{0:c}" )%>
                    </ItemTemplate>
                </asp:TemplateField>
                <asp:TemplateField ItemStyle-Width="19%"
ItemStyle-HorizontalAlign="center">
                    <ItemTemplate>
                        <%# Eval( "TotalPrice" , "{0:c}" )%>
                    </ItemTemplate>
                </asp:TemplateField>
                </Columns>
                </asp:GridView>
            </td>
            <td></td>
        </tr>
        <tr><td><img src="images/spacer.gif" width="1"
            height="3" /></td></tr>
        <tr>
            <td></td>
            <td class="prodUnderlineBG" width="100%">
<img src="images/spacer.gif" width="1" height="1" /></td>
            <td></td>
```

```
            </tr>
            <tr>
                <td></td>
                <td class="prodUnderlineBG" width="100%">
<img src="images/spacer.gif" width="1" height="2" /></td>
                <td></td>
            </tr>
            <tr><td><img src="images/spacer.gif" width="1"
                height="5" /></td></tr>
            <tr>
                <td></td>
                <td align="right">
                    <table border="0" cellpadding="0" cellspacing="0">
                        <tr>
                            <td><b>Total:</b></td>
                            <td style="width: 83px;" align="center">
<asp:Label ID="labelTotal" runat="server" Width="100%">
</asp:Label></td>
                        </tr>
                    </table>
                </td>
                <td></td>
            </tr>
            <tr><td><img src="images/spacer.gif"
                width="1" height="20" /></td></tr>
        </table>
</asp:Content>
```

14. The HTML code is now in place so you can display the items that reside in the shopping cart. The final step is to add the C# code, which will be the entry point to utilize all the code you worked on in this exercise. Let's proceed to the code side of the ShoppingCart.aspx web form, and you will see that as of now there is only the standard code displaying the page load event:

```
using System;
using System.Data;
using System.Configuration;
using System.Collections;
using System.Web;
using System.Web.Security;
using System.Web.UI;
using System.Web.UI.WebControls;
using System.Web.UI.WebControls.WebParts;
using System.Web.UI.HtmlControls;

public partial class ShoppingCart : System.Web.UI.Page
{
    protected void Page_Load( object sender , EventArgs e )
    {
```

```
        }
    }
```

15. Next you need to implement several items within the C# code section of the ShoppingCart.aspx web form. First create a method called LoadShoppingCart, which will be called from within the page load event that will also be wrapped in an If statement to determine whether there is a postback event. Here is the code:

```csharp
using System;
using System.Data;
using System.Configuration;
using System.Collections;
using System.Web;
using System.Web.Security;
using System.Web.UI;
using System.Web.UI.WebControls;
using System.Web.UI.WebControls.WebParts;
using System.Web.UI.HtmlControls;

public partial class ShoppingCart : System.Web.UI.Page
{

    protected void Page_Load( object sender , EventArgs e )
    {
        if ( ! IsPostBack )
        {
            LoadShoppingCart();
        }
    }

    private void LoadShoppingCart()
    {

    }
}
```

16. The next item you have to add is the method LoadShoppingCart to instantiate the business logic code. To achieve this, you first need to add the LittleItalyVineyard.BusinessLogic and LittleItalyVineyard.Common namespaces. After adding the namespaces, you will, as mentioned, instantiate the ProcessGetShoppingCart class from the business logic code along with the necessary ShoppingCart common object class. This common object will then be able to be passed into the business logic code, call the Invoke() method, and if a true value is returned, data bind the gridviewShoppingCart. Here's the code:

```csharp
using System;
using System.Data;
using System.Configuration;
using System.Collections;
using System.Web;
```

```
using System.Web.Security;
using System.Web.UI;
using System.Web.UI.WebControls;
using System.Web.UI.WebControls.WebParts;
using System.Web.UI.HtmlControls;

using LittleItalyVineyard.Common;
using LittleItalyVineyard.BusinessLogic;
using LittleItalyVineyard.Operational;

public partial class ShoppingCart : System.Web.UI.Page
{
    protected void Page_Load( object sender , EventArgs e )
    {
        if ( ! IsPostBack )
        {
            LoadShoppingCart();
        }
    }

    private void LoadShoppingCart()
    {
        LittleItalyVineyard.Common.ShoppingCart shoppingcart = ➥
            new LittleItalyVineyard.Common.ShoppingCart();
        shoppingcart.CartGUID = CartGUID;

        ProcessGetShoppingCart processgetcart➥
            = new ProcessGetShoppingCart();
        processgetcart.ShoppingCart = shoppingcart;

        try
        {
            processgetcart.Invoke();
            gridviewShoppingCart.DataSource = processgetcart.ResultSet;
            gridviewShoppingCart.DataBind();
        }
        catch
        {
            Response.Redirect( "ErrorPage.aspx" );
        }
    }

    private string CartGUID
    {
        get { return Utilities.GetCartGUID(); }
    }
}
```

Notice that you have used the same CartGUID() property to first check whether this user has added items to the shopping cart by checking for a persistent cookie. If not, a new cookie is created with a new GUID.

17. You are approaching the end of the exercise. The shopping cart now has the ability to be displayed, but you need to implement one final item. This final item is to display the running total of all the products that have been added to the shopping cart. This total will be displayed in the labelTotal control, which you placed directly below the GridView. To accomplish this functionality, you will need to loop through the GridView control as it's being data bound. During the data binding, you will be concerned only with actual data rows and with the TotalPrice field that is being data bound. Lastly, you will add a private field named _totalcounter that has a data type of decimal, which will hold the running value and then be set to the labelTotal control and formatted to a currency type. Here's the code:

```csharp
using System;
using System.Data;
using System.Configuration;
using System.Collections;
using System.Web;
using System.Web.Security;
using System.Web.UI;
using System.Web.UI.WebControls;
using System.Web.UI.WebControls.WebParts;
using System.Web.UI.HtmlControls;

using LittleItalyVineyard.Common;
using LittleItalyVineyard.BusinessLogic;
using LittleItalyVineyard.Operational;

public partial class ShoppingCart : System.Web.UI.Page
{
    private decimal _totalcounter;

    protected void Page_Load( object sender , EventArgs e )
    {
        if ( ! IsPostBack )
        {
            LoadShoppingCart();
        }
    }

    private void LoadShoppingCart()
    {
        LittleItalyVineyard.Common.ShoppingCart shoppingcart =➥
            new LittleItalyVineyard.Common.➥
        ShoppingCart();
        shoppingcart.CartGUID = CartGUID();
```

```
            ProcessGetShoppingCart processgetcart =➡
               new ProcessGetShoppingCart();
            processgetcart.ShoppingCart = shoppingcart;

        try
        {
            processgetcart.Invoke();
            gridviewShoppingCart.DataSource = processgetcart.ResultSet;
            gridviewShoppingCart.DataBind();
        }
        catch
        {
            Response.Redirect( "ErrorPage.aspx" );
        }
    }

    private string CartGUID
    {
        get { return Utilities.GetCartGUID(); }
    }

    protected void gridviewShoppingCart_RowDataBound( object sender , ➡
        GridViewRowEventArgs e )
    {
        if ( e.Row.RowType == DataControlRowType.DataRow )
        {
            _totalcounter += Convert.ToDecimal( DataBinder.Eval➡
                ( e.Row.DataItem , "TotalPrice" ) );
        }

        labelTotal.Text = string.Format( "{0:c}" , _totalcounter );
    }
}
```

Finally, you have arrived at the conclusion of yet another quite lengthy exercise that enabled you to show the populated shopping cart. As I have mentioned many times, no products have been added to the database as of yet, but do not despair. Soon you will see how products will be added, and at that time you will be testing your system from beginning to end. Now that you have a shopping cart that can be displayed, you need to add the ability for the user to update the cart.

Updating the Shopping Cart

You now need to implement a mechanism for your users that will allow them to make alterations to their shopping cart. They need to be able to edit the quantity of a single product or several products and be able to completely remove a product from the shopping cart.

In the next exercise, you will add this functionality to allow the user to enter a different numerical value for the quantity and to specify which products they want to remove.

Exercise: Updating the Shopping Cart

This exercise will outline how to enable the functionality to allow the user to update the shopping cart. The update functionality will consist of deleting products and updating the quantity of products within the shopping cart. Follow these steps:

1. The first task is to create two stored procedures: one stored procedure to update the quantity and one stored procedure to delete the product from the shopping cart. Let's start with the update stored procedure where you will be using the update statement and setting the quantity to the specified quantity, which will be specified by the shopping cart ID. Refer to the following database script:

```
CREATE PROCEDURE ShoppingCart_Update

@Quantity int,
@ShoppingCartID int

AS

UPDATE ShoppingCart
SET Quantity = @Quantity
WHERE ShoppingCartID = @ShoppingCartID
```

2. Now let's move to the second stored procedure, the delete stored procedure, after executing the ShoppingCart_Update stored procedure script. This will utilize the standard delete statement to delete the entire record from the database specified again by the shopping cart ID:

```
CREATE PROCEDURE ShoppingCart_Delete

@ShoppingCartID int

AS

DELETE FROM ShoppingCart
WHERE ShoppingCartID = @ShoppingCartID
```

3. Execute both of these scripts against the database, and add the names of these new stored procedures to the StoredProcedure class so you can see the following enumeration of the stored procedures thus far:

```
using System;
using System.Collections.Generic;
using System.Text;

namespace LittleItalyVineyard.DataAccess
{
    public class StoredProcedure
    {
```

```
            public enum Name
            {
                ProductByID_Select ,
                Products_Select ,
                ProductImage_Select ,
                Products_SelectSearch ,
                ShoppingCart_Insert ,
                ShoppingCart_Select ,
                ShoppingCart_Update ,
                ShoppingCart_Delete
            }
        }
    }
```

4. You have created stored procedures and added their respective names to the enumeration within the StoredProcedure class in the data access code. You will now add the first pieces of functionality thus far regarding deleting and updating the database. Therefore, as you have in previous exercises, add Update and Delete folders to the LittleItalyVineyard.DataAccess class library.

5. Next add a new class, ShoppingCartUpdateData, to the newly created Update folder. This class is similar to the prior classes that you created with the data access code. It will also incorporate the associated parameters class and have a method named Update():

```
using System;
using System.Collections.Generic;
using System.Text;
using System.Data.SqlClient;

using LittleItalyVineyard.Common;

namespace LittleItalyVineyard.DataAccess.Update
{
    public class ShoppingCartUpdateData : DataAccessBase
    {
        private ShoppingCart _shoppingcart;
        private ShoppingCartUpdateDataParameters➥
            _shoppingcartupdatedataparameters;

        public ShoppingCartUpdateData()
        {
            StoredProcedureName = StoredProcedure.Name.➥
                ShoppingCart_Update.ToString();
        }

        public void Update()
        {
            _shoppingcartupdatedataparameters =➥
                new ShoppingCartUpdateDataParameters( ShoppingCart );
```

```
            DataBaseHelper dbhelper = new DataBaseHelper➥
                ( StoredProcedureName );
            dbhelper.Parameters =➥
              _shoppingcartupdatedataparameters.➥
                Parameters;
            dbhelper.Run();
    }


    public ShoppingCart ShoppingCart
    {
        get { return _shoppingcart; }
        set { _shoppingcart = value; }
     }
}


public class ShoppingCartUpdateDataParameters
{
    private ShoppingCart _shoppingcart;
    private SqlParameter[] _parameters;

    public ShoppingCartUpdateDataParameters➥
        ( ShoppingCart shoppingcart )
    {
        ShoppingCart = shoppingcart;
        Build();
    }

    private void Build()
    {
        SqlParameter[] parameters =
        {
            new SqlParameter( "@Quantity" ,➥
                ShoppingCart.Quantity ) ,
            new SqlParameter( "@ShoppingCartID" ,➥
                ShoppingCart.ShoppingCartID )
        };

        Parameters = parameters;
    }

    public ShoppingCart ShoppingCart
    {
        get { return _shoppingcart; }
        set { _shoppingcart = value; }
    }
```

```
        public SqlParameter[] Parameters
        {
            get { return _parameters; }
            set { _parameters = value; }
        }
    }
}
```

6. While still in the data access layer, add a similar class in the Delete folder named ShoppingCartDeleteData, which will be the same as the update class with the exception of having a Delete() method:

```csharp
using System;
using System.Collections.Generic;
using System.Text;
using System.Data.SqlClient;

using LittleItalyVineyard.Common;

namespace LittleItalyVineyard.DataAccess.Delete
{
    public class ShoppingCartDeleteData : DataAccessBase
    {
        private ShoppingCart _shoppingcart;
        private ShoppingCartDeleteDataParameters➥
            _shoppingcartdeletedataparameters;

        public ShoppingCartDeleteData()
        {
            StoredProcedureName = StoredProcedure.Name.➥
                ShoppingCart_Delete.ToString();
        }

        public void Delete()
        {
            _shoppingcartdeletedataparameters = new➥
                ShoppingCartDeleteDataParameters( ShoppingCart );
            DataBaseHelper dbhelper = new DataBaseHelper➥
                ( StoredProcedureName );
            dbhelper.Parameters =➥
             _shoppingcartdeletedataparameters.Parameters;
            dbhelper.Run();
        }

        public ShoppingCart ShoppingCart
        {
            get { return _shoppingcart; }
            set { _shoppingcart = value; }
        }
    }
```

```
public class ShoppingCartDeleteDataParameters
{
    private ShoppingCart _shoppingcart;
    private SqlParameter[] _parameters;

    public ShoppingCartDeleteDataParameters➥
        ( ShoppingCart shoppingcart )
    {
        ShoppingCart = shoppingcart;
        Build();
    }

    private void Build()
    {
        SqlParameter[] parameters =
        {
            new SqlParameter( "@ShoppingCartID" ,➥
                ShoppingCart.ShoppingCartID )
        };

        Parameters = parameters;
    }

    public ShoppingCart ShoppingCart
    {
        get { return _shoppingcart; }
        set { _shoppingcart = value; }
    }

    public SqlParameter[] Parameters
    {
        get { return _parameters; }
        set { _parameters = value; }
    }
}
}
```

7. You have now completed the data access code. You can proceed to the business logic code and add
   the two separate classes needed for the update and delete. The first class to add in the LittleItalyVineyard.
   BusinessLogic class library is ProcessUpdateShoppingCart. This class will adhere to the implementation
   of the IBusinessLogic interface, as shown here:

```
using System;
using System.Collections.Generic;
using System.Text;

using LittleItalyVineyard.Common;
using LittleItalyVineyard.DataAccess.Update;
```

```csharp
namespace LittleItalyVineyard.BusinessLogic
{
    public class ProcessUpdateShoppingCart : IBusinessLogic
    {
        private ShoppingCart _shoppingcart;

        public ProcessUpdateShoppingCart()
        {

        }

        public void Invoke()
        {
            ShoppingCartUpdateData shoppingcartdata =➥
                new ShoppingCartUpdateData();
            shoppingcartdata.ShoppingCart = this.ShoppingCart;
            shoppingcartdata.Update();
        }


        public ShoppingCart ShoppingCart
        {
            get { return _shoppingcart; }
            set { _shoppingcart = value; }
        }
    }
}
```

8. You're almost done with the business logic. The final class to add is the ProcessDeleteShoppingCart, which is similar to that of the update class in the prior step in the exercise:

```csharp
using System;
using System.Collections.Generic;
using System.Text;

using LittleItalyVineyard.Common;
using LittleItalyVineyard.DataAccess.Delete;

namespace LittleItalyVineyard.BusinessLogic
{
    public class ProcessDeleteShoppingCart : IBusinessLogic
    {
        private ShoppingCart _shoppingcart;

        public ProcessDeleteShoppingCart()
        {

        }
```

```
public void Invoke()
{
        ShoppingCartDeleteData shoppingcartdata =➡
           new ShoppingCartDeleteData();
        shoppingcartdata.ShoppingCart = this.ShoppingCart;
        shoppingcartdata.Delete();
}

public ShoppingCart ShoppingCart
{
        get { return _shoppingcart; }
        set { _shoppingcart = value; }
}
    }
}
```

9. The code to update the shopping cart for the user is almost complete. The final task is to add the code needed within the presentation tier, or more specifically the ShoppingCart.aspx web form. You first need to alter the HTML code of the shopping cart to add two different values to the DataKeyNames property of the GridView control, add a check box column to the GridView, and add a command button that will execute the update. The two values that will be added to the DataKeyNames property are Quantity and ShoppingCartID. Let's look at the updated portion of the HTML code now for the ShoppingCart.aspx web form:

```
<%@ Page Language="C#" MasterPageFile="~/Main.master"
AutoEventWireup="true" CodeFile="ShoppingCart.aspx.cs"
Inherits="ShoppingCart"
Title="Little Italy Vineyard | Shopping Cart" %>

<asp:Content ID="Content1" ContentPlaceHolderID="contentplaceholderMain"
    Runat="Server">
    <asp:GridView ID="gridviewShoppingCart" runat="server"
        AutoGenerateColumns="false"
        DataKeyNames="Quantity,ShoppingCartID"
            OnRowDataBound="gridviewShoppingCart_RowDataBound"
            Width="100%" BorderWidth="0px" CellPadding="2"
            ShowHeader="false">
                <Columns>
                <asp:TemplateField ItemStyle-Width="16%"
                    ItemStyle-HorizontalAlign="center">
                    <ItemTemplate>
                        <asp:CheckBox ID="checkboxDelete" runat="server" />
                    </ItemTemplate>
                </asp:TemplateField>
```

```
<tr>
        <td></td>
        <td align="right">
            <asp:Button ID="commandContinueShopping"
                runat="server"
              OnClick="commandContinueShopping_Click"
          Text="Continue Shopping"
        CssClass="button" Width="136px" />
            <img src="images/spacer.gif" width="5" height="1" />
            <asp:Button ID="commandUpdate" runat="server"
              OnClick="commandUpdate_Click" Text="Update"
                CssClass="button" />
            <img src="images/spacer.gif" width="5" height="1" />
            <asp:Button ID="commandCheckout" runat="server"
              OnClick="commandCheckout_Click" Text="Check Out"
              CssClass="button" />
            <img src="images/spacer.gif" width="15" height="1" />
        </td>
        <td></td>
    </tr>
</asp:Content>
```

10. The HTML code is now set up so you can proceed to the C# code of the web form. You will implement what in my opinion is the most interesting code to this point. The first task is to add the code to connect to the business logic code in the form of two different methods, Update() and Delete(). Let's look specifically at these new methods:

```csharp
private void Update( int id , int newqty )
{
    ProcessUpdateShoppingCart processupdate =➥
        new ProcessUpdateShoppingCart();

    LittleItalyVineyard.Common.ShoppingCart➥
      shoppingcart = new LittleItalyVineyard.Common.➥
      ShoppingCart();
    shoppingcart.Quantity = newqty;
    shoppingcart.ShoppingCartID = id;
    processupdate.ShoppingCart = shoppingcart;

    try
    {
        processupdate.Invoke();
    }
    catch
    {
        Response.Redirect( "ErrorPage.aspx" );
    }
}
```

```
private void Delete( int id )
{
     ProcessDeleteShoppingCart processdelete =➥
         new ProcessDeleteShoppingCart();

     LittleItalyVineyard.Common.ShoppingCart shoppingcart =➥
          new LittleItalyVineyard.Common.➥
          ShoppingCart();
     shoppingcart.ShoppingCartID = id;
     processdelete.ShoppingCart = shoppingcart;

     try
     {
          processdelete.Invoke();
     }
     catch
     {
          Response.Redirect( "ErrorPage.aspx" );
     }
}
```

11. Finally, you need to add the code for the click event of the command button that will initiate the updating of the shopping cart. The code within this event will loop through the items or rows of the GridView control and determine whether the item is checked; if so, then the row will be deleted. Next, since the user can update the quantity of the product within the text box, you will compare the value within the text box to that of the originally data-bound value, and if they are different, you will call the update method and reload the GridView by calling the LoadShoppingCart() method after you have looped through the GridView rows. Here's the code:

```
protected void commandUpdate_Click( object sender , EventArgs e )
{
     foreach ( GridViewRow row in gridviewShoppingCart.Rows )
     {
          if ( row.RowType == DataControlRowType.DataRow )
          {
               DataKey data = gridviewShoppingCart.➥
                   DataKeys[ row.DataItemIndex ];

               CheckBox check = ( CheckBox ) row.FindControl➥
                   ( "checkboxDelete" );

                if ( check.Checked )
                {
                     Delete( int.Parse( data.Values➥
                        [ "ShoppingCartID" ].ToString() ) );
                }
```

```
              TextBox textNewQuantity = ( TextBox ) row.FindControl➥
                  ( "textQuantity" );
              int integerNewQuantity = int.Parse( textNewQuantity.Text );
              int integerOrigQuantity = int.Parse➥
                ( gridviewShoppingCart.DataKeys➥
                [ row.DataItemIndex ].Value.ToString() );

              if ( integerNewQuantity != integerOrigQuantity )
              {
                  Update( int.Parse( data.➥
                      Values[ "ShoppingCartID" ].➥
                      ToString() ) ,  integerNewQuantity );
              }
          }
      }

      LoadShoppingCart();
  }
```

12. Refer to the complete code:

```
using System;
using System.Data;
using System.Configuration;
using System.Collections;
using System.Web;
using System.Web.Security;
using System.Web.UI;
using System.Web.UI.WebControls;
using System.Web.UI.WebControls.WebParts;
using System.Web.UI.HtmlControls;

using LittleItalyVineyard.Common;
using LittleItalyVineyard.BusinessLogic;
using LittleItalyVineyard.Operational;

public partial class ShoppingCart : System.Web.UI.Page
{
    private decimal _totalcounter;

    protected void Page_Load( object sender , EventArgs e )
    {
        if ( ! IsPostBack )
        {
            LoadShoppingCart();
        }
    }
```

```csharp
private void LoadShoppingCart()
{
    LittleItalyVineyard.Common.ShoppingCart shoppingcart =➥
        new LittleItalyVineyard.Common.➥
        ShoppingCart();
    shoppingcart.CartGUID = CartGUID;

    ProcessGetShoppingCart processgetcart =➥
        new ProcessGetShoppingCart();
    processgetcart.ShoppingCart = shoppingcart;

    try
    {
        processgetcart.Invoke();
        gridviewShoppingCart.DataSource = processgetcart.ResultSet;
        gridviewShoppingCart.DataBind();
    }
    catch
    {
        Response.Redirect( "ErrorPage.aspx" );
    }
}

protected void gridviewShoppingCart_RowDataBound( object sender ,➥
    GridViewRowEventArgs e )
{
    if ( e.Row.RowType == DataControlRowType.DataRow )
    {
        _totalcounter += Convert.ToDecimal( DataBinder.Eval➥
            ( e.Row.DataItem , "TotalPrice" )   );
    }

        labelTotal.Text = string.Format( "{0:c}" , _totalcounter );
    }

protected void commandUpdate_Click( object sender , EventArgs e )
{
    foreach ( GridViewRow row in gridviewShoppingCart.Rows )
    {
        if ( row.RowType == DataControlRowType.DataRow )
        {
            DataKey data = gridviewShoppingCart.DataKeys➥
                [ row.DataItemIndex ];

            CheckBox check = ( CheckBox ) row.FindControl➥
                ( "checkboxDelete" );
```

```csharp
                        if ( check.Checked )
                        {
                            Delete( int.Parse( data.Values➥
                            [ "ShoppingCartID" ].ToString() ) );
                        }

                        TextBox textNewQuantity = ( TextBox ) row.➥
                            FindControl( "textQuantity" );
                        int integerNewQuantity = int.Parse➥
                            ( textNewQuantity.Text );
                        int integerOrigQuantity = int.Parse➥
                            ( gridviewShoppingCart.DataKeys➥
                                [ row.DataItemIndex ].➥
                                    Value.ToString() );

                        if ( integerNewQuantity != integerOrigQuantity )
                        {
                            Update( int.Parse( data.➥
                                Values[ "ShoppingCartID" ].➥
                                ToString() ) , integerNewQuantity );
                        }
                    }
                }
            }

            LoadShoppingCart();
        }

        private void Update( int id , int newqty )
        {
            ProcessUpdateShoppingCart processupdate =➥
                new ProcessUpdateShoppingCart();

            LittleItalyVineyard.Common.ShoppingCart shoppingcart =➥
                new LittleItalyVineyard.Common.➥
                ShoppingCart();
            shoppingcart.Quantity = newqty;
            shoppingcart.ShoppingCartID = id;
            processupdate.ShoppingCart = shoppingcart;

            try
            {
                processupdate.Invoke();
            }
            catch
            {
                Response.Redirect( "ErrorPage.aspx" );
            }
        }
```

```
private void Delete( int id )
{
        ProcessDeleteShoppingCart processdelete = new➥
            ProcessDeleteShoppingCart();

        LittleItalyVineyard.Common.ShoppingCart shoppingcart =➥
            new LittleItalyVineyard.Common.➥
            ShoppingCart();
        shoppingcart.ShoppingCartID = id;
        processdelete.ShoppingCart = shoppingcart;

        try
        {
            processdelete.Invoke();
        }
        catch
        {
            Response.Redirect( "ErrorPage.aspx" );
        }
}

private string CartGUID
{
        get { return Utilities.GetCartGUID(); }
}
}
```

You now have a fully functional shopping cart that will allow the user to update the display and the data of the shopping cart by changing the quantity of the product or by deleting the product added to the shopping cart altogether.

Processing Abandoned Shopping Carts

You may not be familiar with the concept of abandoned shopping carts. Therefore, I'll define what exactly an abandoned shopping cart is. When a user is browsing through your product catalog, they will in most cases be adding items that they are interested in buying to their shopping cart. Some will proceed and finalize their transaction by checking out and paying for the items. However, some customers might not proceed to the end of the transaction. They might want to wait until later that day or some other time before they actually submit their payment information when checking out. They could have several reasons for making this decision; perhaps they want to check with a friend to see whether they like a specific item they are purchasing as a gift, or maybe they have not decided fully to make a purchase at all. In either case, if they add products to the shopping cart and subsequently leave the application, the records will still be contained within the ShoppingCart table in the database, which are referred to as *abandoned* shopping carts.

At this point, you hope this user will return to your online store and continue with the purchase. With that said, you want to remind them of the products that they added to the shopping cart in the past, and therefore you will display those items from the database.

However, undoubtedly some users will not return, and if you did nothing about this, your ShoppingCart table would grow and grow with abandoned items. To keep up with the maintenance of this, you will add a SQL Server job that runs at a given time period to delete any abandoned shopping carts that have existed for longer than a specified window of time.

For the purposes of the case study, you will leave abandoned shopping carts in the database for a period of five days. There is no correct answer as to how long these should be left in the database, and feel free to specify an amount of time you want.

Exercise: Removing Abandoned Shopping Carts

This final exercise will be different from the prior exercises in that you will be dealing exclusively with the database. You will not be adding any C# code; rather, you'll add a SQL Server job that will be scheduled to run at a specified time. Follow these steps:

1. Keeping with the tradition of prior exercises, you will begin by creating the stored procedure that will be needed. This stored procedure will use a delete statement with a WHERE clause, determining whether any shopping carts are older than five days old:

```
CREATE PROCEDURE ShoppingCart_DeleteAbandoned

AS

DELETE FROM ShoppingCart
WHERE
DATEDIFF(dd, DateCreated, GetDate()) > 5
```

2. After executing the previous script against the database, you need to add a SQL Server job. To do so, proceed to Object Explorer in SQL Server Management Studio, expand the SQL Server Agent object, and proceed to the Jobs node, as shown in Figure 17-5. If the SQL Server Agent is not currently running, right-click the SQL Server Agent, and choose the Start menu item command.

Figure 17-5. *The SQL Server Agent*

3. Right-click the Jobs node, and choose the menu item New Job. You will see the New Job dialog box, as shown in Figure 17-6.

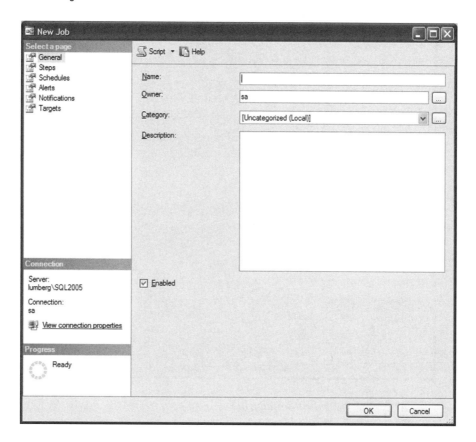

Figure 17-6. *The New Job dialog box*

4. In the Name text box, name the new job **ProcessAbandonedShoppingCarts**. It is not necessary to enter a description, but you can if you want.

5. Click the Steps item in the Select a Page column in the upper-left side of the dialog box. On this page, click the New command button, and you will see the New Job Step dialog box, as shown in Figure 17-7.

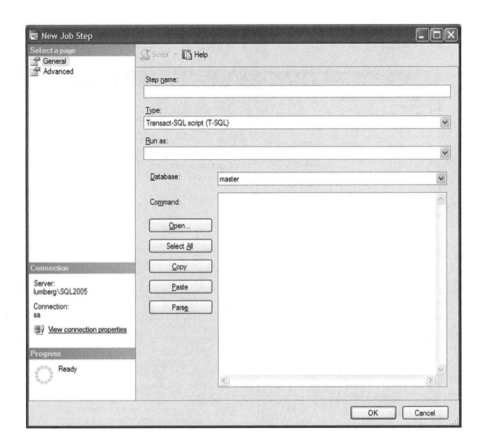

Figure 17-7. *The New Job Step dialog box*

6. In the Step Name text box, enter **Remove**. Keep the type of step as the default selected value of Transact-SQL Script (T-SQL), but change the database name to **LittleItalyVineyard**. Then add the name of the newly created stored procedure by entering the keyword **EXECUTE** followed by the name of the stored procedure, **ShoppingCart_DeleteAbandoned**. The dialog box will now resemble Figure 17-8. Click the OK button.

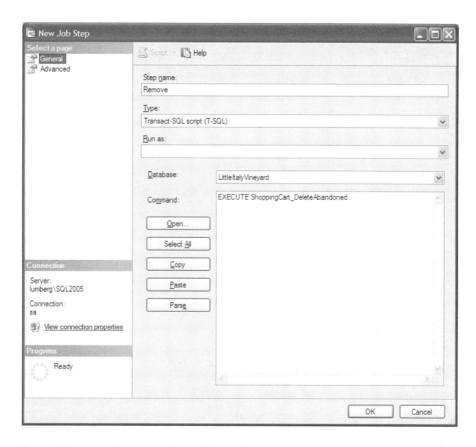

Figure 17-8. *Completing the New Job Step dialog box*

7. After clicking the OK button, you will be returned to the main New Job dialog box. Click the Schedules page in the upper-left column, as shown in Figure 17-9.

Figure 17-9. *The Schedules page*

8. On the Schedules page, you will need to click the New button to add the information required for scheduling the process. After clicking the New button, you will see the New Job Schedule dialog box. In this dialog box, name the schedule **Delete**. Set Schedule Type to Recurring, set the frequency to occur daily, the time to 12 a.m., and finally the start date to today's date with no end date, as shown in Figure 17-10. Click the OK button.

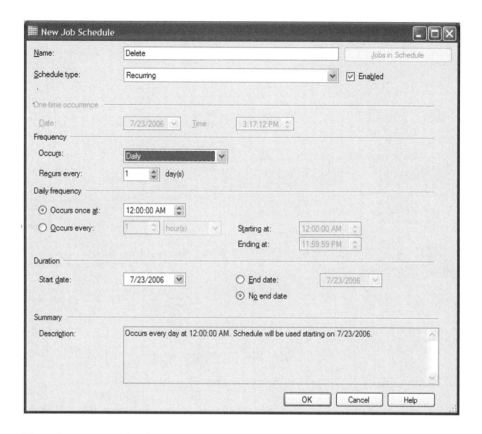

Figure 17-10. *New job schedule*

9. You have now entered all the information necessary for the new SQL Server job. Therefore, click the OK button in the New Job dialog box to save all the information you have added.

The newly created job will not run until the next scheduled time; however, if you want to check your work, you can right-click the job name in the SQL Server Agent node and run the job by selecting the Start Job menu item.

Summary

Congratulations! You have completed the code for adding items to the shopping cart, updating the cart, and processing the maintenance. The e-commerce application is really starting to come together with its functionality. Now that you have a functioning shopping cart, you begin setting up the processing of the credit card payments and allowing your customers to finalize their purchases.

■ ■ ■

CHAPTER 18

Integrating the PayPal SDK

At this point in the book, you have successfully implemented a product catalog and a shopping cart. Naturally, the next step is to finalize the functionality for processing transactions so the user can purchase the products that they have checked out of the shopping cart. To do this, however, you first have to establish the testing environment so that in the following chapters you can add the code to process the credit card transactions via PayPal.

In this chapter, I will discuss the following topics so you are prepared to add the implementation for allowing a customer to pay for their merchandise:

- Introducing the PayPal software development kit (SDK) version 4.2

- Registering the PayPal Developer Central and sandbox accounts

- Creating the certificate

- Preparing the application programming interface (API) code in the PayPalManager class

---

■Note This chapter contains several figures showing the PayPal sandbox. This site could change at any time, so keep this in mind when comparing the figures in this chapter to the actual PayPal sandbox website and utilities.

Introducing the PayPal SDK

It is quite obvious even to a novice that to implement an e-commerce application, you need to accept credit card transactions. That's why there is a great deal of competition between companies that provide credit card processing for online vendors. This competition yields affordable transaction costs for the owners of the e-commerce applications. Some of these companies will be easy to integrate with your system, and others might prove to be a little more difficult.

To process orders for the Little Italy Vineyards application, you'll use PayPal for all your credit card needs. This is for many reasons, explained in detail in the "Why PayPal?" section.

At the time of this writing, the latest version available of the PayPal SDK is version 4.2. However, in subsequent versions, the compatibility will most likely be backward compatible so you will be able to add the latest version with little to no difficulty.

Why PayPal?

Using PayPal for all your credit card needs is a formidable option for many e-commerce sites. As mentioned, one of the prominent advantages is the availability of the SDK. The SDK has extensive documentation and samples that make it easy to implement the PayPal functionality quickly. This is an advantage because not every payment option has this type of an extensive documentation.

The following are several other reasons why PayPal is a great option to use:

Extensive testing environment: PayPal provides a complete testing environment that resembles the actual PayPal account and interface 100 percent.

Thorough documentation: Included within the installation of the SDK is a complete manual about how to set up the environment and implement it within your individual system.

Developer community and support: As a result of PayPal being arguably the most popular credit card transaction system for the Web, fellow developers have implemented PayPal into their respective applications. This has led to others helping others at http://www.paypaldev.org/ and https://developer.paypal.com/. These are forums focused on developing with PayPal, and they have a wealth of information that will aid your development efforts when you encounter difficulties.

Security: PayPal continually increases its efforts and resources to maintain the highest security possible. Taking advantage of this gives you great leverage to incorporate this security in your own applications.

Extensive code examples: Included within the SDK are many samples for using the PayPal API to process credit cards within your e-commerce application.

Those are the primary benefits of using PayPal for your credit card processing needs; these are also the reasons why you are going to incorporate it in the Little Italy Vineyards application and case study.

Next, you'll learn about where to obtain the PayPal SDK and how to begin utilizing it.

Installing the PayPal SDK

We've included the PayPal SDK as an installation package with the accompanying source code for this book for your convenience. However, you can also download the SDK from the PayPal website (http://www.paypal.com) by navigating to the Developers section and locating the latest version. In either case, you must download and install the SDK before proceeding. Installing the SDK is fairly simple; it is a standard installation that will place the files on your local machine. This is where you will find the manual and sample code, along with much more information that is quite useful.

Configuring Your Developer Central Account

After successfully installing the PayPal SDK, you need to establish your test account and environment, which will allow you to thoroughly test the integration of the credit card–processing functionality via PayPal services. You need to complete several steps to register for the account and to configure it locally so that eventually the application can communicate with the PayPal servers.

In this section of the chapter, I will outline all the necessary tasks you need to complete. The first task is to register for the Developer Central test account, which is the account within the PayPal test environment where you will thoroughly set up your application to receive payments. The following exercise shows how to register this account.

Exercise: Registering a Developer Central Account

This exercise shows how to create a free test account for the PayPal Developer Central network and system. Follow these steps:

1. Navigate to the PayPal Developer Central home page, which is located at `https://developer.paypal.com/`. On the home page, click the Sign Up Now link, as shown in Figure 18-1.

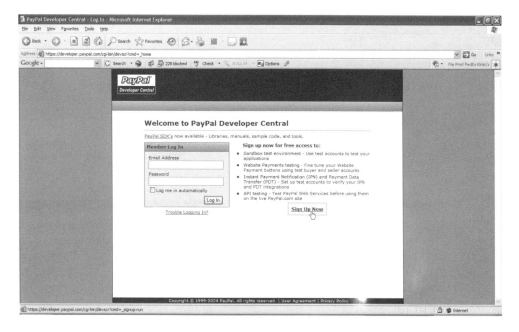

Figure 18-1. *The PayPal Developer Central home page*

2. Upon clicking the Sign Up Now link, you will be directed to the Sign Up page where you need to enter your personalized information, as shown in Figure 18-2. The information required consists of your first name, last name, e-mail address, password, security question and answer, and finally some optional information regarding the name of your company, its website, and how you intend to use the test account.

■**Note** Don't use the same account you might have with the live PayPal system for security purposes. However, you will need a working e-mail account so PayPal can verify the account by sending an e-mail to that address.

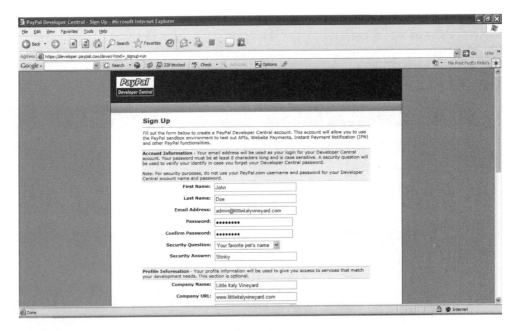

Figure 18-2. *Entering your new account information*

3. Next, agree to the User Agreement and Privacy Policy, and click the Sign Up button, as shown in Figure 18-3.

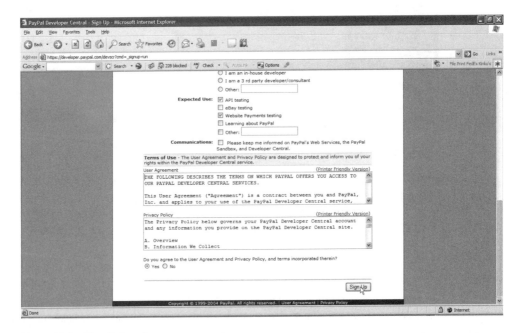

Figure 18-3. *Finalizing the new account*

4. Provided that you have entered all the required information, the new PayPal Developer Central account will be created, and you will see the confirmation message shown in Figure 18-4.

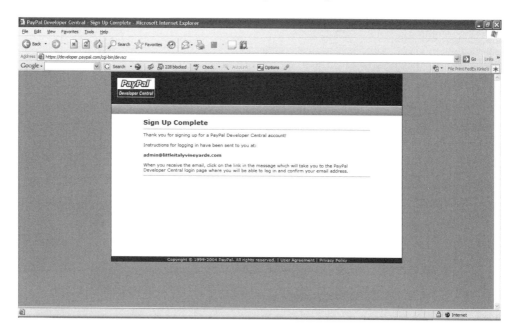

Figure 18-4. *Sign-up complete*

5. The PayPal system will send a confirmation e-mail message to the address you entered. You will need to follow the directions in that message to confirm the newly created account. So, proceed to your e-mail account that you used to sign up for the new account, and you should receive the message within a couple of minutes, as shown in Figure 18-5.

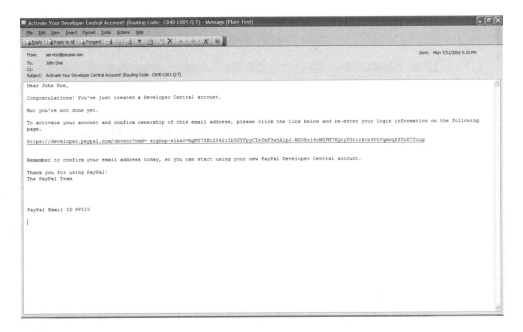

Figure 18-5. *Receiving the sign-up e-mail*

6. Upon receiving the confirmation e-mail, as per the directions in the message, click the link; you will be directed to the PayPal Developer Central account home page, which will display a message that your new account has been successfully confirmed. The next step is to enter your credentials to log in to the newly confirmed account and click the Log In button, as shown in Figure 18-6.

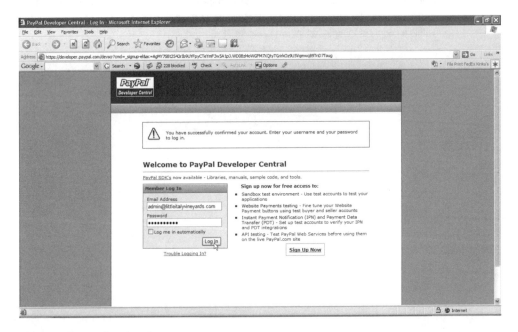

Figure 18-6. *Confirming the new account*

7. Upon successful authentication, you will be directed to the home page within the development account, as shown in Figure 18-7.

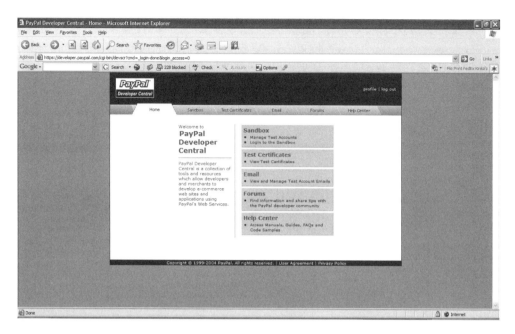

Figure 18-7. *Welcome to PayPal Developer Central*

Congratulations! You have completed the first step of configuring the test environment for processing the credit card transactions with PayPal. In the next phase of the configuration, you will examine additional details of the new test account that you just created and then create the actual sandbox account.

Creating the Sandbox Account

Continuing with configuring the PayPal test account, the next step is to create the sandbox test account. I'll first discuss what the sandbox account is and how it will benefit you.

As is quite apparent from the name of the account, the *sandbox* account is the account PayPal provides to allow you to test the code within the application that processes credit card transactions before the system goes live. The term *sandbox* refers to the fact that as a developer, you can "play around" with the account; it will behave in the same fashion as your "real" PayPal account will.

When logging in to the main test account, you'll see some helpful tips for using the sandbox account. I'll recap some of these tips before showing how to create a new sandbox account. First, the sandbox account and environment is a direct mirror to the live PayPal account; the only difference is that the financial transactions are actually made in the real account only. The sandbox has no connection to a real, live PayPal account. When signing up for the sandbox, it is not necessary to use a real e-mail address or account. The e-mail you enter will be used only as your login name. After completing the registration process, you can also add fictitious banking and credit card information so the testing will resemble the live system as best as possible.

The following exercise shows how to register for a sandbox account.

Exercise: Creating the Sandbox Account

This exercise shows how to create the PayPal sandbox account. After completing this exercise, the testing environment for PayPal will be almost complete for testing purposes. Follow these steps:

1. In the final step of the previous exercise, you verified your new account. While you are still logged in to that account, click the Sandbox tab, which will take you to the main sandbox page, as shown in Figure 18-8.

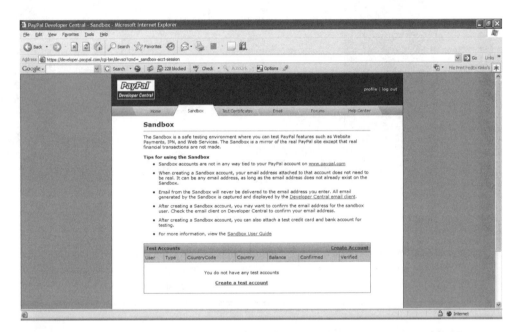

Figure 18-8. *The Sandbox tab*

2. On this page, you'll see a listing of current test accounts along with a link to create a new account. Click the Create a test account link that is located in the Test Accounts table. After clicking this link, you will see a new browser window, as shown in Figure 18-9.

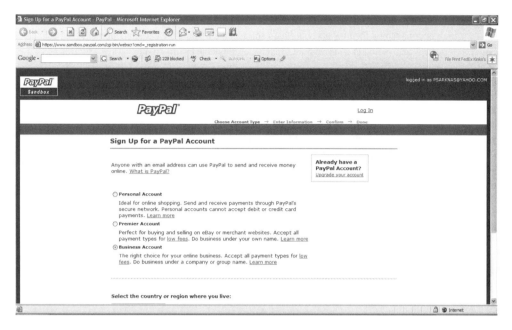

Figure 18-9. *Signing up for a Sandbox PayPal account*

3. From the three different types of accounts, select the Business Account option and the country you live in, and then click the Continue button. You will see the screen shown in Figure 18-10.

Figure 18-10. *Signing up for a sandbox PayPal account—the Getting Started page*

4. You now see the steps that you need to complete. The fist step is to sign up and provide the contact information for the new account. To do so, click the Go button located under the Status column. You will then be directed to enter your information, as shown in Figure 18-11.

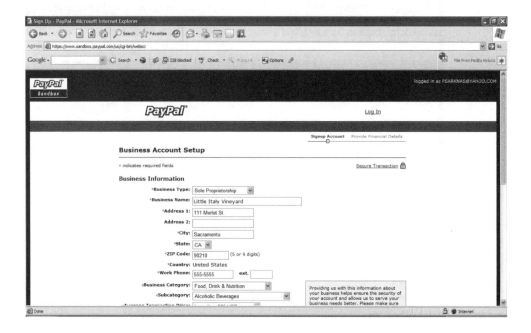

Figure 18-11. *Business information*

5. Enter the required information. Again, since this is a test account, the information can be fictitious. Finally, when you are done entering the information, scroll to the bottom of the page, and click the Continue button, as shown in Figure 18-12.

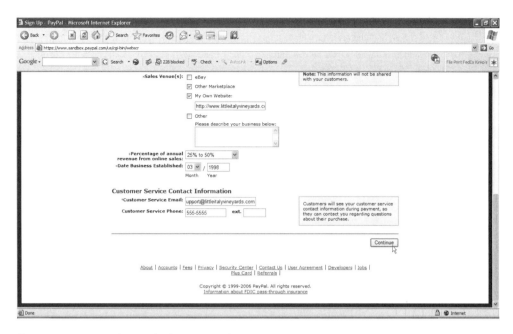

Figure 18-12. *Completing the business information*

6. On the next page, you will be asked to enter the business owner information. Once again, enter the required fields with preferably fictitious information, agree to the terms of service, and then click the Continue button located at the end of the page, as shown in Figure 18-13.

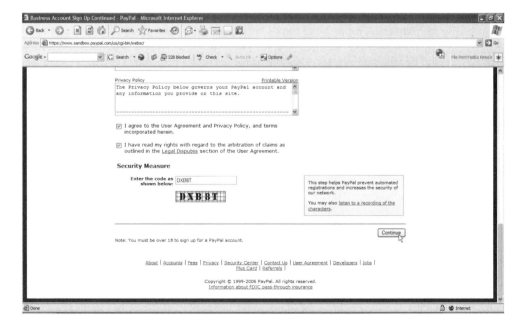

Figure 18-13. *Completing the business owner information*

7. The next step in the process is to enter the bank information associated with the test account. Again, this should be fictitious information. In fact, there will be randomly generated banking information already populated in the text boxes. All that remains is to give the name of the bank and click the Continue button, as shown in Figure 18-14.

Figure 18-14. *Completing the banking information*

8. Upon completion, you will be returned to the page shown in Figure 18-10 that listed the steps to be completed. Proceed to the next step to verify the e-mail by clicking the Go button under the Action column, as shown in Figure 18-15. Again, regardless of what e-mail address you used, this will simulate verifying the account with the internal e-mail account section in the Developer Central account.

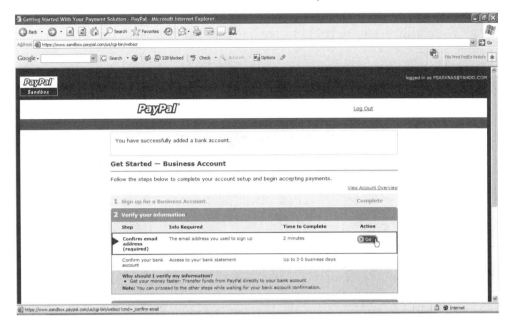

Figure 18-15. *Verifying the new account*

9. You will then be directed to a page that is requesting to verify the e-mail address that you used. Since this is a simulation, you can click the Continue button again, as shown in Figure 18-16.

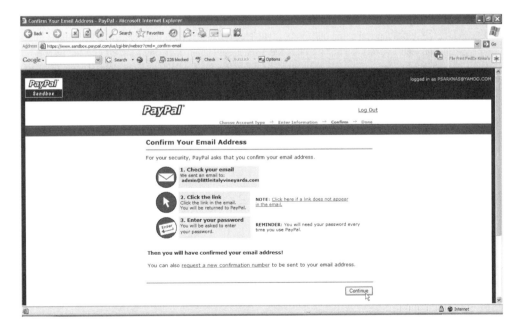

Figure 18-16. *Confirming your e-mail address*

10. Navigate to the original page and then to the sandbox account you just registered. Refresh this page, and you can now view that the new account that has been registered appears in the table, as shown in Figure 18-17.

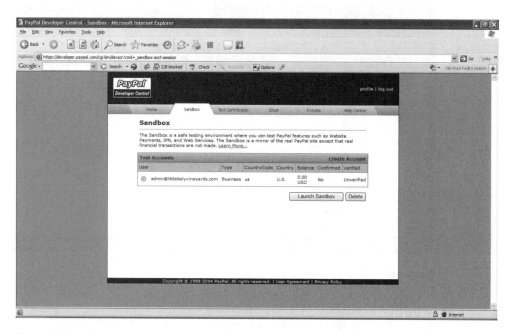

Figure 18-17. *The new test account*

11. The remaining tasks that need to be completed are to verify the new account and the bank information. Because this is a test account, the e-mails sent when using the sandbox account will be simulated and will be able to be viewed from within the PayPal Developer Central account. Therefore, click the Email tab, and you will see the messages shown in Figure 18-18.

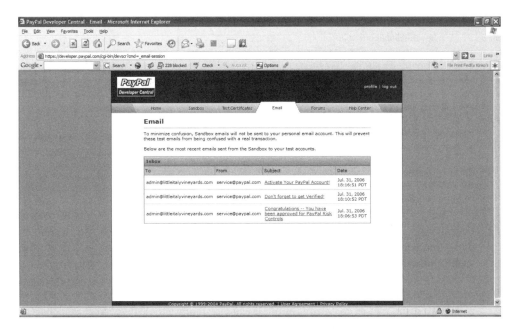

Figure 18-18. *The e-mail messages*

12. Click the e-mail message that has the subject "Activate Your PayPal Account," and navigate to the link that is provided to verify the account. You will then be asked to enter your password, and upon successfully logging in, you will be notified that the e-mail address is now verified, as shown in Figure 18-19.

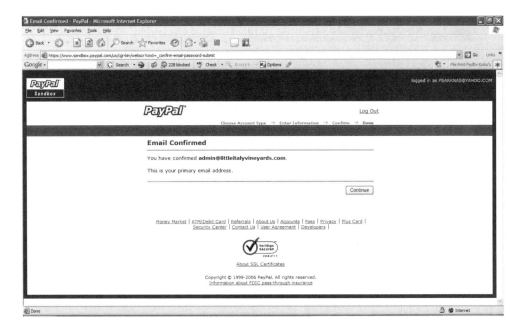

Figure 18-19. *E-mail confirmed*

13. Continue to confirm the bank account as well by clicking the link in the e-mail message and following any additional prompts.

This brings you to the end of the exercise. You now have a functional sandbox test account.

Creating the Test Certificate

You have almost arrived at where you can implement the code and API into your application. To this point, you have entered all the information necessary for the test account, but you must complete one last item. Specifically, you have to create and configure a test certificate for use within the sandbox account, which will provide an additional layer of security. I'll first explain what the test certificate is.

The *test certificate* is linked to the sandbox account and needs to be created to use the PayPal web services and API within the code of your application. You need to submit a username and password to obtain a certificate from the PayPal servers prior to any submission of credit card data or product data that is being tendered. This is not to say that you won't need a Secure Sockets Layer (SSL) certificate installed on the web server, but the certificate does provide additional security because the account that uses the API code will not simply accept a username and password combination. It will also require that the correct associated certificate appears in the same executing file location. In other words, you will need a test certificate for the test environment and then a live certificate for the live PayPal services.

Before you configure the test certificate, be aware that it is not simply as easy as downloading a certificate and adding it to the web project. You need to perform a number of steps to set it up successfully. Don't worry, because I will outline all these details in the following exercise, which shows how to create the test certificate.

Exercise: Creating the Test Certificate

This exercise shows all the intricacies involved in obtaining the test certificate to be prepared for use within the transactions. Follow these steps:

1. If you happen to have the PayPal Development Central (`https://developer.paypal.com/`) account still open in your browser from the previous exercise, it is a good bet that the session has timed out. So, log out of the account, and reenter your credentials. When arriving at the home page, click the Sandbox tab, and then click the Launch Sandbox button with the sandbox account selected that you created earlier in this chapter, as shown in Figure 18-20.

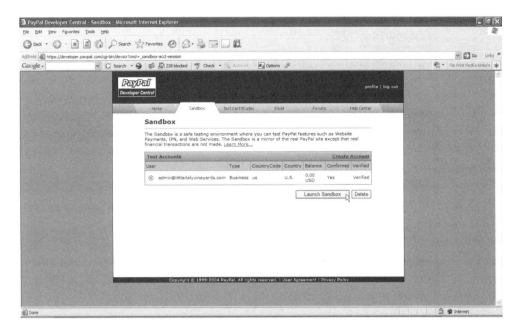

Figure 18-20. *Clicking the Launch Sandbox button*

2. When you click the Launch Sandbox button, the site will launch a new browser window where you will be again asked to log in using your sandbox test account, as shown in Figure 18-21.

Figure 18-21. *Logging into the sandbox account*

3. Once you have logged into the sandbox account successfully, from the home page, click the Profile tab, as shown in Figure 18-22.

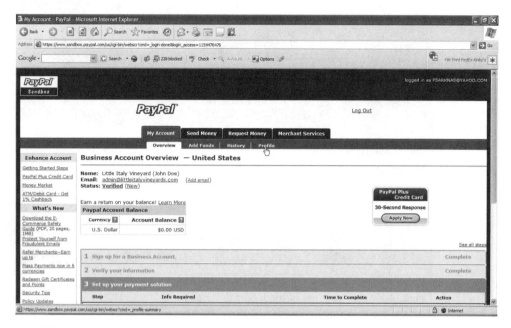

Figure 18-22. *Clicking the Profile tab*

4. When directed to the Profile page, from the column on the left, click the API Access link, as shown in Figure 18-23.

Figure 18-23. *Clicking the API Access link*

5. After clicking the API Access link, you will see the API Set-up page with two options. Select the option on the right, Request API Credentials, as shown in Figure 18-24.

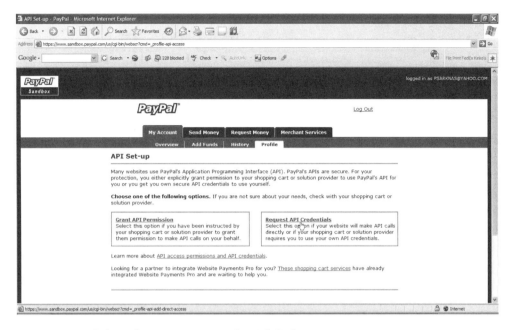

Figure 18-24. *Clicking the Request API Credentials link*

6. From the Request API Credentials page, you'll again see two options of credentials. The first option is to use the API Signature, and the other is the API SSL client-side certificate. Select the second option, API SSL Client-Side Certificate, and then review and agree to the terms and conditions, as shown in Figure 18-25. Then click the Submit button.

Figure 18-25. *Submitting the API credentials*

7. After clicking the Submit button, you will be redirected to the confirmation page. From here, you will see the summary information for the API credentials along with the username and password, as shown in Figure 18-26. For your convenience, copy the username and password to a text file for easy future reference.

Figure 18-26. *API credential request confirmation*

8. Next, download the certificate by clicking the Download Certificate. You will be prompted to save the certificate in a text file format, as shown in Figure 18-27. Save the certificate to an easy place where you will be able to revisit it soon.

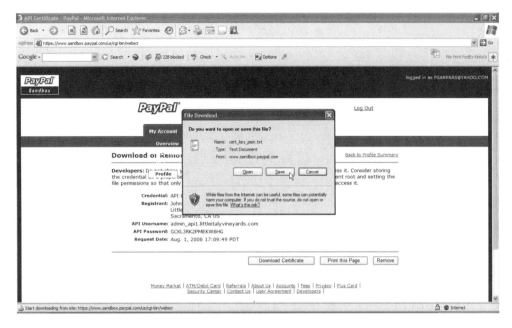

Figure 18-27. *Saving the test certificate*

9. Upon downloading and saving the test certificate, you can now close the sandbox account browser and return to the main PayPal Central account. You were last on the Sandbox tab, so now you need to click the Test Certificates tab. On this page, you can view the new certificate, as shown in Figure 18-28.

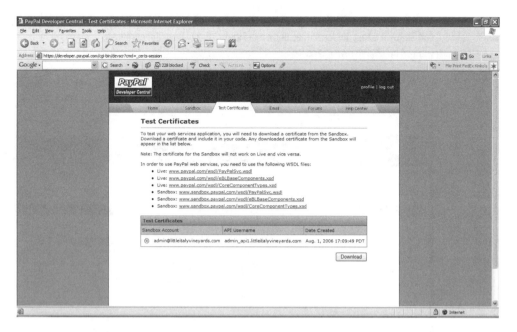

Figure 18-28. *Viewing the test certificate*

Finally, you can see the test certificate that you created and downloaded. From this point, you can log out of the PayPal Developer Central account and focus your attention on configuring the test certificate you just downloaded.

Configuring the Test Certificate

The last task for setting up and configuring the test certificate is to take the downloaded test certificate and convert it to P12 format, which is the format you need to implement the PayPal APIs. A P12-formatted file is used as a certificate in IIS to authenticate a website. When you created and downloaded the test certificate in the previous exercise, the test certificate was in PEM format, saved as an actual text file. You need to convert this format to the P12 format for security reasons, which will require a few different steps to complete, as described in the following exercise.

Exercise: Converting the Test Certificate

This exercise demonstrates how to convert the test certificate to the required format that will be needed to implement the API code. Follow these steps:

1. Install the OpenSSL installation package for Windows that was included within the PayPal SDK download if you have not done so thus far. Next, open a command prompt and ensure that OpenSSL is in the path along with the path of `cert_key_pem.txt`. Execute the following command within the command window:

   ```
   openssl pkcs12 -export -inkey cert_key_pem.txt -inkey cert_key_pem.txt -out
   LittleItalyVineyards.p12
   ```

2. Upon executing this command, you will be prompted to enter a password. Enter your password, and be sure to make note of this because you'll use it later.

3. Finally, this command will now create a file named `LittleItalyVineyards.p12`. This newly created file is your encrypted API certificate.

You will revisit the certificate file in the next section of this chapter.

Integrating the PayPal APIs

You are getting close to the end of the chapter and thus to the explanation of how to set up and configure the testing environment to eventually accept PayPal credit card transactions. So, I need to address one final step in this chapter. This final step is to properly implement the test certificate within your source code solution and then add the API references where you can pick up the development to process the payments for your products that the customers will purchase.

This process will not be as complex and detail oriented as the previous exercises; to complete the tasks in this chapter, you will add the text certificate to the source code base or Visual Studio 2005 solution. At the same time, you will not have a complete integration guide using the PayPal APIs but merely be prepared for the upcoming chapter that will show the thorough details for adding the code to accept and process a credit card payment.

Exercise: Incorporating the Certificate

This exercise shows how to add the test certificate to the web project to prepare the groundwork for adding the actual PayPal API code not only for the sandbox environment but also eventually the live production environment. Follow these steps:

1. Return to the Visual Studio 2005 solution, and relaunch it if you have closed out of the application. Then return to the web project. Right-click the project, and add a new folder named **Certs**, as shown in Figure 18-29.

Figure 18-29. *Adding the Certs folder*

2. Now that you have added the Certs folder to the web project, you need to add the test certificate you created in the previous exercise to this directory. To do so, right-click the Certs directory, choose to add a new item, browse to the file location where the test certificate was saved, and add this P12 file to the directory, as shown in Figure 18-30.

Figure 18-30. *Adding the certificate to the Certs folder*

At this point, you have the certificate added to the web project where you can use it to authenticate the implementation of the API code. As mentioned in this chapter, you are not going to fully implement the API code at this point. Instead, you're preparing it for the following chapter and exercises where you will do just that.

Summary

In this chapter, you set up and configured the PayPal account for testing purposes. To recap, you established a main PayPal Development Central account along with a sandbox account and created and added a test certificate to your source code baseline. All of these exercises were necessary to establish the testing environment to provide seamless integration to the live production credit card transaction account that you will eventually establish. In the next chapter, you will learn how to allow a customer to check out of the shopping cart that they created and to utilize the PayPal services you have implemented to accept payment.

■ ■ ■

CHAPTER 19

Implementing the Checkout Process

In the previous chapter, you finished setting up and implementing the test account, so it is now time to address the functionality that allows the customer to check out of the shopping cart. In this chapter, I will address only the initial part of the checkout process; specifically, you will implement everything up to when users enter their payment information. Chapter 20 will show you how to finalize the checkout process by dealing with the payment information and submitting it to the credit card–processing service for the official payment of the goods.

To summarize, I will address the following topics and implementations in this chapter:

- Checking out of the shopping cart

- Creating a new user account

- Logging into an existing account

Checking Out of the Shopping Cart

Once the customer has added the items to the shopping cart that they are interested in buying, they need to finalize the transaction. This transaction will require several different pieces of functionality. As mentioned earlier, in this chapter, I will address only the segments of the checkout process that lead up to entering the payment information and processing the payment. So, I will cover what happens after the user adds products to their shopping carts.

With that said, after deciding to check out the products they have selected, the user will either be a return customer or be a new customer. More specifically, if they don't have an existing account in the system, they will need to create an account. If the user needs to create a new account, then this process will begin by allowing the user to register a new account. However, since you are picking up where you last left off at the shopping cart, you need to first address how the user will be able to navigate from the shopping cart to the login/register process. The following exercise will show how to accomplish this feat.

Exercise: Implementing the Login

This exercise consists of only a few steps but at the same time demonstrates the steps necessary to begin implementing the checkout functionality. Follow these steps:

1. Revisit your Visual Studio 2005 solution, and proceed to the web project within the solution. Navigate to the ShoppingCart.aspx web form, and add a command button named commandCheckout at the bottom of the GridView control. Set the Text property to Check Out. Then double-click the button so it takes you to code view. Add the following code in the click event handler:

```
protected void commandCheckout_Click( object sender , EventArgs e )
{
    Response.Cookies[ "ReturnURL" ].Value = "CheckOut.aspx";
    Response.Redirect( "Login.aspx" );
}
```

How It Works

The code you added is quite simple. Since the user needs to eventually navigate to the checkout web page, they will either need to log in or create a new account, and you have to take this into account. Therefore, you are creating a nonpersistent cookie named ReturnURL with the value CheckOut.aspx. Finally, you direct the user to the Login.aspx page by using the Response.Redirect method.

2. At this point, you have no web form named Login.aspx; therefore, add a new web form to the web project, and name it **Login.aspx**. In addition, select the associated master page, and then add the following HTML code:

```
<%@ Page Language="C#" MasterPageFile="~/Main.master"
AutoEventWireup="true" CodeFile="Login.aspx.cs"
Inherits="Login" Title="Little Italy Vineyard | Customer Login" %>

<asp:Content ID="Content1" ContentPlaceHolderID="contentplaceholderMain"
Runat="Server">
    <table border="0" cellpadding="3" cellspacing="0" style="width: 360px">
        <tr>
            <td><img src="images/spacer.gif" width="1" height="5" /></td>
        </tr>
        <tr>
            <td><img src="images/spacer.gif" width="50" height="1" /></td>
            <td>Username:</td><td>
<asp:TextBox ID="textUsername"
runat="server" CssClass="textField">
</asp:TextBox><br />
    <asp:RequiredFieldValidator ID="requiredUsername"
runat="server" ErrorMessage="Username required."
    ControlToValidate="textUsername" Display="Dynamic"
```

```
EnableClientScript="False" Width="152px">
</asp:RequiredFieldValidator></td>
        </tr>
        <tr>
            <td></td>
            <td>Password:</td>
<td>
<asp:TextBox ID="textPassword"
runat="server" TextMode="Password"
CssClass="textField"></asp:TextBox>
<br />
<asp:RequiredFieldValidator ID="requiredPassword"
runat="server" ErrorMessage="Password required."
ControlToValidate="textPassword"
Display="Dynamic" Width="152px"
EnableClientScript="False">
</asp:RequiredFieldValidator></td>
        </tr>
        <tr>
            <td colspan="2"></td>
            <td><asp:Button ID="commandLogin" runat="server" Text="Login"
OnClick="commandLogin_Click" CssClass="button" /></td>
        </tr>
        <tr>
          <td colspan="2"></td>
          <td><asp:Label ID="labelMessage" runat="server"></asp:Label></td>
        </tr>
        <tr>
            <td colspan="2"></td>
<td><asp:HyperLink ID="hyperlinkNewAccount" runat="server"
NavigateUrl="Register.aspx" Width="144px">
Register New Account</asp:HyperLink></td>
        </tr>
        <tr>
            <td colspan="2"></td>
            <td></td>
        </tr>
    </table>
</asp:Content>
```

That's all there is to it. This was a brief exercise, but you now have the initial implementation of the login page. You have added the controls that you will revisit later in the chapter when you allow an existing user to log in to their account. However, first you need to allow the users who do not have accounts to click a hyperlink that will navigate them to the Register.aspx web page where they can enter their information.

Creating a New User Account

You need to allow a new customer to register an account if they don't already have one. This process will allow the user to enter their information and establish a username and password. To implement this functionality, you need to add quite a bit of code to your existing code base. Therefore, the following exercise will walk you through all the necessary tasks.

Exercise: Creating a New Account

In this exercise, you will create a stored procedure and add the necessary code to allow the user to enter their information. Then you will save that information in the database so the user can eventually proceed to the final checkout process. Follow these steps:

1. You'll first create the stored procedure that will insert the necessary data. This stored procedure will be different from the previous ones so far in the sense that the information will span three tables: EndUser, Address, and ContactInformation. Therefore, you need to utilize transactions. Here's the stored procedure script:

```
CREATE PROCEDURE EndUser_Insert

@FirstName          nvarchar(50),
@LastName           nvarchar(50),
@AddressLine        nvarchar(50),
@AddressLine2   nvarchar(50),
@City                   nvarchar(50),
@State                  nvarchar(50),
@PostalCode     nvarchar(50),
@Phone                nvarchar(50),
@Phone2             nvarchar(50),
@Fax                    nvarchar(50),
@Email                nvarchar(50),
@EndUserTypeID int,
@Password           nvarchar(50),
@IsSubscribed       bit

AS

--Start the transaction
BEGIN TRANSACTION

DECLARE @AddressID int
DECLARE @ContactInformationID int

INSERT INTO Address
(AddressLine,
AddressLine2,
City,
```

```
State,
PostalCode)
VALUES
(@AddressLine,
@AddressLine2,
@City,
@State,
@PostalCode)

SET @AddressID = @@IDENTITY

-- Roll back the transaction if there are any errors
IF @@ERROR <> 0
BEGIN
-- Roll back the transaction
ROLLBACK

-- Raise an error and return
RAISERROR ('Error INSERT INTO Address.', 16, 1)
RETURN
END

INSERT INTO ContactInformation
(Phone,
Phone2,
Fax,
Email)
VALUES
(@Phone,
@Phone2,
@Fax,
@Email)

SET @ContactInformationID = @@IDENTITY

-- Roll back the transaction if there are any errors
IF @@ERROR <> 0
BEGIN
-- Roll back the transaction
ROLLBACK

-- Raise an error and return
RAISERROR ('Error INSERT INTO ContactInformation', 16, 1)
RETURN
END
```

```
-- Next Step
INSERT INTO EndUser
(EndUserTypeID,
FirstName,
LastName,
AddressID,
ContactInformationID,
Password,
IsSubscribed)
VALUES
(@EndUserTypeID,
@FirstName,
@LastName,
@AddressID,
@ContactInformationID,
@Password,
@IsSubscribed)

SELECT @@IDENTITY

-- Roll back the transaction if there are any errors
IF @@ERROR <> 0
BEGIN
-- Roll back the transaction
ROLLBACK

-- Raise an error and return
RAISERROR ('Error INSERT INTO EndUser', 16, 1)
RETURN
END

COMMIT
```

How It Works

The stored procedure utilizes transactions to first insert the data into the Address table and then retrieve the AddressID value that was just created by the @@IDENTITY variable. In a similar fashion, the ContactInformation table has its respective information inserted and then ends the transaction by taking the two unique IDs from the Address and ContactInformation tables, inserting the remaining information in the EndUser table, and returning the newly created EndUserID value that was created.

2. You now have the stored procedure complete and can proceed to the data access layer of the code. As in the prior exercises, you need to add the name of the stored procedure, EndUser_Insert, to the Name enumeration within the StoredProcedure class. Upon completing that task, proceed to the Insert folder within the LittleItalyVineyard.DataAccess class library, and add a new class named EndUserInsertData. Then add the following code:

```
using System;
using System.Collections.Generic;
using System.Text;
using System.Data;
using System.Data.SqlClient;

using LittleItalyVineyard.Common;

namespace LittleItalyVineyard.DataAccess.Insert
{
    public class EndUserInsertData : DataAccessBase
    {
        private EndUser _enduser;
        private EndUserInsertDataParameters
            _enduserinsertdataparameters;

        public EndUserInsertData()
        {
            StoredProcedureName = StoredProcedure.Name.
                EndUser_Insert.ToString();
        }

        public void Add()
        {
            _enduserinsertdataparameters =
        new EndUserInsertDataParameters( EndUser );
            DataBaseHelper dbhelper = new DataBaseHelper
                ( StoredProcedureName );
            object id = dbhelper.RunScalar
              ( base.ConnectionString ,
                _enduserinsertdataparameters.Parameters );
            EndUser.EndUserID = int.Parse( id.ToString() );
        }

        public EndUser EndUser
        {
            get { return _enduser; }
            set { _enduser = value; }
        }
    }

    public class EndUserInsertDataParameters
```

```
{
    private EndUser _enduser;
    private SqlParameter[ ] _parameters;

    public EndUserInsertDataParameters(EndUser enduser )
    {
        EndUser = enduser;
        Build();
    }

    private void Build()
    {
        SqlParameter[ ] parameters =
        {
            new SqlParameter( "@FirstName" , EndUser.FirstName ) ,
            new SqlParameter( "@LastName" , EndUser.LastName ) ,
            new SqlParameter( "@AddressLine", EndUser.Address.➥
                AddressLine ) ,
            new SqlParameter( "@AddressLine2" , EndUser.Address.➥
                AddressLine2 ) ,
            new SqlParameter( "@City" , EndUser.Address.City ) ,
            new SqlParameter( "@State" , EndUser.Address.State ) ,
            new SqlParameter( "@PostalCode" , EndUser.Address.➥
                PostalCode ) ,
            new SqlParameter( "@Phone" , EndUser.ContactInformation.➥
                Phone ) ,
            new SqlParameter( "@Phone2" , EndUser.ContactInformation.➥
                Phone2 ) ,
            new SqlParameter( "@Fax" , EndUser.ContactInformation.➥
                Fax ) ,
            new SqlParameter( "@Email" , EndUser.ContactInformation.➥
                Email ) ,
            new SqlParameter( "@EndUserTypeID" , EndUser.➥
                EndUserTypeID ) ,
            new SqlParameter( "@Password" , EndUser.Password ) ,
            new SqlParameter( "@IsSubscribed" , EndUser.IsSubscribed )
        };

        Parameters = parameters;
    }
}
```

```
        public EndUser EndUser
        {
            get { return _enduser; }
            set { _enduser = value; }
        }

        public SqlParameter[ ] Parameters
        {
            get { return _parameters; }
            set { _parameters = value; }
        }
    }
}
```

How It Works

You have added two separate classes in the data access layer of the architecture. These classes are similar to the others within the data access layer in that there is a main class and a parameters class. However, notice that you needed to first go to the common class of EndUser and add two fields and properties. These additions were the Address and ContactInformation classes as properties; you also instantiated them within the constructor. The following is the sample of what was added to the EndUser class within the LittleItalyVineyard.Common library project:

```
private Address _address;
private ContactInformation _contactinformation;

public EndUser()
{
    _address = new Address();
    _contactinformation = new ContactInformation();
}

public Address Address
{
    get { return _address; }
    set { _address = value; }
}

public ContactInformation ContactInformation
{
    get { return _contactinformation; }
    set { _contactinformation = value; }
}
```

This addition to the EndUser common class was needed as a result of the information being inserted across multiple tables in the database. If you want to keep the documentation of the class diagrams up-to-date, do not forget to make these adjustments there as well.

3. You are now off to the business logic layer of the code. Add a new class to the LittleItalyVineyard.BusinessLogic class library project named ProcessAddEndUser. You will construct this class similar to the others within this section of the architecture. Therefore, add the following code to the newly added class:

```
using System;
using System.Collections.Generic;
using System.Text;

using LittleItalyVineyard.Common;
using LittleItalyVineyard.DataAccess.Insert;

namespace LittleItalyVineyard.BusinessLogic
{
    public class ProcessAddEndUser : IBusinessLogic
    {
        private EndUser _enduser;

        public ProcessAddEndUser()
        {

        }

        public void Invoke()
        {
                EndUserInsertData enduserdata = new EndUserInsertData();
                enduserdata.EndUser = this.EndUser;
                enduserdata.Add();
                this.EndUser.EndUserID = enduserdata.EndUser.EndUserID;
        }

        public EndUser EndUser
        {
            get { return _enduser; }
            set { _enduser = value; }
        }
    }
}
```

How It Works

This code is no different from the other classes you have created within the business logic layer. It adheres to the IBusinessLogic interface and uses the code created in the previous steps of this exercise.

4. Now you'll move on to the final tier of the architecture that you will need to incorporate, the presentation layer. In the first exercise in this chapter, you created a link that will navigate the user to the Register.aspx web page, which as of the moment does not exist. So now you'll add a new web form to the web project in the solution named Register.aspx and associate it with the master page to which the other web forms adhere. In the Source section of the web form, add the following HTML code:

```
<%@ Page Language="C#" MasterPageFile="~/Main.master"
AutoEventWireup="true" CodeFile="Register.aspx.cs"
Inherits="Register" Title="Little Italy Vineyard | Registration" %>

<asp:Content ID="Content1" ContentPlaceHolderID="contentplaceholderMain"
Runat="Server">
    <table border="0" cellpadding="2" cellspacing="0" style="width: 432px">
        <tr>
            <td style="width: 23px">
<img src="images/spacer.gif" width="1"
height="8" /></td>
        </tr>
        <tr>
            <td style="width: 23px"><img src="images/spacer.gif" width="50"
  height="1" /></td>
            <td style="width: 167px">Firstname:</td>
<td>
<asp:TextBox ID="textFirstname" runat="server"
Width="176px" CssClass="textField">
</asp:TextBox><br />
    <asp:RequiredFieldValidator ID="requiredFirstname"
runat="server" ControlToValidate="textFirstname"
    Display="Dynamic" EnableClientScript="False"
ErrorMessage="Firstname required."
                    Width="152px"></asp:RequiredFieldValidator></td>
        </tr>
        <tr>
            <td style="width: 23px"></td>
            <td style="width: 167px">Lastname:</td>
<td>
<asp:TextBox ID="textLastname" runat="server"
Width="176px" CssClass="textField">
</asp:TextBox><br />
    <asp:RequiredFieldValidator ID="requiredLastname"
runat="server" ControlToValidate="textLastname"
 Display="Dynamic" EnableClientScript="False"
ErrorMessage="Lastname required."
                    Width="152px"></asp:RequiredFieldValidator></td>
        </tr>
        <tr>
            <td style="width: 23px"></td>
            <td style="width: 167px">Address:</td>
```

```
<td>
<asp:TextBox ID="textAddress" runat="server"
Width="176px" CssClass="textField">
</asp:TextBox><br />
<asp:RequiredFieldValidator ID="requiredAddress" runat="server"
ControlToValidate="textAddress"
Display="Dynamic" EnableClientScript="False"
ErrorMessage="Address required."
                        Width="152px"></asp:RequiredFieldValidator></td>
        </tr>
        <tr>
            <td style="width: 23px"></td>
            <td style="width: 167px">Address 2:</td>
<td>
<asp:TextBox ID="textAddress2" runat="server"
Width="176px" CssClass="textField">
</asp:TextBox></td>
 </tr>
  <tr>
  <td style="width: 23px"></td>
  <td style="width: 167px">City:</td>
   <td><asp:TextBox ID="textCity" runat="server" Width="176px"
CssClass="textField"></asp:TextBox><br />
 <asp:RequiredFieldValidator ID="requiredCity" runat="server"
ControlToValidate="textCity"
Display="Dynamic" EnableClientScript="False"
ErrorMessage="City required."
                        Width="152px"></asp:RequiredFieldValidator></td>
        </tr>
        <tr>
            <td style="width: 23px"></td>
            <td style="width: 167px">State:</td>
<td>
<asp:TextBox ID="textState" runat="server"
Width="176px" CssClass="textField">
</asp:TextBox><br />
<asp:RequiredFieldValidator ID="requiredState" runat="server"
ControlToValidate="textState"
 Display="Dynamic" EnableClientScript="False"
ErrorMessage="State required."
                        Width="152px"></asp:RequiredFieldValidator></td>
        </tr>
        <tr>
            <td style="width: 23px"></td>
            <td style="width: 167px">Postal Code:</td>
<td>
<asp:TextBox ID="textPostalCode" runat="server"
```

```
Width="176px" CssClass="textField">
</asp:TextBox><br />
<asp:RequiredFieldValidator ID="requiredPostalCode"
runat="server" ControlToValidate="textPostalCode"
                    Display="Dynamic" EnableClientScript="False"
ErrorMessage="Postal Code required."
 Width="152px"></asp:RequiredFieldValidator></td>
        </tr>
        <tr>
            <td style="width: 23px"></td>
            <td style="width: 167px">Password:</td>
<td><asp:TextBox ID="textPassword" runat="server"
TextMode="Password" Width="176px" CssClass="textField">
</asp:TextBox><br />
<asp:RequiredFieldValidator ID="requiredPassword"
runat="server" ControlToValidate="textPassword"
Display="Dynamic" ErrorMessage="Password required."
Width="152px" EnableClientScript="False">
</asp:RequiredFieldValidator>
<asp:CompareValidator ID="comparePasswords" runat="server"
Display="Dynamic" EnableClientScript="False"
ErrorMessage="The passwords entered do not match"
ControlToCompare="textPassword"
ControlToValidate="textConfirmPassword" Width="240px">
</asp:CompareValidator></td>
        </tr>
        <tr>
            <td style="width: 23px"></td>
<td style="width: 167px">Confirm Password:</td>
<td><asp:TextBox ID="textConfirmPassword" runat="server"
TextMode="Password" Width="176px" CssClass="textField">
</asp:TextBox><br />
<asp:RequiredFieldValidator ID="requiredConfirmPassword"
runat="server" ControlToValidate="textConfirmPassword"
Display="Dynamic" EnableClientScript="False"
ErrorMessage="Confirm password required."
Width="176px"></asp:RequiredFieldValidator></td>
        </tr>
 <tr>
<td style="width: 23px"></td>
<td style="width: 167px">Email:</td>
<td><asp:TextBox ID="textEmail" runat="server"
TextMode="singleLine" Width="176px" CssClass="textField">
</asp:TextBox><br />
<asp:RequiredFieldValidator ID="requiredEmail" runat="server"
ControlToValidate="textEmail"
Display="Dynamic" EnableClientScript="False"
```

```
            ErrorMessage="Email required."
            Width="152px"></asp:RequiredFieldValidator></td>
        </tr>
        <tr>
            <td style="width: 23px"></td>
            <td style="width: 167px">Phone:</td>
<td>
<asp:TextBox ID="textPhone" runat="server"
Width="176px" CssClass="textField">
</asp:TextBox></td>
        </tr>
        <tr>
            <td style="width: 23px"></td>
            <td style="width: 167px">Phone 2:</td>
<td>
<asp:TextBox ID="textPhone2" runat="server"
Width="176px" CssClass="textField">
</asp:TextBox></td>
        </tr>
        <tr>
            <td style="width: 23px"></td>
            <td style="width: 167px">Fax:</td>
<td>
<asp:TextBox ID="textFax" runat="server"
Width="176px" CssClass="textField">
</asp:TextBox></td>
        </tr>
        <tr>
            <td style="width: 23px"></td>
            <td style="width: 167px">Subscribe to Newsletter:</td>
            <td><asp:CheckBox ID="checkboxNewsletter" runat="server"
Width="176px" CssClass="textField" /></td>
        </tr>
        <tr>
            <td colspan="2"></td>
            <td><asp:Button ID="commandRegister" runat="server"
Text="Register Account" OnClick="commandRegister_Click"
CssClass="button" /></td>
        </tr>
    </table>
</asp:Content>
```

How It Works

You added quite a bit of HTML code in this step, so I'll explain some of the details of what it contains. Essentially, the web form contains text boxes for all the information that is asked of the user and required to populate a new user within your system. You also added a number of required field validator controls and associated them with the fields that are necessary when adding a new user account.

A required field validator is a control that is provided within ASP.NET that offers an easy way of ensuring that a user enters a value within the field where you require information. Finally, you added another validator that is incorporated to verify that the password entered is in fact the same as what's entered in the field that asks to confirm the user's password.

5. Now that you have the HTML code and server controls set up on the Register.aspx web form, you can proceed to the code portion. Within the code version, you need to add several items. Add the following code, and I'll then explain the details of what you have incorporated:

```
using System;
using System.Data;
using System.Configuration;
using System.Collections;
using System.Web;
using System.Web.Security;
using System.Web.UI;
using System.Web.UI.WebControls;
using System.Web.UI.WebControls.WebParts;
using System.Web.UI.HtmlControls;

using LittleItalyVineyard.Common;
using LittleItalyVineyard.BusinessLogic;

public partial class Register : System.Web.UI.Page
{
    protected void Page_Load( object sender , EventArgs e )
    {
        textFirstname.Focus();
    }

    protected void commandRegister_Click( object sender , EventArgs e )
    {
        EndUser enduser = new EndUser();
        ProcessAddEndUser processuser = new ProcessAddEndUser();

        if ( IsValid )
        {
            enduser.EndUserTypeID = ( int ) Enums.EndUserType.CUSTOMER;
            enduser.FirstName = textFirstname.Text;
            enduser.LastName = textLastname.Text;
            enduser.Address.AddressLine = textAddress.Text;
            enduser.Address.AddressLine2 = textAddress2.Text;
            enduser.Address.City = textCity.Text;
            enduser.Address.State = textState.Text;
            enduser.Address.PostalCode = textPostalCode.Text;
            enduser.Password = textPassword.Text;
            enduser.ContactInformation.Email = textEmail.Text;
            enduser.ContactInformation.Phone = textPhone.Text;
```

```
                    enduser.ContactInformation.Phone2 = textPhone2.Text;
                    enduser.ContactInformation.Fax = textFax.Text;
                    enduser.IsSubscribed = checkboxNewsletter.Checked;

                    processuser.EndUser = enduser;

                      try
                      {
                            processuser.Invoke();
                      }
                      catch
                    {
                            Response.Redirect( "ErrorPage.aspx" );
                      }

                      if ( Request.Cookies[ "ReturnURL" ].Value != null )
                      {
                            Response.Redirect( Request.Cookies[ "ReturnURL" ]➥
                              .Value );
                      }
                      else
                      {
                            Response.Redirect( "Login.aspx" );
                      }
                }
            }
        }
```

How It Works

How does this work? That's an excellent question; you have been bombarded with a great deal of code up to this point, but everything will become quite clear in a moment. In the previous code that you included in the Register.aspx web form, you did the following: you first added a click event to the command button, and in the click event you instantiated new EndUser and ProcessAddEndUser classes from the common object and business logic layers, respectively. After doing this, you started to populate the ProcessAddEndUser EndUser property with that of the text boxes to pass this information to the business logic layer and ultimately to the data access layer and database to insert the necessary information. Note, however, that this occurs only if the IsValid page property is true as a result of all the validation controls being satisfied.

6. Everything is set up and implemented to allow the new user to add their information and create a new account. However, you need to address a few remaining items so that you can redirect the user to where they originally wanted to go—the checkout. With that being said, I'll now introduce a concept: using a base page from which eventually all the web forms will inherit. Within the base page, a number of items will use session variables to store and maintain state across the application. Therefore, add a class file to the web project named BasePage. You will be prompted that you are adding a code file to the web project, and you'll be asked whether you want to add it to the App_Code directory; you can respond by clicking Yes. Add the following code to the new class file:

```csharp
using LittleItalyVineyard.Common;

public class BasePage : System.Web.UI.Page
{
    internal const string KEY_CURRENTUSER = "Current Logged In User";

    public EndUser CurrentEndUser
    {
        get
        {
            try
            {
                return ( EndUser ) ( Session[ KEY_CURRENTUSER ] );
            }
            catch
            {
                return ( null );  // for design time
            }
        }

        set
        {
            if ( value == null )
            {
                Session.Remove( KEY_CURRENTUSER );
            }
            else
            {
                Session[ KEY_CURRENTUSER ] = value;
            }
        }
    }
}
```

How It Works

The base page is quite simple. To start, the class inherits from the System.Web.UI.Page class, which is what all web forms inherit from by default. Next you added the LittleItalyVineyard.Common namespace so that you can use the common objects within the base page. Then finally, you added a constant string that will be used as the referring session item that is then either accessed or set within the CurrentEndUser property that stores the EndUser common class in the session variable.

7. Now that you have created and implemented the base page, you need to have your web forms inherit from the BasePage class. Doing so is quite simple; you just need to change what Register.aspx inherits from to that of the base page. Finally, you will set the newly created property within the base page of the current user to what was just created and then redirect the user to their original destination:

```csharp
using System;
using System.Data;
using System.Configuration;
using System.Collections;
using System.Web;
using System.Web.Security;
using System.Web.UI;
using System.Web.UI.WebControls;
using System.Web.UI.WebControls.WebParts;
using System.Web.UI.HtmlControls;

using LittleItalyVineyard.Common;
using LittleItalyVineyard.BusinessLogic;

public partial class Register : System.Web.UI.Page
{
    protected void Page_Load( object sender , EventArgs e )
    {
        textFirstname.Focus();
    }

    protected void commandRegister_Click( object sender , EventArgs e )
    {
        EndUser enduser = new EndUser();
        ProcessAddEndUser processuser = new ProcessAddEndUser();

        if ( IsValid )
        {
            enduser.EndUserTypeID = ( int ) Enums.EndUserType➡
              .CUSTOMER;
            enduser.FirstName = textFirstname.Text;
            enduser.LastName = textLastname.Text;
            enduser.Address.AddressLine = textAddress.Text;
            enduser.Address.AddressLine2 = textAddress2.Text;
            enduser.Address.City = textCity.Text;
            enduser.Address.State = textState.Text;
            enduser.Address.PostalCode = textPostalCode.Text;
            enduser.Password = textPassword.Text;
            enduser.ContactInformation.Email = textEmail.Text;
            enduser.ContactInformation.Phone = textPhone.Text;
```

```
                enduser.ContactInformation.Phone2 = textPhone2.Text;
                enduser.ContactInformation.Fax = textFax.Text;
                enduser.IsSubscribed = checkboxNewsletter.Checked;

                processuser.EndUser = enduser;

            try
            {
                processuser.Invoke();
            }
            catch
            {
                Response.Redirect( "ErrorPage.aspx" );
            }

            CurrentEndUser = processuser.EndUser;

            if ( Request.Cookies[ "ReturnURL" ].Value != null )
            {
                Response.Redirect( Request.Cookies[ "ReturnURL" ]➦
                    .Value );
            }
            else
            {
                Response.Redirect( "Login.aspx" );
            }
        }
    }
}
```

How It Works

Within the altered code, you inherited from the base page that was newly created, and upon a successful completion of the user creating a new account, you set the populated EndUser class to the CurrentEndUser property in the BasePage class. Finally, you detect whether the user had an original destination. In other words, did they sign up for a new account without checking out first, or were they in the process of checking out and needed to create an account? You accomplish this by checking whether the cookie, ReturnURL, is present. If the cookie is not null, the user is then redirected to that original location. If the cookie is null or not present, the user is simply redirected to the login page, Login.aspx.

At long last, you have finished the implementation to allow a new user to create an account. Now that users are able to create accounts, you can proceed to implementing the functionality to allow an existing user to log in to their account and eventually check their items out of the shopping cart.

Logging In

You now need to implement the functionality that allows a user to log in—this can be either a new user who has recently created an account or a return customer who has had an account for an extended amount of time. In either case, for the customer to proceed to the checkout process and eventually enter their billing information, you will add the login feature. The following exercise shows you how do to this.

Exercise: Implementing the Login Functionality

This exercise shows how to allow the user to log in to their account and either proceed to the final checkout portion of the process or examine any history within their account. Follow these steps:

1. You will once again begin with creating the stored procedure for accessing the information for the user account. Execute the following stored procedure script:

```
CREATE PROCEDURE EndUserLogin_Select

@Email nvarchar(50),
@Password nvarchar(50)

AS

SELECT EndUserID,
EndUserTypeID,
FirstName,
LastName,
EndUser.AddressID,
EndUser.ContactInformationID,
Password,
IsSubscribed,
Phone,
Phone2,
Fax,
Email
FROM EndUser
INNER JOIN ContactInformation
ON ContactInformation.ContactInformationID = enduser.ContactInformationID
WHERE Email = @Email
AND Password = @Password
AND EndUserTypeID = 1
```

How It Works

The stored procedure script accepts two parameters: the e-mail and the password that will be queried from the EndUser table as well as the inner joined ContactInformation table. Finally, the WHERE clause uses the e-mail, password, and EndUserTypeID that is set to 1, which represents a basic customer and not an administrator.

2. Moving along to the data access tier, first add the name of the stored procedure, EndUserLogin_Select, to the enumeration within the StoredProcedure class. From there, create a new class in the Select portion of the namespace named EndUserLoginSelectData along with its EndUserLoginSelectDataParameters class. The code is as follows:

```csharp
using System;
using System.Collections.Generic;
using System.Text;
using System.Data;
using System.Data.SqlClient;

using LittleItalyVineyard.Common;

namespace LittleItalyVineyard.DataAccess.Select
{
    public class EndUserLoginSelectData : DataAccessBase
    {
        private EndUser _enduser;

        public EndUserLoginSelectData()
        {
            StoredProcedureName = StoredProcedure.Name.➥
                EndUserLogin_Select.ToString();
        }

        public DataSet Get()
        {
            DataSet ds;

            EndUserLoginSelectDataParameters➥
                _enduserselectdataparameters =➥
                new EndUserLoginSelectDataParameters( EndUser );
            DataBaseHelper dbhelper = new DataBaseHelper➥
                ( StoredProcedureName );
            ds = dbhelper.Run( base.ConnectionString ,
                _enduserselectdataparameters.Parameters );

            return ds;
        }

        public EndUser EndUser
        {
            get { return _enduser; }
            set { _enduser = value; }
        }
    }
```

```
public class EndUserLoginSelectDataParameters
{
    private EndUser _enduser;
    private SqlParameter[] _parameters;

    public EndUserLoginSelectDataParameters( EndUser enduser )
    {
        EndUser = enduser;
        Build();
    }

    private void Build()
    {
        SqlParameter[] parameters =
        {
            new SqlParameter( "@Email" , ➡
                EndUser.ContactInformation➡
                .Email ) ,
            new SqlParameter( "@Password" , EndUser.Password )
        };

        Parameters = parameters;
    }

    public EndUser EndUser
    {
        get { return _enduser; }
        set { _enduser = value; }
    }

    public SqlParameter[] Parameters
    {
        get { return _parameters; }
        set { _parameters = value; }
    }
}
```

How It Works

The data access code is similar to the other data access classes you have implemented. A DataSet is returned from the query that uses the stored procedure while specifying the Email and Password parameters that are passed to the stored procedure.

3. Moving along to the business logic layer now, you will keep the similar pattern in that you will add a new class named ProcessEndUserLogin, which will implement the IBusinessLogic interface and subsequently call upon the data access code. The code is as follows:

```csharp
using System;
using System.Collections.Generic;
using System.Text;
using System.Data;

using LittleItalyVineyard.Common;
using LittleItalyVineyard.DataAccess.Select;

namespace LittleItalyVineyard.BusinessLogic
{
    public class ProcessEndUserLogin : IBusinessLogic
    {
        private EndUser _enduser;
        private DataSet _resultset;
        private bool _isauthenticated;

        public ProcessEndUserLogin()
        {

        }

        public void Invoke()
        {
            EndUserLoginSelectData enduserlogin = ➥
                new EndUserLoginSelectData();
            enduserlogin.EndUser = this.EndUser;
            ResultSet = enduserlogin.Get();

            if ( ResultSet.Tables[0].Rows.Count != 0 )
            {
                IsAuthenticated = true;

                EndUser.EndUserID =➥
                    int.Parse( ResultSet.Tables[0]➥
                    .Rows[0]["EndUserID"].ToString() );
                EndUser.EndUserTypeID = ➥
                    int.Parse( ResultSet.Tables[0]➥
                .Rows[0]["EndUserTypeID"].ToString() );
                EndUser.FirstName =➥
                    ResultSet.Tables[ 0 ].Rows[ 0 ]➥
                    [ "Firstname" ].ToString();
                EndUser.LastName =➥
                    ResultSet.Tables[ 0 ].Rows[ 0 ]➥
                    [ "LastName" ].ToString();
                EndUser.AddressID ➥
                 = int.Parse( ResultSet.Tables[0].➥
                     Rows[0]["AddressID"].ToString() );
```

```
                        EndUser.ContactInformationID =➥
                            int.Parse(  ResultSet.Tables[0].➥
                        Rows[0]["ContactInformationID"].ToString() );
                        EndUser.Password = ResultSet.Tables[0].Rows[0]➥
                            [ "Password" ].ToString();

                        // Obtain the Address information.
                        ProcessGetAddress getaddress =➥
                            new ProcessGetAddress();
                        getaddress.Address.AddressID = EndUser.AddressID;

                        getaddress.Invoke();
                        EndUser.Address = getaddress.Address;

                        // Obtain the ContactInformation information.
                        ProcessGetContactInformation getcontactinfo = ➥
                            new  ProcessGetContactInformation();
                            getcontactinfo.➥
                            ContactInformation.ContactInformationID➥
                            =  EndUser.ContactInformationID;

                        getcontactinfo.Invoke();

                        EndUser.ContactInformation = getcontactinfo.➥
                            ContactInformation;
                    }
                    else
                    {
                        EndUser = null;
                        IsAuthenticated = false;
                    }
        }

        public EndUser EndUser
        {
            get { return _enduser; }
            set { _enduser = value; }
        }

        public DataSet ResultSet
        {
            get { return _resultset; }
            set { _resultset = value; }
        }

        public bool IsAuthenticated
        {
```

```
            get { return _isauthenticated; }
            set { _isauthenticated = value; }
        }
    }
}
```

How It Works

Everything within the code is similar to previous business logic classes except this code has an additional step. This additional step is that you will examine the returning DataSet within the Password field and compare that to the password text that was entered by the user. If they match, the Invoke method sets the IsAuthenticated property to true; otherwise, it is false, meaning the passwords do not match, and thus the user cannot proceed.

4. For the final step, you will work with the Login.aspx web form. You have already added the HTML code and controls to this page; however, you now need to add the C# code that will initiate the login process. Therefore, within the click event of the login command button, add the code to commence the process, as follows:

```csharp
using System;
using System.Data;
using System.Configuration;
using System.Collections;
using System.Web;
using System.Web.Security;
using System.Web.UI;
using System.Web.UI.WebControls;
using System.Web.UI.WebControls.WebParts;
using System.Web.UI.HtmlControls;

using LittleItalyVineyard.Common;
using LittleItalyVineyard.BusinessLogic;

public partial class Login : BasePage
{
    protected void Page_Load( object sender , EventArgs e )
    {
        textUsername.Focus();
    }

    protected void commandLogin_Click( object sender , EventArgs e )
    {
        if ( IsValid )
        {
            EndUser enduser = new EndUser();
            ProcessEndUserLogin processlogin = ➥
                new ProcessEndUserLogin();
```

```
        enduser.ContactInformation.Email = textUsername.Text;
        enduser.Password = textPassword.Text;
        processlogin.EndUser = enduser;

        try
        {
            processlogin.Invoke();
        }
        catch
        {
            Response.Redirect( "ErrorPage.aspx" );
        }

        if ( processlogin.IsAuthenticated )
        {
            base.CurrentEndUser = processlogin.EndUser;

            if ( Request.Cookies["ReturnURL"] != null )
            {
                Response.Redirect( Request.Cookies➥
                    ["ReturnURL"].Value );
            }
            else
            {
                // TODO: Implement later.
            }
        }
        else
        {
            labelMessage.Text = "Invalid login!";
        }
    }
  }
}
```

How It Works

Again, the code is similar to that of the other presentation tier code and web forms. First, you set the focus in the page load event to that of the textUsename text box. Then, you check whether the execution of the button click event has valid data and, if so, call the business logic code and the EndUser common class to pass into the ProcessEndUserLogin class in the business logic tier. Finally, if the Invoke method from the ProcessEndUserLogin class returned value is true, you redirect the user to the original page by checking the cookie. If there is no cookie, you will return the user to a page that you will implement in Chapter 22, thus noted by the TODO commented item. If the Invoke method returns a false value, you will alert the user by setting the Text property of the labelMessage to explain that the login is invalid.

With this final implementation of code, you are at the end of the exercise. You now have a fully working login process.

Summary

In this chapter, you completed the functionality that initiates the checkout process for a customer after they have added the desired items to their shopping cart. They now have the ability to register a new account or log in to an existing account. After either of these actions takes place, the user needs to complete the transaction by entering their payment information, or more specifically their credit card information, to pay for their order. The following chapter will explain the next part of the checkout process, which captures the payment information and finalizes the transaction of the order.

CHAPTER 20

■ ■ ■

Processing the Payment

In this chapter, you will address the final portion of the checkout process; specifically, you will implement the functionality to accept a payment from the user. It goes without saying that you certainly hope that this action occurs frequently, because that translates to a lot of sales being made! Knowing this, you have to thoroughly test this functionality and ensure that you take all the necessary security measures.

This chapter will cover the following functionality as well as show how to implement some of the application programming interface (API) source code that is supplied with the PayPal SDK:

- Implementing the PayPal API code

- Entering the billing information

- Submitting the payment

- Finalizing the payment and order

Implementing the PayPal API Code

A few chapters ago, you created the PayPal test account and configured everything you needed to test the credit card–processing functionality of the PayPal account. You briefly addressed the PayPal API code, but you still have a fair amount of implementation to complete before you have the ability to accept a credit card payment for the goods you are selling.

In this section of the chapter, you will add the necessary code and functionality; specifically, the following exercise will show you how to implement the PayPal API credentials.

Exercise: Implementing PayPal API Credentials

In this chapter, you will focus on the functionality to allow users to submit the credit card payment information to PayPal, determine whether the transaction is successful, and if not, alert the user why it wasn't. In this exercise, you'll implement the PayPal API credentials. Follow these steps:

1. Return to the LittleItalyVineyard.Operational class library within your source code and then to the PayPalManager class. You first need to add some references: System.Security, System.Web, the local project LittleItalyVineyard.Common class library project, and the namespace that was added for the PayPal sandbox (LittleItalyVineyard.Operational.PayPalAPI.Sandbox). After adding the references, add these namespaces to the PayPalManager class:

```
using System.Web;
using System.IO;
using System.Security.Cryptography.X509Certificates;

using LittleItalyVineyard.Common;
using LittleItalyVineyard.Operational.PayPalAPI.Sandbox;
```

2. After adding the necessary references, proceed to the constructor of the PayPalManager class. In the constructor, you will first address the credentials and security that will be needed each time you utilize the PayPal API calls. The first step is to instantiate two classes from the PayPal APIs, namely, PayPalAPIAASoapBinding and PayPalAPISoapBinding, as shown in the following code sample:

```
using System;
using System.Configuration;
using System.Collections.Generic;
using System.Text;
using System.Web;
using System.IO;
using System.Security.Cryptography.X509Certificates;

using LittleItalyVineyard.Common;
using LittleItalyVineyard.Operational.PayPalAPI.Sandbox;

namespace LittleItalyVineyard.Operational
{
    public class PayPalManager
    {
        private PayPalAPIAASoapBinding PPInterface =➥
         new PayPalAPIAASoapBinding();
        private PayPalAPISoapBinding service =➥
         new PayPalAPISoapBinding();

        public PayPalManager()
        {
```

```
            }
        }
    }
```

3. Continuing building the PayPalManager constructor; specifically, implement the username and password for accessing and implementing the PayPal APIs. Add the following code to the constructor:

```
using System;
using System.Configuration;
using System.Collections.Generic;
using System.Text;
using System.Web;
using System.IO;
using System.Security.Cryptography.X509Certificates;

using LittleItalyVineyard.Common;
using LittleItalyVineyard.Operational.PayPalAPI.Sandbox;

namespace LittleItalyVineyard.Operational
{
    public class PayPalManager
    {
        private PayPalAPIAASoapBinding PPInterface =➥
         new PayPalAPIAASoapBinding();
        private PayPalAPISoapBinding service =➥
            new PayPalAPISoapBinding();

        public PayPalManager()
        {
            UserIdPasswordType user = new UserIdPasswordType();

            user.Username = ConfigurationManager.➥
              AppSettings["PayPalAPIUsername"];
            user.Password = ConfigurationManager.➥
              AppSettings["PayPalAPIPassword"];
        }
    }
}
```

How It Works

The previous code utilizes the UserPasswordType class and then sets the Username and Password properties to what was registered when a sandbox account was established. Notice that you stored the username and password, appropriately named PayPalAPIUsername and PayPalAPIPassword, in the Web.config file within the appSettings. To complete this exercise step, add the PayPal API username and password to the Web.config file.

4. Moving along, you need to now specify the uniform resource locator (URL) for the PayPal API. In this case, you are still going to use the PayPal sandbox. Make the following addition to the constructor code:

```
using System;
using System.Configuration;
using System.Collections.Generic;
using System.Text;
using System.Web;
using System.IO;
using System.Security.Cryptography.X509Certificates;

using LittleItalyVineyard.Common;
using LittleItalyVineyard.Operational.PayPalAPI.Sandbox;

namespace LittleItalyVineyard.Operational
{
    public class PayPalManager
    {
        private PayPalAPIAASoapBinding PPInterface =➡
          new PayPalAPIAASoapBinding();
        private PayPalAPISoapBinding service =➡
          new PayPalAPISoapBinding();

        public PayPalManager()
        {
            UserIdPasswordType user = new UserIdPasswordType();

            user.Username = ConfigurationManager.➡
              AppSettings["PayPalAPIUsername"];
            user.Password = ConfigurationManager.➡
              AppSettings["PayPalAPIPassword"];

            PPInterface.Url = ConfigurationManager.➡
              AppSettings["PayPalAPIURL"];

            PPInterface.RequesterCredentials =➡
              new CustomSecurityHeaderType();
            PPInterface.RequesterCredentials.Credentials =➡
              new UserIdPasswordType();
            PPInterface.RequesterCredentials.Credentials = user;
        }
    }
}
```

How It Works

The PPInterface class specifies the URL, which is then obtained from the Web.config file within the appSettings. As mentioned, you are utilizing the sandbox, so the URL specified within the Web.config file is as follows:

```
<appSettings>
    <add key="PayPalAPIURL"
      value="https://api-aa.sandbox.paypal.com/2.0/"/>
</appSettings>
```

You finalize this code by instantiating the CustomSecurityHeaderType class and by setting the Credentials property to that of the UserIdPasswordType class that you implemented earlier in the exercise.

5. The final step in the exercise is to incorporate the certificate that will be used for the API access. You will implement that access to the certificate, LittleItalyVineyards.p12, by means of the file system:

```
using System;
using System.Configuration;
using System.Collections.Generic;
using System.Text;
using System.Web;
using System.IO;
using System.Security.Cryptography.X509Certificates;

using LittleItalyVineyard.Common;
using LittleItalyVineyard.Operational.PayPalAPI.Sandbox;

namespace LittleItalyVineyard.Operational
{
    public class PayPalManager
    {
        private PayPalAPIAASoapBinding PPInterface =➥
          new PayPalAPIAASoapBinding();
        private PayPalAPISoapBinding service =➥
          new PayPalAPISoapBinding();

        public PayPalManager()
        {
            UserIdPasswordType user = new UserIdPasswordType();

            user.Username = ConfigurationManager.➥
              AppSettings["PayPalAPIUsername"];
            user.Password = ConfigurationManager.➥
              AppSettings["PayPalAPIPassword"];

            PPInterface.Url = ConfigurationManager.➥
              AppSettings["PayPalAPIURL"];
```

```
        PPInterface.RequesterCredentials =➡
          new CustomSecurityHeaderType();
        PPInterface.RequesterCredentials.Credentials =➡
          new UserIdPasswordType();
        PPInterface.RequesterCredentials.Credentials = user;

        FileStream fstream = File.Open( CertPath ,➡
          FileMode.Open , FileAccess.Read );
        byte[ ] buffer = new byte[ fstream.Length ];

        int count = fstream.Read( buffer , 0 , buffer.Length );

        fstream.Close();

        X509Certificate2 cert = new X509Certificate2( buffer ,➡
          CertPassword );
        PPInterface.ClientCertificates.Add( cert );
    }

    private string CertPath
    {
        get { return HttpContext.Current.Server.MapPath(➡
        ConfigurationManager.AppSettings[ "CertificatePath" ] ); }
    }

    private string CertPassword
    {
        get { return ConfigurationManager.➡
        AppSettings["CertificatePassword"]; }
    }
  }
}
```

How It Works

The first item I need to discuss is the property that you added, CertPath. This property is a read-only property that will return the file path of the certificate file by obtaining the value from the Web.config file and then returning that value using the Server.MapPath function to return the full path. The value of the CertificatePath from the Web.config file is as follows:

```
<appSettings>
    <add key="CertificatePath" value="Certs/LittleItalyVineyards.p12"/>
</appSettings>
```

This full file path of the certificate is then used within a FileStream to open and read the certificate into a byte array, and then the FileStream is then closed. The X509Certificate2 class is then instantiated along with passing the byte array with the password that was used when you created the certificate in Chapter 18. This password is retrieved from the CertPassword property, which in turn retrieves the certificate password from the Web.config file.

You have completed the implementation of the PayPalManager class constructor where the credentials will be established. Now, anytime the class is instantiated, all the credentials will be set up automatically. Then another method can be called from within the PayPalManager without having to be concerned with the password and credentials for accessing the PayPal APIs.

Implementing the Direct Payment

You have only begun the overall implementation of the PayPal API code. In the previous section of the chapter, you established a methodology that will create all the necessary credentials for accessing the APIs within the PayPalManager class constructor. The next step is to address the functionality that will allow a user to submit a payment to the PayPal web service to transact a complete order.

The following exercise will demonstrate all the necessary steps.

Exercise: Implementing the Direct Payment

In this exercise, you will add the functionality to allow a user to submit a payment to the PayPal web service to transact a complete order. Follow these steps:

1. While you are still in the PayPalManager class, create a method named ProcessDirectPayment:

```
public void ProcessDirectPayment()
{

}
```

2. The ProcessDirectPayment method contained in the PayPalManager class requires quite a lot of code. However, you will take it step by step. First, add the PayPal API classes that are needed, and then specify that the transaction will be that of a sale by adding the following code to the ProcessDirectPayment method:

```
public void ProcessDirectPayment()
{
    DoDirectPaymentRequestType DoDirectPmtReqType =➡
    new DoDirectPaymentRequestType();
DoDirectPmtReqType.DoDirectPaymentRequestDetails =➡
    new DoDirectPaymentRequestDetailsType();

    // Set payment action
    DoDirectPmtReqType.DoDirectPaymentRequestDetails.➡
PaymentAction = PaymentActionCodeType.Sale;
```

```
        DoDirectPmtReqType.DoDirectPaymentRequestDetails.➥
IPAddress = HttpContext.Current.Request.UserHostAddress;
}
```

How It Works

The previously implemented code utilizes the DoDirectPaymentRequestType class from the PayPal APIs. After this class is instantiated, the DoDirectPaymentRequestDetails class is instantiated. Finally, the PaymentActionCodeType enumeration is set to that of the type Sale since this functionality will be used only to process orders that are being sold. The final line of code sets the IPAddress property of the DoDirectPaymentRequestDetails class to that of the IP address of the user making the purchase. The IP address is retrieved by using Request.UserHostAddress from the current HTTPContext.

3. To add the remainder of the code, you have to address the parameters you will need to populate the PayPal API classes and eventually submit the payment. With that said, this information has to be passed into the ProcessDirectPayment method as a parameter. These parameters will consist of a struct named PayPalInformation. So, you first need to create this struct within the same filename, PayPalManger, but outside of the PayPalManager class. The code will look like the following:

```
public struct PayPalInformation
{
    public Orders Order;
}
```

How It Works

The struct added, PayPalInformation, contains only one common object or class. More specifically, it is that of the Orders class. This essentially means you will be able to populate an Orders class that is part of the PayPalInformation struct.

4. Now that you have the PayPalInformation struct completed, you need to utilize it by adding it to the ProcessDirectPayment method as a parameter. The method will now resemble the following:

```
public void ProcessDirectPayment( PayPalInformation paypalinformation )
{

}
```

5. Moving along, you can now begin to populate the credit card details needed to be eventually used in the ProcessDirectPayment method. Add the following code:

```
// Set CreditCard info.
DoDirectPmtReqType.DoDirectPaymentRequestDetails.CreditCard =➥
    new CreditCardDetailsType();

DoDirectPmtReqType.DoDirectPaymentRequestDetails.CreditCard.➥
CreditCardNumber = paypalinformation.Order.CreditCard.Number;

DoDirectPmtReqType.DoDirectPaymentRequestDetails.CreditCard.➥
CreditCardType = ( CreditCardTypeType ) StringToEnum➥
```

```
( typeof( CreditCardTypeType ) ,
    paypalinformation.Order.CreditCard.CardType );
```

```
DoDirectPmtReqType.DoDirectPaymentRequestDetails.CreditCard.CVV2 =➡
paypalinformation.Order.CreditCard.SecurityCode;
```

```
DoDirectPmtReqType.DoDirectPaymentRequestDetails.CreditCard.ExpMonth =➡
paypalinformation.Order.CreditCard.ExpMonth;
```

```
DoDirectPmtReqType.DoDirectPaymentRequestDetails.CreditCard.ExpYear =➡
paypalinformation.Order.CreditCard.ExpYear;
```

How It Works

In the code you just added, you have viewed for the first time how you will use the struct PayPalInformation. As I mentioned when you added the struct, there will be a common object of the class Orders. You can witness that this is then used from the struct to populate the information needed for the credit card. Therefore, the previous code instantiates the CreditCardDetailsType class from the PayPal APIs and then subsequently is populated by the PayPalInformation struct. Lastly, with regard to the CreditCardTypeType, you introduced a new function in the overall PayPalManager class. This new function is named StringToEnum, and it allows the matching of the credit card type to that of the enumeration of the credit card type provided by PayPal. The following is the new function:

```
private static object StringToEnum( Type typ , string val )
{
    object objectOut = null;

    foreach ( System.Reflection.FieldInfo fieldinfo in typ.GetFields() )
    {
        if ( fieldinfo.Name == val )
        {
            objectOut = fieldinfo.GetValue( null );
        }
    }

    return objectOut;
}
```

In this new function, an object is returned as a result of the enumeration type being passed in as a parameter, and the string value of the credit card type is returned. Using the reflection classes of the framework, the object is returned upon there being a match to the enumeration and thus having the PayPal API credit card type set to the enumerated value.

6. The next portion of the method you're implementing is the credit card billing address and the name of the cardholder. This information too will be supplied from the Orders class that is part of the struct. This is the next portion of code you need to add:

```
// Set the billing address

DoDirectPmtReqType.DoDirectPaymentRequestDetails.CreditCard.CardOwner =➥
    new PayerInfoType();

DoDirectPmtReqType.DoDirectPaymentRequestDetails.CreditCard.CardOwner.➥
    PayerName = new PersonNameType();

DoDirectPmtReqType.DoDirectPaymentRequestDetails.CreditCard.CardOwner.➥
    PayerName.FirstName = paypalinformation.Order.EndUser.FirstName;

DoDirectPmtReqType.DoDirectPaymentRequestDetails.CreditCard.CardOwner.➥
    PayerName.LastName = paypalinformation.Order.EndUser.LastName;

DoDirectPmtReqType.DoDirectPaymentRequestDetails.CreditCard.CardOwner.➥
    Address = new AddressType();

DoDirectPmtReqType.DoDirectPaymentRequestDetails.CreditCard.CardOwner.➥
    Address.Street1 = paypalinformation.Order.CreditCard.Address.AddressLine;

DoDirectPmtReqType.DoDirectPaymentRequestDetails.CreditCard.CardOwner.➥
    Address.Street2 = paypalinformation.Order.CreditCard.Address.➥
    AddressLine2;

DoDirectPmtReqType.DoDirectPaymentRequestDetails.CreditCard.CardOwner.➥
    Address.CityName = paypalinformation.Order.CreditCard.Address.City;

DoDirectPmtReqType.DoDirectPaymentRequestDetails.CreditCard.CardOwner.➥
    Address.StateOrProvince = paypalinformation.Order.CreditCard.➥
    Address.State;

DoDirectPmtReqType.DoDirectPaymentRequestDetails.CreditCard.CardOwner.➥
    Address.PostalCode = paypalinformation.Order.CreditCard.Address.➥
    PostalCode;

DoDirectPmtReqType.DoDirectPaymentRequestDetails.CreditCard.CardOwner.➥
    Address.CountrySpecified = true;
DoDirectPmtReqType.DoDirectPaymentRequestDetails.CreditCard.CardOwner.➥
    Address.Country = CountryCodeType.US;

DoDirectPmtReqType.DoDirectPaymentRequestDetails.CreditCard.CardOwner.➥
    Address.Phone = paypalinformation.Order.EndUser.ContactInformation.Phone;
```

How It Works

In this added code, you can see that in the same fashion that the credit card information is populated, the credit card owner's information and the cardholder's address are populated.

7. To proceed, you will now address how the PayPal APIs will be populated with the products the customer is wanting to buy. In a similar fashion, this information will be populated, but as you will be able to see, you need to loop through all the products that were originally added to the shopping cart when the customer decided to check out and finalize. The following is the code:

```
PaymentDetailsItemType[ ] itemArray = new PaymentDetailsItemType[➡
paypalinformation.Order.OrderDetails.Products.Length ];
PaymentDetailsItemType items = null;

// Loop through all items that were added to the shopping cart.
for ( int i = 0 ; i < paypalinformation.Order.OrderDetails.Products.➡
    Length ; i++ )
{
    items = new PaymentDetailsItemType();
    items.Amount = new BasicAmountType();
    items.Amount.Value = paypalinformation.Order.OrderDetails.➡
      Products[i].Price.ToString();
    items.Amount.currencyID = CurrencyCodeType.USD;
    items.Quantity = paypalinformation.Order.OrderDetails.Products[i].➡
      Quantity.ToString();

    items.Name = paypalinformation.Order.OrderDetails.Products[i].Name;
    items.Number = paypalinformation.Order.OrderDetails.Products[i].➡
      ProductID.ToString();

    itemArray.SetValue( items , i );
}

// set payment Details
DoDirectPmtReqType.DoDirectPaymentRequestDetails.PaymentDetails =➡
  new PaymentDetailsType();

DoDirectPmtReqType.DoDirectPaymentRequestDetails.PaymentDetails.➡
Custom = System.DateTime.Now.ToLongTimeString();

DoDirectPmtReqType.DoDirectPaymentRequestDetails.PaymentDetails.➡
  OrderDescription = "";

DoDirectPmtReqType.DoDirectPaymentRequestDetails.PaymentDetails.➡
  PaymentDetailsItem = new PaymentDetailsItemType[ itemArray.Length ];

DoDirectPmtReqType.DoDirectPaymentRequestDetails.PaymentDetails.➡
  PaymentDetailsItem = itemArray;

for ( int ii = 0 ; ii < itemArray.Length ; ii++ )
{ DoDirectPmtReqType.DoDirectPaymentRequestDetails.PaymentDetails.➡
    PaymentDetailsItem.SetValue( itemArray[ ii ] , ii );
}
```

How It Works

The previous code, as mentioned, will loop through the individual products that are eventually being paid for by the customer. As a result of the Orders class that is part of the PayPalInformation struct, there is an array of the Products class as part of the OrderDetails. From this array, the PaymentDetailsItemType is populated with each of the products that the user selected for purchase.

8. The next step in this exercise (prior to submitting the information to be officially processed) is to complete some additional details. These details, more specifically, are the details of the order and the shipping address of where the merchandise will be sent. Add the following code:

```
// Order summary.
DoDirectPmtReqType.DoDirectPaymentRequestDetails.PaymentDetails.➡
OrderTotal = new BasicAmountType();

DoDirectPmtReqType.DoDirectPaymentRequestDetails.PaymentDetails.➡
  OrderTotal.currencyID = CurrencyCodeType.USD;

DoDirectPmtReqType.DoDirectPaymentRequestDetails.PaymentDetails.➡
  OrderTotal.Value = paypalinformation.Order.OrderTotal.ToString();

DoDirectPmtReqType.DoDirectPaymentRequestDetails.PaymentDetails.➡
  ShippingTotal = new BasicAmountType();

DoDirectPmtReqType.DoDirectPaymentRequestDetails.PaymentDetails.➡
  ShippingTotal.currencyID = CurrencyCodeType.USD;

DoDirectPmtReqType.DoDirectPaymentRequestDetails.PaymentDetails.➡
  ShippingTotal.Value = paypalinformation.Order.ShippingTotal.ToString();

DoDirectPmtReqType.DoDirectPaymentRequestDetails.PaymentDetails.➡
  TaxTotal = new BasicAmountType();

DoDirectPmtReqType.DoDirectPaymentRequestDetails.PaymentDetails.➡
  TaxTotal.currencyID = CurrencyCodeType.USD;

DoDirectPmtReqType.DoDirectPaymentRequestDetails.PaymentDetails.➡
  TaxTotal.Value = paypalinformation.Order.Tax.ToString();

DoDirectPmtReqType.DoDirectPaymentRequestDetails.PaymentDetails.➡
  ItemTotal = new BasicAmountType();

DoDirectPmtReqType.DoDirectPaymentRequestDetails.PaymentDetails.➡
  ItemTotal.currencyID = CurrencyCodeType.USD;

DoDirectPmtReqType.DoDirectPaymentRequestDetails.PaymentDetails.➡
  ItemTotal.Value = paypalinformation.Order.SubTotal.ToString();

//set ship to address
```

```
DoDirectPmtReqType.DoDirectPaymentRequestDetails.PaymentDetails.➥
  ShipToAddress = new AddressType();

DoDirectPmtReqType.DoDirectPaymentRequestDetails.PaymentDetails.➥
  ShipToAddress.Name = paypalinformation.Order.EndUser.➥
  FirstName + " " + paypalinformation.Order.EndUser.LastName;

DoDirectPmtReqType.DoDirectPaymentRequestDetails.PaymentDetails.➥
  ShipToAddress.Street1 = paypalinformation.Order.➥
  ShippingAddress.AddressLine;

DoDirectPmtReqType.DoDirectPaymentRequestDetails.PaymentDetails.➥
  ShipToAddress.CityName = paypalinformation.Order.➥
  ShippingAddress.City;

DoDirectPmtReqType.DoDirectPaymentRequestDetails.PaymentDetails.➥
  ShipToAddress.StateOrProvince = paypalinformation.Order.➥
  ShippingAddress.State;

DoDirectPmtReqType.DoDirectPaymentRequestDetails.PaymentDetails.➥
  ShipToAddress.PostalCode = paypalinformation.Order.➥
  ShippingAddress.PostalCode;

DoDirectPmtReqType.DoDirectPaymentRequestDetails.PaymentDetails.➥
  ShipToAddress.CountrySpecified = true;

DoDirectPmtReqType.DoDirectPaymentRequestDetails.PaymentDetails.➥
    ShipToAddress.Country = CountryCodeType.US;

// credentials
DoDirectPaymentReq DoDPReq = new DoDirectPaymentReq();
DoDPReq.DoDirectPaymentRequest = DoDirectPmtReqType;
DoDPReq.DoDirectPaymentRequest.Version = "2.20";
```

How It Works

The previously added code follows the same methodology as in earlier steps. The summary details of the complete order are populated to the PayPal APIs along with the shipping address, all originating from the PayPalInformation struct that has been passed as a parameter into the method.

9. The final task to implement within the API code is to submit the actual request to the PayPal service. When accomplishing this task, you will have information returned to you that will provide the information about what the result was with the posted transaction. The code is as follows:

```
try
{
    //make call return response
    DoDirectPaymentResponseType DPRes = new DoDirectPaymentResponseType();
```

```
            DPRes = PPInterface.DoDirectPayment( DoDPReq );
            string errors = CheckForErrors( DPRes );

            if ( errors == string.Empty )
            {
                IsSubmissionSuccess = true;
                 paypalinformation.Order.TransactionID = DPRes.TransactionID;
            }
            else
            {
                IsSubmissionSuccess = false;
                SubmissionError = errors;
            }
    }
    catch ( Exception ex )
    {
        throw ex;
    }
```

How It Works

When examining the newly added code, you will notice that there is a new function that will validate the response that is returned. The name of this new function is CheckForErrors, and the response is passed in as a parameter. Therefore, you also need to add this function, as outlined in the following code:

```
private string CheckForErrors( AbstractResponseType abstractResponse )
{
    bool errorsExist = false;
    string errorList = "";

    // First, check if Ack is not Success
    if ( !abstractResponse.Ack.Equals( AckCodeType.Success ) )
    {
        errorsExist = true;
    }

    // Check for nothing in the Errors Collection
    if ( abstractResponse.Errors != null )
    {
        if ( abstractResponse.Errors.Length > 0 )
        {
            errorsExist = true;
            errorList = "ERROR: ";
            for ( int i = 0 ; i < abstractResponse.Errors.Length ; i++ )
            {
                errorList += abstractResponse.Errors[i].LongMessage +
        " (" +  abstractResponse.Errors[i].ErrorCode + ")" +
```

```
                    Environment.NewLine;
            }
        }
    }

    return errorList;
}
```

The CheckForErrors function examines the return response from the PayPal API payment submission to determine whether any errors have occurred. These types of errors are not errors that will cause the processing to fail completely, but rather to not complete the payment transaction. Some examples could be an invalid credit card number, the incorrect calculation of the order total, or perhaps the credit card being declined. In any case, a string of the errors will be returned from the function, and if everything is successful, the string returned will be that of an empty string.

Lastly, you also need to add some properties to the class. These are IsSubmissionSuccess and SubmissionError. Add the following to the code as well:

```
private bool _issubmissionsuccess;
private string _submissionerror;

public bool IsSubmissionSuccess
{
    get { return _issubmissionsuccess; }
    set { _issubmissionsuccess = value; }
}

public string SubmissionError
{
    get { return _submissionerror; }
    set { _submissionerror = value; }
}
```

After you add these properties and field names, you can address the actual posting of the payment to PayPal. The DoDirectPaymentResponseType class is instantiated, and the DoDirectPayment method of the PPInterface is called, which is the explicit call to submit the payment to the PayPal APIs. The result of this transmission is then checked for either the success or the failure of the direct payment. Upon the submission being returned, the IsSubmissionSuccess Boolean property is set to either true or false, and if there are any errors detected, the SubmissionError property is populated with the error message.

Now that you are done with this exercise, users have the ability to submit a direct payment to PayPal by means of the supplied APIs and web service. You'll now move along to the remaining sections of the chapter that will outline how to assemble the entire process.

Entering the Billing and Shipping Information

In the previous section, you implemented the code that you will utilize for processing the payments for the products that the customers purchase. I will now explain the necessary steps to implement and capture the information that will be populated with the PayPal APIs to ultimately accept the payment for the goods; see the next exercise.

Exercise: Obtaining the Billing and Shipping Information

In this exercise, you will pick up where you left off when the customer either registered for a new account or logged in to their existing account when they decided they were finished shopping for products. Therefore, they will arrive at the page that requires the shipping address, credit card information, and credit card billing address information. This exercise will explain all these tasks that you need to incorporate in your code. Follow these steps:

1. First add the CheckOut.aspx web form to the web project. As mentioned, this page will allow the user to enter their shipping address, credit card information, and credit card billing address information. After adding the new web form and associating it with the respective master page, add a GridView control to display the contents of the shopping cart along with the total cost of the items contained within the cart. The HTML code is as follows:

```
<%@ Page Language="C#" MasterPageFile="~/Main.master"
AutoEventWireup="true" CodeFile="CheckOut.aspx.cs"
Inherits="CheckOut" Title="Little Italy Vineyard | Check Out" %>

<asp:Content ID="Content1" ContentPlaceHolderID="contentplaceholderMain"
    Runat="Server">

    <table cellpadding="0" cellspacing="0" border="0"
        width="95%" align="center">
        <tr>
            <td><img src="images/spacer.gif" width="10" height="15" /></td>
            <td width="100%"></td>
            <td><img src="images/spacer.gif" width="10" height="1" /></td>
        </tr>
        <tr>
            <td></td>
            <td class="prodUnderlineBG" width="100%">
        <img src="images/spacer.gif"
            width="1" height="4" />
            </td>
            <td></td>
        </tr>
        <tr><td><img src="images/spacer.gif" width="1"
    height="3" /></td></tr>
        <tr>
            <td></td>
```

```
                        <td>
    <asp:GridView ID="gridviewShoppingCart" runat="server"
       AutoGenerateColumns="false" ShowHeader="True"
       Width="100%"
       DataKeyNames="Quantity,ShoppingCartID"
OnRowDataBound="gridviewShoppingCart_RowDataBound"
       BorderWidth="0px">
                            <Columns>


     <asp:TemplateField ItemStyle-Width="25%"
ItemStyle-HorizontalAlign="center"
HeaderStyle-HorizontalAlign="center" HeaderText="Product">
                                <ItemTemplate>
                                    <%# Eval("ProductName") %>
                                </ItemTemplate>
                            </asp:TemplateField>
          <asp:TemplateField ItemStyle-HorizontalAlign="center"
ItemStyle-Width="25%" HeaderStyle-HorizontalAlign="center"
HeaderText="Quantity">
                                <ItemTemplate>
                                    <%# Eval("Quantity") %>
                                </ItemTemplate>
                            </asp:TemplateField>
        <asp:TemplateField ItemStyle-HorizontalAlign="center"
ItemStyle-Width="25%" HeaderStyle-HorizontalAlign="center"
HeaderText="Unit Cost">
                                <ItemTemplate>
                                    <%# Eval( "UnitPrice" , "{0:c}" )%>
                                </ItemTemplate>
                            </asp:TemplateField>
 <asp:TemplateField ItemStyle-HorizontalAlign="center"
ItemStyle-Width="25%" HeaderStyle-HorizontalAlign="center"
HeaderText="Subtotal">
                                <ItemTemplate>
                                    <%# Eval( "TotalPrice" , "{0:c}" )%>
                                </ItemTemplate>
                            </asp:TemplateField>
                        </Columns>
                    </asp:GridView>
            </td>
            <td></td>
        </tr><tr><td>
<img src="images/spacer.gif" width="1" height="3" />
</td></tr>
    </table>
</asp:Content>
```

How It Works

The previous HTML code you added contains the GridView control named gridviewShoppingCart and has designated four individual columns for the grid. The columns that are data bound are ProductName, Quantity, UnitPrice, and TotalPrice. The last two columns are formatted to display a currency type.

2. Upon adding the GridView for displaying the shopping cart items, you need to add the text boxes for the shipping address. The following is the HTML code:

```
<tr>
    <td></td>
    <td class="prodUnderlineBG" width="100%">
      <img src="images/spacer.gif" width="1" height="1" />
      </td>
            <td></td>
        </tr>
        <tr>
            <td></td>
    <td class="prodUnderlineBG" width="100%">
<img src="images/spacer.gif" width="1"
 height="2" /></td>
            <td></td>
        </tr>
<tr><td><img src="images/spacer.gif" width="1"
height="5" />
</td></tr>
        <tr>
            <td></td>
            <td align="right">
                <table border="0" cellpadding="2" cellspacing="0">
                    <tr>
            <td><b>Subtotal:</b></td>
        <td><img src="images/spacer.gif" width="15"
          height="1" /></td>
        <td style="width: 69px;">
<asp:Label ID="labelSubTotal"
runat="server" Width="100%">
    </asp:Label></td>
        </tr>
        <tr>
<td><b>Tax:</b></td>
 <td></td>
<td><asp:Label ID="labelTax" runat="server"
Width="100%"></asp:Label></td>
                    </tr>
                </table>
            </td>
            <td></td>
        </tr>
```

```
    </table>
    <br />
<table border="0" cellpadding="0" cellspacing="2"
   width="90%" align="center">
        <tr>
            <td colspan="3"><b>Shipping Information</b></td>
        </tr>
        <tr>
            <td align="center" colspan="3">
<table cellpadding="0" cellspacing="0" border="0"
   width="100%">
                    <tr>
 <td width="100%" class="separatorBG">
<img src="images/spacer.gif" width="1" height="1"
border="0" /></td>
 <td>
<img src="images/textSeparatorRight.gif" />
</td>
        </tr>
        </table>
            </td>
        </tr>
   <tr><td>
<img src="images/spacer.gif" width="1"
    height="3" /></td></tr>
        <tr>
            <td><img src="images/spacer.gif" width="10" height="1" /></td>
            <td>First Name:</td>
       <td>
<asp:TextBox ID="textFirstname" runat="server"
CssClass="textField"></asp:TextBox></td>
        </tr>
        <tr>
            <td></td>
            <td>Last Name:</td>
<td>
<asp:TextBox ID="textLastname" runat="server"
CssClass="textField"></asp:TextBox></td>
        </tr>
        <tr>
            <td></td>
            <td>Address:</td>
<td><asp:TextBox ID="textAddress" runat="server"
CssClass="textField"></asp:TextBox>
<asp:RequiredFieldValidator ID="requiredAddress"
runat="server" Display="Dynamic"
EnableClientScript="False"
```

```
                ErrorMessage="Address Required."
                ControlToValidate="textAddress" Width="152px">
                </asp:RequiredFieldValidator></td>
                    </tr>
                    <tr>
                        <td></td>
                        <td>Address 2:</td>
                <td><asp:TextBox ID="textAddress2" runat="server"
                CssClass="textField"></asp:TextBox></td>
                    </tr>
                    <tr>
                        <td></td>
                        <td>City:</td>
                <td><asp:TextBox ID="textCity" runat="server"
                CssClass="textField"></asp:TextBox>
                <asp:RequiredFieldValidator ID="requiredCity"
                runat="server" Display="Dynamic"
                EnableClientScript="False"
                ErrorMessage="<br />
                City Required." ControlToValidate="textCity">
                </asp:RequiredFieldValidator></td>
                    </tr>
                    <tr>
                        <td></td>
                        <td>State:</td>
                <td><asp:TextBox ID="textState" runat="server"
                CssClass="textField"></asp:TextBox>
                <asp:RequiredFieldValidator ID="requiredState"
                runat="server" Display="Dynamic"
                EnableClientScript="False"
                ErrorMessage="State Required."
                ControlToValidate="textState">
                </asp:RequiredFieldValidator></td>
                    </tr>
                    <tr>
                        <td></td>
                        <td>Postal Code:</td>
                <td><asp:TextBox ID="textPostalCode" runat="server"
                CssClass="textField"></asp:TextBox>
                <asp:RequiredFieldValidator ID="requiredPostalCode"
                runat="server" Display="Dynamic"
                EnableClientScript="False" ErrorMessage="Postal Code Required."
                ControlToValidate="textPostalCode" Width="152px">
                </asp:RequiredFieldValidator></td>
                    </tr>
                    <tr>
                        <td></td>
```

```
            <td>Shipping Options:</td>
<td><asp:DropDownList ID="dropdownlistShippingOption"
runat="server" CssClass="textField">
    <asp:ListItem Value="5.99">Ground $5.99</asp:ListItem>
   <asp:ListItem Value="8.99">2nd Day $8.99</asp:ListItem>
    <asp:ListItem Value="10.99">Next Day Air $10.99</asp:ListItem>
</asp:DropDownList></td>
        </tr>
<tr><td><img src="images/spacer.gif" width="1" height="15" />
</td></tr>
```

How It Works

The previous HTML code adds the text boxes along with the necessary validation controls to capture the customer's name, their shipping address, and how they would like to have their merchandise shipped. More specifically, the customer will be given three options for the shipping method: ground, second day, or next day. These different shipping options and costs are hard-coded into the application for demonstration purposes. Depending on your needs, certain services can dynamically generate the shipping options and costs as a result of entering the originating postal code and the destination postal code.

3. After the shipping information, the next section you need is for the actual credit card information along with the billing address information. This will be followed by a CheckBox control that will serve as the terms for the customer to agree to that they are "of age" to make purchases from the winery. Therefore, add the following HTML code:

```
<tr>
            <td colspan="3"><b>Payment</b></td>
        </tr>
        <tr>
    <td align="center" colspan="3">
<table cellpadding="0" cellspacing="0"
    border="0"
        width="100%">
                    <tr>
    <td width="100%"
class="separatorBG">
<img src="images/spacer.gif"
width="1" height="1"
    border="0" /></td>
<td>
<img src="images/textSeparatorRight.gif" />
</td>
                    </tr>
                </table>
            </td>
        </tr>
 <tr><td>
<img src="images/spacer.gif" width="1" height="3" />
```

```
</td></tr>
        <tr>
            <td></td>
            <td>Credit Card:</td>
    <td><asp:DropDownList ID="dropdownlistCreditCardType"
runat="server" CssClass="textField">
<asp:ListItem Text="American Express" Value="Amex">
</asp:ListItem>
<asp:ListItem Text="Master Card" Value="MasterCard">
</asp:ListItem>
<asp:ListItem Text="Visa" Value="Visa"></asp:ListItem>
<asp:ListItem Text="Discover" Value="Discover">
</asp:ListItem>
                </asp:DropDownList></td>
        </tr>
        <tr>
            <td></td>
            <td>Credit Card Number:</td>
<td>
<asp:TextBox ID="textCreditCardNumber" runat="server"
CssClass="textField"></asp:TextBox>
<asp:RequiredFieldValidator ID="requireCreditCardNumber"
runat="server" Display="Dynamic"
EnableClientScript="False"
ErrorMessage="Credit Card Number Required."
ControlToValidate="textCreditCardNumber">
</asp:RequiredFieldValidator></td>
        </tr>
        <tr>
            <td></td>
            <td>Security Code:</td>
<td><asp:TextBox ID="textSecurityCode" runat="server"
CssClass="textField"></asp:TextBox>
<asp:RequiredFieldValidator ID="requireSecurityCode"
runat="server" Display="Dynamic"
EnableClientScript="False"
ErrorMessage="Security Code Required."
ControlToValidate="textSecurityCode">
</asp:RequiredFieldValidator></td>
        </tr>
        <tr>
            <td></td>
            <td>Expiration Date:</td>
<td><asp:DropDownList ID="dropdownlistExpMonth"
runat="server" CssClass="monthYear">
                    <asp:ListItem Text="01" Value="01"></asp:ListItem>
                    <asp:ListItem Text="02" Value="02"></asp:ListItem>
```

```
                    <asp:ListItem Text="03" Value="03"></asp:ListItem>
                    <asp:ListItem Text="04" Value="04"></asp:ListItem>
                    <asp:ListItem Text="05" Value="05"></asp:ListItem>
                    <asp:ListItem Text="06" Value="06"></asp:ListItem>
                    <asp:ListItem Text="07" Value="07"></asp:ListItem>
                    <asp:ListItem Text="08" Value="08"></asp:ListItem>
                    <asp:ListItem Text="09" Value="09"></asp:ListItem>
                    <asp:ListItem Text="10" Value="10"></asp:ListItem>
                    <asp:ListItem Text="11" Value="11"></asp:ListItem>
                    <asp:ListItem Text="12" Value="12"></asp:ListItem>
                </asp:DropDownList>
                <asp:DropDownList ID="dropdownlistExpYear" runat="server"
                    CssClass="monthYear">
                    <asp:ListItem Text="2006" Value="2006"></asp:ListItem>
                    <asp:ListItem Text="2007" Value="2007"></asp:ListItem>
                    <asp:ListItem Text="2008" Value="2008"></asp:ListItem>
                    <asp:ListItem Text="2009" Value="2009"></asp:ListItem>
                    <asp:ListItem Text="2010" Value="2010"></asp:ListItem>
                    <asp:ListItem Text="2011" Value="2011"></asp:ListItem>
                    <asp:ListItem Text="2012" Value="2012"></asp:ListItem>
                </asp:DropDownList></td>
        </tr>
    <tr><td>
<img src="images/spacer.gif" width="1"
    height="15" /></td></tr>
        <tr>
            <td colspan="3"><b>Billing Address</b></td>
        </tr>
        <tr>
            <td align="center" colspan="3">
        <table cellpadding="0" cellspacing="0" border="0"
        width="100%">
                    <tr>
                        <td width="100%" class="separatorBG">
<img src="images/spacer.gif"
    width="1" height="1" border="0" />
    </td>
                        <td><img src="images/textSeparatorRight.gif" /></td>
                    </tr>
                </table>
            </td>
        </tr>
<tr><td>
<img src="images/spacer.gif" width="1"
    height="3" /></td></tr>
        <tr>
            <td></td>
```

```
        <td>Address:</td>
<td><asp:TextBox ID="textBillingAddress" runat="server"
CssClass="textField"></asp:TextBox>
<asp:RequiredFieldValidator ID="requireBillingAddress"
runat="server" Display="Dynamic"
EnableClientScript="False"
ErrorMessage="Billing Address Required."
ControlToValidate="textBillingAddress">
</asp:RequiredFieldValidator></td>
        </tr>
        <tr>
            <td></td>
            <td>Address 2:</td>
<td><asp:TextBox ID="textBillingAddress2" runat="server"
CssClass="textField"></asp:TextBox></td>
        </tr>
        <tr>
            <td></td>
            <td>City:</td>
<td><asp:TextBox ID="textBillingCity" runat="server"
CssClass="textField"></asp:TextBox>
<asp:RequiredFieldValidator ID="requireBillingCity"
runat="server" Display="Dynamic"
EnableClientScript="False"
ErrorMessage="Billing City Required."
ControlToValidate="textBillingCity">
</asp:RequiredFieldValidator></td>
        </tr>
        <tr>
            <td></td>
            <td>State:</td>
<td>
<asp:TextBox ID="textBillingState" runat="server"
CssClass="textField"></asp:TextBox>
<asp:RequiredFieldValidator ID="requireBillingState"
runat="server" Display="Dynamic"
EnableClientScript="False"
ErrorMessage="Billing State Required."
ControlToValidate="textBillingState">
</asp:RequiredFieldValidator></td>
        </tr>
        <tr>
            <td></td>
            <td>Postal Code:</td>
<td><asp:TextBox ID="textBillingPostalCode"
runat="server" CssClass="textField"></asp:TextBox>
<asp:RequiredFieldValidator ID="requireBillingPostalCode"
```

```
runat="server" Display="Dynamic"
EnableClientScript="False"
ErrorMessage="Billing Postal Code Required."
ControlToValidate="textBillingPostalCode">
</asp:RequiredFieldValidator></td>
</tr>
<tr>
<td>
</td><td></td><td>
<asp:CheckBox ID="checkboxVerify" runat="server"
AutoPostBack="True"
OnCheckedChanged="checkboxVerify_CheckedChanged"
Text="I certify that I am of legal age to purchase."
Width="100%" /></td>
        </tr>
<tr><td>
<img src="images/spacer.gif" width="1"
   height="15" /></td></tr>
        <tr>
            <td colspan="2"></td>
            <td></td>
        </tr>
<tr><td><img src="images/spacer.gif" width="1"
   height="5" /></td></tr>
    </table>
```

How It Works

The previous HTML code allows the customer to add the billing address that is associated with their credit card. All validation is incorporated to ensure that all the necessary fields are populated with values. You will notice that the different types of credit cards and the expiration dates are hard-coded into the web form. This implementation is hard-coded for simplicity in the overall demonstration; however, it is certainly possible to generate this information dynamically if your requirements dictate this.

4. Now you'll turn your attention to the C# code portion of the web form. Here in the code, you will address a number of items, such as checking whether the connection is a secure connection. If it is not, you will redirect the user to the secure connection. Lastly, you will need to load the shopping cart information along with the information from the user who has just logged in. The code is as follows:

```
using System;
using System.Data;
using System.Configuration;
using System.Collections;
using System.Web;
using System.Web.Security;
using System.Web.UI;
using System.Web.UI.WebControls;
using System.Web.UI.WebControls.WebParts;
using System.Web.UI.HtmlControls;
```

```csharp
using LittleItalyVineyard.Common;
using LittleItalyVineyard.BusinessLogic;
using LittleItalyVineyard.Operational;

public partial class CheckOut : BasePage
{
    private decimal _totalcounter;

    protected void Page_Load( object sender , EventArgs e )
    {
        if ( ! Request.IsSecureConnection )
        {
            Response.Redirect( base.UrlBaseSSL );
        }

        if ( ! IsPostBack )
        {
            LoadShoppingCart();
            LoadInformation();
        }
    }

    private void LoadInformation()
    {
        textFirstname.Text = base.CurrentEndUser.FirstName;
        textLastname.Text = base.CurrentEndUser.LastName;

        // Populate shipping address information.
        textAddress.Text = base.CurrentEndUser.Address.AddressLine;
        textAddress2.Text = base.CurrentEndUser.Address.AddressLine2;
        textCity.Text = base.CurrentEndUser.Address.City;
        textState.Text = base.CurrentEndUser.Address.State;
        textPostalCode.Text = base.CurrentEndUser.Address.PostalCode;
    }

    protected void gridviewShoppingCart_RowDataBound( object sender , ➥
        GridViewRowEventArgs e )
    {
        if ( e.Row.RowType == DataControlRowType.DataRow )
        {
            _totalcounter += Convert.ToDecimal( DataBinder.Eval➥
                ( e.Row.DataItem , "TotalPrice" ) );
        }
```

```
            labelSubTotal.Text = string.Format( "{0:c}" , _totalcounter );
            labelTax.Text = string.Format( "{0:c}" , ➥
               ( CalculationManager.CalcSalesTax( _totalcounter ) ) );
    }

    private void LoadShoppingCart()
    {
            LittleItalyVineyard.Common.ShoppingCart shoppingcart = new➥
LittleItalyVineyard.Common.ShoppingCart();
            shoppingcart.CartGUID = Utilities.GetCartGUID();

            ProcessGetShoppingCart processgetcart =➥
              new ProcessGetShoppingCart();
            processgetcart.ShoppingCart = shoppingcart;

            try
            {
                processgetcart.Invoke();
                gridviewShoppingCart.DataSource = processgetcart.ResultSet;
                gridviewShoppingCart.DataBind();
            }
            catch
            {
                Response.Redirect( "ErrorPage.aspx" );
            }
    }
}
```

How It Works

As mentioned, within the page load event, the first task is to check whether the incoming request is a secure connection, or more specifically whether it uses the SSL certificate. The reason for this is because on this page, you will be asking the customer to enter their credit card information, and you certainly want this to be over the secure channel. You achieve this by first examining the request with the IsSecureConnection property. If this property is false, you will redirect the application to the secure connection. You will be able to determine the secure connection of the page by adding the following property to the BasePage in the App_Code folder:

```
public string UrlBaseSSL
{
    get { return Request.Url.AbsoluteUri.Replace➥
        ( @"http://" , @"https://" ); }
}
```

The UrlBaseSSL property in the BasePage is a read-only property that will return a string utilizing the request's Url.AbsoluteUri property. This will then utilize the Replace function to remove the unsecure specification with that of the secure specification.

■**Note** Depending on your development configuration, it is advisable to possibly disable or comment the redirection to the secure connection if an SSL certificate is not installed and configured. However, ensure that this is enabled when deploying to the production environment.

Lastly, you will finalize loading the page because the next request that will be handled will be a secure connection, thus moving along to load the shopping cart items as well as the name of the person by using the CurrentOrder class in the BasePage.

5. You now need to add the command button to take the information and direct users to a web page that will summarize the information they have entered. With that being said, finalize the HTML code by adding this segment:

```
<asp:Button ID="commandSubmit" runat="server"
Text="Continue" Width="136px"
OnClick="commandSubmit_Click"
CssClass="button" Enabled="False" />
```

6. With the HTML code in place, you will now add the respective C# code for the commandSubmit click event. However, notice that this command button's Enabled property is false. The reasoning for this is that you will prevent the user from continuing until they click the check box and subsequently agree that they are "of age" to make the purchase. The checkboxVerify control has the AutoPostBack property set to true so that when it's clicked, you will also enable or disable the commandSubmit button. Add the following code in the Checked Changed event:

```
protected void checkboxVerify_CheckedChanged( object sender , EventArgs e )
{
    commandSubmit.Enabled = checkboxVerify.Checked;
}

protected void commandSubmit_Click( object sender , EventArgs e )
{
    if ( IsValid )
    {
        base.CurrentEndUser.FirstName = textFirstname.Text;
        base.CurrentEndUser.LastName = textLastname.Text;
        base.CurrentEndUser.Address.AddressLine = textAddress.Text;
        base.CurrentEndUser.Address.AddressLine2 = textAddress2.Text;
        base.CurrentEndUser.Address.City = textCity.Text;
        base.CurrentEndUser.Address.State = textState.Text;
        base.CurrentEndUser.Address.PostalCode = textPostalCode.Text;

        base.CurrentOrder = new Orders();
```

```
    base.CurrentOrder.EndUser.FirstName = textFirstname.Text;
    base.CurrentOrder.EndUser.LastName = textLastname.Text;

    base.CurrentOrder.ShippingAddress.AddressLine = textAddress.Text;
    base.CurrentOrder.ShippingAddress.AddressLine2 =➥
        textAddress2.Text;
    base.CurrentOrder.ShippingAddress.City = textCity.Text;
    base.CurrentOrder.ShippingAddress.State = textState.Text;
    base.CurrentOrder.ShippingAddress.PostalCode =➥
        textPostalCode.Text;

base.CurrentOrder.CreditCard.CardType = ➥
        dropdownlistCreditCardType.SelectedItem.Value;
base.CurrentOrder.CreditCard.Number = textCreditCardNumber.Text;
base.CurrentOrder.CreditCard.SecurityCode = textSecurityCode.Text;
base.CurrentOrder.CreditCard.ExpMonth = int.Parse➥
    ( dropdownlistExpMonth.SelectedItem.Text );
base.CurrentOrder.CreditCard.ExpYear = int.Parse➥
    ( dropdownlistExpYear.SelectedItem.Text );

base.CurrentOrder.CreditCard.Address.AddressLine = ➥
    textBillingAddress.Text;
base.CurrentOrder.CreditCard.Address.AddressLine2 = ➥
    textBillingAddress2.Text;
base.CurrentOrder.CreditCard.Address.City = textBillingCity.Text;
base.CurrentOrder.CreditCard.Address.State =➥
  textBillingState.Text;
base.CurrentOrder.CreditCard.Address.PostalCode = ➥
   textBillingPostalCode.Text;

labelTax.Text = labelTax.Text.Replace( "$" , "" );
base.CurrentOrder.Tax = Convert.ToDecimal( labelTax.Text );

labelSubTotal.Text = labelSubTotal.Text.Replace( "$" , "" );
base.CurrentOrder.SubTotal = Convert.ToDecimal➥
  ( labelSubTotal.Text );

base.CurrentOrder.ShippingTotal = Convert.ToDecimal➥
  ( dropdownlistShippingOption.SelectedItem.Value );

Response.Redirect( "CheckOutConfirm.aspx" );
    }
}
```

How It Works

Within the click event for the button, the first item that is implemented is to check whether the request on the page is valid by using the IsValid property. This property will return true if all the validation on the page passes, and it will return false if there is a problem and will simply exit from the click event. Moving along, since on this page you will not be officially submitting the information for payment just yet, you will load the information into the CurrentOrder within the base page and redirect the user to the CheckOutConfirm.aspx page where they will be able to review what they have entered.

You have arrived at the end of another exercise, and now I will demonstrate how to process the actual payment.

Submitting the Payment

You have now implemented all the code to process the payment and all the web pages to capture the required information. The next step is to submit the actual payment to PayPal, determine whether the payment is successful, and then give the customer an acknowledgment of the payment. The following exercise shows how to do this.

Exercise: Submitting the Payment

You have now arrived at the section of the application where you collect all the information from the customer and submit it for processing to complete the credit card transaction. Follow these steps:

1. In the previous exercise, you added the web page that collects all the information that is required. You now need to add the web page that will display that information to allow the customer to confirm what they entered. To do so, you need to add a new web form named CheckOutConfrm.aspx and associate it with the appropriate master page to the web project. Upon adding the new web form, as with the prior web form, you will add the display of the shopping cart items, the respective totals, and the information that was entered by the user on the CheckOut.aspx web form:

```
<%@ Page Language="C#" MasterPageFile="~/Main.master"
AutoEventWireup="true" CodeFile="CheckOutConfirm.aspx.cs"
Inherits="CheckOutConfirm"
Title="Little Italy Vineyard | Check Out Confirmation" %>

<asp:Content ID="Content1" ContentPlaceHolderID="contentplaceholderMain"
Runat="Server">
<table cellpadding="0" cellspacing="0" border="0"
    width="95%" align="Center">
        <tr>
            <td><img src="images/spacer.gif" width="10" height="15" /></td>
            <td width="100%"></td>
            <td><img src="images/spacer.gif" width="10" height="1" /></td>
        </tr>

        <tr>
            <td></td>
```

```
<td class="prodUnderlineBG" width="100%">
<img src="images/spacer.gif" width="1" height="4" />
</td>
            <td></td>
        </tr>
<tr><td>
<img src="images/spacer.gif" width="1"
   height="3" /></td></tr>
        <tr>
            <td></td>
            <td>
<asp:GridView ID="gridviewShoppingCart" runat="server"
AutoGenerateColumns="false" ShowHeader="true"
Width="100%"
DataKeyNames="Quantity,ShoppingCartID,ProductID"
BorderWidth="0px">
<Columns>

<asp:TemplateField ItemStyle-Width="25%"
ItemStyle-HorizontalAlign="center"
HeaderStyle-HorizontalAlign="center"
HeaderText="Product">
<ItemTemplate>
<asp:Label id="labelProductName" runat="server"
Text='<%# Eval("ProductName") %>'>
</asp:Label>
    </ItemTemplate>
        </asp:TemplateField>
      <asp:TemplateField ItemStyle-HorizontalAlign="center"
ItemStyle-Width="25%" HeaderStyle-HorizontalAlign="center"
HeaderText="Quantity">
     <ItemTemplate>
      <asp:Label id="labelQuantity" runat="server"
Text='<%# Eval("Quantity") %>'></asp:Label>
                            </ItemTemplate>
                        </asp:TemplateField>
         <asp:TemplateField ItemStyle-HorizontalAlign="center"
ItemStyle-Width="25%" HeaderStyle-HorizontalAlign="center"
HeaderText="Unit Cost">
     <ItemTemplate>
 <asp:Label id="labelUnitPrice" runat="server"
Text='<%# Eval( "UnitPrice" , "{0:c}" )%>'>
</asp:Label>
         </ItemTemplate>
         </asp:TemplateField>
<asp:TemplateField ItemStyle-HorizontalAlign="center"
ItemStyle-Width="25%"
```

```
HeaderStyle-HorizontalAlign="center"
HeaderText="Subtotal">
  <ItemTemplate>
     <asp:Label id="labelTotalPrice" runat="server"
Text='<%# Eval( "TotalPrice" , "{0:c}" )%>'>
</asp:Label>
                             </ItemTemplate>
                        </asp:TemplateField>
                   </Columns>
              </asp:GridView>
          </td>
          <td></td>
      </tr>
<tr><td>
<img src="images/spacer.gif" width="1"
   height="3" /></td></tr>
      <tr>
          <td></td>
<td class="prodUnderlineBG" width="100%">
<img src="images/spacer.gif" width="1" height="1" />
</td>
<td></td>
      </tr>
      <tr>
          <td></td>
          <td class="prodUnderlineBG" width="100%">
<img src="images/spacer.gif" width="1" height="2" />
</td>
          <td></td>
      </tr>
<tr><td>
<img src="images/spacer.gif" width="1"
   height="5" /></td></tr>
      <tr>
          <td></td>
          <td align="right">
              <table border="0" cellpadding="2" cellspacing="0">
                  <tr>
                      <td><b>Subtotal:</b></td>
<td><img src="images/spacer.gif" width="15" height="1" />
</td>
<td style="width: 69px;">
<asp:Label ID="labelSubTotal" runat="server"
Width="100%"></asp:Label></td>
                  </tr>
                  <tr>
                      <td><b>Tax:</b></td>
```

```
                                    <td></td>
<td><asp:Label ID="labelTax" runat="server"
Width="100%">
</asp:Label></td>
                        </tr>
                        <tr>
                            <td><b>Shipping:</b></td>
                            <td></td>
<td><asp:Label ID="labelShippingCost" runat="server"
Width="100%"></asp:Label></td>
                        </tr>
<tr><td><img src="images/spacer.gif" width="1"
height="1" /></td></tr>
                        <tr>
<td colspan="3" class="prodUnderlineBG">
<img src="images/spacer.gif" width="1" height="2" />
</td>
</tr>
<tr><td><img src="images/spacer.gif" width="1"
height="1" /></td></tr>
<tr>
<td><b>Order Total:</b></td>
<td></td>
<td><asp:Label ID="labelTotal" runat="server"
Width="100%"></asp:Label></td>
     </tr>
                    </table>
            </td>
            <td></td>
        </tr>
    </table>
    <br />
<table border="0" cellpadding="0" cellspacing="3"
   width="90%" align="Center">
        <tr>
            <td colspan="3"><b>Shipping Information</b></td>
        </tr>
        <tr>
            <td align="center" colspan="3">
  <table cellpadding="0" cellspacing="0"
    border="0" width="100%">
                    <tr>
<td width="100%" class="separatorBG">
<img src="images/spacer.gif" width="1" height="1"
 border="0" /></td>
<td><img src="images/textSeparatorRight.gif" /></td>
     </tr>
```

```
                    </table>
                </td>
            </tr>
    <tr><td>
    <img src="images/spacer.gif" width="1"
        height="3" /></td></tr>
            <tr>
                <td><img src="images/spacer.gif" width="10" height="1" /></td>
                <td nowrap="nowrap">First Name:</td>
    <td width="60%">
    <asp:Label ID="labelFirstname"
    runat="server"></asp:Label></td>
            </tr>
            <tr>
                <td></td>
                <td nowrap="nowrap">Last Name:</td>
    <td>
    <asp:Label ID="labelLastname" runat="server">
    </asp:Label></td>
            </tr>
            <tr>
                <td></td>
                <td>Address:</td>
    <td>
    <asp:Label ID="labelAddress" runat="server">
    </asp:Label></td>
            </tr>
            <tr>
                <td></td>
                <td nowrap="nowrap">Address 2:</td>
    <td>
    <asp:Label ID="labelAddress2" runat="server">
    </asp:Label></td>
            </tr>
            <tr>
                <td></td>
                <td>City:</td>
                <td><asp:Label ID="labelCity" runat="server"></asp:Label></td>
            </tr>
            <tr>
                <td></td>
                <td>State:</td>
                <td><asp:Label ID="labelState" runat="server"></asp:Label></td>
            </tr>
            <tr>
                <td></td>
                <td nowrap="nowrap">Postal Code:</td>
```

```
<td>
<asp:Label ID="labelPostalCode" runat="server">
</asp:Label></td>
        </tr>
        <tr>
            <td></td>
            <td nowrap="nowrap">Shipping Options:</td>
            <td></td>
        </tr>
<tr><td>
<img src="images/spacer.gif" width="1"
height="15" /></td></tr>
        <tr>
            <td colspan="3"><b>Payment</b></td>
        </tr>
        <tr>
            <td align="center" colspan="3">
<table cellpadding="0" cellspacing="0"
    border="0" width="100%">
                    <tr>
<td width="100%" class="separatorBG">
<img src="images/spacer.gif" width="1"
height="1" border="0" /></td>
<td><img src="images/textSeparatorRight.gif" /></td>
</tr>
  </table>
            </td>
        </tr>
<tr><td>
<img src="images/spacer.gif" width="1"
  height="3" /></td></tr>
        <tr>
            <td></td>
            <td nowrap="nowrap">Credit Card:</td>
   <td><asp:Label ID="labelCreditCardType" runat="server">
</asp:Label></td>
        </tr>
        <tr>
            <td></td>
            <td nowrap="nowrap">Credit Card Number:</td>
<td><asp:Label ID="labelCreditCardNumber" runat="server">
</asp:Label></td>
        </tr>
        <tr>
            <td></td>
            <td nowrap="nowrap">Security Code:</td>
<td><asp:Label ID="labelCreditCardSecurityCode" runat="server">
```

```
    </asp:Label></td>
        </tr>
        <tr>
            <td></td>
            <td nowrap="nowrap">Expiration Date:</td>
<td><asp:Label ID="labelExpirationDate" runat="server">
</asp:Label></td>
        </tr>
<tr><td>
<img src="images/spacer.gif" width="1"
height="15" /></td></tr>
        <tr>
            <td colspan="3"><b>Billing Address</b></td>
        </tr>
        <tr>
            <td align="center" colspan="3">
 <table cellpadding="0" cellspacing="0"
border="0" width="100%">
                    <tr>
<td width="100%" class="separatorBG">
<img src="images/spacer.gif" width="1" height="1"
border="0" /></td>
    <td><img src="images/textSeparatorRight.gif" /></td>
                    </tr>
                </table>
            </td>
        </tr>
<tr><td>
<img src="images/spacer.gif" width="1"
height="3" /></td></tr>
        <tr>
            <td></td>
            <td>Address:</td>
<td><asp:Label ID="labelBillingAddress" runat="server">
</asp:Label></td>
        </tr>
        <tr>
            <td></td>
            <td nowrap="nowrap">Address 2:</td>
<td><asp:Label ID="labelBillingAddress2" runat="server">
</asp:Label></td>
        </tr>
        <tr>
            <td></td>
            <td>City:</td>
```

```
<td>
<asp:Label ID="labelBillingCity" runat="server">
</asp:Label></td>
        </tr>
        <tr>
            <td></td>
            <td>State:</td>
<td>
<asp:Label ID="labelBillingState" runat="server">
</asp:Label></td>
        </tr>
        <tr>
            <td></td>
            <td nowrap="nowrap">Postal Code:</td>
            <td><asp:Label ID="labelBillingPostalCode" runat="server">
</asp:Label></td>
        </tr>
<tr><td>
<img src="images/spacer.gif" width="1"
height="15" /></td></tr>
        <tr>
            <td colspan="3" align="right">
                <table cellpadding="3" cellspacing="0" border="0">
                    <tr>
<td><asp:Button ID="commandEdit" runat="server"
Text="Edit Information" Width="136px"
OnClick="commandEdit_Click"
CssClass="button" /></td>
<td><asp:Button ID="commandConfirm"
runat="server" OnClick="commandConfirm_Click"
Text="Confirm Payment" CssClass="button" />
</td>
        </tr>
      </table>
      </td>
        </tr>
        <tr><td><img src="images/spacer.gif" width="1" height="5" />
</td></tr>
    </table>
</asp:Content>
```

How It Works

In the previously added HTML code, you have a series of labels, after the display of the shopping cart display, that will be populated with the information that was entered by the user on the CheckOut.aspx web page.

2. You'll now turn attention to the C# code that will populate the information that the user can verify just prior to officially submitting their payment. Here's the code:

```csharp
using System;
using System.Data;
using System.Configuration;
using System.Collections;
using System.Web;
using System.Web.Security;
using System.Web.UI;
using System.Web.UI.WebControls;
using System.Web.UI.WebControls.WebParts;
using System.Web.UI.HtmlControls;

using LittleItalyVineyard.Common;
using LittleItalyVineyard.BusinessLogic;
using LittleItalyVineyard.Operational;

public partial class CheckOutConfirm : BasePage
{
    protected void Page_Load( object sender , EventArgs e )
    {
        if ( ! Request.IsSecureConnection )
        {
            Response.Redirect( base.UrlBaseSSL );
        }

        if ( ! IsPostBack )
        {
            LoadShoppingCart();
            LoadInformation();
        }
    }

    private void LoadInformation()
    {
        labelFirstname.Text = base.CurrentEndUser.FirstName;
        labelLastname.Text = base.CurrentEndUser.LastName;
        labelAddress.Text = base.CurrentEndUser.Address.AddressLine;
        labelAddress2.Text = base.CurrentEndUser.Address.AddressLine2;
        labelCity.Text = base.CurrentEndUser.Address.City;
        labelState.Text = base.CurrentEndUser.Address.State;
        labelPostalCode.Text = base.CurrentEndUser.Address.PostalCode;

        labelCreditCardType.Text = base.CurrentOrder.CreditCard.CardType;
        labelCreditCardNumber.Text = base.CurrentOrder.CreditCard.Number;
        labelCreditCardSecurityCode.Text = base.CurrentOrder.➥
            CreditCard.SecurityCode;
        labelExpirationDate.Text = base.CurrentOrder.CreditCard.➥
            ExpMonth. ToString() + " / " +
```

```
                base.CurrentOrder.CreditCard.➦
                ExpYear.ToString();

        labelBillingAddress.Text = base.CurrentOrder.CreditCard.➦
            Address.AddressLine;
        labelBillingAddress2.Text = base.CurrentOrder.CreditCard.➦
            Address.AddressLine2;
        labelBillingCity.Text = base.CurrentOrder.CreditCard.➦
            Address.City;
        labelBillingState.Text = base.CurrentOrder.CreditCard.➦
            Address.State;
        labelBillingPostalCode.Text = base.CurrentOrder.CreditCard.➦
            Address.PostalCode;

        labelSubTotal.Text = string.Format( "{0:c}" , ➦
            base.CurrentOrder.SubTotal );
        labelTax.Text = string.Format( "{0:c}" , base.CurrentOrder.Tax );
        labelShippingCost.Text = string.Format( "{0:c}" , ➦
            base.CurrentOrder.ShippingTotal );

        labelTotal.Text = string.Format( "{0:c}" , Convert.ToDecimal➦
            ( base.CurrentOrder.SubTotal ) +
                base.CurrentOrder.Tax +
                base.CurrentOrder.ShippingTotal );
    }

private void LoadShoppingCart()
{
        LittleItalyVineyard.Common.ShoppingCart shoppingcart =➦
            new LittleItalyVineyard.Common.ShoppingCart();
        shoppingcart.CartGUID = Utilities.GetCartGUID();

        ProcessGetShoppingCart processgetcart =➦
         new ProcessGetShoppingCart();
        processgetcart.ShoppingCart = shoppingcart;

        try
        {
            processgetcart.Invoke();
            gridviewShoppingCart.DataSource = processgetcart.ResultSet;
            gridviewShoppingCart.DataBind();
        }
        catch
        {
            Response.Redirect( "ErrorPage.aspx" );
        }
    }
```

How It Works

The first task is to check whether the incoming request is being processed over a secure channel. If it is not, the request will be redirected to the same location but with the secure connection. As mentioned, during your development process, you might want to disable this code or comment it out because you will probably not have an SSL certificate installed on your development machine. The remaining code is similar to the code you added in previous exercises. You will load the shopping cart items and set the labels for read-only display to that of the BasePage's CurrentOrder class, which in fact is of the common type Orders.

3. After the information is displayed for the user to verify, you will present the user with two options. They will be able to navigate to the CheckOut.aspx page or officially submit the information for payment. The code is as follows:

```
protected void commandConfirm_Click( object sender , EventArgs e )
{
    Product[] prods = new Product[ gridviewShoppingCart.Rows.Count ];

    foreach ( GridViewRow grow in gridviewShoppingCart.Rows )
    {
        if ( grow.RowType == DataControlRowType.DataRow )
        {
            Product prod = new Product();

            DataKey data = gridviewShoppingCart.DataKeys➥
              [ grow.DataItemIndex ];

            prod.ProductID = int.Parse➥
              ( data.Values["ProductID"].ToString() );

            Label labelProductName = ( Label ) grow.FindControl➥
              ( "labelProductName" );
            prod.Name = labelProductName.Text;

            Label labelQuantity = (Label ) grow.FindControl➥
              ( "labelQuantity" );
            prod.Quantity = int.Parse( labelQuantity.Text );

            Label labelUnitPrice = (Label ) grow.FindControl➥
              ( "labelUnitPrice" );
            labelUnitPrice.Text = labelUnitPrice.Text.Replace➥
              ( "$" , "" );
            prod.Price = Convert.ToDecimal( labelUnitPrice.Text );

            prods.SetValue( prod , grow.DataItemIndex );
        }
    }

    CurrentOrder.OrderDetails.Products = prods;
```

```
        // Order Total.
        labelTotal.Text = labelTotal.Text.Replace( "$" , "" );
        CurrentOrder.OrderTotal = Convert.ToDecimal( labelTotal.Text );
        CurrentOrder.EndUserID = CurrentEndUser.EndUserID;

        string URL = "CheckOutReceipt.aspx";
        Response.Redirect( "Loading.aspx?Page=" + URL );
}

protected void commandEdit_Click( object sender , EventArgs e )
{
    // Navigate back to the previous page.
    Response.Redirect( "CheckOut.aspx" );
}
```

How It Works

Redirecting the user to edit their information is quite simple. It is a standard Response.Redirect call to the CheckOut.aspx web form. Now, the more detailed and extensive code to actually submit the payment to PayPal is contained in the Confirm button click event. This code begins by declaring the common class, Product, as an array, which is set to the gridviewShoppingCart total rows. These are all the products that the customer is going to purchase. You are using an array so the payment process can be dynamic and the code can handle one product or many products via the array. You then populate the product array with the details of each product by looping through each of the GridView rows and finally officially adding each product with the details to the array by using the SetValue method.

At the conclusion of looping through the GridView rows, you will take the BasePage's CurrentOrder class and then the OrderDetails Product array and set it to the product array that was initially declared. Finally, the total and EndUserID will be populated, and then the code will redirect the process to the Loading.aspx web form, which I will discuss in more detail in the next exercise step.

4. As a result of the payment information being sent via a web service to the PayPal processing system, the request may take several seconds and thus take the web page a little while to complete loading. Since this is the case, you will implement a page that will inform the user that the payment is currently being processed. When the payment submission is complete, you can redirect the user to a page that indicates this. Given this information, add a new web form named Loading.aspx, but don't associate it with a master page since you do not want to display any links that could potentially allow the user to navigate to another location. After adding the Loading.aspx web form, add the following HTML code as well as some JavaScript:

```
<%@ Page Language="C#"  AutoEventWireup="true"
CodeFile="Loading.aspx.cs"
Inherits="Loading"
Title="Untitled Page" %>

<html>
<head id="Head1" runat="server">
    <title>Processing....</title>
```

```
        <meta http-equiv="Content-Style-Type" content="text/css" />
        <link href="Css/style.css" type="text/css" rel="stylesheet" />

<script language="javascript">
    var LoopCounter = 1;
    var MaxLoop = 5;
    var IntervalId;

    function BeginLoad()
    {
      location.href = "<%= Request.QueryString["Page"]%>";
      IntervalId = window.setInterval("LoopCounter=UpdateProgress➥
        (LoopCounter, MaxLoop)", 500);
    }

    function EndLoad()
    {
       window.clearInterval(IntervalId);
       Progress.innerText = "Page Loaded -- Not Transferring";
    }

    function UpdateProgress(LoopCounter, MaxLoops)
    {
      LoopCounter += 1;

      if (LoopCounter <= MaxLoops)
      {
        Progress.innerText += ".";
        return LoopCounter;
      }
      else
      {
         Progress.innerText = "";
         return 1;
      }
    }
  }
</script>
</head>
<body onload="BeginLoad()" onunload="EndLoad()">
    <form id="form1" runat="server">
        <table width="100%" height="100%" border="0" cellpadding="0"
cellspacing="0"
style="background-image:
url(images/til_1.jpg);">
            <tr>
                <td> </td>
                <td width="490" align="left" valign="top">
```

```
<table width="490" border="0" cellspacing="0"
   cellpadding="0">
                        <tr>
                            <td width="10"> </td>
                            <td width="470" align="left" valign="top">
<table width="470" height="100%" border="0"
cellpadding="0" cellspacing="0">
<tr>
    <td height="164" align="left"
valign="top" background="images/top_1.jpg">
<div style="padding-left: 156px;
padding-top: 69px">
<img src="images/logo.jpg"
width="159"
height="36" border="0"></div>
        </td>
          </tr>
          <tr>
        <td height="172" align="right"
valign="top" background="images/back_1.jpg">
<div style="padding-left:
0px; padding-top: 14px; padding-right: 23px;
padding-bottom: 0px">
      </div>
            </td>
            </tr>
            <tr>
<td height="100%" align="left" valign="top">
<table width="100%" height="100%"
border="0" cellpadding="0" cellspacing="0"
background="images/rep_3.jpg">
    <tr align="left" valign="top">
    <td background="images/rep_left.jpg"
style="width: 10px">
   <img src="images/rep_left.jpg"
width="10" height="1"></td>
     <td height="100%">
    <table width="450" height="100%" border="0"
cellpadding="0" cellspacing="0">
                 <tr align="left" valign="top">
 <td background="images/rep_line.jpg"
bgcolor-"#F3E9BF"
style="background-repeat: repeat-y;
   background-position: top left;">
      <br />
    <br />
      <br />
      <table border="0" cellpadding="0"
```

```
cellspacing="0" width="99%" height="99%"
align="center" valign="middle">
<tr>
<td align="center" valign="middle">
<font color="Red" size="3">
<span id="Message">
<img src="Images/pleasewait.gif" /><br />
<br />
Processing Payment -- Please Wait
<span id="Progress" style="WIDTH:25px;TEXT-ALIGN:left">
</span>
<br />
<br />
<br />
<br />
</span>
</font>
</td>
</tr>
</table>
</td>
</tr>
</table>
    </td>
 <td width="10"
background="images/rep_right.jpg">
<img src="images/rep_right.jpg"
width="10" height="1"></td>
            </tr>
          <tr>
<td colspan="3" valign="top" align="center">
<img src="images/bottom_1.jpg" width="470"
height="23"></td>
        </tr>
        </table>
      </td>
        </tr>
</table>
</td>
<td></td>
    </tr>
</table>
                </td>
                <td> </td>
            </tr>
            <tr>
                <td></td>
                <td height="100%">
```

```
<table cellpadding="0" cellspacing="0" border="0"
width="100%" height="100%">
                        <tr>
<td style="height: 100%; background-image:
url(images/rep_bot.jpg); background-repeat: repeat-y;
background-position: center;"></td>
                        </tr>
                    </table>
                </td>
                <td></td>
            </tr>
        </table>
    </form>
</body>
</html>
```

How It Works

The HTML code you added is fairly straightforward. There is an animated GIF image, the text "Processing Payment – Please Wait," and most of the HTML from the master page with the exception of any of the links. When you examine the JavaScript, you'll see that this is where it gets quite interesting. The JavaScript contains three functions: BeginLoad, EndLoad, and UpdateProgress. The BeginLoad method, which is subsequently set within the onload method of the body of the page, initially sets the web page that will be the final destination by using the Request.QueryString. After determining the destination page, this will cause the delay when loading the destination page. During the submission, the UpdateProgress method will be called and subsequently write a period to the text, giving an animation effect. Finally, when the payment submission is returned and the destination page is completely loaded, the page will be redirected to the destination and is able to be displayed.

5. No C# code accompanies the Loading.aspx web form, but now you need to add the CheckOutReceipt.aspx web form and associate it with the respective master page. In this HTML, add two separate panels that initially have the Visible property to false. One panel is for a successful payment submission, and the other is for a failure. Let's look at the HTML code:

```
<%@ Page Language="C#" MasterPageFile="~/Main.master"
AutoEventWireup="true" CodeFile="CheckOutReceipt.aspx.cs"
Inherits="CheckOutReceipt"
Title="Little Italy Vineyard | Check Out Receipt" %>

<asp:Content ID="Content1" ContentPlaceHolderID="contentplaceholderMain"
Runat="Server">
     <br />
    <table border-"0" cellpadding-"0" cellspacing-"0" width="100%">
        <tr>
            <td width="100%">
    <asp:Panel ID="panelSuccess" runat="server" Height="100%"
     Visible="False" Width="100%">
        <table border="0" cellpadding="0" cellspacing="0"
```

```
            width="100%">
                            <tr>
                                <td width="25%" style="text-align: center">
                                    <img src="Images/Success.gif" /></td>
                                <td width="75%">
    <strong>Your order has been processed
successfully. 
                                    <br />
                                    <br />
                                    Little Italy Vineyard thanks
                                    you for your business.</strong></td>
                            </tr>
                            <tr>
                                <td width="25%">
                Transaction ID:</td>
                                <td width="75%">
        <asp:Label ID="labelTransactionID"
runat="server"></asp:Label></td>
                            </tr>
                            <tr>
                                <td width="25%">
                Order Total:</td>
                                <td width="75%">
            <asp:Label ID="labelOrderTotal"
runat="server"></asp:Label></td>
                            </tr>
                        </table>
                         </asp:Panel>
                </td>
            </tr>
            <tr>
                <td width="100%">
<asp:Panel ID="panelFailure" runat="server" Height="100%"
Visible="False" Width="100%">
    <table border="0" cellpadding="0" cellspacing="0"
width="100%">
                            <tr>
                                <td width="25%" style="text-align: center">
                                    <img src="Images/error.gif" /></td>
                                <td width="75%">
    <strong>We apologize for the inconvenience,
but an error occurred with the payment of
                                    your order.<br />
                                    <br />
            Error Message:</strong></td>
                            </tr>
                            <tr>
```

```
                        <td>
                        </td>
                        <td width="25%">
<asp:Label ID="labelErrorMessage"
runat="server"></asp:Label></td>
                        </tr>
                    </table>
                </asp:Panel>
            </td>
        </tr>
    </table>
    <br />
</asp:Content>
```

How It Works

As mentioned, there are two panels: panelSuccess and panelFailure. You set both the Visible properties to false. The panelSuccess panel has a small image of a check mark and some text informing the user that the payment has been successful; it also displays the transaction ID and the order total. The panelFailure panel has a small image of a red *X* and subsequently tells the user that the payment has failed and why it failed.

6. You now need to add the associated C# code to the CheckOutReceipt.aspx web form that will officially submit the order and payment information to PayPal. Upon the order and payment information being submitted, the respective panel will be set to visible if the payment is successful or if there is a failure:

```
using System;
using System.Data;
using System.Configuration;
using System.Collections;
using System.Web;
using System.Web.Security;
using System.Web.UI;
using System.Web.UI.WebControls;
using System.Web.UI.WebControls.WebParts;
using System.Web.UI.HtmlControls;

using LittleItalyVineyard.Operational;
using LittleItalyVineyard.BusinessLogic;

public partial class CheckOutReceipt : BasePage
{
    protected void Page_Load( object sender , EventArgs e )
    {
        if ( !IsPostBack )
        {
            SubmitOrder();
        }
```

```
        }

        private void SubmitOrder()
        {
            PayPalManager paypal = new PayPalManager();
            PayPalInformation _paypalinformation = new PayPalInformation();

            _paypalinformation.Order = CurrentOrder;
            paypal.ProcessDirectPayment( _paypalinformation );

            if ( paypal.IsSubmissionSuccess )
            {
                panelSuccess.Visible = true;
                labelOrderTotal.Text = string.Format( "{0:c}" , ➥
                    _paypalinformation.Order.OrderTotal );
                labelTransactionID.Text = CurrentOrder.TransactionID;
            }
            else
            {
                panelFailure.Visible = true;
                labelErrorMessage.Text = paypal.SubmissionError;
            }
        }
    }
}
```

How It Works

The code begins with the SubmitOrder method where it instantiates the PayPalManager class from the Operational namespace along with the PayPalInformation struct. The Order class from the struct is subsequently populated with the CurrentOrder of the base page, and then the ProcessDirectPayment method is called from the PayPalManager class, passing in the PayPalInformation struct as its parameter. This line of code is what will take a few seconds to process. Upon the completion of the submission, the IsSubmissionSuccess property will be checked, and if true, the paneSuccess will be shown along with the transaction ID and order total. If the IsSubmissionSuccess property is false, the panelFailure will be shown, and the SubmissionError property will be displayed along with the reason for the payment failure.

Now that you have completed the exercise to accept a payment for the merchandise, you have one final step to add to the overall process.

Finalizing the Payment

You have completed the functionality to submit and process a payment to PayPal. There is a final piece to add to the payment submission process—you need to add the completed order to the database if in fact the payment is successful.

You'll implement each of these remaining features in the forthcoming exercises.

Exercise: Finalizing the Order

This exercise outlines all the steps to now insert the order and the order details into the database in the form of a transaction. Follow these steps:

1. Begin at the database level to add two stored procedures, Order_Insert and OrderDetails_Insert:

```
CREATE PROCEDURE Order_Insert

@EndUserID int,
@TransactionID nvarchar(50)

AS

INSERT INTO Orders
(EndUserID,
TransactionID)
VALUES
(@EndUserID,
@TransactionID)

SELECT @@IDENTITY

CREATE PROCEDURE OrderDetails_Insert

@OrderID int,
@ProductID int,
@Quantity int

AS

INSERT INTO OrderDetails
(OrderID,
ProductID,
Quantity)
VALUES
(@OrderID,
@ProductID,
@Quantity)
```

2. Now add each of the stored procedure names to the StoredProcedure Name enumeration. You then need to add two classes to the Insert folder in the LittleItalyVineyard.DataAccess class library. The two classes are OrderInsertData and OrderDetailsInsertData:

```
using System;
using System.Collections.Generic;
using System.Text;
```

```csharp
using System.Data;
using System.Data.SqlClient;

using LittleItalyVineyard.Common;

namespace LittleItalyVineyard.DataAccess.Insert
{
    public class OrderInsertData : DataAccessBase
    {
        private Orders _orders;
        private OrderInsertDataParameters _orderinsertdataparameters;

        public OrderInsertData()
        {
            StoredProcedureName = StoredProcedure.Name.➥
              Order_Insert.ToString();
        }

        public void Add( SqlTransaction transaction )
        {
            _orderinsertdataparameters =➥
             new OrderInsertDataParameters( Orders );
            DataBaseHelper dbhelper = new DataBaseHelper➥
             ( StoredProcedureName );
            object id = dbhelper.RunScalar( transaction , ➥
             _orderinsertdataparameters.Parameters );
            Orders.OrderID = int.Parse( id.ToString() );
        }

    public Orders Orders
    {
        get { return _orders; }
         set { _orders = value; }
      }
    }

    public class OrderInsertDataParameters
    {
        private Orders _orders;
        private SqlParameter[] _parameters;

        public OrderInsertDataParameters(Orders orders )
        {
            Orders = orders;
            Build();
        }
```

```
            private void Build()
            {
                SqlParameter[] parameters =
                {
                    new SqlParameter( "@EndUserID" , ➥
                        Orders.EndUserID ) ,
                    new SqlParameter( "@TransactionID" , ➥
                        Orders.TransactionID )
                };

                Parameters = parameters;
            }

            public Orders Orders
            {
                get { return _orders; }
                set { _orders = value; }
            }

            public SqlParameter[] Parameters
            {
                get { return _parameters; }
                set { _parameters = value; }
            }
        }
    }
}

using System;
using System.Collections.Generic;
using System.Text;
using System.Data;
using System.Data.SqlClient;

using LittleItalyVineyard.Common;

namespace LittleItalyVineyard.DataAccess.Insert
{
    public class OrderDetailsInsertData : DataAccessBase
    {
        private OrderDetails _orderdetails;
        private OrderDetailsInsertDataParameters ➥
            _orderdetailsinsertdataparameters;

        public OrderDetailsInsertData()
        {
            OrderDetails = new OrderDetails();
            StoredProcedureName = StoredProcedure.Name.➥
```

```csharp
            OrderDetails_Insert.ToString();
    }

    public void Add( SqlTransaction transaction )
    {
        _orderdetailsinsertdataparameters = new➥
            OrderDetailsInsertDataParameters➥
              ( OrderDetails );
          DataBaseHelper dbhelper = new DataBaseHelper➥
            ( StoredProcedureName );
          dbhelper.Run( transaction , ➥
          _orderdetailsinsertdataparameters.Parameters );
     }

     public OrderDetails OrderDetails
     {
       get { return _orderdetails; }
       set { _orderdetails = value; }
     }
}

public class OrderDetailsInsertDataParameters
{
    private OrderDetails _orderdetails;
    private SqlParameter[] _parameters;

    public OrderDetailsInsertDataParameters➥
      ( OrderDetails orderdetails )
    {
      OrderDetails = orderdetails;
      Build();
    }

    private void Build()
    {
      SqlParameter[] parameters =
      {
        new SqlParameter( "@OrderID" , OrderDetails.OrderID ) ,
        new SqlParameter( "@ProductID" , OrderDetails.ProductID ) ,
        new SqlParameter( "@Quantity" , OrderDetails.Quantity )
      };

      Parameters = parameters;
    }

    public OrderDetails OrderDetails
    {
```

```
        get { return _orderdetails; }
        set { _orderdetails = value; }
      }

    public SqlParameter[] Parameters
    {
        get { return _parameters; }
        set { _parameters = value; }
      }
    }
}
```

How It Works

The two classes you added are similar to the others in the data access layer. At the same time, they have a few slight differences. The first difference is with the Add method; it has a parameter of a transaction that is passed in. In the next step of the exercise, the reasons for this will become more apparent.

3. While you are still within the data access layer of the application, you now need to add a new folder named Transaction, which will subsequently create a new namespace. In this new folder, you will add two new classes, TransactionBase and OrderInsertTransaction. Let's first look at the TransactionBase class and its code and then the OrderInsertTransaction:

```
using System;
using System.Collections.Generic;
using System.Text;
using System.Configuration;
using System.Data;
using System.Data.SqlClient;

namespace LittleItalyVineyard.DataAccess.Transaction
{
    public class TransactionBase
    {
        protected SqlTransaction transaction = null;
        protected SqlConnection connection = null;
        protected SqlCommand command = null;

        public TransactionBase()
        {
            connection = new SqlConnection( ConfigurationManager.➡
              ConnectionStrings[ "SQLCONN" ].ToString() );
            connection.Open();
            command = connection.CreateCommand();
        }
    }
}
```

```csharp
using System;
using System.Collections.Generic;
using System.Text;

using LittleItalyVineyard.Common;
using LittleItalyVineyard.DataAccess.Insert;

namespace LittleItalyVineyard.DataAccess.Transaction
{
    public class OrderInsertTransaction : TransactionBase
    {
      public OrderInsertTransaction()
      {

      }

     public void Begin( Orders orders )
     {

       command = connection.CreateCommand();
       transaction = connection.BeginTransaction( "OrderInsert" );
       command.Connection = connection;
       command.Transaction = transaction;

       OrderInsertData orderadd = new OrderInsertData();
       OrderDetailsInsertData orderdetailsadd =➡
           new OrderDetailsInsertData();

      try
      {
        // Insert Order.
        orderadd.Orders = orders;
        orderadd.Add( transaction );

        // Insert Order Details.
        for ( int i = 0 ; i < orders.OrderDetails.Products.Length ; i++ )
        {
           orderdetailsadd.OrderDetails.OrderID = orders.OrderID;
           orderdetailsadd.OrderDetails.ProductID =➡
             orders.OrderDetails.Products[i].➡
             ProductID;
           orderdetailsadd.OrderDetails.Quantity =➡
             orders.OrderDetails.Products[i].➡
             Quantity;

           orderdetailsadd.Add( transaction );
        }
```

```
    transaction.Commit();
    }
    catch ( Exception ex )
    {
       transaction.Rollback( "OrderInsert" );
       throw ex;
    }
   }
  }
}
```

How It Works

You first added the TransactionBase class that establishes the connection within the transaction. After this is completed, you then implemented the OrderInsertTransaction, which will then inherit the TransactionBase class. The Begin method is then added, which will take an Orders class as a parameter. Immediately the transaction is set up by naming the transaction OrderInsert, and then it adds the order to the database via the transaction. After the order is inserted, an order detail record is inserted for each product that the OrderDetail class contains. All this activity is wrapped within a try/catch statement, and if any activity is not successful, the transaction is rolled back. If all is successful, the transaction is committed.

4. The next class to be added is within the business logic layer. Specifically, add a class named ProcessAddOrder that has the following code:

```csharp
using System;
using System.Collections.Generic;
using System.Text;

using LittleItalyVineyard.Common;
using LittleItalyVineyard.DataAccess.Transaction;

namespace LittleItalyVineyard.BusinessLogic
{
    public class ProcessAddOrder : IBusinessLogic
    {
       private Orders _orders;

       public ProcessAddOrder()
       {

       }

       public void Invoke()
       {
          OrderInsertTransaction ordertransaction =➥
            new OrderInsertTransaction();
          ordertransaction.Begin( this.Orders );
       }
```

```
        public Orders Orders
        {
            get { return _orders; }
            set { _orders = value; }
        }
    }
}
```

How It Works

The class added to the business logic layer is similar to the other business logic classes; the only difference is that the transaction class in the data access layer will be called upon. The Order class will subsequently be passed into the Begin method.

5. Now return to the CheckOutReceipt.aspx web form. Add the following code within the section that will occur only if there is a successful payment processed:

```
private void SubmitOrder()
{
    PayPalManager paypal = new PayPalManager();
    PayPalInformation _paypalinformation = new PayPalInformation();

    _paypalinformation.Order = CurrentOrder;
    paypal.ProcessDirectPayment( _paypalinformation );

    // If payment successful - add Order to database and display.
    if ( paypal.IsSubmissionSuccess )
    {
        panelSuccess.Visible = true;
        labelOrderTotal.Text = string.Format( "{0:c}" , ➥
            _paypalinformation.Order.OrderTotal );
        labelTransactionID.Text = CurrentOrder.TransactionID;

        ProcessAddOrder addorder = new ProcessAddOrder();
        addorder.Orders = CurrentOrder;
        try
        {
            addorder.Invoke();
        }
        catch
        {
            Response.Redirect( "ErrorPage.aspx" );
        }
    }
    else
    {
        panelFailure.Visible = true;
        labelErrorMessage.Text = paypal.SubmissionError;
    }
}
```

How It Works

The previous code has expanded upon the code you added earlier in the chapter. The new code to add the order to the database contains the ProcessAddOrder class and sets the base page CurrentOrder object to the ProcessAddOrder's Orders property. Lastly, the Invoke method will be called and will execute the entire process to add the order and the associated order details to the database.

You have finished the final exercise in this chapter, so you now have code in place to populate your database with the information from the customer's order.

Summary

Congratulations! You have enabled your application to accept payments for the products your client is selling. This is a major accomplishment in the development process. Now that customers have the ability to purchase products from your client's company, you need to finalize the overall development and add sections where the administrator cannot only manage the products for sale but can also process the orders. In addition to the administrator's needs, you will also incorporate the customer account and allow users to view the status of the orders they have placed. You will also give them the ability to log in and check the status of the order at any time.

CHAPTER 21

■ ■ ■

Creating the Administrator's Control Panel

You're approaching the finish line of the core development of your application—you have arrived at the administrator's control panel. This control panel is the password-protected segment of the application where the owners of Little Italy Vineyards (or anyone who has been given permission) can alter content of the website. The administrator's control panel will play a vital role in the overall maintenance of the application. In this chapter, I'll cover the following functionality:

- Setting up the administrator's area

- Creating the administrator login

- Creating a new product

- Updating an existing product

- Viewing the products in the catalog

Setting Up the Control Panel

The first task to address as you implement a complete administrator's control panel is to return to the Visual Studio 2005 solution and add the necessary files and configurations. The following exercise shows how to perform the setup.

Exercise: Performing the Visual Studio 2005 Setup

In this exercise, you will perform the necessary setup work for the application to have a secure administrator's control panel. Follow these steps:

1. You will need to add a new physical directory to your web project. To accomplish this, right-click the web project, choose to add a new folder, and name the folder **Admin**, as shown in Figure 21-1.

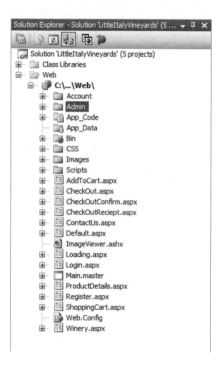

Figure 21-1. *The Admin folder*

2. Now that you have added the Admin folder to the web project, you have to specify that this new directory is where the administrator section will be and secure it with forms authentication. You'll add this configuration to the Web.config file. Therefore, open the Web.config file, and add the following in the System.Web tags:

```
<authentication mode="Forms">
    <forms name="LITTLEITALYAUTH" loginUrl="~/Admin/Login.aspx"
      protection="All" timeout="120" path="/">
    </forms>
</authentication>
<authorization>
    <allow users="*"/>
</authorization>
```

How It Works

By adding the previous authentication to the web project's Web.config file, you are enabling the security in the Admin directory. At the same time that you are adding security to the Admin folder, you also are specifying that you are opening the root of the web project to anonymous users by specifying the <allow users="*"/> element.

3. You have the necessary configurations specified in the Web.config file, so now you need to return to the Admin folder and begin building upon it. The first item to add to the Admin directory is a new Web.config file. To accomplish this, right-click the Admin folder, and choose to add a new item. In the Add New Item dialog box, choose Web Configuration File, and name it simply **Web.config**. Click the Add button, and finally add the following to the Web.config file that you added:

```xml
<?xml version="1.0"?>
<configuration>
    <appSettings/>
    <connectionStrings/>
    <system.web>
        <authorization>
            <deny users="?" />
        </authorization>
    </system.web>
</configuration>
```

How It Works

As mentioned, you have enabled the security for the Admin folder. However, by placing an additional Web.config file in the Admin directory, the configurations in the Web.config file in the Admin directory will override those in the root directory.

4. Now that all the configurations are in place for the administrator's section, you need to add the necessary web forms. Therefore, in the Admin folder, add the Login.aspx web form, and then add a new master page named Admin.master. In the master page, add the following Hypertext Markup Language (HTML) code:

```html
<%@ Master Language="C#" AutoEventWireup="true"
CodeFile="Admin.master.cs" Inherits="Admin_Admin" %>

<html xmlns="http://www.w3.org/1999/xhtml" >
<head runat="server">
    <title>Untitled Page</title>
    <link href="../CSS/Style.css" type="text/css" rel="stylesheet">
</head>
<body style="text-align: center" background="../Images/til_1.jpg">
    <form id="form1" runat="server">
        <br />

        <table border="0" cellpadding="0" cellspacing="0" width="90%">
           <tr>
          <td style="width: 100%; background-color:
             #f3e9bf; text-align: center">
               </td>
```

```
            </tr>
            <tr>
        <td style="width: 100%; background-color:
            #f3e9bf; text-align: center">
                <img border="0" height="36" src="../images/logo.jpg"
            width="159" /><br />
                </td>
            </tr>
            <tr>
        <td style="width: 100%; background-color:
            #f3e9bf; text-align: center">
                    <strong>Administrative Control Panel</strong></td>
            </tr>
            <tr>
                <td style="width: 100%">
                <div class="shadetabs">
        <ul>
        <li runat="server" id="Products">
        <a href="Products.aspx">Products</a>
        </li>
        </ul>
        </div>
                </td>
            </tr>
            <tr>
                <td style="width: 100%; text-align: center;">
        <div style="background-color: #f3e9bf; width: 100%; text-align: center;
            height: 205px;">
        <asp:contentplaceholder id="contentplaceholderAdmin"
            runat="server">
            </asp:contentplaceholder>
        </div>
                </td>
            </tr>
        </table>
    </form>
</body>
</html>
```

How It Works

The master page has added the logo to the top of the page with a label indicating that it's the administrator's control panel. You'll also see a link that is styled as a tab that will allow for easy navigation within the control panel.

These additions bring you to the conclusion of the first exercise in the chapter. All the necessary configurations are in place, so you can move along to incorporating the login and eventually adding and editing the products within the catalog.

Creating the Administrator Login

As mentioned, you need to ensure that the administrator's control panel is secure with a password-protected login. This section of the chapter will show you how to implement a login that is similar to the one you implemented in Chapter 19 when a new user registered for an account or revisited the application to log in. However, the login for the administrator's control panel will restrict everyone except those with sufficient access to log in. The following exercise shows how to implement the login.

Exercise: Implementing the Login

This exercise walks you through all the steps to implement a secure login for the administrators of the application. Follow these steps:

1. Start at the database level, and create the stored procedure that will query the user according to the username and password entered:

```
CREATE PROCEDURE AdminLogin_Select

@Email nvarchar(50),
@Password nvarchar(50)

AS

SELECT EndUserID,
EndUserTypeID,
FirstName,
LastName,
EndUser.AddressID,
EndUser.ContactInformationID,
Password,
IsSubscribed,
Phone,
Phone2,
Fax,
Email
FROM EndUser
INNER JOIN ContactInformation ON
ContactInformation.ContactInformationID = enduser.ContactInformationID
WHERE Email = @Email
AND Password = @Password
AND EndUserTypeID = 2
```

2. After executing the stored procedure script, add the name of the stored procedure to the Name enumeration in the StoredProcedure class in the data access layer. With that complete, you can add the classes that the data access portion of the architecture needs. Proceed to the LittleItalyVineyard. DataAccess class library project and then to the Select directory and namespace. Add a new class named AdminLoginSelectData with the following code:

```csharp
using System;
using System.Collections.Generic;
using System.Text;
using System.Data;
using System.Data.SqlClient;

using LittleItalyVineyard.Common;

namespace LittleItalyVineyard.DataAccess.Select
{
    public class AdminLoginSelectData : DataAccessBase
    {
        private EndUser _enduser;

        public AdminLoginSelectData()
        {
            StoredProcedureName = StoredProcedure.Name.➥
          AdminLogin_Select.ToString();
        }

        public DataSet Get()
        {
            DataSet ds;

        AdminLoginSelectDataParameters➥
         _adminselectdataparameters =➥
         new AdminLoginSelectDataParameters( EndUser );
                DataBaseHelper dbhelper = new DataBaseHelper➥
        ( StoredProcedureName );
            ds = dbhelper.Run( base.ConnectionString ,➥
        adminselectdataparameters.Parameters     );

            return ds;
        }

        public EndUser EndUser
        {
            get { return _enduser; }
            set { _enduser = value; }
        }
    }

    public class AdminLoginSelectDataParameters
    {
        private EndUser _enduser;
        private SqlParameter[] _parameters;
```

```
        public AdminLoginSelectDataParameters( EndUser enduser )
        {
            EndUser = enduser;
            Build();
        }

        private void Build()
        {
            SqlParameter[] parameters =
            {
                new SqlParameter( "@Email" ,➥
              EndUser.ContactInformation.Email ) ,
                new SqlParameter( "@Password" , EndUser.Password )
            };

            Parameters = parameters;
        }

    public EndUser EndUser
    {
        get { return _enduser; }
        set { _enduser = value; }
    }

    public SqlParameter[] Parameters
    {
        get { return _parameters; }
        set { _parameters = value; }
    }
    }
  }
}
```

How It Works

The previous code is similar to the other data access layer classes you added. A DataSet will be returned from the EndUser class and is passed with the credentials.

3. Proceed to the business logic tier and to the LittleItalyVineyard.BusinessLogic class library. Add a new class named ProcessAdminLogin. Then add the following code:

```
using System;
using System.Collections.Generic;
using System.Text;
using System.Data;

using LittleItalyVineyard.Common;
using LittleItalyVineyard.DataAccess.Select;
```

```csharp
namespace LittleItalyVineyard.BusinessLogic
{
    public class ProcessAdminLogin : IBusinessLogic
    {
        private EndUser _enduser;
        private DataSet _resultset;
        private bool _isauthenticated;

        public ProcessAdminLogin()
        {

        }

        public void Invoke()
        {
            AdminLoginSelectData adminlogin = new AdminLoginSelectData();
            adminlogin.EndUser = this.EndUser;
            ResultSet = adminlogin.Get();

            if ( ResultSet.Tables[ 0 ].Rows.Count != 0 )
            {
                IsAuthenticated = true;
            }
            else
            {
                IsAuthenticated = false;
            }
        }

        public EndUser EndUser
        {
            get { return _enduser; }
            set { _enduser = value; }
        }

        public DataSet ResultSet
        {
            get { return _resultset; }
            set { _resultset = value; }
        }

        public bool IsAuthenticated
        {
            get { return _isauthenticated; }
            set { _isauthenticated = value; }
        }
    }
}
```

How It Works

The business logic class will pass the EndUser class into the data access layer. As a result, the DataSet named ResultSet will be returned, which will then be analyzed to see whether there are any rows within the DataSet; this will result in a match being made by the credentials being passed to those in the database and in subsequently authenticating the user.

4. Now move to the presentation tier of the architecture and to the Login.aspx web form you created in the Admin folder. Add the following HTML code to the Login.aspx web form, and notice that you are not going to use a master page for this web form:

```
<%@ Page Language="C#" AutoEventWireup="true"
CodeFile="Login.aspx.cs" Inherits="Admin_Login" %>

<html>
<head id="Head1" runat="server">
    <title>Admin Log In</title>
    <meta http-equiv="Content-Style-Type" content="text/css" />
    <link href="../Css/style.css" type="text/css" rel="stylesheet" />
</head>
<body>
    <form id="form1" runat="server">
    <table width="100%" height="100%" border="0" cellpadding="0"
  cellspacing="0" style="background-image: url(../images/til_1.jpg);">
            <tr>
        <td> </td>
        <td width="490" align="left" valign="top">
        <table width="490" border="0" cellspacing="0" cellpadding="0">
         <tr>
           <td width="10"> </td>
           <td width="470" align="left" valign="top">
     <table width="470" height="100%" border="0"
        cellpadding="0" cellspacing="0">
     <tr>
            <td height="164" align="left" valign="top"
               background="../images/top_1.jpg">
           <div style="padding-left: 156px; padding-top: 69px">
     <img src="../images/logo.jpg" width="159" height="36"
         border="0">
               <br />
                    </div>
                 </td>
               </tr>
             <tr>
         <td height="172" align="right" valign="top"
            background="../images/back_1.jpg">
        <div style="padding-left: 0px; padding-top: 14px;
           padding-right: 23px; padding-bottom: 0px">
         </div>
```

```
        </td>
      </tr>
       <tr>
      <td height="100%" align="left" valign="top">
      <table width="100%" height="100%" border="0"
      cellpadding="0" cellspacing="0"
          background="../images/rep_3.jpg">
              <tr align="left" valign="top">
      <td background="../images/rep_left.jpg" style="width: 10px">
      <img src="../images/rep_left.jpg" width="10" height="1">
        </td>
      <td height="100%">
      <table width="450" height="100%" border="0"
         cellpadding="0" cellspacing="0">
      <tr align="left" valign="top">
      <td background="../images/rep_line.jpg"
         bgcolor="#F3E9BF" style="background-repeat: repeat-y;
         background-position: top left; text-align: center;">
         <br />
        <strong>Administrator Control Panel Log In</strong>
      <br />
        <table border="0" cellpadding="0" cellspacing="0"
    width="99%" height="99%" align="center" valign="middle">
        <tr>
        <td align="center" valign="top">
         <br />

         <table border="0" cellpadding="3" cellspacing="0"
         style="width: 360px">
    <tr>
      <td style="width: 28px">
    <img height="5" src="../images/spacer.gif" width="1" /></td>
        </tr>
      <tr>
        <td style="width: 28px">
          <img height="1" src="../images/spacer.gif" width="50" /></td>
          <td>
           Username:</td>
          <td>
    <asp:TextBox ID="textUsername" runat="server" CssClass="textField">
    </asp:TextBox><br />
    <asp:RequiredFieldValidator ID="requiredUsername" runat="server"
    ControlToValidate="textUsername"
    Display="Dynamic" EnableClientScript="False"
    ErrorMessage="Username required."
    Width="152px"></asp:RequiredFieldValidator></td>
                        </tr>
```

```
            <tr>
             <td style="width: 28px">
                </td>
                <td>
             Password:</td>
         <td>
<asp:TextBox ID="textPassword" runat="server"
CssClass="textField" TextMode="Password">
</asp:TextBox><br />
<asp:RequiredFieldValidator ID="requiredPassword" runat="server"
ControlToValidate="textPassword"
Display="Dynamic" EnableClientScript="False"
ErrorMessage="Password required."
Width="152px"></asp:RequiredFieldValidator></td>
        </tr>
        <tr>
        <td colspan="2">
        </td>
        <td>
<asp:Button ID="commandLogin" runat="server"
CssClass="button" OnClick="commandLogin_Click"
Text="Login" /></td>
 </tr>
  <tr>
 <td colspan="2">
 </td>
  <td>
 <asp:Label ID="labelMessage" runat="server">
</asp:Label></td>
    </tr>
    </table>
    </td>
</tr>
</table>
    </td>
</tr>
  </table>
 </td>
<td width="10" background="../images/rep_right.jpg">
<img src="../images/rep_right.jpg" width="10" height="1">
</td>
    </tr>
    <tr>
<td colspan="3" valign="top" align="center">
<img src="../images/bottom_1.jpg" width="470"
height="23"></td>
       </tr>
```

```
                </table>
            </td>
        </tr>
        </table>
                                  </td>
                                  <td></td>
                             </tr>
                         </table>
                 </td>
                 <td> </td>
             </tr>
             <tr>
                 <td></td>
                 <td height="100%">
<table cellpadding="0" cellspacing="0" border="0"
width="100%" height="100%">
                             <tr>
<td style="height: 100%;
background-image: url(../images/rep_bot.jpg);
 background-repeat: repeat-y; background-position: center;">
</td>
</tr>
    </table>
        </td>
   <td></td>
</tr>
</table>
    </form>
</body>
</html>
```

How It Works

The HTML code you have added is not overly complex. It specifies two text boxes, a command button, and validation controls.

5. For the final step within this exercise, you'll add the code to the login form that takes the username and password entered by the user and eventually compares that to the information in the database. Add the following code to the Login.aspx web form:

```
using System;
using System.Data;
using System.Configuration;
using System.Collections;
using System.Web;
using System.Web.Security;
using System.Web.UI;
using System.Web.UI.WebControls;
```

```csharp
using System.Web.UI.WebControls.WebParts;
using System.Web.UI.HtmlControls;

using LittleItalyVineyard.Common;
using LittleItalyVineyard.BusinessLogic;

public partial class Admin_Login : System.Web.UI.Page
{
    protected void Page_Load( object sender , EventArgs e )
    {
        textUsername.Focus();
    }

    protected void commandLogin_Click( object sender , EventArgs e )
    {
        if ( IsValid )
        {
            EndUser enduser = new EndUser();
            ProcessAdminLogin processlogin = new ProcessAdminLogin();

            enduser.ContactInformation.Email = textUsername.Text;
            enduser.Password = textPassword.Text;
            processlogin.EndUser = enduser;

            try
            {
                processlogin.Invoke();

                if ( processlogin.IsAuthenticated )
                {
                    FormsAuthentication.RedirectFromLoginPage➥
                      ( textUsername.Text , false );
                }
                else
                {
                    labelMessage.Text = "Invalid login!";
                }
            }
            catch
            {
                Response.Redirect( "../ErrorPage.aspx" );
            }
        }
    }
}
```

How It Works

The previous code you added to the Login.aspx web form checks that the page is valid, or in other words that all the validation controls have evaluated all the information and will allow the process to continue. Upon the IsValid property being true, an EndUser class and the business logic (the ProcessAdminUser classes) are instantiated. The EndUser class has both the Email and Password properties populated with the input that is entered by the user. Finally, within a try/catch statement, the Invoke() method is called, and then the IsAuthenticated property is checked. If this is true, the user is redirected to the location that is specified within the Web.config file and the forms authentication. If the IsAuthenticated property is false, the login is not valid, and therefore a message is displayed to the user. If an error occurs during this process, the user is redirected to the error page that is specified within the catch part of the try/catch statement.

You have arrived at the end of the exercise, so you have a working login for the administrators of the application.

Creating a New Product

At this point, you have the initial workings of what will eventually be a fully featured administrator control panel. Thus far, you have implemented the necessary structure and configurations, along with a secure login. The next functionality to implement within the administrator's control panel is to add products to the catalog. This will be a vital piece of the administrator's capabilities. Throughout the life of the application, the administrator will have to continually add products to the catalog and change and update information.

Exercise: Adding a Product to the Catalog

This exercise shows how to add a product to the product catalog and thus allow the customers to browse and (you hope) make numerous purchases. Follow these steps:

1. As you might have guessed, you will begin the exercise at the database and create the stored procedure that will be required. It is evident that you will need a script that will insert the information in the Products table in the database and that will associate the product image. Let's look at the following script:

```
CREATE PROCEDURE Product_Insert

@ProductCategoryID int,
@ProductName nvarchar(50),
@ProductImage image,
@Description text,
@Price smallmoney

AS
```

```
--Start the transaction
BEGIN TRANSACTION

DECLARE @ProductImageID int

INSERT INTO ProductImages
(ProductImage)
VALUES
(@ProductImage)

-- Roll back the transaction if there were any errors
IF @@ERROR <> 0
 BEGIN
    -- Rollback the transaction
    ROLLBACK

    -- Raise an error and return
    RAISERROR ('Error INSERT INTO ProductImage.', 16, 1)
    RETURN
 END

SET @ProductImageID = @@IDENTITY

INSERT INTO Products
(ProductCategoryID,
ProductName,
ProductImageID,
Description,
Price)
VALUES
(@ProductCategoryID,
@ProductName,
@ProductImageID,
@Description,
@Price)

-- Roll back the transaction if there were any errors
IF @@ERROR <> 0
 BEGIN
    -- Rollback the transaction
    ROLLBACK

    -- Raise an error and return
    RAISERROR ('Error INSERT INTO Products', 16, 1)
    RETURN
 END

COMMIT
```

How It Works

The Product_Insert stored procedure inserts information across two tables. As a result of this, the scripts are wrapped within a transaction by first inserting the image data into the ProductImages table and then utilizing the @@IDENTITY variable to retrieve the last ID entered so that it can subsequently be entered in the Products table. If an error occurs at any point, the transaction is rolled back to its original state. If no errors are encountered, the transaction is committed.

2. Following in a similar trend, you will move along to the data access tier of the architecture and add the necessary code. First add the new stored procedure name to the Name enumeration, and then add a new class to the LittleItalyVineyard.DataAccess class library project within the Insert folder named ProductInsertData. Upon successfully adding the new class, add the following code:

```
using System;
using System.Collections.Generic;
using System.Text;
using System.Data;
using System.Data.SqlClient;

using LittleItalyVineyard.Common;

namespace LittleItalyVineyard.DataAccess.Insert
{
    public class ProductInsertData : DataAccessBase
    {
        private Product _product;
        private ProductInsertDataParameters ➥
            _productinsertdataparameters;

        public ProductInsertData()
        {
            StoredProcedureName = StoredProcedure.Name.Product_Insert.➥
                ToString();
        }

        public void Add()
        {
            _productinsertdataparameters =➥
            new ProductInsertDataParameters( Product );
                DataBaseHelper dbhelper = new DataBaseHelper➥
                    ( StoredProcedureName );
                dbhelper.Parameters = _productinsertdataparameters.➥
                    Parameters;
                dbhelper.Run();
        }
```

```
        public Product Product
        {
            get { return _product; }
            set { _product = value; }
        }
    }

    public class ProductInsertDataParameters
    {
        private Product _product;
        private SqlParameter[] _parameters;

        public ProductInsertDataParameters( Product product )
        {
          Product = product;
          Build();
        }

        private void Build()
        {
          SqlParameter[] parameters =
          {
            new SqlParameter( "@ProductCategoryID", ➥
              Product.ProductCategoryID ) ,
            new SqlParameter( "@ProductName" , Product.Name ) ,
            new SqlParameter( "@ProductImage" , Product.ImageData ) ,
            new SqlParameter( "@Description" , Product.Description ) ,
            new SqlParameter( "@Price" , Product.Price )
          };

          Parameters = parameters;
        }

      public Product Product
      {
        get { return _product; }
        set { _product = value; }
      }

      public SqlParameter[] Parameters
      {
        get { return _parameters; }
        set { _parameters = value; }
      }
    }
}
```

How It Works

In the code added to the data access layer, you stay true to form in that you specify the name of the stored procedure followed by the standard method named Add. You then pair this class with the associated parameters class for finalization.

3. The next step is to proceed to the business logic tier of the application. This is similar to the other code you have incorporated into the application within the business logic. Specifically, add the following in a new class named ProcessAddProduct:

```
using System;
using System.Collections.Generic;
using System.Text;

using LittleItalyVineyard.Common;
using LittleItalyVineyard.DataAccess.Insert;

namespace LittleItalyVineyard.BusinessLogic
{
    public class ProcessAddProduct : IBusinessLogic
    {
        private Product _product;

        public ProcessAddProduct()
        {

        }

        public void Invoke()
        {
            ProductInsertData productdata = new ProductInsertData();
            productdata.Product = this.Product;
            productdata.Add();
        }

        public Product Product
        {
            get { return _product; }
            set { _product = value; }
        }
    }
}
```

How It Works

The previous code implements the Invoke() method from which the code in the data access layer is called and implemented. A Product class is declared as a property, which will allow it to be populated from the calling code.

4. Typically at this point in exercises, you would proceed to the presentation tier of the application and add the necessary HTML code as well as the C# code. However, since you are going to have different categories for each of the products, you will need to first address that issue. Therefore, identify each of the categories, and insert them into the database. Say that you have determined you have the following categories:

- Appetizer Wines

- White Wines

- Rose Wines

- Sparkling Wines

- Red Wines

- Desert Wines

- Glasses

- Accessories

Now that you have identified the individual category names, add each of them to the ProductCategory table by executing the following scripts:

```
INSERT INTO ProductCategory(ProductCategoryName) VALUES('Appetizer Wine')
INSERT INTO ProductCategory(ProductCategoryName) VALUES('White Wine')
INSERT INTO ProductCategory(ProductCategoryName) VALUES('Rose Wine')
INSERT INTO ProductCategory(ProductCategoryName) VALUES('Red Wine')
INSERT INTO ProductCategory(ProductCategoryName) VALUES('Desert Wine')
INSERT INTO ProductCategory(ProductCategoryName) VALUES('Glasses')
INSERT INTO ProductCategory(ProductCategoryName) VALUES('Accessories')
```

5. The individual product categories are populated within the database; therefore, the next step is to create a new stored procedure that will select all these categories. Execute the following within the database:

```
CREATE PROCEDURE ProductCategory_Select

AS

SELECT ProductCategoryID,
ProductCategoryName
FROM ProductCategory
```

6. Moving along, add the name of the new stored procedure, ProductCategory_Select, to the Name enumeration within the StoredProcedure class. Next, add a new class to the LittleItalyVineyard.DataAccess class library project within the Select folder named ProductCategorySelectData, and add the following code:

```
using System;
using System.Collections.Generic;
using System.Text;
using System.Data;
```

```
namespace LittleItalyVineyard.DataAccess.Select
{
    public class ProductCategorySelectData : DataAccessBase
    {
        public ProductCategorySelectData()
        {
            base.StoredProcedureName = StoredProcedure.Name.➥
                ProductCategory_Select.ToString();
        }

        public DataSet Get()
        {
            DataSet ds;

            DataBaseHelper dbhelper = new DataBaseHelper➥
                ( base.StoredProcedureName );
            ds = dbhelper.Run( base.ConnectionString );

            return ds;
        }
    }
}
```

How It Works

The previous is standard code following the pattern you have established within the architecture. After
the stored procedure name is declared, a DataSet is then returned from the Get method that will ultimately return a listing of the product categories.

7. The next step is to add the business logic class named ProcessGetProductCategory. With that said, add
   this as a new class to the LittleItalyVineyard.BusinessLogic class library, and add the following code:

```
using System;
using System.Collections.Generic;
using System.Text;
using System.Data;

using LittleItalyVineyard.Common;
using LittleItalyVineyard.DataAccess.Select;

namespace LittleItalyVineyard.BusinessLogic
{
    public class ProcessGetProductCategory : IBusinessLogic
    {
        private DataSet _resultset;
        public ProcessGetProductCategory()
        {
```

```
        }

        public void Invoke()
        {
            ProductCategorySelectData productcategorydata =➥
                new ProductCategorySelectData();
            ResultSet = productcategorydata.Get();
        }

        public DataSet ResultSet
        {
            get { return _resultset; }
            set { _resultset = value; }
        }
    }
}
```

How It Works

Nothing is all that different within the business logic class and code that has been added. The Invoke() method is declared, which will call upon the data access code.

8. At this point within the exercise, you have everything implemented that is necessary to move along to the presentation tier and the web form itself. So, add a new web form to the Admin directory in the web project named AddProduct.aspx, and associate it with the Admin.master page you created earlier in the chapter. Add the following HTML code to the new web form:

```
<%@ Page Language="C#" MasterPageFile="~/Admin/Admin.master"
AutoEventWireup="true" CodeFile="AddProduct.aspx.cs"
Inherits="Admin_AddProduct" Title="
Admin Control Panel | Add Product " %>

<asp:Content ID="Content1" ContentPlaceHolderID="contentplaceholderAdmin"
  Runat="Server">
    <br />
    <table border="0" cellpadding="0" cellspacing="0" style="width: 432px">
        <tr>
            <td style="width: 100px">
                Product Name:</td>
            <td style="width: 100px">
    <asp:TextBox ID="textProductName" runat="server"
CssClass="textField"></asp:TextBox>
    <asp:RequiredFieldValidator ID="requireName" runat="server"
ErrorMessage="Product name required."
ControlToValidate="textProductName" Display="Dynamic"
EnableClientScript="False" Width="160px">
</asp:RequiredFieldValidator></td>
        </tr>
```

```
<tr>
    <td style="width: 100px">
        Category:</td>
    <td style="width: 100px">
<asp:DropDownList ID="dropdownlistCategory" runat="server"
CssClass="textField">
 </asp:DropDownList></td>
</tr>
<tr>
    <td style="width: 100%; height: 124px;">
    </td>
    <td style="width: 100%; height: 124px;">
<asp:TextBox ID="textDescription" runat="server"
Height="136px" TextMode="MultiLine"
                Width="100%"></asp:TextBox>
        </td>
</tr>
<tr>
    <td style="width: 100px">
        Price:</td>
    <td style="width: 100px">
<asp:TextBox ID="textPrice" runat="server" CssClass="textField">
</asp:TextBox>
<asp:RequiredFieldValidator ID="requirePrice" runat="server"
ErrorMessage="Price required." ControlToValidate="textPrice"
Display="Dynamic" EnableClientScript="False">
</asp:RequiredFieldValidator></td>
</tr>
<tr>
    <td style="width: 100px; height: 22px">
        Image:</td>
    <td style="width: 100px; height: 22px">
<asp:FileUpload ID="fileuploadImage" runat="server"
 Width="320px" CssClass="textField" /></td>
</tr>
<tr>
    <td style="width: 100px">
    </td>
    <td style="width: 100px">
    </td>
</tr>
<tr>
    <td style="width: 100px">
    </td>
    <td style="width: 100px">
         <table border="0" cellpadding="0" cellspacing="0">
            <tr>
```

```
                            <td style="width: 100px">
<asp:Button ID="commandAdd" runat="server"
OnClick="commandAdd_Click" Text="Add Product"
CssClass="button" /></td>
                            <td style="width: 58px">
<asp:Button ID="commandCancel" runat="server"
Text="Cancel" CausesValidation="False"
  OnClick="commandCancel_Click"
CssClass="button" /></td>
                        </tr>
                    </table>
                </td>
                <td style="width: 100px">
                </td>
            </tr>
        </table>
</asp:Content>
```

How It Works

The AddProduct.aspx web form adds a series of controls to the page that will capture the information that the user enters when adding a new product and that will provide the necessary validation.

9. Proceed to the code section of the AddProduct.aspx web form. Set the focus to the first text box on the page, and then call a method to populate the different category choices within the DropDownList control. Here's the code:

```
using System;
using System.Data;
using System.Configuration;
using System.Collections;
using System.Web;
using System.Web.Security;
using System.Web.UI;
using System.Web.UI.WebControls;
using System.Web.UI.WebControls.WebParts;
using System.Web.UI.HtmlControls;

using LittleItalyVineyard.Common;
using LittleItalyVineyard.BusinessLogic;

public partial class Admin_AddProduct : System.Web.UI.Page
{
    protected void Page_Load( object sender , EventArgs e )
    {
        if ( !IsPostBack )
        {
            textProductName.Focus();
```

```
                    LoadCategories();
            }
    }

    private void LoadCategories()
    {
        ProcessGetProductCategory processgetcategory =➡
          new ProcessGetProductCategory();

        try
        {
            processgetcategory.Invoke();
        }
        catch
        {
            Response.Redirect( "../ErrorPage.aspx" );
        }

        dropdownlistCategory.DataTextField = "ProductCategoryName";
        dropdownlistCategory.DataValueField = "ProductCategoryID";
        dropdownlistCategory.DataSource = processgetcategory.ResultSet;
        dropdownlistCategory.DataBind();
    }

    protected void commandCancel_Click( object sender , EventArgs e )
    {
        Response.Redirect( "Products.aspx" );
    }
}
```

How It Works

The code added accomplishes two separate tasks. First it sets the focus to the textProductName text box within the page load event, and then it populates the category drop-down list. You accomplish this by implementing the LoadCategories method that will call upon the code within the business logic and data access layers that were previously addressed.

10. To complete the exercise and fully implement the ability for an administrator to add a product to the catalog, you will address the code needed to insert data or cancel the process. Place the following code within the commandAdd button's click event:

```
protected void commandAdd_Click( object sender , EventArgs e )
{
    if ( IsValid )
    {
        ProcessAddProduct addproduct = new ProcessAddProduct();
        Product prod = new Product();
```

```
        prod.ProductCategoryID = int.Parse( dropdownlistCategory.↪
          SelectedItem.Value );
        prod.Name = textProductName.Text;
        prod.Description = textDescription.Text;
        prod.ImageData = fileuploadImage.FileBytes;
        prod.Price = Convert.ToDecimal( textPrice.Text );
        addproduct.Product = prod;

        try
        {
            addproduct.Invoke();
        }
        catch
        {
            Response.Redirect( "../ErrorPage.aspx" );
        }

        Response.Redirect( "Products.aspx" );
    }
}
```

How It Works

The code you added to the AddProduct.aspx web form allows an administrator to add a product to the catalog. A Product class will be instantiated and subsequently populated with the entered product information from the administrator. Finally, the Invoke() method will be called from the ProcessAddProduct class within the business logic layer, and upon success, execution will then redirect the user to the main products page where they can view the newly added product. Note, however, that you'll add the Products.aspx web form later in this chapter, and all the functionality from this chapter will come fully together then.

With this final implementation of code, you have a fully operational section of the administrator's control panel that will allow you to add products to the catalog.

Updating a Product

The functionality for the administrator's control panel is shaping up quite nicely thus far. However, you still need some additional functionality. In the following exercise, you will begin to add new functionality that will allow you to edit and update an existing product in the catalog.

Exercise: Implementing Product Update Functionality

In this exercise, you will create the functionality to take an existing product from the catalog and allow the administrator to make alterations and finally save the new updates. Follow these steps:

1. First create the necessary stored procedure that will take the information and update the product from the user's input:

```
CREATE PROCEDURE Product_Update

@ProductCategoryID int,
@ProductName nvarchar(50),
@ProductImageID int,
@ProductImage image,
@Description text,
@Price smallmoney,
@ProductID int

AS

--Start the transaction
BEGIN TRANSACTION

UPDATE ProductImages
SET ProductImage = @ProductImage
WHERE ProductImageID = @ProductImageID

-- Roll back the transaction if there were any errors
IF @@ERROR <> 0
  BEGIN
     -- Roll back the transaction
     ROLLBACK

     -- Raise an error and return
     RAISERROR ('Error UPDATE ProductImage.', 16, 1)
     RETURN
  END

UPDATE Products
SET ProductCategoryID = @ProductCategoryID,
ProductName = @ProductName,
ProductImageID = @ProductImageID,
Description = @Description,
Price = @Price
WHERE ProductID = @ProductID
```

```
-- Roll back the transaction if there were any errors
IF @@ERROR <> 0
 BEGIN
    -- Roll back the transaction
    ROLLBACK

    -- Raise an error and return
    RAISERROR ('Error UPDATE Products', 16, 1)
    RETURN
 END

COMMIT
```

How It Works

When updating a product within the database, the information spans two tables. These tables are the Products and ProductImages tables. As a result of the information spanning multiple tables, you use a transaction. If an error is encountered, the entire process or transaction is rolled back to its original state. On the other hand, if no errors occur, the information is committed to the database.

2. The stored procedure is now in place. Add the name of the newly created stored procedure to the Name enumeration within the StoreProcedure class. Next, proceed to the LittleItalyVineyard.DataAccess class library and then to the Update folder and namespace. Create a new class here named ProductUpdateData, and add the following code to the class:

```
using System;
using System.Collections.Generic;
using System.Text;
using System.Data.SqlClient;

using LittleItalyVineyard.Common;

namespace LittleItalyVineyard.DataAccess.Update
{
    public class ProductUpdateData : DataAccessBase
    {
        private Product _product;
        private ProductUpdateDataParameters➥
          _productupdatedataparameters;

        public ProductUpdateData()
        {
            StoredProcedureName = StoredProcedure.Name.➥
              Product_Update.ToString();
        }
```

```csharp
        public void Update()
        {
            _productupdatedataparameters =➡
                new ProductUpdateDataParameters➡
                    ( Product );
            DataBaseHelper dbhelper = new DataBaseHelper➡
                    ( StoredProcedureName );
            dbhelper.Parameters =➡
                _productupdatedataparameters.Parameters;
            dbhelper.Run();
        }

        public Product Product
        {
            get { return _product; }
            set { _product = value; }
        }
    }

public class ProductUpdateDataParameters
{
    private Product _product;
    private SqlParameter[] _parameters;

    public ProductUpdateDataParameters( Product product )
    {
        Product = product;
        Build();
    }

    private void Build()
    {
        SqlParameter[] parameters =
        {
          new SqlParameter( "@ProductCategoryID" , ➡
            Product.ProductCategoryID ) ,
          new SqlParameter( "@ProductName" , Product.Name ) ,
          new SqlParameter( "@ProductImageID" , Product.ImageID ) ,
          new SqlParameter( "@ProductImage"   , Product.ImageData ) ,
          new SqlParameter( "@Description" , Product.Description ) ,
          new SqlParameter( "@Price" , Product.Price ) ,
          new SqlParameter( "@ProductID" , Product.ProductID )
        };

        Parameters = parameters;
    }
```

```
        public Product Product
        {
            get { return _product; }
            set { _product = value; }
        }

        public SqlParameter[] Parameters
        {
            get { return _parameters; }
            set { _parameters = value; }
        }
    }
}
```

How It Works

This code establishes the name of the stored procedure and implements the Update method, which will execute the stored procedure with the subsequent parameters that are built in the ProductUpdateDataParameters class.

3. Moving along, you can now address the business logic code by adding a new class named ProcessUpdateProduct to the LittleItalyVineyard.BusinessLogic class library:

```
using System;
using System.Collections.Generic;
using System.Text;

using LittleItalyVineyard.Common;
using LittleItalyVineyard.DataAccess.Update;

namespace LittleItalyVineyard.BusinessLogic
{
    public class ProcessUpdateProduct : IBusinessLogic
    {
     private Product _product;

     public ProcessUpdateProduct()
     {

     }

     public void Invoke()
     {
        ProductUpdateData productdata = new ProductUpdateData();
        productdata.Product = this.Product;
        productdata.Update();
     }
```

```
        public Product Product
        {
            get { return _product; }
            set { _product = value; }
        }
    }
}
```

How It Works

The business logic code establishes a Product class that will be populated from the calling code. This Product class will then be submitted to the data access code from within the Invoke() method.

4. You can now proceed to the presentation portion and to the web form itself. Within the web project, add a new web form to the Admin directory named EditProduct.aspx. When adding this web form, associate it to the Admin.master page, and add the following HTML code:

```
<%@ Page Language="C#" MasterPageFile="~/Admin/Admin.master"
AutoEventWireup="true" CodeFile="EditProduct.aspx.cs"
Inherits="Admin_EditProduct" Title="
Admin Control Panel | Edit Product " %>

<asp:Content ID="Content1" ContentPlaceHolderID="contentplaceholderAdmin"
Runat="Server">
<table cellSpacing="0" cellPadding="0" width="100%" border="0"
style="height: 362px">
        <tr>
            <td colSpan="2">

            </td>
        </tr>
        <tr>
            <td vAlign="top" style="width: 21px">

            </td>
            <td vAlign="top" align="left">
  <table height="100%" cellSpacing="0" cellPadding="0"
   width="620" align="left" border="0">
                    <tr vAlign="top">
                        <td>
                            <br>
 <table cellSpacing="0" cellPadding="0"
width="100%" border="0">
        <tr>
<td class="ContentHead" style="width: 60px; height: 13px">
                Name:</td>
    <td class="ContentHead" style="height: 13px">
<asp:TextBox ID="textName" runat="server"
```

```
CssClass="textField"></asp:TextBox>
<asp:RequiredFieldValidator ID="requireName"
runat="server" ErrorMessage="Product name required."
ControlToValidate="textName" Display="Dynamic"
EnableClientScript="False">
</asp:RequiredFieldValidator></td>
                                        </tr>
                                        <tr>
            <td class="ContentHead" style="width: 60px">
                                                Description:
            </td>
             <td class="ContentHead">
        <asp:TextBox ID="textDescription" runat="server" Height="104px"
TextMode="MultiLine"
        Width="352px" CssClass="textField"></asp:TextBox></td>
                                        </tr>
                                        <tr>
          <td class="ContentHead" style="width: 60px; height: 24px;">
                                                Price:</td>
        <td class="ContentHead"
style="height: 24px">
<asp:TextBox ID="textPrice" runat="server" CssClass="textField">
</asp:TextBox>
<asp:RequiredFieldValidator ID="requirePrice" runat="server"
ErrorMessage="Price Required." ControlToValidate="textPrice"
Display="Dynamic" EnableClientScript="False">
</asp:RequiredFieldValidator></td>
                                        </tr>
                                        <tr>
<td class="ContentHead" style="width: 60px">
                                                Category:</td>
            <td class="ContentHead">
<asp:DropDownList ID="dropdownlistCategory"
        runat="server" CssClass="textField">
        </asp:DropDownList></td>
                                        </tr>
                                        <tr>
      <td class="ContentHead" style="width: 60px">
                                                Image:</td>
<td class="ContentHead">
<asp:Image ID="imageProductDetail" runat="server"
BorderColor="#92775C" BorderStyle="Double"
        BorderWidth="3px" Width="100px" /></td>
                                        </tr>
                                        <tr>
            <td class="ContentHead" style="width: 60px">
                                        </td>
```

```
                                    <td class="ContentHead">
                                    </td>
                                </tr>
                                <tr>
                    <td class="ContentHead" style="width: 60px">
                    </td>
                <td class="ContentHead">
<asp:FileUpload ID="fileuploadProductImage" runat="server"
Width="320px" CssClass="textField" /></td>
        </tr>
    </table>
<table cellSpacing="0" cellPadding="0"
width="100%" border="0" valign="top">
 <tr>
<td rowspan="1" style="width: 4px">
         
<table border="0" cellpadding="0" cellspacing="0"
style="width: 120px">
        <tr>
        <td style="width: 59px">
<asp:Button ID="commandUpdate" runat="server"
OnClick="commandUpdate_Click"
Text="Update" CssClass="button" /></td>
        <td style="width: 59px">
        </td>
        <td style="width: 100px">
<asp:Button ID="commandCancel" runat="server"
OnClick="commandCancel_Click" Text="Cancel"
CssClass="button" /></td>
    </tr>
    </table>
</td>
 </tr>
    </table>
    </td>
 </tr>
</table>
</td>
</tr>
</table>
</asp:Content>
```

How It Works

The HTML code you added to the EditProduct.aspx web form is similar to what you created in the AddProduct.aspx web form. Several text boxes capture the user input. However, the EditProduct.aspx web form has one additional item—an image control to display the current image that is associated with the product.

5. Proceed to the C# code section of the web form. In this area, you will add the code necessary to populate the current information about the selected product for update and to update the newly entered information. To start this process, within the page load event, set the focus to the first text box, and again populate the DropDownList control with the different product categories:

```csharp
using System;
using System.Data;
using System.Configuration;
using System.Collections;
using System.Web;
using System.Web.Security;
using System.Web.UI;
using System.Web.UI.WebControls;
using System.Web.UI.WebControls.WebParts;
using System.Web.UI.HtmlControls;

using LittleItalyVineyard.BusinessLogic;
using LittleItalyVineyard.Common;

public partial class Admin_EditProduct : System.Web.UI.Page
{
    protected void Page_Load( object sender , EventArgs e )
    {
        if ( !IsPostBack )
        {
            textName.Focus();
            LoadCategories();
        }
    }

    private void LoadCategories()
    {
        ProcessGetProductCategory processgetcategory =➥
            new ProcessGetProductCategory();

        try
        {
            processgetcategory.Invoke();
        }
        catch
        {
            Response.Redirect( "../ErrorPage.aspx" );
        }

        dropdownlistCategory.DataTextField = "ProductCategoryName";
        dropdownlistCategory.DataValueField = "ProductCategoryID";
        dropdownlistCategory.DataSource = processgetcategory.ResultSet;
        dropdownlistCategory.DataBind();
    }
}
```

How It Works

This code first sets the focus to the textName text box and then populates the individual product categories in the drop-down list.

6. The next order of business is to take the selected product that has been chosen to be updated and populate the current information about the product to the respective text boxes along with the image:

```
private const string SAVEDPRODUCTIMAGEID = "SavedProductImageID";

protected void Page_Load( object sender , EventArgs e )
{
    if ( !IsPostBack )
    {
        textName.Focus();
        LoadCategories();
        LoadProduct();
    }
}

private void LoadProduct()
{
    Product prod = new Product();
    prod.ProductID = int.Parse( Request.QueryString["ProductID"] );

    ProcessGetProductByID getProduct = new ProcessGetProductByID();
    getProduct.Product = prod;

    try
    {
        getProduct.Invoke();

        textName.Text = getProduct.Product.Name;
        textDescription.Text = getProduct.Product.Description;
        textPrice.Text = getProduct.Product.Price.ToString();
        imageProductDetail.ImageUrl =➡
          "../ImageViewer.ashx?ImageID=" +
            getProduct.Product.ImageID.ToString();
        dropdownlistCategory.SelectedIndex =➡
        dropdownlistCategory.Items.IndexOf➡
          (dropdownlistCategory.➡
        Items.FindByText(getProduct.Product.➡
          ProductCategory.➡
          ProductCategoryName));

        // Save product image id in case user does not want to update image.
        SavedProductImageID = getProduct.Product.ImageID;
    }
```

```
        catch
        {
            Response.Redirect( "../ErrorPage.aspx" );
        }
    }

    private int SavedProductImageID
    {
        get { return ( int ) ViewState[ SAVEDPRODUCTIMAGEID ]; }
        set { ViewState[ SAVEDPRODUCTIMAGEID ] = value; }
    }
```

How It Works

This code is a little more involved compared to other sections in this chapter thus far. You added a constant string field, SAVEDPRODUCTIMAGEID, which will represent the name of the object you want to save within the ViewState. Subsequently, you added property named SavedProductImageID, which is an integer value.

7. The final piece of functionality to implement is to add the code that will take the new information and subsequently update the newly entered information. Place this code in the commandUpdate click event:

```
protected void commandUpdate_Click( object sender , EventArgs e )
{
    if ( IsValid )
    {
        Product prod = new Product();
        prod.ProductID = int.Parse( Request.QueryString["ProductID"] );
        prod.Name = textName.Text;
        prod.Description = textDescription.Text;
        prod.Price = Convert.ToDecimal( textPrice.Text );
        prod.ProductCategoryID = int.Parse( dropdownlistCategory.➥
          SelectedItem.Value );
        prod.ImageID = SavedProductImageID;

        if ( fileuploadProductImage.HasFile )
        {
            prod.ImageData = fileuploadProductImage.FileBytes;
        }
        else
        {
            ProcessGetProductImage processgetimg =➥
              new ProcessGetProductImage();
            processgetimg.Product = prod;

            try
            {
                processgetimg.Invoke();
            }
```

```
        catch
        {
            Response.Redirect( "../ErrorPage.aspx" );
        }

        prod.ImageData = processgetimg.Product.ImageData;
    }

    ProcessUpdateProduct processupdate = new ProcessUpdateProduct();
    processupdate.Product = prod;

    try
    {
        processupdate.Invoke();
    }
    catch
    {
        Response.Redirect( "../ErrorPage.aspx" );
    }

    Response.Redirect( "Products.aspx" );
    }
}
```

How It Works

To complete the updating and editing functionality in this exercise, you used the SavedProductImageID property, which then sets or retrieves the specified value within the ViewState. You saved the image ID of the product so that if the user does not want to update the image of the product, you can simply retrieve the existing image ID from that property. However, if they do want to update the image, you will handle that as well by first checking the HasFile property of the fileuploadProductImage control. If this upload control has a file associated, you will then process the selected image. Finally, after a successful update, the user will be redirected to the Products.aspx web form.

You will implement the Products.aspx web form in the following section of the chapter.

Viewing All the Products

At long last you have arrived at the last section of the chapter. This final section will tie up the loose ends of the previous functionality that you have implemented thus far. To clarify this further, you implemented the functionality that allows an administrator to log in, add a new product to the catalog, and update an existing product. However, once an administrator logs in, they need a landing page, or home page, and they need to be able to view the current products in the catalog and select a product that should be updated.

The following exercise is where you will add the aforementioned home page with the ability to view the current product catalog.

Exercise: Viewing the Product Catalog

This final exercise of the chapter will not be as lengthy as the previous ones have been. The main reason for this is that you have already created a good deal of the functionality. Follow these steps:

1. Add a new web form to the Admin directory named Products.aspx, and associate it with the Admin.master page. Upon adding the new web form, add the following HTML code to the web form:

```
<%@ Page Language="C#" MasterPageFile="~/Admin/Admin.master"
AutoEventWireup="true" CodeFile="Products.aspx.cs"
Inherits="Admin_Products"
Title=" Admin Control Panel | Products " %>

<asp:Content ID="Content1" ContentPlaceHolderID="contentplaceholderAdmin"
Runat="Server">
    <br />
    <asp:Button ID="commandAddProduct" runat="server"
 OnClick="commandAddProduct_Click"
        Text="Add Product" CssClass="button" /><br />
    <br />

    <asp:DataList ID="datalistProducts" runat="server" RepeatColumns="1"
      Width="100%">
        <ItemTemplate>
            <table border="0" cellpadding="1" cellspacing="0" width="100%">
                <tr>
                    <td>
    <img border="0" height="1" src="../images/spacer.gif"
            width="50" /></td>
    <td align="right" valign="top">
<a href='EditProduct.aspx?productID=
<%# Eval("ProductID") %>&ImageID=
<%# Eval("ProductImageID") %>'>
    <img border="0" class="prodBorder" height="85"
src='../ImageViewer.ashx?ImageID=<%# Eval("ProductImageID") %>'>
    </a>
    </td>
    <td valign="top" width="100%">
 <table border="0" cellpadding="0" cellspacing="0" width="100%">
        <tr>
        <td width="17">
<img border="0" height="3" src="../images/spacer.gif" width="17" /></td>
        <td>
    </td>
 </tr>
  <tr>
  <td>
```

```
    </td>
  <td class="ProductListHead">
 <a href='EditProduct.aspx?productID=
<%# Eval("ProductID") %>&ImageID=
<%# Eval("ProductImageID") %>'><b>
      <%# Eval("ProductName") %>
    </b></a>
  </td>
     </tr>
       <tr>
     <td>
  <img border="0" height="5"
src="../images/spacer.gif" width="1" />
</td>
</tr>
<tr>
    <td colspan="2">
    <table border="0" cellpadding="0" cellspacing="0"
    width="75%">
  <tr>
  <td class="prodUnderlineBG" width="100%">
      </td>
        </tr>
      <tr>
      <td>
    <img border="0" height="1" src="../images/spacer.gif"
     width="1" /></td>
      </tr>
      <tr>
    <td>
    <img src="../images/prodDecorRight.gif" />
      </td>
    </tr>
      </table>
    </td>
       </tr>
       <tr>
         <td>
         </td>
         <td>
      <%# Eval("Description") %>
    </td>
       </tr>
    <tr>
<td>
<img border="0" height="5" src="../images/spacer.gif"
    width="1" /></td>
```

```
      </tr>
        <tr>
    <td>
    </td>
    <td>
    <span class="ProductListItem"><b>Price: </b>
      <%# Eval("Price", "{0:c}") %>
  </span>
</td>
</tr>
 <tr>
    <td>
    <img border="0" height="5" src="../images/spacer.gif"
      width="1" /></td>
    </tr>
      <tr>
    <td>
        </td>

        </tr>
        </table>
        </td>
    <td>
<img border="0" height="1" src="../images/spacer.gif"
    width="15" /></td>
 </tr>
    </table>
 </ItemTemplate>
    </asp:DataList>
</asp:Content>
```

How It Works

This HTML code is similar to that within the public portion of the site, in other words in the Winery.aspx web form. The code contains a DataList control and shows the name, a short description, the cost, and the image of the product. When the user clicks the title or the image, the user will be navigated to the EditProduct.aspx web form where the appropriate updates can be performed. Lastly, you added a command button, commandAddProduct, that will redirect the user to the AddProduct.aspx web form.

2. For the next task, proceed to the code portion of the web form, and add the following C# code that will populate the product catalog:

```
using System;
using System.Data;
using System.Configuration;
using System.Collections;
using System.Web;
using System.Web.Security;
```

```
using System.Web.UI;
using System.Web.UI.WebControls;
using System.Web.UI.WebControls.WebParts;
using System.Web.UI.HtmlControls;

using LittleItalyVineyard.Common;
using LittleItalyVineyard.BusinessLogic;

public partial class Admin_Products : System.Web.UI.Page
{
    protected void Page_Load( object sender , EventArgs e )
    {
        if ( !IsPostBack )
        {
            LoadProducts();
        }
    }

    private void LoadProducts()
    {
        ProcessGetProducts processproducts = new ProcessGetProducts();

        try
        {
            processproducts.Invoke();
        }
        catch
        {
            Response.Redirect( "../ErrorPage.aspx" );
        }

        datalistProducts.DataSource = processproducts.ResultSet;
        datalistProducts.DataBind();
    }

    protected void commandAddProduct_Click( object sender , EventArgs e )
    {
        Response.Redirect( "AddProduct.aspx" );
    }
}
```

How It Works

This code loads the entire product catalog to the DataList control by using the ProcessGetProducts business logic class and subsequently data binds the DataList with the results.

You now have the ability to view the products within your catalog.

Summary

In this chapter, you implemented the administrator's control panel; specifically, you added the functionality to allow only those users with administrative privileges to log in, subsequently view the current products in the catalog, add a new product, and then update or edit an existing product. These areas are fully functional at this point; however, you will revisit the administrator's control panel in Chapter 23 to add some functionality.

■ ■ ■

CHAPTER 22

Building the Customer's Account

You have completed implementing the administrator's account, also referred to as the administrator's *control panel*. With this chapter, you are fast approaching the end of the core development for the Little Italy Vineyards winery's application.

In this chapter, you will create the functionality to allow the customer to view what they have ordered and see a real-time snapshot of the order status. Specifically, you'll implement the following functionality:

- Setting up the customer account

- Setting up the customer login

- Viewing the customer's orders

- Viewing the customer's order details

Setting Up the Customer Account

Your first task for implementing the customer's account is to perform the initial setup within Visual Studio 2005. This initial setup will not be overly complex; in fact, it is similar to how you set up the administrator's account in the previous chapter. The following exercise shows you how.

Exercise: Setting Up the Customer Account

In this exercise, you will create the customer account in Visual Studio 2005. The process is similar to setting up the administrator's account in the previous chapter. Follow these steps:

1. Proceed to the web project, right-click the web project, and choose New Folder. Finally, change the name of the new folder to **Account**, as shown in Figure 22-1.

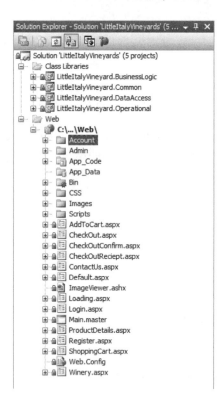

Figure 22-1. *The Account folder*

2. Add a new master page named Account.master with the following Hypertext Markup Language (HTML) code:

```
<%@ Master Language="C#" AutoEventWireup="true"
CodeFile="Account.master.cs" Inherits="Main" %>

<html>
<head runat="server">
    <title></title>
    <meta http-equiv="Content-Style-Type" content="text/css" />
    <link href="../Css/style.css" type="text/css" rel="stylesheet" />
    <script language="javascript" src="../Scripts/scriptLibrary.js">
    </script>
</head>
```

```
<body>
    <form id="form1" runat="server">
 <table width="100%" height="100%" border="0" cellpadding="0"
cellspacing="0" style="background-image: url(../images/til_1.jpg);">
            <tr>
                <td> </td>
                <td width="490" align="left" valign="top">
 <table width="490" border="0" cellspacing="0"
    cellpadding="0">
                        <tr>
                            <td width="10"> </td>
                            <td width="470" align="left" valign="top">
 <table width="470" height="100%" border="0"
   cellpadding="0" cellspacing="0">
                                    <tr>
 <td height="164" align="left" valign="top"
background="../images/top_1.jpg" style="width: 475px">
  <div style="padding-left: 156px; padding-top: 69px; text-align: left;">
<a href="../Default.aspx"><img src="../images/logo.jpg" width="159"
height="36" border="0"></a><br />
     <br />
     <br />
     <br />
      </div>
                    </td>
                    </tr>
                    <tr>
    <td height="172" align="right" valign="top"
     background="../images/back_1.jpg" style="width: 475px">
     <div style="padding-left: 0px; padding-top: 14px;
    padding-right: 23px; padding-bottom: 0px">
       <asp:Label ID="labelWelcome" runat="server"></asp:Label>
      <br />
      <asp:HyperLink ID="hyperlinkReturn" runat="server"
    NavigateUrl="~/Default.aspx">Return to Little Italy Vineyards
    </asp:HyperLink><a href="../login.aspx"></a></div>
        </td>
        </tr>
          <tr>
        <td height="100%" align="left" valign="top" style="width: 475px">
        <table width="100%" height="100%" border="0" cellpadding="0"
        cellspacing="0" background="../images/rep 3.jpg">
        <tr align="left" valign="top">
        <td background="../images/rep_left.jpg" style="width: 10px">
        <img src="../images/rep_left.jpg" width="10" height="1"></td>
        <td height="100%">
        <table width="450" height="100%" border="0" cellpadding="0"
         cellspacing="0">
```

```
                <tr align="left" valign="top">
    <td background="../images/rep_line.jpg" bgcolor="#F3E9BF"
      style="background-repeat: repeat-y;
    background-position: top left;">
    <asp:ContentPlaceHolder ID="contentplaceholderMain" runat="server">
        </asp:ContentPlaceHolder>
          </td>
          </tr>
        </table>
        </td>
        <td width="10" background="../images/rep_right.jpg">
    <img src="../images/rep_right.jpg" width="10" height="1"></td>
          </tr>
          <tr>
          <td colspan="3" valign="top" align="center">
    <img src="../images/bottom_1.jpg" width="470" height="23">
    </td>
        </tr>
            </table>
             </td>
             </tr>
              </table>
                              </td>
                              <td></td>
                      </tr>
                    </table>
                  </td>
                  <td> </td>
                </tr>
                <tr>
                      <td></td>
      <td height="100%">
    <table cellpadding="0" cellspacing="0"
      border="0" width="100%" height="100%">
        <tr>
    <td style="height: 100%; background-image: url(../images/rep_bot.jpg);
    background-repeat: repeat-y; background-position: center;">
    </td>
        </tr>
         </table>
             </td>
              <td></td>
             </tr>
          </table>
        </form>
  </body>
  </html>
```

3. Add a web form named CustomerOrders.aspx, and associate it to the Account.master master page.

4. The final task in this first exercise is to add the other web form that you will need. Specifically, add another web form to the Account directory named CustomerOrderDetails.aspx, and associate it to the Account.master master page as well.

You have now arrived at the end of the first exercise within the chapter; in the next section, you'll further enhance the customer login.

Extending the Customer Login

The customer login is actually a piece of functionality that already exists in your application. If you rewind to when you implemented the shopping cart, you'll remember that you built an existing login for the customer. If they are returning customers, they can log in. Otherwise, they can register for a new account. In the following exercise, you will revisit the login you created and expand upon it to eventually allow the user to view what they have ordered from your application.

Exercise: Extending the Customer Login

In this exercise, you'll revisit the login functionality that you created when you implemented the shopping cart. Perform this step:

1. Return to the Login.aspx web form and then to the commandLogin click event. You'll see existing code in this click event; however, you'll extend the functionality to handle when a customer is logging in to their account but not adding any products to the shopping cart. Here's the code:

```
protected void commandLogin_Click( object sender , EventArgs e )
{
    if ( IsValid )
    {
        EndUser enduser = new EndUser();
        ProcessEndUserLogin processlogin = new ProcessEndUserLogin();

        enduser.ContactInformation.Email = textUsername.Text;
        enduser.Password = textPassword.Text;
        processlogin.EndUser = enduser;

        try
        {
            processlogin.Invoke();
        }
        catch
        {
            Response.Redirect( "ErrorPage.aspx" );
        }
    }
```

```
        if ( processlogin.IsAuthenticated )
        {
            Response.Cookies["Authenticated"].Value = "True";

            base.CurrentEndUser = processlogin.EndUser;

            if ( Request.Cookies["ReturnURL"] != null )
            {
                Response.Redirect( Request.Cookies["ReturnURL"].Value );
            }
            else
            {
                Response.Redirect( "Account/CustomerOrders.aspx" );
            }
        }
        else
        {
            labelMessage.Text = "Invalid login!";
        }
    }
}
```

How It Works

This code first checks to see whether the page is valid as a result of the validation controls. If in fact the page is valid, meaning the user has input all the necessary information, the ProcessEndUserLogin business logic class is then populated with the EndUser class property. ProcessEndUserLogin subsequently calls the Invoke() method. Following this, the IsAuthenticated property is checked, and if it is true, since this login is not coming from the user registration process, the ReturnURL cookie will be null. As a result, the user will be redirected to the CustomerOrders.aspx web form. If the credentials entered are not valid, the user will be informed because an error message within the labelMessage control will appear.

You now have the ability for a customer to log in to their account.

Viewing the Orders

One of the major facets of the customer's account will be the ability for a customer to view the existing orders they have placed in the shopping cart and the associated details of the order. It is quite simple to understand why it's important to include this functionality. When a customer makes a purchase from your client's company, they want to have a receipt of what they have purchased. The following exercise shows how to create the functionality to allow the user to view the orders.

Exercise: Viewing the Orders

In this exercise, you will allow a customer to view the history of the orders they have placed. Follow these steps:

1. As with many of the exercises, you will start with the database and create the stored procedure needed to query the orders for a specific user. Here's the stored procedure:

```
CREATE PROCEDURE Orders_Select

@EndUserID int

AS

SELECT OrderID,TransactionID, OrderDate, OrderStatusName,
ShipDate, TrackingNumber FROM Orders
INNER JOIN orderstatus ON orderstatus.orderstatusid = orders.orderstatusid
WHERE EndUserID = @EndUserID
ORDER BY OrderDate DESC
```

How It Works

The Orders_Select stored procedure queries the orders from the Orders table and joins the table to the OrderStatus table via inner joins so the resulting query can display the status of the order.

2. The next step is to add the name of the new stored procedure to the Name enumeration within the StoredProcedure class after executing the script from step 1. Following this, you need to add a new class named OrdersSelectData to the Select directory within the LittleItalyVineyard.DataAccess class library project. In the new class, add the following code:

```
using System;
using System.Collections.Generic;
using System.Text;
using System.Data;
using System.Data.SqlClient;

using LittleItalyVineyard.Common;

namespace LittleItalyVineyard.DataAccess.Select
{
    public class OrdersSelectData : DataAccessBase
    {
        private EndUser _enduser;

        public OrdersSelectData()
        {
            StoredProcedureName = StoredProcedure.Name.➥
             Orders_Select.ToString();
        }
```

```
    public DataSet Get()
    {
      DataSet ds;

      OrdersSelectDataParameters _ordersselectdataparameters =➥
        new OrdersSelectDataParameters( EndUser );
      DataBaseHelper dbhelper = new DataBaseHelper➥
        ( StoredProcedureName );
      ds = dbhelper.Run( base.ConnectionString ,➥
        _ordersselectdataparameters.Parameters );

      return ds;
    }

    public EndUser EndUser
    {
      get { return _enduser; }
      set { _enduser = value; }
    }
  }

  public class OrdersSelectDataParameters
  {
    private EndUser _enduser;
    private SqlParameter[] _parameters;

    public OrdersSelectDataParameters( EndUser enduser )
    {
      EndUser = enduser;
      Build();
    }

private void Build()
{
    SqlParameter[] parameters =
     {
       new SqlParameter( "@EndUserID" , EndUser.EndUserID )
     };

    Parameters = parameters;
}

public EndUser EndUser
{
    get { return _enduser; }
  set { _enduser = value; }
 }
```

```
        public SqlParameter[] Parameters
        {
          get { return _parameters; }
          set { _parameters = value; }
        }
      }
    }
}
```

How It Works

The data access code populates the parameters from the EndUser property and, upon building the parameters with the associated parameters class, returns a DataSet from the Get function.

3. As usual, you need to go to the business logic tier and add a new class to the LittleItalyVineyard. BusinessLogic class library project. The name of the new class is ProcessGetOrders, and you will add the following code:

```
using System;
using System.Collections.Generic;
using System.Text;
using System.Data;

using LittleItalyVineyard.Common;
using LittleItalyVineyard.DataAccess.Select;

namespace LittleItalyVineyard.BusinessLogic
{
    public class ProcessGetOrders : IBusinessLogic
    {
        private EndUser _enduser;
        private DataSet _resultset;

        public ProcessGetOrders()
        {

        }

        public void Invoke()
        {
            OrdersSelectData ordersselect = new OrdersSelectData();
            ordersselect.EndUser = this.EndUser;
            ResultSet = ordersselect.Get();
        }

        public EndUser EndUser
        {
            get { return _enduser; }
            set { _enduser = value; }
        }
```

```
        public DataSet ResultSet
        {
            get { return _resultset; }
            set { _resultset = value; }
        }
    }
}
```

How It Works

The business logic code added as usual implements the Invoke() method that will execute the data access code. The EndUser property will be populated from the calling code and will pass that property to the data access classes. Finally, a DataSet will be returned with the queried results.

4. Next, you will add the HTML code to the presentation tier and more specifically the CustomerOrders.aspx web form located in the Account directory that you added in the first exercise in this chapter. So, add the following HTML code to the web form:

```
<%@ Page Language="C#" MasterPageFile="Account.master"
AutoEventWireup="true" CodeFile="CustomerOrders.aspx.cs"
Inherits="Account_CustomerOrders"
Title="Little Italy Vineyards | Orders" %>

<asp:Content ID="Content1" ContentPlaceHolderID="contentplaceholderMain"
    Runat="Server">
    <br />
    <table border="0" cellpadding="0" cellspacing="0" width="90%">
        <tr>
            <td>
                <strong>My Orders</strong></td>
        </tr>
        <tr>
            <td>
            </td>
        </tr>
        <tr>
            <td>
    <asp:GridView ID="gridviewOrders" runat="server"
      AutoGenerateColumns="false" Width="100%">
    <Columns>
    <asp:TemplateField HeaderText="Transaction ID">
        <ItemTemplate>
<a href="CustomerOrderDetails.aspx?TransID=
<%# Eval("TransactionID") %>&OrderID=<%# Eval("OrderID") %>">
<%# Eval("TransactionID") %></a>
        </ItemTemplate>
    </asp:TemplateField>
    <asp:TemplateField HeaderText="Order Date">
```

```
            <ItemTemplate>
                <%# Eval("OrderDate") %>
            </ItemTemplate>
        </asp:TemplateField>
        <asp:TemplateField HeaderText="Status">
            <ItemTemplate>
                <%# Eval("OrderStatusName") %>
            </ItemTemplate>
        </asp:TemplateField>
   <asp:TemplateField HeaderText="Ship Date">
            <ItemTemplate>
                <%# Eval("ShipDate") %>
            </ItemTemplate>
        </asp:TemplateField>
        <asp:TemplateField HeaderText="Tracking Number">
            <ItemTemplate>
                <%# Eval( "TrackingNumber" )%>
            </ItemTemplate>
        </asp:TemplateField>
        </Columns>
        </asp:GridView>
            </td>
        </tr>
    </table>
    <br />
</asp:Content>
```

How It Works

In this code, you added a GridView control that will display three individual columns. The three columns will display the TransactionID, OrderDate, and OrderStatusName fields that were specified within the stored procedure used to query the result set. Lastly, the TransactionID field will link to the CustomerOrderDetails.aspx web form and pass specific query strings.

5. For the conclusion of the exercise, proceed to the code view of CustomerOrders.aspx, and add the following code, which will populate the orders based upon the user:

```
using System;
using System.Data;
using System.Configuration;
using System.Collections;
using System.Web;
using System.Web.Security;
using System.Web.UI;
using System.Web.UI.WebControls;
using System.Web.UI.WebControls.WebParts;
using System.Web.UI.HtmlControls;
```

```
using LittleItalyVineyard.BusinessLogic;

public partial class Account_CustomerOrders : BasePage
{
    protected void Page_Load( object sender , EventArgs e )
    {
        if ( !IsPostBack )
        {
            Label labelWelcome = ( Label ) Master.FindControl➥
                ( "labelWelcome" );
            labelWelcome.Text = "Welcome, " + base.CurrentEndUser.FirstName +
                " " +   base.CurrentEndUser.LastName;

            LoadOrders();
        }
    }

    private void LoadOrders()
    {
        ProcessGetOrders getorders = new ProcessGetOrders();
        getorders.EndUser = CurrentEndUser;

        try
        {
            getorders.Invoke();
        }
        catch
        {
            Response.Redirect( "../ErrorPage.aspx" );
        }

        gridviewOrders.DataSource = getorders.ResultSet;
        gridviewOrders.DataBind();
    }
}
```

How It Works

Within the previously added code, if the request is not a postback, the labelWelcome control within the Account.master page is retrieved by using the Master.FindControl method. Subsequently, the text of this control is then set to a welcome message utilizing the logged-in user's first and last names. After this information is set up, the orders for the logged-in user are queried by instantiating the ProcessGetOrders class within the business logic tier and finally binding the gridviewOrders GridView control to the DataSet result set of the ProcessGetOrders class.

You now have the ability for an administrator to view the customers' orders.

Viewing the Order Details

The final step of giving your customers the ability to view their orders is to allow the customer to view the details of the main order they placed. To be more specific, in the following exercise, you'll implement the ability to view what exactly the order contains.

Exercise: Viewing the Order Details

To complete the final exercise, you will continue the implementation of viewing the orders from a customer and take it to the next level. This next level is to view the details of each order that the customer has placed. Follow these steps:

1. Again, you will begin with the stored procedure to query the order details from the supplied order as follows:

```
CREATE PROCEDURE OrderDetails_Select

@OrderID int

AS

SELECT Quantity, ProductName, Price FROM OrderDetails
INNER JOIN Products ON Products.ProductID = OrderDetails.ProductID
WHERE OrderID = @OrderID
```

How It Works

The OrderDetails_Select stored procedure queries the OrderDetails table and joins it with the Products table via inner joins based on the OrderID passed as a parameter.

2. As with the other exercises, add the name of the newly executed stored procedure to the Name enumeration in the StoredProcedure class within the LittleItalyVineyard.DataAccess class library project. Then add a new class to the Select directory and namespace named OrderDetailsSelectData, and add the following code:

```
using System;
using System.Collections.Generic;
using System.Text;
using System.Data;
using System.Data.SqlClient;

using LittleItalyVineyard.Common;

namespace LittleItalyVineyard.DataAccess.Select
{
    public class OrderDetailsSelectData : DataAccessBase
    {
        private OrderDetails _orderdetails;
```

```
      public OrderDetailsSelectData()
      {
        StoredProcedureName = StoredProcedure.Name.➥
          OrderDetails_Select.ToString();
      }

      public DataSet Get()
      {
        DataSet ds;

        OrderDetailsSelectDataParameters➥
          _orderdetailsselectdataparameters =➥
          new OrderDetailsSelectDataParameters( OrderDetails );
        DataBaseHelper dbhelper = new DataBaseHelper➥
          ( StoredProcedureName );
        ds = dbhelper.Run( base.ConnectionString , ➥
          _orderdetailsselectdataparameters.Parameters );

        return ds;
      }

      public OrderDetails OrderDetails
      {
          get { return _orderdetails; }
          set { _orderdetails = value; }
      }
    }

  public class OrderDetailsSelectDataParameters
  {
      private OrderDetails _orderdetails;
      private SqlParameter[] _parameters;

  public OrderDetailsSelectDataParameters( OrderDetails orderdetails )
  {
   OrderDetails = orderdetails;
   Build();
  }

  private void Build()
  {
      SqlParameter[] parameters =
      {
         new SqlParameter( "@OrderID" , OrderDetails.OrderID ) ,
      };

      Parameters = parameters;
  }
```

```
    public OrderDetails OrderDetails
    {
       get { return _orderdetails; }
       set { _orderdetails = value; }
    }

    public SqlParameter[] Parameters
    {
       get { return _parameters; }
       set { _parameters = value; }
      }
    }
  }
```

How It Works

In this code, which you added to the data access tier, a DataSet is returned from the Get method after the parameters have been built with the associated parameter class.

3. Next, proceed to the business logic portion of the code base. Specifically, add a new class named ProcessGetOrderDetails to the LittleItalyVineyard.BusinessLogic class library, and add the following code:

```
using System;
using System.Collections.Generic;
using System.Text;
using System.Data;

using LittleItalyVineyard.Common;
using LittleItalyVineyard.DataAccess.Select;

namespace LittleItalyVineyard.BusinessLogic
{
    public class ProcessGetOrderDetails : IBusinessLogic
    {
        private OrderDetails _orderdetails;
        private DataSet _resultset;

        public ProcessGetOrderDetails()
        {

        }

        public void Invoke()
        {
            OrderDetailsSelectData orderdetailsselect =➠
              new OrderDetailsSelectData();
            orderdetailsselect.OrderDetails = this.OrderDetails;
            ResultSet = orderdetailsselect.Get();
        }
```

```
        public OrderDetails OrderDetails
        {
            get { return _orderdetails; }
            set { _orderdetails = value; }
        }

        public DataSet ResultSet
        {
            get { return _resultset; }
            set { _resultset = value; }
        }
    }
}
```

How It Works

The business logic code is similar in that it implements the standard IBusinessLogic interface with the Invoke() method that calls upon the data access code. Finally, the ResultSet property is populated with the queried results.

4. Next go to the presentation tier of the functionality of this exercise, and place the following HTML code in the CustomerOrderDetails.aspx web form:

```
<%@ Page Language="C#" MasterPageFile="Account.master"
AutoEventWireup="true" CodeFile="CustomerOrderDetails.aspx.cs"
Inherits="Account_CustomerOrderDetails"
Title="Little Italy Vineyards | Order Details" %>

<asp:Content ID="Content1" ContentPlaceHolderID="contentplaceholderMain"
  Runat="Server">
    <br />
    <table border="0" cellpadding="0" cellspacing="0" width="90%">
        <tr>
            <td style="width: 151px">
            </td>
            <td style="width: 100px">
            </td>
        </tr>
        <tr>
            <td style="width: 151px; height: 13px;">
                Transaction ID</td>
            <td style="width: 100px; height: 13px;">
    <asp:Label ID="labelTransactionID" runat="server" Text="">
    </asp:Label></td>
        </tr>
        <tr>
            <td style="width: 151px">
            </td>
```

```
                <td style="width: 100px">
                </td>
        </tr>
        <tr>
            <td style="width: 151px">
                Purchased Items:</td>
            <td style="width: 100px">
<asp:GridView ID="gridviewOrderDetailsProducts"
  runat="server" AutoGenerateColumns="false"
  Width="100%">
                <Columns>
                    <asp:TemplateField HeaderText="Qty.">
                        <ItemTemplate>
                            <%# Eval("Quantity") %>
                        </ItemTemplate>
                    </asp:TemplateField>
                    <asp:TemplateField HeaderText="Product">
                        <ItemTemplate>
                            <%# Eval("ProductName") %>
                        </ItemTemplate>
                    </asp:TemplateField>
                    <asp:TemplateField HeaderText="Price">
                        <ItemTemplate>
                            <%# Eval( "Price" , "{0:c}" )%>
                        </ItemTemplate>
                    </asp:TemplateField>
                </Columns>
                </asp:GridView>
            </td>
        </tr>
        <tr>
            <td style="width: 151px; height: 16px;">
                Tax:</td>
            <td style="width: 100px; height: 16px;">
                <asp:Label ID="labelTax" runat="server"></asp:Label></td>
        </tr>
        <tr>
            <td style="width: 151px; height: 16px;">
                Order Total:</td>
            <td style="width: 100px; height: 16px;">
<asp:Label ID="labelOrderTotal" runat="server">
</asp:Label></td>
        </tr>
        <tr>
            <td style="width: 151px; height: 19px">
            </td>
            <td style="width: 100px; height: 19px">
```

```
                </td>
            </tr>
            <tr>
                <td style="width: 151px">
                </td>
                <td style="width: 100px">
<asp:Button ID="commandReturn" runat="server"
Text="Return"
CssClass="button" OnClick="commandReturn_Click" />
</td>
            </tr>
        </table>
</asp:Content>
```

How It Works

The order details display the individual products along with the price and give the amount of tax paid and the order total. Finally, a command button returns the user to the listing of all their orders.

5. Now that the HTML code is in place to display order details, you can move along to the C# code portion of the CustomerOrderDetails.aspx web form. Add the following code to the web form:

```csharp
using System;
using System.Data;
using System.Configuration;
using System.Collections;
using System.Web;
using System.Web.Security;
using System.Web.UI;
using System.Web.UI.WebControls;
using System.Web.UI.WebControls.WebParts;
using System.Web.UI.HtmlControls;


using LittleItalyVineyard.Common;
using LittleItalyVineyard.BusinessLogic;
using LittleItalyVineyard.Operational;

public partial class Account_CustomerOrderDetails : BasePage
{
    protected void Page_Load( object sender , EventArgs e )
    {
        if ( !IsPostBack )
        {
            Label labelWelcome = ( Label ) Master.FindControl➥
              ( "labelWelcome" );
            labelWelcome.Text = "Welcome, " +
              base.CurrentEndUser.FirstName +
                " " +    base.CurrentEndUser.LastName;
```

```
            LoadOrderDetails();
        }
    }

    private void LoadOrderDetails()
    {
        ProcessGetOrderDetails processdetails =➥
          new ProcessGetOrderDetails();

        OrderDetails orderdetails = new OrderDetails();
        orderdetails.OrderID = int.Parse( Request.QueryString["OrderID"] );
        processdetails.OrderDetails = orderdetails;

        try
        {
            processdetails.Invoke();
        }
        catch
        {
            Response.Redirect( "../ErrorPage.aspx" );
        }

        gridviewOrderDetailsProducts.DataSource = processdetails.ResultSet;
        gridviewOrderDetailsProducts.DataBind();

        labelTransactionID.Text = Request.QueryString[ "TransID" ];
    }

    protected void commandReturn_Click( object sender , EventArgs e )
    {
        Response.Redirect( "CustomerOrders.aspx" );
    }
}
```

How It Works

In the page load event, the first task is to write the welcome message to the master page with the logged-in user. You accomplish this by using the Master.FindControl method and then setting the text of the Label control to that of the welcome message using the base page's CurrentEndUser property. Finally, the individual products are displayed within the gridviewOrderDetailsProducts GridView control by utilizing the ProcessGetOrderDetails class. To complete the display, the transaction ID is displayed by using the query string. Finally, you use the response.redirect method within the commandReturn click event to navigate the user to the main orders web page.

6. Some items still need to be displayed within the CustomerOrderDetails.aspx web form. To accomplish this, proceed to the LittleItalyVineyard.Operational class library project and then to the PayPalManager class. In this class, you need to implement a method that will utilize the PayPal application programming interfaces (APIs) to query the details of an order that was placed according to the transaction ID. To accomplish this, add the following method to the PayPalManager class:

```
public void GetTransactionDetails( Orders order )
{

}
```

7. You have added a new method named GetTransactionDetails with a parameter of the common class Orders being passed. Prior to addressing the code within this new method, you need to make some additions to the constructor as well as to the property that specifies the path to the certificate. Let's examine these items:

```
public PayPalManager()
{
    UserIdPasswordType user = new UserIdPasswordType();

    //set api credentials
    user.Username = ConfigurationManager.AppSettings["PayPalAPIUsername"];
    user.Password = ConfigurationManager.AppSettings["PayPalAPIPassword"];

    PPInterface.Url = ConfigurationManager.AppSettings["PayPalAPIURL"];
    PPInterface.RequesterCredentials = new CustomSecurityHeaderType();
    PPInterface.RequesterCredentials.Credentials =➥
      new UserIdPasswordType();
    PPInterface.RequesterCredentials.Credentials = user;

    service.Url = ConfigurationManager.AppSettings["PayPalAPIURL"];
    service.RequesterCredentials = new CustomSecurityHeaderType();
    service.RequesterCredentials.Credentials = new UserIdPasswordType();
    service.RequesterCredentials.Credentials = user;

    //this is .NET 2.0 specific portion of the code that
    //allows us to have the .p12 on the filesystem and
    //not have to register it with WinHttpCertCfg
    //uses X509Certificate2 class.
    FileStream fstream = File.Open➥
      ( CertPath , FileMode.Open , FileAccess.Read );
    byte[] buffer = new byte[ fstream.Length ];

    int count = fstream.Read( buffer , 0 , buffer.Length );

    fstream.Close();

    //use .NET 2.0  X509Certificate2 class to read .p12 from filesystem
    // where "12345678" is the private key password
```

```
    X509Certificate2 cert = new X509Certificate2( buffer , CertPassword );
    PPInterface.ClientCertificates.Add( cert );
    service.ClientCertificates.Add( cert );
}
```

How It Works

In the constructor, nothing all that new is added; there are simply additional declarations. In addition to the PPInterface that specifies the URL and the user credentials, the PayPalAPISoapBinding class is instantiated as the variable service:

```
<appSettings>
<!-- Sandbox PayPal -->
    <add key="CertificatePath" value="~/Certs/LittleItalyVineyards.p12"/>
</appSettings>
```

How It Works

A property within the PayPalManager class named CertPath returns the physical path of the certificate that is needed for the PayPal APIs. This property uses the Server.MapPath with the value that is specified within the Web.config appSetting values. However, since the request will be coming from a subfolder, you needed to adjust the value of the CertificatePath key within the appSettings. Therefore, the new value should specify the root directory by using the tilde (~) character, which will force the value to use the root path of the certificate.

8. All the additions are now in place; therefore, you can address the GetTransactionDetails method itself. With that said, add the following code to the method:

```
public void GetTransactionDetails( Orders order )
{
    GetTransactionDetailsRequestType detailRequest =➥
       new GetTransactionDetailsRequestType();
    detailRequest.TransactionID = order.TransactionID;
    detailRequest.Version = "2.0";
    GetTransactionDetailsReq request = new GetTransactionDetailsReq();
    request.GetTransactionDetailsRequest = detailRequest;

    GetTransactionDetailsResponseType response = service.➥
       GetTransactionDetails( request );
}
```

How It Works

In this code, the GetTransactionDetailsRequestType class is instantiated and subsequently sets the version of the PayPal APIs along with the more important property, the transaction ID. Following this, you specify that the GetTransactionDetailsResponseType class uses the GetTransactionDetails method to submit to the PayPal servers. The next step of the exercise will outline the resulting response and check for any errors that might occur.

9. To complete the final implementation of the GetTransactionDetails method, append code to the method that will first check for any errors in the submission and if successful will set the IsSubmissionSuccess property to true. If there are errors, the IsSubmissionSuccess property will be set to false. The following is the code:

```
public void GetTransactionDetails( Orders order )
{
    GetTransactionDetailsRequestType detailRequest =➥
       new GetTransactionDetailsRequestType();
    detailRequest.TransactionID = order.TransactionID;
    detailRequest.Version = "2.0";
    GetTransactionDetailsReq request = new GetTransactionDetailsReq();
    request.GetTransactionDetailsRequest = detailRequest;

    GetTransactionDetailsResponseType response = service.➥
      GetTransactionDetails( request );

    string sErrors = this.CheckForErrors( response );

    if ( sErrors == string.Empty )
    {
        PaymentInfoType payment = response.➥
          PaymentTransactionDetails.PaymentInfo;

        order.OrderTotal = GetAmountValue( payment.GrossAmount );
        order.Tax = GetAmountValue( payment.TaxAmount );
        IsSubmissionSuccess = true;
    }
    else
    {
        IsSubmissionSuccess = false;
    }
}
```

How It Works

After setting the IsSubmissionSuccess property to true, the Orders class that is passed into the method as a parameter has the OrderTotal and Tax properties populated. However, before populating these properties, you need to add a new method that will parse the amounts that are desired:

```
private decimal GetAmountValue( BasicAmountType amount )
{
    decimal sOut;

    try
    {
        sOut = Convert.ToDecimal( amount.Value );
        amount.currencyID = CurrencyCodeType.USD;
    }
```

```
catch
{
   sOut = 0;
}

return sOut;
}
```

The GetAmountValue function converts the value to a decimal and subsequently to a property of the Orders class. Lastly, if an error occurs by checking the sErrors variable by running it through the CheckForErrors function, the IsSubmissionSuccess is set to false, which can then be determined from the calling code.

10. You'll now complete the additions to the CustomerOrderDetails.aspx C# code portion of the web form. You will instantiate the PayPalManager class along with an Orders class that sets the TransactionID property to the query string passed along to the page. Therefore, the LoadOrderDetails method of the CustomerOrderDetails.aspx web form is as follows:

```
private void LoadOrderDetails()
{
    ProcessGetOrderDetails processdetails = new ProcessGetOrderDetails();

    OrderDetails orderdetails = new OrderDetails();
    orderdetails.OrderID = int.Parse( Request.QueryString["OrderID"] );
    processdetails.OrderDetails = orderdetails;

    try
    {
       processdetails.Invoke();
    }
    catch
    {
       Response.Redirect( "../ErrorPage.aspx" );
    }

    gridviewOrderDetailsProducts.DataSource = processdetails.ResultSet;
    gridviewOrderDetailsProducts.DataBind();

    labelTransactionID.Text = Request.QueryString[ "TransID" ];

    PayPalManager paypal = new PayPalManager();
    Orders ord = new Orders();

    ord.TransactionID = Request.QueryString[ "TransID" ];
    paypal.GetTransactionDetails( ord );
```

```
        if ( paypal.IsSubmissionSuccess )
        {
            labelOrderTotal.Text = ord.OrderTotal.ToString( "c" );
            labelTax.Text = ord.Tax.ToString( "c" );
        }
        else
        {
            Response.Redirect( "../ErrorPage.aspx" );
        }
    }
```

In this code that populates the order details, if the IsSubmissionSuccess property has a value of true, the labelOrderTotal and labelTax controls' text properties are set to the subsequent values of the Orders class. If there is an error, the user will be redirected to the error page.

Summary

You have finished the core development for the application and case study. Congratulations! This is not to say that there will not be any additional development, but the majority of the coding is complete. As a result of most of the coding being complete, you will now focus on issues of fulfilling the orders, accessing the money from the purchases, and finally deploying the application to the production server in preparation for the application to launch.

PART 6

Order Fulfillment and Promotion

In the previous parts of this book, you added a great deal of functionality and code to the overall application. You are still not completely finished with the coding aspect, however, even though the vast majority of the code and structure is intact. In this part, you will focus on viewing the orders placed by customers, fulfilling the orders, and updating the customers in a timely fashion.

CHAPTER 23

■ ■ ■

Managing the Orders

The first chapter in this part of the book will focus on managing the orders placed by your customers. Specifically, I'll address the following aspects:

- Viewing all the customers' orders

- Viewing the order details

- Updating the status of the order

- Fulfilling the order

- Informing the customer of a new order's status

- Refunding customer orders

Viewing the Orders

In the previous chapter regarding the customer's account, you implemented the ability for customers to view their orders. However, now that you have shifted the focus to fulfilling the orders, the administrator needs the ability to view all the orders from all the customers. You'll learn how to do this in the following exercise.

Exercise: Viewing the Orders

This exercise shows how to enable an administrator to view all the orders that have been placed by customers. Follow these steps:

1. Add and execute the stored procedure to query the orders that have been placed by customers. Here's the stored procedure script:

```
CREATE PROCEDURE OrdersAll_Select

AS

SELECT
OrderID,TransactionID, OrderDate, OrderStatusName,
FirstName, LastName,
```

```
AddressLine, AddressLine2, City, State, PostalCode,
Phone, Email
FROM Orders
INNER JOIN orderstatus
ON orderstatus.orderstatusid = orders.orderstatusid
INNER JOIN EndUser
ON EndUser.EndUserID = Orders.EndUserID
INNER JOIN Address
ON Address.AddressID = EndUser.AddressID
INNER JOIN ContactInformation
ON ContactInformation.ContactInformationID = EndUser.ContactInformationID
ORDER BY OrderDate DESC
```

How It Works

The OrdersAll_Select stored procedure will query the Orders table for all the orders that have been placed. Then you joined four other tables via inner joins so you can display the name of the customer, their address, their e-mail address, their phone number, and the status of the order.

2. Add the name of the new stored procedure, OrdersAll_Select, to the Name enumeration in the StoredProcedure class located in the data access tier of the code. Since you are still working in the data access layer of the code, add a new class to the Select directory and namespace named OrdersAllSelectData. Add the following code to the class:

```csharp
using System;
using System.Collections.Generic;
using System.Text;
using System.Data;
using System.Data.SqlClient;

using LittleItalyVineyard.Common;

namespace LittleItalyVineyard.DataAccess.Select
{
    public class OrdersAllSelectData : DataAccessBase
    {
        public OrdersAllSelectData()
        {
          StoredProcedureName = StoredProcedure.Name.➥
            OrdersAll_Select.ToString();
        }

        public DataSet Get()
        {
          DataSet ds;

          DataBaseHelper dbhelper = new DataBaseHelper➥
            ( base.StoredProcedureName );
          ds = dbhelper.Run( base.ConnectionString );
```

```
            return ds;
        }
    }
}
```

How It Works

The code added to the OrdersAllSelectData class doesn't contain any associated parameters class because no parameters are required for the associated stored procedure. Lastly, a DataSet is returned from the Get function with the result set being all the orders that have been placed in the system.

3. You'll now address the business logic code, so open the LittleItalyVineyard.BusinessLogic class library project. Add a new class named ProcessGetAllOrders, and then add the following code:

```
using System;
using System.Collections.Generic;
using System.Text;
using System.Data;

using LittleItalyVineyard.Common;
using LittleItalyVineyard.DataAccess.Select;

namespace LittleItalyVineyard.BusinessLogic
{
    public class ProcessGetAllOrders : IBusinessLogic
    {
        private DataSet _resultset;

        public ProcessGetAllOrders()
        {

        }

        public void Invoke()
        {
          OrdersAllSelectData ordersall = new OrdersAllSelectData();
          ResultSet = ordersall.Get();
        }

        public DataSet ResultSet
        {
          get { return _resultset; }
          set { _resultset = value; }
        }
    }
}
```

How It Works

In the business logic class, ProcessGetAllOrders will implement the IBusinessLogic interface and thus include the Invoke() method. Finally, a property named ResultSet will hold a DataSet from the returned Get function of the OrdersAllSelectData class in the data access tier.

4. Thus far, you have addressed the stored procedure and the data access and business logic layers of the code. Now you need to turn your attention to the presentation segments of the code and architecture so that an administrator can view and eventually manage the customer orders. To proceed, locate the Admin.master master page located in the Admin directory of the web project. First add an Orders tab to the Hypertext Markup Language (HTML) by adding the following HTML code to the master page:

```
<li runat="server" id="Orders"><a href="Orders.aspx">Orders</a></li>
```

After adding the new link, the complete HTML code for the Admin.master page is as follows:

```
<%@ Master Language="C#" AutoEventWireup="true"
CodeFile="Admin.master.cs" Inherits="Admin_Admin" %>

<html xmlns="http://www.w3.org/1999/xhtml" >
<head runat="server">
    <title>Untitled Page</title>
    <link href="../CSS/Style.css" type="text/css" rel="stylesheet">
</head>
<body style="text-align: center" background="../Images/til_1.jpg">
    <form id="form1" runat="server">
        <br />
        <table border="0" cellpadding="0" cellspacing="0" width="90%">
            <tr>
                <td style="width: 100%; background-color:
             #f3e9bf; text-align: center">
                </td>
            </tr>
            <tr>
                <td style="width: 100%; background-color:
             #f3e9bf; text-align: center">
                    <img border="0" height="36" src="../images/logo.jpg"
         width="159" /><br />
                </td>
            </tr>
            <tr>
                <td style="width: 100%; background-color:
              #f3e9bf; text-align: center">
                    <strong>Administrative Control Panel</strong></td>
            </tr>
            <tr>
                <td style="width: 100%">
                <div class="shadetabs">
            <ul>
```

```
         <li runat="server" id="Products">
        <a href="Products.aspx">Products
        </a></li>
        <li runat="server" id="Orders">
        <a href="Orders.aspx">Orders</a></li>
      </ul>
        </div>
            </td>
        </tr>
        <tr>
            <td style="width: 100%; text-align: center;">
    <div style="background-color: #f3e9bf; width: 100%; text-align:
        center; height: 205px;">
     <asp:contentplaceholder id="contentplaceholderAdmin"
        runat="server">
     </asp:contentplaceholder>
    </div>
            </td>
        </tr>
      </table>
    </form>
</body>
</html>
```

How It Works

The master page is not much different now from when you first created it. It simply has another link in the form of a tab that will link to the Order.aspx web form.

5. Now that you have modified the master page to include an Orders link, you need to add the Orders.aspx web form to the Admin directory and associate it to the Admin.master master page. Upon adding the new web form, add the following HTML code:

```
<%@ Page Language="C#" MasterPageFile="~/Admin/Admin.master"
AutoEventWireup="true" CodeFile="Orders.aspx.cs"
Inherits="Admin_Orders"
Title="Admin Control Panel | Orders" %>

<asp:Content ID="Content1" ContentPlaceHolderID="contentplaceholderAdmin"
    Runat="Server">
    <br />
    <table border="0" cellpadding="0" cellspacing="0" width="95%">
        <tr>
            <td><strong>All Orders</strong></td>
        </tr>
        <tr>
            <td>
            </td>
        </tr>
```

```
            <tr>
                <td>
<asp:GridView ID="gridviewAllOrders" runat="server"
AutoGenerateColumns="false">
    <Columns>
    <asp:TemplateField HeaderText="Transaction ID">
        <ItemTemplate>
<a href="OrderDetails.aspx?TransID=<%# Eval("TransactionID") %>&OrderID=
    <%# Eval("OrderID") %>"><%# Eval("TransactionID") %></a>
        </ItemTemplate>
    </asp:TemplateField>
    <asp:TemplateField HeaderText="Name">
        <ItemTemplate>
            <%# Eval("FirstName") %> <%# Eval("LastName") %><br />
            <%# Eval("AddressLine") %> <%# Eval("AddressLine2") %><br />
            <%# Eval("City") %>, <%# Eval("State") %>
            <%# Eval("PostalCode") %>
        </ItemTemplate>
    </asp:TemplateField>
    <asp:TemplateField HeaderText="Email">
        <ItemTemplate>
            <%# Eval("Email") %>
        </ItemTemplate>
    </asp:TemplateField>
    <asp:TemplateField HeaderText="Phone">
        <ItemTemplate>
            <%# Eval("Phone") %>
        </ItemTemplate>
    </asp:TemplateField>
    <asp:TemplateField HeaderText="Order Date">
        <ItemTemplate>
            <%# Eval("OrderDate") %>
        </ItemTemplate>
    </asp:TemplateField>
    <asp:TemplateField HeaderText="Status">
        <ItemTemplate>
            <%# Eval("OrderStatusName") %>
        </ItemTemplate>
    </asp:TemplateField>
    </Columns>
    </asp:GridView>
            </td>
        </tr>
    </table>
    <br />
    <br />
</asp:Content>
```

How It Works

This HTML code is fairly straightforward. You added a GridView control with several columns to be data bound. The individual columns are TransactionID and a formatted column that displays the name of the customer with their address. Finally, the name of the customer is followed by the customer's e-mail address and phone number along with the order date and order status. You formatted the TransactionID column as a hyperlink that will direct the user to the OrderDetails.aspx web form.

6. Now that you have created the web form and implemented the mechanics for an administrator to view the orders, you need to populate the GridView control with the orders queried from the database. To do so, add the following code:

```
using System;
using System.Data;
using System.Configuration;
using System.Collections;
using System.Web;
using System.Web.Security;
using System.Web.UI;
using System.Web.UI.WebControls;
using System.Web.UI.WebControls.WebParts;
using System.Web.UI.HtmlControls;

using LittleItalyVineyard.BusinessLogic;

public partial class Admin_Orders : System.Web.UI.Page
{
    protected void Page_Load( object sender , EventArgs e )
    {
        if ( !IsPostBack )
        {
            LoadOrders();
        }
    }

    private void LoadOrders()
    {
        ProcessGetAllOrders getallorders = new ProcessGetAllOrders();

        try
        {
            getallorders.Invoke();
        }
        catch
        {
            Response.Redirect( "../ErrorPage.aspx" );
        }
```

```
            gridviewAllOrders.DataSource = getallorders.ResultSet;
            gridviewAllOrders.DataBind();
        }
    }
```

How It Works

In the Orders.aspx web form, gridviewAllOrders, which is a GridView control, is data bound to the DataSet that is returned from the query of all the customers' orders. The Invoke() method is called from the ProcessGetAllOrders business logic class and finally will data bind the results to the GridView control.

The exercise is complete, and you can now address the details of allowing the administrator to view the details of the order and eventually fulfill and ship the order.

Viewing the Order Details

The next portion of functionality is to view the individual order details. Implementing the details of the orders will be similar to what you implemented for the customer account. This has one major difference, however. For the customer account, the information was read-only so that the customer could view all the information about their order but not modify it. For the administrator access, only a portion of the order information will be read-only. For instance, the products that have been purchased and the tax, shipping, and total will be read-only, but the administrator will need to be able to update the order by modifying the status, the tracking information, and the ship date. This will all be handled in the order details section of the application.

In the following exercise, you will implement the ability to view the order details.

Exercise: Viewing the Order Details

This exercise shows how to implement the functionality to allow the administrator to view the order details. Follow these steps:

1. You have already created the stored procedure to query the order details; however, you need to populate the different choices for the order status and add another stored procedure that will query the Orders table by a specified order ID. Therefore, add the stored procedures and execute them:

```
CREATE PROCEDURE OrderStatus_Select

AS

SELECT OrderStatusID, OrderStatusName FROM OrderStatus

CREATE PROCEDURE OrdersByID_Select

@OrderID int

AS
```

```
SELECT OrderDate, ShipDate,
OrderStatusID, TrackingNumber
FROM Orders
WHERE OrderID = @OrderID
```

How It Works

The OrderStatus_Select stored procedure simply selects both the OrderStatusID and the OrderStatusName so that the result set can be displayed. Finally, the OrdersByID_Select stored procedure will query the individual information from the Orders table based on the order ID that was selected.

2. In this step, you'll add the new stored procedures to the Name enumeration located in the StoredProcedure class in the data access layer. Then you'll add two new classes to the Select directory and namespace for the order status query. Add two new classes named OrderStatusSelectData and OrderSelectByIDData with the following code included:

```
using System;
using System.Collections.Generic;
using System.Text;
using System.Data;

namespace LittleItalyVineyard.DataAccess.Select
{
    public class OrderStatusSelectData : DataAccessBase
    {
        public OrderStatusSelectData()
        {
            base.StoredProcedureName = StoredProcedure.Name.➥
              OrderStatus_Select.ToString();
        }

        public DataSet Get()
        {
            DataSet ds;

            DataBaseHelper dbhelper = new DataBaseHelper➥
              ( base.StoredProcedureName );
            ds = dbhelper.Run( base.ConnectionString );

            return ds;
        }
    }
}

using System;
using System.Collections.Generic;
using System.Text;
using System.Data;
using System.Data.SqlClient;
```

```
using LittleItalyVineyard.Common;

namespace LittleItalyVineyard.DataAccess.Select
{
    public class OrderSelectByIDData : DataAccessBase
    {
        private Orders _orders;

        public OrderSelectByIDData()
        {
            StoredProcedureName = StoredProcedure.Name.➥
             OrdersByID_Select.ToString();
        }

        public DataSet Get()
        {
            DataSet ds;

            OrderSelectByIDDataParameters➥
                _orderselectbyiddataparameters =➥
                new OrderSelectByIDDataParameters( Orders );
        DataBaseHelper dbhelper = new DataBaseHelper( StoredProcedureName );
            ds = dbhelper.Run( base.ConnectionString ,
                _orderselectbyiddataparameters.➥
                 Parameters );

            return ds;
        }

        public Orders Orders
        {
            get { return _orders; }
            set { _orders = value; }
        }
    }

    public class OrderSelectByIDDataParameters
    {
        private Orders _orders;
        private SqlParameter[] _parameters;

        public OrderSelectByIDDataParameters( Orders orders )
        {
            Orders = orders;
            Build();
        }
```

```
    private void Build()
    {
      SqlParameter[] parameters =
      {
         new SqlParameter( "@OrderID" , Orders.OrderID )
      };

      Parameters = parameters;
    }

    public Orders Orders
    {
       get { return _orders; }
       set { _orders = value; }
    }

    public SqlParameter[] Parameters
    {
       get { return _parameters; }
       set { _parameters = value; }
      }
    }
}
```

How It Works

The data access code is not too complex so far; you are simply looking to return a DataSet with all the order status types. The OrderSelectByIDData class will query the individual record from the Orders table based upon the order ID.

3. You'll now move along to the business logic layer to add the necessary classes. Therefore, add a new class named ProcessGetOrderStatus and a class named ProcessGetOrderByID to the LittleItalyVineyard.BusinessLogic class library project with the following code:

```
using System;
using System.Collections.Generic;
using System.Text;
using System.Data;

using LittleItalyVineyard.Common;
using LittleItalyVineyard.DataAccess.Select;

namespace LittleItalyVineyard.BusinessLogic
{
    public class ProcessGetOrderStatus : IBusinessLogic
    {
        private DataSet _resultset;
```

```csharp
        public ProcessGetOrderStatus()
        {

        }

        public void Invoke()
        {
            OrderStatusSelectData orderstatusdata =➥
              new OrderStatusSelectData();
            ResultSet = orderstatusdata.Get();
        }

        public DataSet ResultSet
        {
            get { return _resultset; }
            set { _resultset = value; }
        }
    }
}

using System;
using System.Collections.Generic;
using System.Text;
using System.Data;

using LittleItalyVineyard.Common;
using LittleItalyVineyard.DataAccess.Select;

namespace LittleItalyVineyard.BusinessLogic
{
    public class ProcessGetOrderByID
    {
        private Orders _orders;
        private DataSet _resultset;

        public ProcessGetOrderByID()
        {

        }

        public void Invoke()
        {
            OrderSelectByIDData orderbyid = new OrderSelectByIDData();
            orderbyid.Orders = this.Orders;
            ResultSet = orderbyid.Get();
```

```
      if ( ResultSet.Tables[0].Rows.Count > 0 )
      {
        if ( ResultSet.Tables[0].Rows[0]["ShipDate"].ToString() != "" )
        {
          Orders.ShipDate = Convert.ToDateTime( ResultSet.➥
            Tables[0].Rows[0]➥
            ["ShipDate"].ToString() );
        }

        Orders.TrackingNumber = ResultSet.➥
            Tables[0].Rows[0]["TrackingNumber"].➥
            ToString();
        Orders.OrderStatusID = int.Parse( ResultSet.➥
            Tables[0].Rows[0]➥
            ["OrderStatusID"].ToString() );
      }
    }

    public Orders Orders
    {
        get { return _orders; }
        set { _orders = value; }
    }

    public DataSet ResultSet
    {
        get { return _resultset; }
        set { _resultset = value; }
    }
  }
}
```

How It Works

The business logic layer code will simply implement the necessary Invoke() method and populate the ResultSet property that can be used from the calling code for both of the classes. In the ProcessGetOrderByID class, the Order class will be populated by iterating through the DataSet returned. Regarding the ShipDate property, you need to first check whether it is a null value since the property is a DateTime format. In other words, if the value is null, an exception will occur.

4. Now add the web form OrderDetails.aspx to the Admin directory, and associate it with the respective master page. Upon doing so, add the following HTML code:

```
 <%@ Page Language="C#" MasterPageFile="~/Admin/Admin.master"
AutoEventWireup="true"
CodeFile="OrderDetails.aspx.cs"
Inherits="Admin_OrderDetails"
Title="Admin Control Panel | Order Details" %>
```

```
<asp:Content ID="Content1" ContentPlaceHolderID="contentplaceholderAdmin"
    Runat="Server">
    <table border="0" cellpadding="0" cellspacing="0" width="75%">
        <tr>
            <td></td><td></td>
        </tr>
        <tr>
            <td>
                Transaction ID</td>
            <td>
<asp:Label ID="labelTransactionID" runat="server"></asp:Label></td>
        </tr>
        <tr>
            <td></td><td></td>
        </tr>
        <tr>
            <td></td><td></td>
        </tr>
        <tr>
            <td>
                Purchased Items:</td>
            <td>
<asp:GridView ID="gridviewOrderDetailsProducts" runat="server"
    AutoGenerateColumns="false">
                    <Columns>
                        <asp:TemplateField HeaderText="Qty.">
                            <ItemTemplate>
                                <%# Eval("Quantity") %>
                            </ItemTemplate>
                        </asp:TemplateField>
                        <asp:TemplateField HeaderText="Product">
                            <ItemTemplate>
                                <%# Eval("ProductName") %>
                            </ItemTemplate>
                        </asp:TemplateField>
                        <asp:TemplateField HeaderText="Price">
                            <ItemTemplate>
                                <%# Eval( "Price" , "{0:c}" )%>
                            </ItemTemplate>
                        </asp:TemplateField>
                    </Columns>
                </asp:GridView>
            </td>
        </tr>
        <tr>
            <td></td><td></td>
        </tr>
```

```
        <tr>
            <td>
                Shipped Date:</td>
            <td>
<asp:TextBox ID="textShippedDate" runat="server"
    CssClass="textField">
</asp:TextBox>
            </td>
        </tr>
        <tr>
            <td></td>
            <td>
                 </td>
        </tr>
        <tr>
            <td>
                Tracking Number:</td>
            <td>
 <asp:TextBox ID="textTrackingNumber" runat="server"
     CssClass="textField"></asp:TextBox></td>
        </tr>
        <tr>
            <td></td><td></td>
        </tr>
        <tr>
            <td>
                Order Status:</td>
            <td>
<asp:DropDownList ID="dropdownlistOrderStatus" runat="server"
CssClass="textField">
                </asp:DropDownList></td>
        </tr>
        <tr>
            <td></td><td></td>
        </tr>
        <tr>
            <td>
            </td>
            <td>
    <table border="0" cellpadding="0" cellspacing="0"
        style="width: 224px">
                    <tr>
                        <td style="width: 59px">
 <asp:Button ID="commandReturn" runat="server" Text="Return"
     CssClass="button" OnClick="commandReturn_Click" /></td>
                    </tr>
                </table>
```

```
                    </td>
                </tr>
            </table>
        </asp:Content>
```

How It Works

The HTML code you just added to the OrderDetails.aspx web form will display the general details of the selected order along with the individual products that are contained in the order. In addition to the order details, you will also have the ability to update the order with respect to the shipping date and the tracking number, which I'll discuss in the next exercise.

5. The code that needs to be added to the C# portion of the web form is fairly lengthy. However, you first need to populate the order status types in the drop-down list, populate the individual products in the order, and populate the shipping date and tracking number, as shown here:

```
using System;
using System.Data;
using System.Configuration;
using System.Collections;
using System.Web;
using System.Web.Security;
using System.Web.UI;
using System.Web.UI.WebControls;
using System.Web.UI.WebControls.WebParts;
using System.Web.UI.HtmlControls;

using LittleItalyVineyard.Common;
using LittleItalyVineyard.BusinessLogic;
using LittleItalyVineyard.Operational;

public partial class Admin_OrderDetails : System.Web.UI.Page
{
    protected void Page_Load( object sender , EventArgs e )
    {
        if ( !IsPostBack )
        {
            LoadOrderStatus();
            LoadOrderDetails();
        }
    }

    private void LoadOrderDetails()
    {
        ProcessGetOrderDetails processdetails =➡
            new ProcessGetOrderDetails();
        ProcessGetOrderByID processorder =➡
            new ProcessGetOrderByID();
```

```csharp
OrderDetails orderdetails = new OrderDetails();
orderdetails.OrderID = int.Parse( Request.QueryString➥
    [ "OrderID" ] );
processdetails.OrderDetails = orderdetails;

Orders orders = new Orders();
orders.OrderID = int.Parse( Request.QueryString➥
    [ "OrderID" ] );
processorder.Orders = orders;

try
{
   processdetails.Invoke();
   processorder.Invoke();
}
catch
{
   Response.Redirect( "../ErrorPage.aspx" );
}

gridviewOrderDetailsProducts.DataSource =➥
   processdetails.ResultSet;
gridviewOrderDetailsProducts.DataBind();

labelTransactionID.Text = Request.QueryString[ "TransID" ];

if ( orders.ShipDate != DateTime.MinValue )
{
    textShippedDate.Text = orders.ShipDate.ToShortDateString();
}
textTrackingNumber.Text = orders.TrackingNumber;

dropdownlistOrderStatus.SelectedIndex =➥
   dropdownlistOrderStatus.Items.➥
   IndexOf( dropdownlistOrderStatus.Items.FindByValue➥
   ( orders.OrderStatusID.ToString() ) );
}

private void LoadOrderStatus()
{
   ProcessGetOrderStatus processorderstatus =➥
      new ProcessGetOrderStatus();
```

```
try
{
    processorderstatus.Invoke();
}
catch
{
    Response.Redirect( "../ErrorPage.aspx" );
}

dropdownlistOrderStatus.DataTextField = "OrderStatusName";
dropdownlistOrderStatus.DataValueField = "OrderStatusID";
dropdownlistOrderStatus.DataSource =➡
    processorderstatus.ResultSet;
dropdownlistOrderStatus.DataBind();
    }
}
```

How It Works

As mentioned, you had to address a number of issues in the OrderDetails.aspx web form. The first item was to populate the dropdownlistOrderStatus DropDownList control with all the available status types for the order. You accomplished this by utilizing the ProcessGetOrderStatus class from the business logic layer of the architecture. You data bound the resulting DataSet after setting the DataTextField property to the OrderStatusName and the DataValueField property to the OrderStatusID fields so that the DropDownList control will show the text name of the status and the value to the associated status ID of the name. To finalize this code in this exercise, you query specifically the ship date and the tracking number and populate the respective controls, taking into account that if the ShipDate property is the minimum value of a date, the text box will not be populated and will be left as an empty string.

You now have the individual status types populated in the DropDownList control. You can now move along to addressing the remaining items needed, which I'll discuss in the following section.

Creating the Order Fulfillment

The administrator now has the ability to view all the orders that the customers have placed. Let's reverse a bit to review how an order is placed from a customer: first, the customer enters their credit card information, and upon acceptance, a new order appears in the system. This new order will eventually have to be fulfilled. Therefore, the default status for a new order that is placed is New. The administrator will physically need to obtain the items that were purchased, prepare the packaging, and make arrangements with the shipping company that will be delivering the goods to the customer. When making these arrangements, the shipping company will provide the administrator with a tracking number. The administrator will need to add this to the order for recording-keeping purposes and to inform the customer that they can track the progress of their shipment while it is en route to their delivery destination.

In the following exercise, you'll implement functionality to allow the administrator to update the order with this information.

Exercise: Fulfilling the Order

This exercise show how to implement the functionality where an administrator can fulfill the order and update the status, the tracking information, and the date the goods are shipped. Follow these steps:

1. As with most of the exercises you have dealt with, you will initiate the implementation at the database level by creating the stored procedure that is necessary to update the status of a specific order:

```
CREATE PROCEDURE Orders_Update

@OrderID int,
@OrderStatusID int,
@ShipDate smalldatetime,
@TrackingNumber nvarchar(50)

AS

UPDATE Orders
SET OrderStatusID = @OrderStatusID,
ShipDate = @ShipDate,
TrackingNumber = @TrackingNumber
WHERE OrderID = @OrderID
```

How It Works

The Orders_Update stored procedure accepts four parameters: @OrderID, @OrderStatusID, @ShipDate, and @TrackingNumber. All the information is updated in the Orders table based on the OrderID.

2. You will now move to the data access tier of the architecture. Similar to other exercises, add the name of the new stored procedure created in the enumeration. In this implementation will be an update to the database, so add a new class to the Update directory or namespace in the LittleItalyVineyard.DataAccess class library project named OrderUpdateData. In this new class, add the following code:

```
using System;
using System.Collections.Generic;
using System.Text;
using System.Data.SqlClient;

using LittleItalyVineyard.Common;

namespace LittleItalyVineyard.DataAccess.Update
{
    public class OrderUpdateData : DataAccessBase
    {
        private Orders _orders;
        private OrderUpdateDataParameters _orderupdatedataparameters;
```

```
        public OrderUpdateData()
        {
            StoredProcedureName = StoredProcedure.Name.➥
                Orders_Update.ToString();
        }

        public void Update()
        {
            _orderupdatedataparameters =➥
                new OrderUpdateDataParameters( Orders );
                DataBaseHelper dbhelper =➥
                new DataBaseHelper( StoredProcedureName );
                dbhelper.Parameters =➥
                _orderupdatedataparameters.Parameters;
                dbhelper.Run();
        }

    public Orders Orders
    {
        get { return _orders; }
        set { _orders = value; }
    }
}

public class OrderUpdateDataParameters
{
    private Orders _orders;
    private SqlParameter[] _parameters;

    public OrderUpdateDataParameters( Orders orders )
    {
        Orders = orders;
        Build();
    }

    private void Build()
    {
        SqlParameter[] parameters =
        {
            new SqlParameter( "@OrderID", Orders.OrderID ) ,
            new SqlParameter( "@OrderStatusID" ,➥
                Orders.OrderStatusID ) ,
            new SqlParameter( "@ShipDate", Orders.ShipDate ) ,
            new SqlParameter( "@TrackingNumber", Orders.TrackingNumber )
        };

        Parameters = parameters;
    }
```

```csharp
        public Orders Orders
        {
           get { return _orders; }
           set { _orders = value; }
        }

        public SqlParameter[] Parameters
        {
           get { return _parameters; }
           set { _parameters = value; }
        }
      }
  }
```

How It Works

The code in the data access layer will be similar to that of the others. An associated parameters class will be utilized to execute the stored procedure Orders_Update.

3. The next task will be the business logic tier of the application. Therefore, proceed to the LittleItalyVineyard.BusinessLogic class library project, and add a new class named ProcessUpdateOrder. Add the following code to the newly created class:

```csharp
using System;
using System.Collections.Generic;
using System.Text;
using System.Data.SqlClient;

using LittleItalyVineyard.Common;
using LittleItalyVineyard.DataAccess.Update;

namespace LittleItalyVineyard.BusinessLogic
{
    public class ProcessUpdateOrder : IBusinessLogic
    {
        private Orders _orders;

        public ProcessUpdateOrder()
        {

        }

        public void Invoke()
        {
            OrderUpdateData orderupdate = new OrderUpdateData();
            orderupdate.Orders = this.Orders;
            orderupdate.Update();
        }
```

```
            public Orders Orders
            {
                get { return _orders; }
                set { _orders = value; }
            }
        }
    }
```

How It Works

The ProcessUpdateOrder class in the business logic tier of the architecture uses the required Invoke() method to pass the common class Orders into the data access portion and eventually update the order specified.

4. Now you'll proceed to the OrderDetails.aspx web form. Now that you are going to be enabling the administrator to enter the update information, you need to provide a simple method in which the administrator can enter a date value for when the order ships. To do so, you will add a Calendar control and an image control, as shown in the following updated HTML code:

```
<td>
        <asp:TextBox ID="textShippedDate" runat="server"
CssClass="textField">
</asp:TextBox>
    <asp:ImageButton ID="imagebuttonDatePicker" runat="server"
    ImageUrl="~/Images/icon-calendar.gif"
    OnClick="imagebuttonDatePicker_Click" />
    <asp:Calendar ID="calendarDatePicker"
        runat="server
    OnSelectionChanged="calendarDatePicker_SelectionChanged"
        Visible="False" Width="128px"></asp:Calendar>
</td>
```

How It Works

You added a button with an associated image along with a Calendar control where the Visible property is set to false.

5. The HTML code is in place for allowing the administrator to choose a date from the Calendar control, so you now need to address the C# code of enabling this functionality:

```
protected void imagebuttonDatePicker_Click( object sender ,➥
    ImageClickEventArgs e )
{
    if ( calendarDatePicker.Visible )
    {
        calendarDatePicker.Visible = false;
    }
    else
    {
```

```
            calendarDatePicker.Visible = true;
        }
}

protected void calendarDatePicker_SelectionChanged( object sender ,➥
    EventArgs e )
{
    textShippedDate.Text = calendarDatePicker.SelectedDate.➥
        ToShortDateString();
    calendarDatePicker.Visible = false;
}
```

How It Works

The code added spans two events. These two events are the click event of the image button and the selection changed event of the Calendar control. I'll first explain the image button click event: the code will first check whether the Calendar control is visible, and if it is, the calendar's visible property will be set to false. If not, the calendar's visible property will be set to true. This will enable the Calendar control to be displayed when the administrator clicks the image button, and if they click the image button when the calendar is being displayed, the calendar display will simply be removed or the Visible property set to false. Lastly, the selection changed event of the Calendar control, which will be fired when the administrator selects a date on the calendar, will take that value and populate the textShippedDate text box with that date in a short date format. After the text box is populated, the calendar's display will be removed.

6. You now need to implement the code that will allow for updating the order. However, you need to first add a command button to the OrderDetails.aspx web form, followed by adding a click event to the commandUpdate button, as shown here:

```
<tr>
    <td style="width: 115px">
        </td>
        <td style="width: 100px">
            <table border="0" cellpadding="0" cellspacing="0"
    style="width: 224px">
                <tr>
                <td style="width: 59px">
<asp:Button ID="commandReturn" runat="server" Text="Return"
    CssClass="button" OnClick="commandReturn_Click" /></td>
                <td style="width: 62px">
<asp:Button ID="commandUpdate" runat="server" Text="Update"
    OnClick="commandUpdate_Click" CssClass="button" /></td>
                </tr>
        </table>
    </td>
</tr>
```

You have added the HTML for the commandUpdate button. The following is the C# code portion in the click event:

```csharp
protected void commandUpdate_Click( object sender , EventArgs e )
{
    Orders orders = new Orders();
    ProcessUpdateOrder updateorder = new ProcessUpdateOrder();

    orders.OrderID = int.Parse( Request.QueryString["OrderID"] );
    orders.OrderStatusID = int.Parse➥
      ( dropdownlistOrderStatus.SelectedItem.Value );
    orders.ShipDate = Convert.ToDateTime( textShippedDate.Text );
    orders.TrackingNumber = textTrackingNumber.Text;

    updateorder.Orders = orders;

    try
    {
       updateorder.Invoke();
     }
    catch
    {
       Response.Redirect( "../ErrorPage.aspx" );
    }

     Response.Redirect( "Orders.aspx" );
}
```

How It Works

The click event, which will ultimately update the order that has been selected, will utilize the ProcessUpdateOrder class from in the business logic tier. The information that needs to be updated will be populated from the Orders common class and subsequently passed to the business logic class. Finally, the Invoke() method will be called from in a try/catch statement, and if there are no errors, the user will be redirected to the Orders.aspx web form where the updates will be reflected.

In this exercise, you enabled the administrator to add or update the remaining pieces of information regarding a specific customer order.

Informing the Customer

All your customers are important to you because you want them to return to the application and make additional purchases. With that said, it is always a good idea to keep each customer informed about what is going on with their order each step of the way. Simply put, each time the status changes for an order, the customer should be notified of the update status. You'll implement this functionality in the following exercise.

In this exercise, you will implement the ability to automatically e-mail the customer when you have updated their order. Follow these steps:

1. Since the method used to update the customer will be via e-mail, you will revisit the EmailManager class found in the LittleItalyVineyard.Operational class library you created in Chapter 14. Proceed to the OrderDetails.aspx web form and to the C# code portion. Add the LittleItalyVineyard.Operational name-space to the top of the code as follows:

```
using LittleItalyVineyard.Operational;
```

2. Prior to adding the code that will populate the EmailManager class and eventually send the e-mail, you need the e-mail address of the customer to which to send the e-mail message. To accomplish this, you will proceed to the Orders.aspx web form and add a query string to the hyperlink that displays the transaction ID. Therefore, update the following HTML in the Orders.aspx web form:

```
<asp:TemplateField HeaderText="Transaction ID">
   <ItemTemplate>
    <a href="OrderDetails.aspx?TransID=
       <%# Eval("TransactionID") %>&OrderID=
    <%# Eval("OrderID") %>&Email=<%# Eval("Email") %>">
<%# Eval("TransactionID") %></a>
      </ItemTemplate>
</asp:TemplateField>
```

How It Works

As mentioned, a new query string is added to the hyperlink named Email; it uses the Eval data-binding method to populate the query string with the customer's e-mail address.

3. Now that you will be able to easily obtain the customer's e-mail address as a result of the newly added query string, proceed to the commandUpdate click event in the OrderDetails.aspx web form. The fol-lowing code will populate the content of the e-mail message and finally send the update message:

```
protected void commandUpdate_Click( object sender , EventArgs e )
{
    Orders orders = new Orders();
    ProcessUpdateOrder updateorder = new ProcessUpdateOrder();

    orders.OrderID = int.Parse( Request.QueryString["OrderID"] );
    orders.OrderStatusID = int.Parse( dropdownlistOrderStatus.➥
      SelectedItem.Value );
    orders.ShipDate = Convert.ToDateTime( textShippedDate.Text );
    orders.TrackingNumber = textTrackingNumber.Text;

    updateorder.Orders = orders;

    try
    {
      updateorder.Invoke();
```

```
                    EmailManager emailmngr = new EmailManager();
                    EmailContents mailcontents = new EmailContents();

                    mailcontents.To = Request.QueryString[ "Email" ];
                    mailcontents.Subject = "Little Italy Vineyard Update - Order ID: " +
                     Request.QueryString["OrderID"];
                    mailcontents.Body = "Your order has been updated. ➥
                    Please log into your account for details.";

                    emailmngr.Send( mailcontents );

                    if ( !emailmngr.IsSent )
                    {
                        Response.Redirect("../ErrorPage.aspx");
                    }
                }
                catch
                {
                  Response.Redirect( "../ErrorPage.aspx" );
                }

                Response.Redirect( "Orders.aspx" );
            }
```

How It Works

The EmailContents struct is first populated with all the basic information from the customer's order and then is used to populate the EmailManager class to execute sending the e-mail message from the LittleItalyVineyard.Operational class library, which informs the customer that the status of their order has changed and they are able to view the updates by logging into their account.

In this exercise, you added functionality to keep the customer informed when their order has been updated.

Issuing Refunds

As the company sells the products on its website to customers, the products are paid in full by means of a credit card payment when an order is placed. However, sometimes the company will have to issue a refund to the customer for their purchase. This could be for many reasons; for instance, maybe there is going to be a long delay when fulfilling the order, and as a result, the customer does not want to wait. They instead want to cancel the order and get a refund of the money they spent.

As part of the overall fulfillment of the orders, the administrator will certainly need the ability to refund the amount of an order that has been placed by a customer. In the following exercise, you'll implement the functionality to refund an order.

Exercise: Refunding an Order

For this final exercise in the chapter, you will add the necessary functionality to allow the administrator to issue a refund for an order that has already been placed by a customer. Follow these steps:

1. Return to the PayPalManager class located in the LittleItalyVineyard.Operational class library project. In this class, you need to add a method that will refund a transaction. Examine the following code in the method that you need to add:

```
public void RefundTransaction( string TransactionID )
{
    RefundTransactionRequestType refundRequest =➡
      new RefundTransactionRequestType();
    BasicAmountType amount = new BasicAmountType();
    amount.currencyID = CurrencyCodeType.USD;
    refundRequest.Memo = "Transaction ID: " + TransactionID;
    refundRequest.RefundType = RefundPurposeTypeCodeType.Full;
    refundRequest.TransactionID = TransactionID;
    refundRequest.Version = "2.0";

    RefundTransactionReq request = new RefundTransactionReq();
    request.RefundTransactionRequest = refundRequest;

    try
    {
      RefundTransactionResponseType response =➡
         service.RefundTransaction(request);
      string errors = CheckForErrors( response );

      if (errors == string.Empty)
      {
        IsSubmissionSuccess = true;
      }
      else
      {
        IsSubmissionSuccess = false;
        SubmissionError = errors;
      }
    }
    catch (Exception ex)
    {
      throw ex;
    }
}
```

How It Works

In the RefundTransaction method, the transaction ID will be passed as a string parameter. You'll use the PayPal application programming interfaces (APIs) to issue a full refund to this order, which is specified by the transaction ID.

2. The next task is to add a command button HTML code to the OrderDetails.aspx web form and then add the associated click event. This code in the click event will initiate the refund of the customer's order:

```
<td>
  <table border="0" cellpadding="0" cellspacing="0" style="width: 224px">
    <tr>
      <td style="width: 59px">
<asp:Button ID="commandReturn" runat="server" Text="Return"
CssClass="button" OnClick="commandReturn_Click" /></td>
    <td style="width: 62px">
<asp:Button ID="commandUpdate" runat="server"
  Text="Update"
  OnClick="commandUpdate_Click"
  CssClass="button" /></td>

<td style="width: 100px">
<asp:Button ID="commandRefund"
  runat="server"
Text="Issue Refund"
OnClick="commandRefund_Click"
CssClass="button" />
</td>

</tr>
  </table>
</td>

protected void commandRefund_Click( object sender , EventArgs e )
{
    PayPalManager paypal = new PayPalManager();
    paypal.RefundTransaction( Request.QueryString[ "TransID" ] );
}
```

How It Works

The code to initiate the refund simply instantiates the PayPalManager class and then calls the Refund-Transaction method, passing in the TransID query string.

3. After implementing the refunding functionality, you will need to update the order in your database. The code will be similar to what you added in the update click event. The updated code is as follows:

```
protected void commandRefund_Click( object sender , EventArgs e )
{
    PayPalManager paypal = new PayPalManager();
```

```
  paypal.RefundTransaction( Request.QueryString[ "TransID" ] );

  Orders orders = new Orders();
  ProcessUpdateOrder updateorder = new ProcessUpdateOrder();

  int refundedstatustype = 3;

  orders.OrderID = int.Parse( Request.QueryString["OrderID"] );
  orders.OrderStatusID = refundedstatustype;
  orders.ShipDate = ( DateTime ) SqlDateTime.Null;
  updateorder.Orders = orders;

  try
  {
    updateorder.Invoke();
  }
  catch
  {
    Response.Redirect("../ErrorPage.aspx");
  }

  Response.Redirect("Orders.aspx");
}
```

How It Works

As mentioned, the code to update the order is similar to the code added in the previous exercise. However, there are a few differences. The first item that is different is that you need to add a new namespace to the code in the declarations:

```
using System.Data.SqlTypes;
```

You need this so you can set the ShipDate of the Orders common class to the SqlDateTime.Null value and then cast it to a DateTime data type. This will prevent an exception when updating the Orders table because you are not going to be adding a ShipDate. Lastly, you will set the status of the order to the refunded status, which has an ID of 3 in the OrderStatus table.

4. For the final task, you will need to be able to alert the customer that their order has been refunded. Similar to how you alerted the customer when the order was fulfilled, you will add the following code to send an e-mail message indicating the refund:

```
protected void commandRefund_Click( object sender , EventArgs e )
{
  PayPalManager paypal = new PayPalManager();
  paypal.RefundTransaction( Request.QueryString[ "TransID" ] );

  Orders orders = new Orders();
  ProcessUpdateOrder updateorder = new ProcessUpdateOrder();

  int refundedstatustype = 3;
```

```
      orders.OrderID = int.Parse( Request.QueryString["OrderID"] );
      orders.OrderStatusID = refundedstatustype;
      orders.ShipDate = ( DateTime ) SqlDateTime.Null;
      updateorder.Orders = orders;

      try
      {
         updateorder.Invoke();

         if (paypal.IsSubmissionSuccess)
         {
            EmailManager emailmngr = new EmailManager();
            EmailContents mailcontents = new EmailContents();

            mailcontents.To = Request.QueryString["Email"];
            mailcontents.Subject =➥
  "Little Italy Vineyard Update - Order ID: " +
    Request.QueryString["OrderID"];
            mailcontents.Body = "Your order has been refunded.  ➥
    Please log into your account for details.";

     emailmngr.Send(mailcontents);

          if (!emailmngr.IsSent)
          {
              Response.Redirect("../ErrorPage.aspx");
          }
        }
      }
      catch
      {
         Response.Redirect("../ErrorPage.aspx");
      }

      Response.Redirect("Orders.aspx");
}
```

How It Works

The final code added to the click event of the command button for issuing a refund is to utilize the EmailManager class once again along with the associated EmailContents struct. Basic information is provided in the e-mail message to inform the customer that their order has been refunded. Finally, if the e-mail is sent successfully by checking the IsSent property, the administrator will be redirected to the Orders.aspx web form where the updated information will be displayed.

The administrator is now able to issue a refund for a customer's order.

Summary

Throughout this chapter, you enabled the functionality to manage the orders that customers have placed. You built functionality to view the orders as well as the details in the individual order. Lastly, you enabled the application to update the Orders table with the date the order will ship and with the tracking information. In addition to the updating, you expanded the PayPal APIs to issue a refund for an order if necessary.

CHAPTER 24

■ ■ ■

Promoting the Site and Upselling

You are nearing the end of this book, and you have addressed quite a bit of functionality up to this point. A customer has the ability to order products from your catalog; in addition, an administrator has the ability to fulfill orders, add new products to the catalog, and make any alterations necessary to existing products within the product catalog. Therefore, the functionality thus far could be considered sufficient for the first version of your e-commerce application.

However, prior to releasing the first version of the application, you want to have the ability to promote the products that you or your clients are selling. For example, say you have a fast-food restaurant. A customer will go inside the store (or through the drive-through) and will place their order. Inevitably, the person taking your order will ask you one of the following questions: Would you like fries with that? Would you like to "value size" your order? Would you like dessert with that? All of these questions relate to the concept of *upselling*. The restaurant has already sold a product to you, but they are attempting to sell an add-on product or increase the volume or size of the order you just placed.

Selling merchandise via e-commerce is not much different. However, in place of asking to "value size" a product, the most common technique is to display products that are related to what the customer is already buying in the hope that they will add the related product to their final order.

In this chapter, I will discuss how to implement such techniques in an attempt to maximize your sales. More specifically, I will discuss and offer exercises for the following topics:

- Upselling by showing related products

- Sending e-newsletters to advertise sales and product information

Upselling with Related Products

When a customer makes a purchase from your online store, you want to allow them to view other closely related products that are for sale. Take, for example, when a customer adds a bottle or several bottles of wine to their shopping cart; on the shopping cart page, you should be able to show them some products that have been purchased by other customers who made similar purchases. Displaying this information for customers can often result in the customers viewing the associated product and saying to themselves, "That looks good—I'm going to purchase that too!" If the customer adds this related product to their order, you have just increased your sales by means of upselling.

Upselling is common with e-commerce applications, so you have probably already seen it in action. Therefore, the following exercise will explain all the details of implementing upselling into your e-commerce application for Little Italy Vineyards.

Exercise: Upselling

This exercise shows how to display related products to the customers when they add products to their shopping carts. The related products will be based on querying orders placed by other customers who have ordered the same products. Follow these steps:

1. At the database level, you need to create a stored procedure that queries the necessary information and thus returns the values for display to the customer. Here's the stored procedure script:

```
CREATE PROCEDURE ProductPromotion_Select

@ProductID int

AS

SELECT
ProductID,
ProductName,
SUBSTRING(Description, 1, 150) + '...'
  AS Description
FROM Products

WHERE ProductID IN
(
    SELECT TOP 5 details2.ProductID
    FROM OrderDetails details1
    INNER JOIN OrderDetails details2
    ON details1.OrderID = details2.OrderID
    WHERE details1.ProductID = @ProductID
    AND details2.ProductID != @ProductID
    GROUP BY details2.ProductID
)
```

How It Works

With the ProductPromotion_Select stored procedure, the goal is to query the Products table for five purchases of the same product by other customers. The really effective part of this stored procedure is within the WHERE clause because a subquery is used. In the subquery, the top five results are taken from the OrderDetails table, which is inner joined to itself, so you can display any other products that were included in the other customers' completed orders (excluding the product that the current customer has just added to their shopping cart); this is how you find the related products.

2. After adding and executing the stored procedure script, now move to the data access tier and more specifically the LittleItalyVineyard.DataAccess class library project. First add the name of the newly created stored procedure to the Name enumeration. Then, in the Select directory and namespace, add the new class, ProductPromotionSelectData, with the following code:

```
using System;
using System.Collections.Generic;
using System.Text;
using System.Data;
using System.Data.SqlClient;

using LittleItalyVineyard.Common;

namespace LittleItalyVineyard.DataAccess.Select
{
    public class ProductPromotionSelectData : DataAccessBase
    {
        private Product _product;

        public ProductPromotionSelectData()
        {
            base.StoredProcedureName = StoredProcedure.Name.➥
                ProductPromotion_Select.ToString();
        }

        public DataSet Get()
        {
            DataSet ds;

            ProductPromotionSelectDataParameters _productpromotion =➥
                new ProductPromotionSelectDataParameters( Product );
            DataBaseHelper dbhelper = new DataBaseHelper➥
                ( StoredProcedureName );
            ds = dbhelper.Run( base.ConnectionString , ➥
                _productpromotion.Parameters );

            return ds;
        }

        public Product Product
        {
            get { return _product; }
            set { _product = value; }
        }
    }

    public class ProductPromotionSelectDataParameters
    {
```

```csharp
        private Product _product;
        private SqlParameter[] _parameters;

        public ProductPromotionSelectDataParameters( Product product )
        {
           Product = product;
           Build();
        }

        private void Build()
        {
           SqlParameter[ ] parameters =
           {
              new SqlParameter( "@ProductID" , Product.ProductID )
           };

           Parameters = parameters;
        }

        public Product Product
        {
          get { return _product; }
          set { _product = value; }
        }

        public SqlParameter[] Parameters
        {
           get { return _parameters; }
           set { _parameters = value; }
        }
      }
    }
```

3. The next step is to proceed to the business logic portion of the code and more specifically the LittleItalyVineyard.BusinessLogic class library project. Add a new class named ProcessGetPromotions with the following code:

```csharp
using System;
using System.Collections.Generic;
using System.Text;
using System.Data;

using LittleItalyVineyard.Common;
using LittleItalyVineyard.DataAccess.Select;

namespace LittleItalyVineyard.BusinessLogic
{
    public class ProcessGetPromotions : IBusinessLogic
```

```
    {
       private DataSet _resultset;
       private Product _product;

       public ProcessGetPromotions()
       {

       }

       public void Invoke()
       {
          ProductPromotionSelectData promotiondata =➥
            new ProductPromotionSelectData();
          promotiondata.Product = this.Product;
          ResultSet = promotiondata.Get();
       }

       public Product Product
       {
          get { return _product; }
          set { _product = value; }
       }

       public DataSet ResultSet
       {
          get { return _resultset; }
        set { _resultset = value; }
       }
    }
  }
}
```

4. Now you'll incorporate the functionality into the presentation tier of the application. In this case, you need to address two aspects. First, you need to adjust the AddToCart.aspx web form, and then you need to adjust the ShoppingCart.aspx web form. So, add the following Hypertext Markup Language (HTML) code to the AddToCart.aspx web form:

```
protected void Page_Load( object sender , EventArgs e )
{
    LittleItalyVineyard.Common.ShoppingCart shoppingcart =➥
      new LittleItalyVineyard.Common.ShoppingCart();
    shoppingcart.ProductID = int.Parse( Request.QueryString["ProductID"] );
    shoppingcart.CartGUID = CartGUID;
    shoppingcart.Quantity = 1;

    ProcessAddShoppingCart procshoppingcart =➥
      new ProcessAddShoppingCart();
    procshoppingcart.ShoppingCart = shoppingcart;
```

```
    try
    {
        procshoppingcart.Invoke();
    }
    catch
    {
        Response.Redirect( "ErrorPage.aspx" );
    }

    Response.Redirect( "ShoppingCart.aspx?ProductID=" +
        Request.QueryString["ProductID"] );
}
```

How It Works

In the page load event of the AddToCart.aspx web form, there is no major addition in terms of functionality. In fact, the only addition is a new query string, ProductID, that is appended to the ShoppingCart.aspx redirection where the value is taken from the same query string that is passed into the AddToCart.aspx web form.

5. Now, you will address the ShoppingCart.aspx where you first need to add the following bold HTML code to the original ShoppingCart.aspx web form:

```
<%@ Page Language="C#" MasterPageFile="~/Main.master"
AutoEventWireup="true" CodeFile="ShoppingCart.aspx.cs"
Inherits="ShoppingCart" Title="Little Italy Vineyard | Shopping Cart" %>

<asp:Content ID="Content1" ContentPlaceHolderID="contentplaceholderMain"
Runat="Server">
    <table cellpadding="0" cellspacing="0" border="0" width="100%">
        <tr>
            <td style="width: 11px"><img src="images/spacer.gif"
width="10" height="15" /></td>
            <td width="100%"></td>
            <td><img src="images/spacer.gif" width="10" height="1" />
</td>
        </tr>
        <tr>
            <td style="width: 11px"></td>
            <td>
        <table cellpadding="0" cellspacing="0" border="0"
            width="100%">
                <tr>
                    <td width="16%" align="center"><b>Remove</b>
                     </td>
                    <td width="30%"><b>Product</b></td>
                    <td width="17%" align="center"><b>Quantity</b>
                     </td>
```

```
                        <td width="18%" align="center"><b>Unit Cost</b>
                          </td>
                        <td width="19%" align="center"><b>Subtotal</b>
                            </td>
                    </tr>
                </table>
            </td>
            <td></td>
        </tr>
        <tr>
            <td style="width: 11px"></td>
            <td class="prodUnderlineBG" width="100%">
<img src="images/spacer.gif" width="1" height="4" /></td>
            <td></td>
        </tr>
        <tr><td style="width: 11px">
<img src="images/spacer.gif" width="1" height="3" /></td></tr>
        <tr>
            <td style="width: 11px"></td>
            <td>
                <asp:GridView ID="gridviewShoppingCart"
runat="server" AutoGenerateColumns="false"
DataKeyNames="Quantity,ShoppingCartID"
                    OnRowDataBound="gridviewShoppingCart_
RowDataBound" Width="100%" BorderWidth="0px"
CellPadding="2" ShowHeader="false">
                <Columns>
    <asp:TemplateField ItemStyle-Width="16%"
ItemStyle-HorizontalAlign="center">
                    <ItemTemplate>
    <asp:CheckBox ID="checkboxDelete" runat="server" />
                    </ItemTemplate>
                </asp:TemplateField>
                <asp:TemplateField ItemStyle-Width="30%">
                    <ItemTemplate>
                        <%# Eval("ProductName") %>
                    </ItemTemplate>
                </asp:TemplateField>
                <asp:TemplateField ItemStyle-Width="17%"
ItemStyle-HorizontalAlign="center">
                    <ItemTemplate>
                        <asp:TextBox id="textQuantity" runat="server"
Columns="4" MaxLength="3" Text='<%# Eval("Quantity") %>'
width="30px" CssClass="textfield" />
                    </ItemTemplate>
                </asp:TemplateField>
            <asp:TemplateField ItemStyle-Width="18%"
```

```
                            ItemStyle-HorizontalAlign="center">
                             <ItemTemplate>
                                 <%# Eval( "UnitPrice" , "{0:c}" )%>
        </ItemTemplate>
        </asp:TemplateField>
        <asp:TemplateField ItemStyle-Width="19%"
            ItemStyle-HorizontalAlign="center">
                             <ItemTemplate>
                                 <%# Eval( "TotalPrice" , "{0:c}" )%>
                             </ItemTemplate>
                     </asp:TemplateField>
                     </Columns>
                     </asp:GridView>
              </td>
              <td></td>
         </tr>
         <tr><td style="width: 11px">
<img src="images/spacer.gif" width="1" height="3" /></td></tr>
         <tr>
             <td style="width: 11px"></td>
             <td class="prodUnderlineBG" width="100%">
<img src="images/spacer.gif" width="1" height="1" /></td>
             <td></td>
         </tr>
         <tr>
             <td style="width: 11px"></td>
             <td class="prodUnderlineBG" width="100%">
<img src="images/spacer.gif" width="1" height="2" /></td>
             <td></td>
         </tr>
         <tr><td style="width: 11px">
<img src="images/spacer.gif" width="1" height="5" /></td></tr>
         <tr>
             <td style="width: 11px"></td>
             <td align="right">
                 <table border="0" cellpadding="0" cellspacing="0">
                     <tr>
     <td><b>Total:</b></td>
      <td style="width: 83px;" align="center">
<asp:Label ID="labelTotal" runat="server" Width="100%"></asp:Label></td>
                     </tr>
                 </table>
             </td>
             <td></td>
         </tr>
         <tr><td style="width: 11px">
<img src="images/spacer.gif" width="1" height="20" /></td></tr>
```

```
        <tr>
            <td style="width: 11px">
            </td>
 <td align="right" style="text-align: center">
                <asp:Panel ID="panelPromotion" runat="server"
Height="50px" Visible="False" Width="85%">
                Customers have also purchased the following:<br />
                    <br />
                <asp:GridView ID="gridviewAssociated" runat="server"
ShowHeader="False" Width="100%" AutoGenerateColumns="false">
                <Columns>
                <asp:TemplateField>
                 <ItemTemplate>
    <a href="ProductDetails.aspx?ProductID=<%# Eval("ProductID")%>">
<%# Eval("ProductName") %></a>
                </ItemTemplate>
                    <ItemStyle Width="30%" />
                </asp:TemplateField>
                <asp:TemplateField>
                 <ItemTemplate>
                    <%# Eval("Description") %>
                 </ItemTemplate>
                    <ItemStyle Width="70%" />
                </asp:TemplateField>
                </Columns>
                </asp:GridView>
                </asp:Panel>
                 </td>
            <td>
            </td>
        </tr>
        <tr>
            <td style="width: 11px; height: 22px"></td>
            <td align="right" style="height: 22px">
     <asp:Button ID="commandContinueShopping" runat="server"
OnClick="commandContinueShopping_Click" Text="Continue Shopping"
CssClass="button" Width="136px" />
                <img src="images/spacer.gif" width="5" height="1" />
                <asp:Button ID="commandUpdate" runat="server"
OnClick="commandUpdate_Click" Text="Update" CssClass="button" />
                <img src="images/spacer.gif" width="5" height="1" />
                <asp:Button ID="commandCheckout" runat="server"
OnClick="commandCheckout_Click" Text="Check Out" CssClass="button" />
                <img src="images/spacer.gif" width="15" height="1" />
            </td>
            <td style="height: 22px"></td>
        </tr>
```

```
        <tr><td style="width: 11px"><img src="images/spacer.gif"
width="1" height="15" /></td></tr>
    </table>
</asp:Content>
```

How It Works

In this HTML code, you first added a new panel named panelPromotion, and in the panel control there is a GridView control named gridviewAssociated. The panel control's Visible property is set to False, so for it to display, you will need to set the Visible property to true. The reasoning for this is that when the e-commerce application first starts or a new product is added to the product catalog, there will be a period of time that zero orders have been placed for the product, thus not being related with any other orders. When this is the case, you will not show any results in the panel, thus keeping the Visible property set to False.

6. Now add the code that will show the customer's related products within the ShoppingCart.aspx web form after adding a new item to the shopping cart:

```
protected void Page_Load( object sender , EventArgs e )
{
    if ( !IsPostBack )
    {
        LoadShoppingCart();
        LoadPromotion();
    }
}

private void LoadPromotion()
{
    ProcessGetPromotions getpromotions = new ProcessGetPromotions();
    Product product = new Product();

    if ( Request.QueryString["ProductID"] != null )
    {
        product.ProductID = int.Parse( Request.QueryString["ProductID"] );
    }
    else
    {
        return;
    }

    getpromotions.Product = product;

    try
    {
        getpromotions.Invoke();
```

```
      if ( getpromotions.ResultSet.Tables[0].Rows.Count > 0 )
      {
         panelPromotion.Visible = true;
         gridviewAssociated.DataSource = getpromotions.ResultSet;
         gridviewAssociated.DataBind();
      }
   }
   catch
   {
      Response.Redirect( "ErrorPage.aspx" );
   }
}
```

How It Works

The code added will first call the method LoadPromotion from within the page load event. In the LoadPromotion method, the code will first instantiate the ProcessGetPromotions class along with a new Product common class. From that point, you will check whether there is a ProductID query string. This needs to be checked because if the user is navigating to the shopping cart page from a location that does not provide a query string, you will simply exit the method that is specified by the return keyword in the else portion of the If statement. However, when there is a specified query string, you will cast the query string of the product ID to an integer data type and set the ProductID property of the Product common class. Moving along, the Product property of the ProcessGetPromotions class will be set to the Product class that was earlier instantiated, and then the Invoke() method is wrapped within a try/catch statement and will be called to query the related products. The ResultSet DataSet property is then checked to determine whether there are any resulting records. If there are, the panelPromotion's Visible property is set to true, and subsequently the gridviewAssociated GridView control will be data bound to the ResultSet. If there are no resulting records, the code will continue leaving the method, thus keeping the panelPromotion control's Visible property set to False.

In this exercise, you established some new functionality in an attempt to upsell to customers as they add products to their shopping cart. You should keep the upselling simple in an effort not to annoy the customer but instead to simply show related products where they can easily see them.

Promoting with the E-newsletter

Another technique to promote and advertise the products for sale is to keep the customers informed by means of a newsletter that is delivered as an e-mail message. In this e-mail message, you might announce a sale or perhaps an end-of-the-season special. You want to be able to broadcast these messages to all the subscribed customers. The following exercise shows how to implement the e-newsletter.

Exercise: Implementing the E-newsletter

This exercise shows how to compile a single newsletter and have it broadcast to all the subscribed customers. It will also provide functionality to allow a customer to be removed from the subscribed newsletter list at any time. Follow these steps:

1. Once again you will start at the database level and add the necessary stored procedure. With that said, add and execute the following script for the stored procedure:

```
CREATE PROCEDURE Newsletter_Select

AS

SELECT EndUserID,
FirstName,
LastName,
Email
FROM EndUser
INNER JOIN ContactInformation
ON ContactInformation.ContactInformationID = EndUser.ContactInformationID
WHERE IsSubscribed = 1
AND EndUserTypeID = 1
```

How It Works

The Newsletter_Select stored procedure simply queries from the EndUser table while inner joining the ContactInformation table for only those users who are declared as customers from the EndUserTypeID being equal to the number 1 and the IsSubscribed field being equal to 1, meaning that they have agreed to receive newsletters.

2. After adding and executing the stored procedure script followed by adding the name of the stored procedure to the Name enumeration, you can stay within the data access tier of the code and add the necessary class. So, add a new class named NewsletterSelectData to the LittleItalyVineyard.DataAccess class library project within the Select directory and namespace. This new class will contain the following code:

```
using System;
using System.Collections.Generic;
using System.Text;
using System.Data;

namespace LittleItalyVineyard.DataAccess.Select
{
    public class NewsletterSelectData: DataAccessBase
    {
        public NewsletterSelectData()
        {
            StoredProcedureName = StoredProcedure.Name.➥
                Newsletter_Select.ToString();
        }
```

```
    public DataSet Get()
    {
      DataSet ds;

      DataBaseHelper dbhelper = new DataBaseHelper➥
        ( StoredProcedureName );
      ds = dbhelper.Run( ConnectionString );

      return ds;
    }
  }
}
```

How It Works

The body code added to the data access portion of the application first specifies the name of the stored procedure being used within the constructor and then has a function named Get that will return a DataSet by way of using the DataBaseHelper class.

3. The next segment to implement is the business logic code into the architecture. Therefore, proceed to the LittleItalyVineyard.BusinessLogic class library project, and add a new class named ProcessNewsletter. Within this class, add the following code:

```
using System;
using System.Collections.Generic;
using System.Text;
using System.Data;

using LittleItalyVineyard.DataAccess.Select;

namespace LittleItalyVineyard.BusinessLogic
{
    public class ProcessNewsletter : IBusinessLogic
    {
      private DataSet _resultset;

      public ProcessNewsletter()
      {

      }

      public void Invoke()
      {
        NewsletterSelectData newsletterdata =➥
          new NewsletterSelectData();
        ResultSet = newsletterdata.Get();
      }
```

```
        public DataSet ResultSet
        {
            get { return _resultset; }
            set { _resultset = value; }
        }
    }
}
```

How It Works

In a similar fashion to the other business logic classes, you implement the IBusinessLogic interface and subsequently implement the Invoke() method that will call upon the NewsletterSelectData class that you created in the previous exercise step. Finally, a DataSet property named ResultSet will be used for the returned DataSet from the data access code.

4. You need to add several pieces to the presentation layer of the application. You'll first focus your attention on the actual HTML template that will be used within the e-mail newsletter message being sent. To do so, return to the Admin directory within the web project, and add a new folder named EmailTemplates. After you add this new folder, add an HTML page to that directory named CustomerNewsletter.htm. Since this is an HTML page and not a web form, there will be no master page associated, and it will have only HTML code. Therefore, add the following HTML code:

```html
<html>
<head>
<link href="https://www.littleitalyvineyards.com/Css/style.css"
type="text/css" rel="stylesheet" />
</head>
<body>
<table width="100%" height="100%" border="0"
cellpadding="0" cellspacing="0"
style="background-image:
url(https://www.littleitalyvineyards.com➥
    /images/til_1.jpg);">
<tr>
<td> </td>
<td width="490" align="left" valign="top">
<table width="490" border="0" cellspacing="0"
cellpadding="0">
<tr>
<td style="width: 10px"> </td>
<td width="470" align="left" valign="top">
<table width="470" height="100%" border="0"
cellpadding="0" cellspacing="0">
<tr>
<td height="164" align="left" valign="top"
background="https://www.littleitalyvineyards.com➥
    /images/top_1.jpg"
style="width: 475px">
<div style="padding-left: 156px; padding-top: 69px; text-align: left;">
```

```
<a href="http://www.littleitalyvineyards.com/Default.aspx">
<img src="https://www.littleitalyvineyards.com/images/logo.jpg"
width="159" height="36" border="0"></a><br />
<br />
<br />
<br />
 </div>
</td>
</tr>
<tr>
<td height="172" align="right" valign="top"
background="https://www.littleitalyvineyards.com~CC
/images/back_1.jpg"
style="width: 475px">
<div style="padding-left: 0px; padding-top: 14px; padding-right: 23px;
padding-bottom: 0px">
 
<br />
</div>
</td>
</tr>
<tr>
<td height="100%" align="left" valign="top"
style="width: 475px">
<table width="100%" height="100%" border="0"
cellpadding="0" cellspacing="0"
background="https://www.littleitalyvineyards.com➥
/images/rep_3.jpg">
<tr align="left" valign="top">
<td background="https://www.littleitalyvineyards.com/images/rep_left.jpg"
style="width: 10px">
<img src="https://www.littleitalyvineyards.com/images/rep_left.jpg"
width="10" height="1"></td>
<td height="100%">
<table width="450" height="100%" border="0" cellpadding="0"
cellspacing="0">
<tr align="left" valign="top">
<td background="https://www.littleitalyvineyards.com/images/rep_line.jpg"
bgcolor="#F3E9BF" style="background-repeat: repeat-y;
background-position: top left; text-align: center;">
 <br />
<br />
<table border="0" cellpadding="0" cellspacing="0" width="95%">
<tr>
    <td>
        Dear `+Name+,<br />
        <br />
        `+MessageBody+</td>
```

```
</tr>
</table>
<br />
<br />
<br />
`+Clickhere+ to be removed from this newsletter mailing list.</td>
</tr>
</table>
</td>
<td width="10"
background="https://www.littleitalyvineyards.com/images/rep_right.jpg">
<img src="https://www.littleitalyvineyards.com/images/rep_right.jpg"
width="10" height="1"></td>
</tr>
<tr>
<td colspan="3" valign="top" align="center">
<img src="https://www.littleitalyvineyards.com/images/bottom_1.jpg"
width="470" height="23"></td>
</tr>
</table>
</td>
</tr>
</table>
</td>
<td></td>
</tr>
</table>
</td>
<td> </td>
</tr>
<tr>
<td></td>
<td height="100%">
<table cellpadding="0" cellspacing="0" border="0"
width="100%" height="100%">
<tr>
<td style="height: 100%; background-image:
url(https://www.littleitalyvineyards.com➥
/images/rep_bot.jpg);
background-repeat: repeat-y; background-position: center;">
</td>
</tr>
</table>
</td>
</tr>
</table>
</body>
</html>
```

How It Works

The HTML code you added is almost the same layout as you have been using for the application thus far. The most notable differences are the links for the style sheet and the images. Notice that they are full uniform resource locator (URL) links; because this HTML will be e-mailed to the customer, the images and styles will need to have a publicly available location for them to display. For added security, you have used the HTTPS secure connection for the links. Figure 24-1 shows the end result.

Figure 24-1. *The HTML newsletter template*

Lastly, you will notice there is some text added to the main body of the template, namely, `+Name+, `+MessageBody+, and `+Clickhere+. These are placeholders where the customer's name and the body of the message will be placed.

5. As mentioned, you will need to add several pieces to the Admin directory within the web project and presentation section. Specifically, you will add three separate web forms: Newsletter.aspx, SendingNewsletter.aspx, and NewsletterConfirmation.aspx. The Newsletter.aspx and the NewsletterConfirmation.aspx web forms will be associated to the Admin.master master page. Before adding these new web forms, you need to add a new tab to the Admin.master page, as shown in the following HTML:

```
<div class="shadetabs">
    <ul>
    <li runat="server" id="Products">
<a href="Products.aspx">Products</a></li>
    <li runat="server" id="Orders">
<a href="Orders.aspx">Orders</a></li>
    <li runat="server" id="Newsletter">
```

```
<a href="Newsletter.aspx">Newsletter</a></li>
    </ul>
</div>
```

6. Now add the Newsletter.aspx web form and the NewsletterConfirmation.aspx web form, which will both be associated to the Admin.master master page. The following is the HTML for these pages:

```
<%@ Page Language="C#" MasterPageFile="~/Admin/Admin.master"
AutoEventWireup="true" CodeFile="Newsletter.aspx.cs"
Inherits="Admin_Newsletter"
Title="Admin Control Panel | Newsletter" %>

<asp:Content ID="Content1"
ContentPlaceHolderID="contentplaceholderAdmin"
Runat="Server">
    <br />
    <table border="0" cellpadding="0" cellspacing="0"
width="85%">
        <tr>
            <td>
        <strong>Compose Newsletter</strong></td>
        </tr>
        <tr>
            <td>
  <asp:TextBox ID="textMessageBody" runat="server"
CssClass="textField" Height="208px"
  TextMode="MultiLine" Width="100%">
</asp:TextBox></td>
        </tr>
        <tr>
            <td>
            </td>
    </tr>
     <tr>
       <td style="text-align: center">
       <asp:Button ID="commandSend" runat="server"
CssClass="button" OnClick="commandSend_Click"
     Text="Send Newsletter" /></td>
        </tr>
    </table>
</asp:Content>
```

In the HTML you just added to the Newsletter.aspx web form, there is a multiline text box and a command button named commandSend:

```
<%@ Page Language="C#" MasterPageFile="~/Admin/Admin.master"
AutoEventWireup="true" CodeFile="NewsletterConfirmation.aspx.cs"
Inherits="Admin_NewsletterConfirmation"
Title="Admin Control Panel | Newsletter Confirmation" %>
```

```
<asp:Content ID="Content1"
ContentPlaceHolderID="contentplaceholderAdmin"
Runat="Server">
    <br />
    <br />
    <br />
    <table border="0" cellpadding="0" cellspacing="0"
width="75%">
    <tr>
    <td style="width: 100px; height: 10px; text-align: center">
    <strong>The newsletters have been sent.</strong></td>
    </tr>
    </table>
</asp:Content>
```

Within the HTML you added to the NewsletterConfirmation.aspx web form, you simply have an HTML table with a message informing the administrator that the newsletters have been sent.

7. Now add the final web form, which will not be associated to the Admin.master master page, and add the following HTML to the SendingNewsletter.aspx web form:

```
<%@ Page Language="C#" AutoEventWireup="true"
CodeFile="SendingNewsletter.aspx.cs"
Inherits="Admin_SendingNewsletter" %>

<html>
<head id="Head1" runat="server">
    <title>Processing....</title>
    <meta http-equiv="Content-Style-Type" content="text/css" />
    <link href="../Css/style.css" type="text/css" rel="stylesheet" />
    <script language="javascript">
        var LoopCounter = 1;
        var MaxLoop = 5;
        var IntervalId;

        function BeginLoad()
        {
            location.href = "<%= Request.QueryString["Page"]%>";
            IntervalId = window.setInterval("LoopCounter=UpdateProgress➥
              (LoopCounter, MaxLoop)", 500);
        }

        function EndLoad()
        {
            window.clearInterval(IntervalId);
            Progress.innerText = "Page Loaded -- Not Transferring";
        }
```

```
            function UpdateProgress(LoopCounter, MaxLoops)
            {
                LoopCounter += 1;

                if (LoopCounter <= MaxLoops)
                {
                    Progress.innerText += ".";
                    return LoopCounter;
                }
                else
                {
                    Progress.innerText = "";
                    return 1;
                }
            }
    </script>
    </head>
    <body onload="BeginLoad()" onunload="EndLoad()"
    style="text-align: center"
    background="../Images/til_1.jpg">
        <form id="form2" runat="server">
            <br />

            <table border="0" cellpadding="0" cellspacing="0" width="90%">
                <tr>
        <td style="width: 100%; background-color:
            #f3e9bf; text-align: center">
                    </td>
                </tr>
                <tr>
        <td style="width: 100%; background-color:
            #f3e9bf; text-align: center">
        <img border="0" height="36" src="../images/logo.jpg"
            width="159" /><br />
                    </td>
                </tr>
                <tr>
        <td style="width: 100%; background-color: #f3e9bf;
            text-align: center">
                        <strong>Administrative Control Panel</strong></td>
                </tr>
                <tr>
                    <td style="width: 100%">
```

```
            </td>
        </tr>
        <tr>
            <td style="width: 100%; text-align: center;">
    <div style="background-color: #f3e9bf; width: 100%;
        text-align: center; height: 205px;">
            <br />
            <br />
    <table align="center" border="0" cellpadding="0"
        cellspacing="0" height="99%" valign="middle"
            width="99%">
            <tr>
                <td align="center" valign="middle">
                    <font color="red" size="3"><span id="Message">
            <img src="../Images/pleasewait.gif" /><br />
                        <br />
                        Sending Newsletter
             -- Please Wait
        <span id="Progress" style="width: 25px; text-align: left">
                        </span>
                        <br />
                        <br />
                        <br />
                        <br />
                    </span></font>
                </td>
            </tr>
        </table>
    </div>
            </td>
        </tr>
    </table>
    </form>
</body>
</html>
```

How It Works

The HTML added to the SendingNewsletter.aspx web form is similar to the page you added when processing a customer's payment and submitting the information to the PayPal application programming interfaces (APIs) in Chapter 20. Over time when the customer list grows and there are several hundred or even several thousand customers who are subscribed to the newsletter, processing the sending of the e-mail newsletters can be a lengthy process. So, if this is the case, you want to have this page displayed during the processing and sending of the e-mails.

8. Proceed to the LIttleItalyVineyard.Operational class library and then to the EmailManager class. In this class, add a new class within the class file that will process the sending of the newsletter e-mail messages. Add the following code, and then I'll discuss it in more detail:

```csharp
public class NewsletterManager
{
    private DataSet _userdata;
    private string _messagebody;

    public NewsletterManager()
    {

    }

    public void SendNewsletter()
    {
        string msgbody = string.Empty;
        EmailManager mailmanager = new EmailManager();
        EmailContents mailcontents = new EmailContents();

        using ( StreamReader sr = new StreamReader( HttpContext.➥
            Current.Server.MapPath( "~/Admin/EmailTemplates➥
            /CustomerNewsletter.htm" ) ) )
        {
            string stringBody = sr.ReadToEnd();

            foreach ( DataRow dr in UserData.Tables[0].Rows )
            {
                msgbody = stringBody;
                msgbody = msgbody.Replace( "`+Name+" ,➥
                    dr["FirstName"].ToString() +
                    " " +    dr["LastName"].ToString() );
                msgbody = msgbody.Replace( "`+MessageBody+" , MessageBody );

                mailcontents.To = dr["Email"].ToString();
                mailcontents.FromName = "Little Italy Vineyards";
                mailcontents.FromEmailAddress =➥
                    "info@littleitalyvineyards.com";
                mailcontents.Subject = "Newsletter";
                mailcontents.Body = msgbody;

                mailmanager.Send( mailcontents );
            }
        }
    }

    public string MessageBody
    {
        get { return _messagebody; }
        set { _messagebody = value; }
    }
```

```
    public DataSet UserData
    {
        get { return _userdata; }
        set { _userdata = value; }
    }
}
```

How It Works

You have added a fair amount of code to the operational portion of the application and code. The name of the new class is called NewsletterManager, which has a method named SendNewsletter and two separate properties, MessageBody and UserData. Within the SendNewsletter method, you will first instantiate the EmailManager class and EmailContents struct, followed by using a StreamReader to read the HTML template page, CustomerNewsletter.htm. The entire usage of the StreamReader is enclosed within a using statement so that when the processing is complete, the resources for the StreamReader will be disposed of automatically. Within the using statement, the first task looks for the placeholders that you placed within the HTML template. To refresh your memory, the placeholders that were used are `+Name+ and `+MessageBody+, which you will utilize within the stringBody string variable that was used to read the entire contents of the HTML template with the StreamReader's ReadToEnd function. You will first take the complete stringBody variable and then use the Replace method to look for the placeholders and use the name of the customer and the message body of the newsletter, respectively. You will finally populate the EmailContents struct followed by using the EmailManager class to send the email. All of this is within a loop of the DataSet that is returned and that contains the information from those who are subscribed to the newsletter.

9. You have added the underlying functionality to the application, which will query the subscribed customers and send the e-mail newsletter messages. You now need to add the functionality to capture the information entered by the administrator and pass it along to be processed for the sending of the newsletters. Here's the Newsletter.aspx code:

```
using System;
using System.Data;
using System.Configuration;
using System.Collections;
using System.Web;
using System.Web.Security;
using System.Web.UI;
using System.Web.UI.WebControls;
using System.Web.UI.WebControls.WebParts;
using System.Web.UI.HtmlControls;

using LittleItalyVineyard.Operational;

public partial class Admin_Newsletter : BasePage
{
    protected void Page_Load( object sender , EventArgs e )
    {
```

```
        if ( !IsPostBack )
        {
           textMessageBody.Focus();
        }
     }

     protected void commandSend_Click( object sender , EventArgs e )
     {
        string URL = "NewsletterConfirmation.aspx";
        base.NewsletterBody = Utilities.FormatText➥
           ( textMessageBody.Text , true );
        Response.Redirect( "SendingNewsletter.aspx?Page=" + URL );
     }
}
```

How It Works

This code is not overly complex. First notice that this page inherits from the BasePage because you will
need to add a string property to the BasePage class. This string property is named NewsletterBody. Within
the page load event, you first set the focus to the textMessageBody text box. Finally, within the click event
of the commandSend button, you specify that the target location is the NewsletterConfirmation.aspx
web page, and then you set the new BasePage property, NewsletterBody, to that of the text entered
into the textMessageBody text box after it is formatted using the FormatText function of the Utilities
class. Finally, the user is redirected to the SendingNewsletter.aspx web form with the Page query string
you specified earlier.

10. Now you will address the NewsletterConfirmation.aspx web form where the actual code will be placed
to call upon the functionality to process and send the e-mail newsletters:

```
using System;
using System.Data;
using System.Configuration;
using System.Collections;
using System.Web;
using System.Web.Security;
using System.Web.UI;
using System.Web.UI.WebControls;
using System.Web.UI.WebControls.WebParts;
using System.Web.UI.HtmlControls;

using LittleItalyVineyard.Operational;
using LittleItalyVineyard.BusinessLogic;

public partial class Admin_NewsletterConfirmation : BasePage
{
    protected void Page_Load( object sender , EventArgs e )
    {
```

```
        if ( !IsPostBack )
        {
           SendNewsletters();
        }
    }

    private void SendNewsletters()
    {
        ProcessNewsletter processnewsletter = new ProcessNewsletter();
        NewsletterManager newslettermngr = new NewsletterManager();

        try
        {
           processnewsletter.Invoke();
           newslettermngr.MessageBody = base.NewsletterBody;
           newslettermngr.UserData = processnewsletter.ResultSet;
           newslettermngr.SendNewsletter();
        }
        catch
        {
           Response.Redirect( "../ErrorPage.aspx" );
        }
    }
}
```

How It Works

In this code that you added to the NewsletterConfirmation.aspx web form, you need to have the page inherit from the BasePage class, and then within the page load event, you will check whether there is a postback. If not, you will call the SendNewsletters method. Now within the SendNewsletter method, you will instantiate the ProcessNewsletter and NewsletterManager classes. Then finally, you call the Invoke() method of the ProcessNewsletter followed by the MessageBody and UserData properties being populated with the NewsletterBody and the ResultSet properties, respectively. The SendNewsletter method will then be called to complete the processing of the e-mail newsletters.

You now have complete functionality for sending e-mail newsletter messages to all the customers.

Allowing the Customer to Unsubscribe

Now that you have solid functionality to send e-mail messages to the customers who are subscribed to receive these transmissions, you will add one final piece of functionality. This final piece is to allow any of the customers to unsubscribe from the newsletter at any time if they happen to decide they do not want it sent to them anymore. This is an important aspect to implement within any type of mass e-mailing functionality. You do not want any of your customers to be annoyed by the newsletter if they decide they do not want it anymore. The following exercise shows how to allow the customers to unsubscribe from the newsletter.

Exercise: Unsubscribing from the Newsletter

In this exercise, you will finalize the e-mail newsletter functionality so that a customer can unsubscribe from the newsletter e-mail without any interaction from an administrator. Follow these steps:

1. As usual, you will begin with the stored procedure that is needed to remove the customer from the mailing list:

```
CREATE PROCEDURE NewsletterUnsubscribe_Update

@EndUserID int

AS

UPDATE EndUser SET IsSubscribed = 0
WHERE EndUserID = @EndUserID
```

How It Works

The NewsletterUnsubscribe_Update stored procedure accepts one parameter, EndUserID, which will then subsequently update the EndUser table and then set the IsSubscribed field to false or zero in this case where the EndUserID is specified.

2. After executing the new stored procedure and adding it to the Name enumeration within the data access tier, add a new class to the Update folder named NewsletterUpdateData with the following code:

```
using System;
using System.Collections.Generic;
using System.Text;
using System.Data.SqlClient;

using LittleItalyVineyard.Common;

namespace LittleItalyVineyard.DataAccess.Update
{
    public class NewsletterUpdateData : DataAccessBase
    {
        private EndUser _enduser;
        private NewsletterUpdateDataParameters➥
            _newsletterupdatedataparameters;

        public NewsletterUpdateData()
        {
          StoredProcedureName = StoredProcedure.Name.➥
            NewsletterUnsubscribe_Update.ToString();
        }
```

```csharp
    public void Update()
    {
        _newsletterupdatedataparameters =➥
            new NewsletterUpdateDataParameters( EndUser );
        DataBaseHelper dbhelper =➥
            new DataBaseHelper( StoredProcedureName );
        dbhelper.Parameters =➥
            _newsletterupdatedataparameters.Parameters;
        dbhelper.Run();
    }


    public EndUser EndUser
    {
        get { return _enduser; }
        set { _enduser = value; }
    }
}

public class NewsletterUpdateDataParameters
{
    private EndUser _enduser;
    private SqlParameter[] _parameters;

    public NewsletterUpdateDataParameters( EndUser enduser )
    {
      EndUser = enduser;
      Build();
    }

    private void Build()
    {
        SqlParameter[] parameters =
        {
            new SqlParameter( "@EndUserID" , EndUser.EndUserID )
        };

        Parameters = parameters;
    }

    public EndUser EndUser
    {
      gct { return _enduser; }
      set { _enduser = value; }
    }

    public SqlParameter[] Parameters
    {
```

```
            get { return _parameters; }
            set { _parameters = value; }
          }
        }
    }
```

How It Works

The code added to the data access layer of the architecture and application is similar to the other code in this section. An update method executes the stored procedure that you created in the first step of this exercise by using the EndUser common class to pass in the required parameter.

3. The next step is to add a new class to the LittleItalyVineyard.BusinessLogic, named ProcessNewsletterUnsubscribe, and add the following code:

```csharp
using System;
using System.Collections.Generic;
using System.Text;

using LittleItalyVineyard.Common;
using LittleItalyVineyard.DataAccess.Update;

namespace LittleItalyVineyard.BusinessLogic
{
    public class ProcessNewsletterUnsubscribe : IBusinessLogic
    {
        private EndUser _enduser;

        public ProcessNewsletterUnsubscribe()
        {

        }

        public void Invoke()
        {
            NewsletterUpdateData newsletterupdatedata =➥
                new NewsletterUpdateData();
            newsletterupdatedata.EndUser = this.EndUser;
            newsletterupdatedata.Update();
        }

        public EndUser EndUser
        {
          get { return _enduser; }
          set { _enduser = value; }
        }
    }
}
```

How It Works

The code within the business logic layer has the standard and required Invoke() method that will pass along the EndUser common class property to the NewsletterUpdateData class.

4. In the previous exercise, you added full functionality to read the HTML newsletter template and send the e-mail messages. However, in the SendNewsletter method of the NewsletterManager class within the LittleItalyVineyard.Operational class library, you will need to add some code, which is in bold in the following updated SendNewsletter method:

```
public void SendNewsletter()
{
    string unsubscr = string.Empty;
    string msgbody = string.Empty;
    EmailManager mailmanager = new EmailManager();
    EmailContents mailcontents = new EmailContents();

     using ( StreamReader sr = new StreamReader( HttpContext.Current.➥
        Server.MapPath( "~/Admin/EmailTemplates➥
        /CustomerNewsletter.htm" ) ) )
    {
        string stringBody = sr.ReadToEnd();

        foreach ( DataRow dr in UserData.Tables[0].Rows )
        {
            msgbody = stringBody;

            unsubscr = "<a  href=\"http://www.littleitalyvineyards.com/➥
                Admin/Unsubscribe.aspx?EndUserID=" +
            dr["EndUserID"].ToString() + "?FullName=" +
            dr["FirstName"].ToString() +
            " " + dr["LastName"].ToString() +
            "\"Target=\"_blank\"\">Click here</a>";

            msgbody = msgbody.Replace( "`+Name+" , ➥
                dr["FirstName"].ToString() +
                 " " +   dr["LastName"].ToString() );
            msgbody = msgbody.Replace( "`+MessageBody+" , MessageBody );
            msgbody = msgbody.Replace( "`+Clickhere+" , unsubscr );

            mailcontents.To = dr["Email"].ToString();
            mailcontents.FromName = "Little Italy Vineyards";
            mailcontents.FromEmailAddress =➥
              "info@littleitalyvineyards.com";
            mailcontents.Subject = "Newsletter";
            mailcontents.Body = msgbody;
```

```
                    mailmanager.Send( mailcontents );
                }
            }
    }
}
```

How It Works

The newly appended code within the SendNewsletter method will address the last placeholder;
`+Clickhere+, which will be replaced with a hyperlink that will direct a customer to a site where they
can unsubscribe from the e-mail newsletter.

5. Moving along, you now need to add the web form to the Admin section of the web project that the
   customer will be directed to if they so want to be removed from the subscription of the newsletter.
   Therefore, add a new web form named Unsubscribe.aspx to the Admin directory with the following
   HTML:

```
<%@ Page Language="C#" AutoEventWireup="true"
CodeFile="UnSubscribe.aspx.cs"
Inherits="Admin_UnSubscribe"
Title="Admin Control Panel | Unsubscribe" %>

<html>
<head id="Head1" runat="server">
<title></title>
<meta http-equiv="Content-Style-Type" content="text/css" />
<link href="../Css/style.css" type="text/css" rel="stylesheet" />
</head>
<body>
<form id="form1" runat="server">
<table width="100%" height="100%" border="0"
cellpadding="0" cellspacing="0"
style="background-image: url(../images/til_1.jpg);">
<tr>
<td> </td>
<td width="490" align="left" valign="top">
<table width="490" border="0" cellspacing="0"
cellpadding="0">
<tr>
<td width="10"> </td>
<td width="470" align="left" valign="top">
<table width="470" height="100%" border="0"
cellpadding="0" cellspacing="0">
<tr>
<td height="164" align="left" valign="top"
background="../images/top_1.jpg">
<div style="padding-left: 156px; padding-top: 69px">
<img src="../images/logo.jpg" width="159" height="36"
border="0"><br />
```

```
 </div>
</td>
</tr>
<tr>
<td height="172" align="right" valign="top"
background="../images/back_1.jpg">
<div style="padding-left: 0px; padding-top: 14px; padding-right:
23px; padding-bottom: 0px">
 </div>
</td>
</tr>
<tr>
<td height="100%" align="left" valign="top">
<table width="100%" height="100%" border="0" cellpadding="0"
cellspacing="0" background="../images/rep_3.jpg">
<tr align="left" valign="top">
<td background="../images/rep_left.jpg" style="width: 10px">
<img src="../images/rep_left.jpg" width="10" height="1"></td>
<td height="100%">
<table width="450" height="100%" border="0" cellpadding="0"
cellspacing="0">
<tr align="left" valign="top">
<td background="../images/rep_line.jpg" bgcolor="#F3E9BF"
style="background-repeat: repeat-y;
background-position: top left; text-align: center;">
 <br />
<strong>Unsubscribe From Newsletter</strong><br />
<table border="0" cellpadding="0" cellspacing="0"
width="99%" height="99%" align="center" valign="middle">
<tr>
<td align="center" valign="top">
<br />
<br />

<table border="0" cellpadding="3" cellspacing="0"
style="width: 360px">
<tr>
<td>
Dear
<asp:Label ID="labelName" runat="server">
</asp:Label>, you have been successfully
removed from the newsletter mailing list.</td>
</tr>
</table>
</td>
</tr>
</table>
```

```
        </td>
       </tr>
      </table>
     </td>
     <td width="10" background="../images/rep_right.jpg">
     <img src="../images/rep_right.jpg" width="10" height="1"></td>
    </tr>
    <tr>
     <td colspan="3" valign="top" align="center">
     <img src="../images/bottom_1.jpg" width="470" height="23"></td>
    </tr>
   </table>
  </td>
 </tr>
</table>
</td>
<td></td>
</tr>
</table>
</td>
<td> </td>
</tr>
<tr>
<td></td>
<td height="100%">
<table cellpadding="0" cellspacing="0" border="0"
width="100%" height="100%">
<tr>
<td style="height: 100%;
background-image: url(../images/rep_bot.jpg); background-repeat:
repeat-y; background-position: center;"></td>
</tr>
</table>
</td>
<td></td>
</tr>
</table>
</form>
</body>
</html>
```

How It Works

The HTML you added contains a Label control named labelName along with a brief message informing the customer that they have been removed from the newsletter mailing list.

6. As a result of the Admin directory being password protected with forms authentication, you will need to specify that Unsubscribe.aspx will be the exception to the forms authentication by appending the following to the Web.config file within the Admin directory:

```
<?xml version="1.0"?>
<configuration>
    <appSettings/>
    <connectionStrings/>
    <system.web>
        <authorization>
            <deny users="?" />
        </authorization>
    </system.web>
    <location path="UnSubscribe.aspx">
        <system.web>
            <authorization>
                <allow users="*" />
            </authorization>
        </system.web>
    </location>
</configuration>
```

How It Works

The Web.config file originally specifies that all pages within the directory are inaccessible without being authenticated. However, by adding the path of the file Unsubscribe.aspx using the location tag, you can specify that this page is actually accessible without the user being authenticated. You accomplish this by using an asterisk for the users element.

7. Now add the following C# code to the Unsubscribe.aspx web form:

```
using System;
using System.Data;
using System.Configuration;
using System.Collections;
using System.Web;
using System.Web.Security;
using System.Web.UI;
using System.Web.UI.WebControls;
using System.Web.UI.WebControls.WebParts;
using System.Web.UI.HtmlControls;

using LittleItalyVineyard.Common;
using LittleItalyVineyard.BusinessLogic;

public partial class Admin_UnSubscribe : System.Web.UI.Page
{
    protected void Page_Load( object sender , EventArgs e )
    {
```

```
        if ( !IsPostBack )
        {
            UnsubscribeCustomer();
            labelName.Text = Request.QueryString["FullName"];
        }
    }

    private void UnsubscribeCustomer()
    {
        ProcessNewsletterUnsubscribe unsubscribe =➥
          new ProcessNewsletterUnsubscribe();
        EndUser enduser = new EndUser();
        enduser.EndUserID = int.Parse( Request.QueryString["EndUserID"] );

        unsubscribe.EndUser = enduser;

        try
        {
            unsubscribe.Invoke();
        }
        catch
        {
            Response.Redirect( "../ErrorPage.aspx" );
        }
    }
}
```

How It Works

The final piece of functionality you just added checks for a postback, and within the UnsubscribeCustomer method, you instantiate the ProcessNewsletterUnsubscribe class from the business logic tier, populate the EndUserID from the query string, and finally call the Invoke() method. Lastly, by using the FullName query string, the labelName's text will be set to the customer's full name.

This brings you to the completion of another exercise; you now have the functionality that will allow the customers who are subscribed to the newsletter to unsubscribe, if necessary.

Summary

In this chapter, you explored a few techniques you can use to promote additional products and attempt to upsell the products from an online store. With the completion of this functionality, you can be confident that you have the fully functional e-commerce application that you initially set out to build. Not only can customers search and browse through the product catalog, but you can also attempt to promote related products and try to upsell the orders being placed by the customers.

CHAPTER 25

■■■

Accessing the Money from the Credit Card Transaction

At this point in the book, you have not only implemented the functionality to allow the administrator to fulfill orders and fully process them but also to promote additional sales. Now that you have completed the sales portion of the application, I'll discuss another important aspect of the overall process of selling online: accessing the money from the credit card transaction. Obviously, when the products are sold and shipped to the customer, the business wants access to that money as quickly as possible.

Once a customer pays for their products with their credit card, the funds are not readily available for use for the company. The funds are still within the credit card–processing company, which in this case is PayPal. In this chapter, I will discuss the methods that are available for obtaining the funds from the PayPal account, specifically by placing them into a checking account for the business, which can then use the funds.

■**Note** All your previous work regarding PayPal involved the PayPal test account, or the *sandbox* account. The sandbox account does not have the ability to transfer any funds because the funds are fictitious. Because of this, in this chapter, the figures and discussion will be directly related to the live PayPal account.

Transferring Funds

The most common way to access the funds from PayPal is to have PayPal transfer the money to the bank account registered within your PayPal profile. Using a direct transfer of funds is also the fastest and cheapest method. There is no cost involved, and the funds are available in your bank account within three to four days.

The following exercise will demonstrate how to transfer the funds in PayPal to your bank account.

Exercise: Transferring Your Money

This exercise shows how to transfer the funds that are available in your PayPal account to your business bank account. Follow these steps:

1. Log in to your PayPal account located at `https://www.paypal.com`. Enter your username and password, and within a few seconds, you will arrive at the home page, as shown in Figure 25-1.

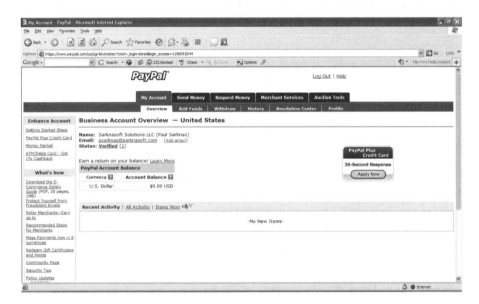

Figure 25-1. *The PayPal account home page*

2. Prior to transferring any funds, you need to be sure you have a registered bank account on file with PayPal. To do so, click the Profile tab and then the link Bank Accounts in the Financial Information section. This will navigate you to the page that lists the currently registered bank accounts, as shown in Figure 25-2.

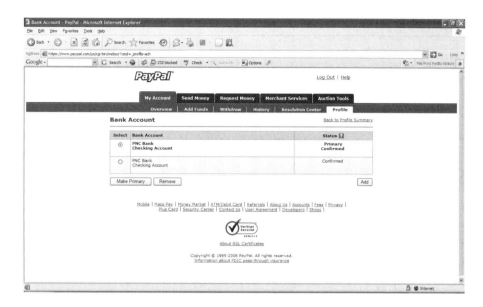

Figure 25-2. *The bank accounts*

3. On this web page, you can select the primary bank account you want to use. Or, if you do not have any current accounts registered, click the Add button to complete the registration process for a new bank account. Next, click the Withdraw tab, and you will be taken to the page shown in Figure 25-3 that presents the different options for withdrawing the funds from PayPal.

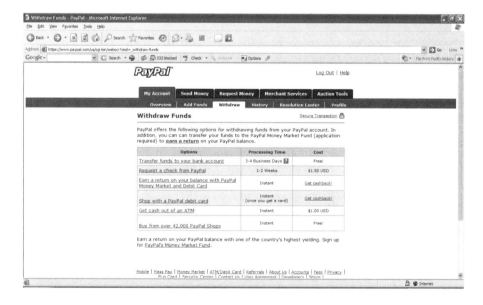

Figure 25-3. *Withdraw options*

4. From the different options available, click the first option, Transfer Funds to Your Bank Account. You'll then see the screen shown in Figure 25-4.

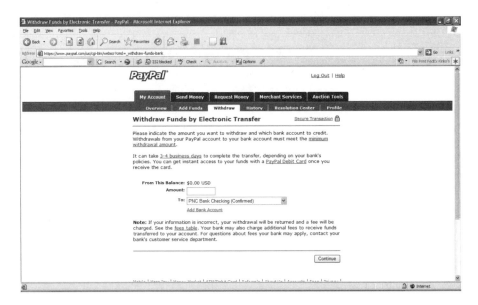

Figure 25-4. *Electronic transfer*

5. To complete the transfer, enter the amount you want to transfer from the available balance within the PayPal account, and click the Continue button. After confirming the transfer, the funds will be readily available in your bank account within three to four days.

This exercise showed you how to receive the funds that you have collected from the sales and showed how to transfer the funds to your checking account.

Accessing the Money in Other Ways

Although transferring the funds is the most common method used, it is important to realize that PayPal offers additional methods to access your funds. In the following sections, I will discuss some of the highlights of the additional options that are available.

Requesting a Check

Another option for accessing the funds from your PayPal account is to request a physical check. This costs an additional $1.50 (at the time of this writing), and it takes longer for the check to be processed and mailed to the address you specify.

Money Market

PayPal offers a money market where you can keep your funds and earn a return. This isn't really a way to gain access to your funds like the other methods discussed, but nonetheless it is an option available to you.

Debit Card

A debit card is available where you can access the funds directly from PayPal. Once you have requested and obtained your debit card, you can utilize the funds in your PayPal account by using the card to make purchases wherever MasterCard is accepted. This could make a perfect backup method for your transfers.

Cash with ATM

Along with making purchases with the debit card, the ability to withdraw your funds from the PayPal account in the form of cash from an ATM machine is also available. Some associated fees are involved.

Purchase from PayPal Shops

The final option is to shop directly with the PayPal funds at one of the PayPal shops indicated online within the PayPal account. Although this is not a method of withdrawing the funds, it could come in handy if you need to make a purchase with your funds.

Summary

In this chapter, I discussed an important aspect of selling products online. As mentioned, once a customer makes a purchase and pays for the merchandise, ideally you want to gain access to the funds as soon as possible. I demonstrated the various methods to gain access to your funds when using PayPal to process your credit cards. If you are not using PayPal to process your credit card payments, check with your processing company to learn how to withdraw your money. Lastly, it's a good idea to keep some of the funds in either the PayPal account (or the account that you use for credit card transactions) so that when you need to issue a refund, you'll have sufficient funds.

PART 7

■ ■ ■

Deployment

It has been quite an experience developing the application thus far. You have completed the code and development that is required for the official release of the application. As a result, you need to prepare the code for eventual deployment to the production environment. This part will outline the options that are available for compiling, building, and copying the code to the production servers.

CHAPTER 26

■ ■ ■

Exploring Your Compilation and Deployment Options

You are almost ready to deploy the finalized application and source code to the production environment and servers. Before placing the compiled code in the production environment, though, you need to do some necessary preparation work.

In this chapter, I will discuss the options for making as smooth a transition as possible when deploying the application to production and officially "going live." Specifically, I will cover the following topics:

- Building the code

- Precompiling and publishing the application

- Finalizing the application

Building the Code

Throughout the course of developing the application for the case study, you have compiled and built the complete source code several times. Now that you have completed the development, you will build the source code for a final time. When doing so, pay special attention to any errors that you might discover, and examine any of the warnings that are present.

Any warnings that have accumulated during the development will not prevent you from compiling and running the source code, but nevertheless you should address these warnings prior to officially launching the application. Warnings could appear for many reasons. It could be that variables being used are not initialized to a value when defined; or perhaps you added some code that originated from a previous version of the framework, and the functionality is being phased out.

Regardless, it is always considered a best practice to address these warning even though they will not prohibit you from running the application; it's more of an overall maintenance or housekeeping task.

Precompiling and Publishing

The latest release of Visual Studio 2005 allows you to prepare your source code prior to deploying to production. Take a step back, and recall how ASP.NET applications were deployed in previous versions: essentially the source code was built, and upon success, the web forms and only the DLLs were copied to the production server. Once the code was copied to the production server, the first request of the application would encounter a brief delay. This was not something that hampered your efforts in a major capacity, but with the latest release of Visual Studio 2005 and the .NET Framework 2.0, you have some additional options.

The most prominent option with regards to compiling and deploying the application is the ability to *precompile* the web application. Choosing this option will shorten the processing time that is experienced when your application is requested for the first time on the production server. Instead of your customers experiencing this first hit on the application, the precompilation will act as the first hit on the application by forcing all the pages and code to compile into assemblies.

The following exercise will demonstrate how you precompile your application.

Exercise: Precompiling the Source Code

This exercise is fairly brief in nature, but it outlines the necessary steps to precompile your source code. Follow these steps:

1. Create a new folder on your local machine where you will save the precompiled code. I like to create a new folder named precomp on my desktop. However, you can create a new folder wherever you want and give it the name of your choosing.

2. Right-click the web project, and select Publish Web Site, as shown in Figure 26-1.

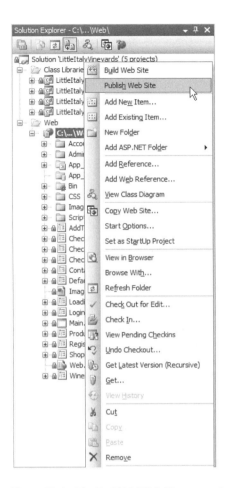

Figure 26-1. *The Publish Web Site menu item*

3. You will now see the Publish Web Site dialog box, as shown in Figure 26-2.

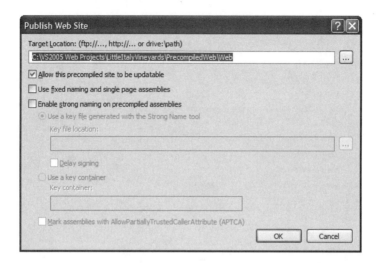

Figure 26-2. *The Publish Web Site dialog box*

Notice that there are three options when publishing. The first option, Allow This Precompiled Site to Be Updatable, will be checked. With this option, all the code of the application will be compiled into assemblies, and any web forms (.aspx files) will be copied as is to the folder that was specified for the publishing results. The second option, Use Fixed Naming and Single Page Assemblies, results in the compilation creating user-friendly names of the assemblies as opposed to the hashed values being used for the naming. Lastly, the third option, Enable Strong Naming on Precompiled Assemblies, tells the publishing process to use strong-named assemblies with a key file or a key container, which will result in additional security.

4. The next task is to navigate to the newly created folder you created in step 1 and set the target location for the publishing. Then click the OK button. In a few seconds, the publishing will complete, which is indicated in the lower-left section of the Visual Studio 2005 integrated development environment (IDE). Proceed to the folder where Visual Studio placed the published files, as shown in Figure 26-3.

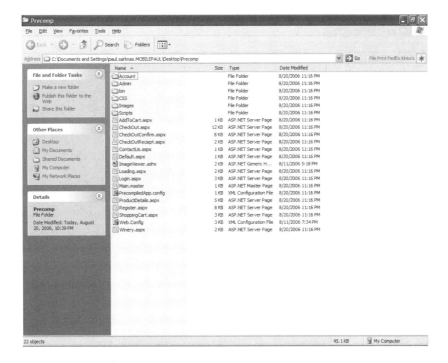

Figure 26-3. *The published files*

These are the published files that are ready to be copied to the production servers. For now, though, you will hold off on copying any of the files; instead, you will wait until the next chapter when the configurations are complete and then copy them to production.

Finalizing the Application

To finalize preparing the compiled source code for the production environment, you still have one aspect to address—taking the precompiled code that is generated and disabling the debugging feature. Turning off debugging is not an absolute requirement for deploying the code to production; however, it is not necessary for the compiled code to generate any debugging overhead when running on the production server. Eliminating this overhead will enhance the performance of the overall application. At first, when only a few users are utilizing the application, it may not be readily apparent that this increases performance, but as the application expands in popularity and you see increased traffic, the benefit of eliminating the debugging overhead will then become obvious. The following exercise shows you how to finalize the application.

Exercise: Finalizing the Application

This exercise shows how to turn off the debugging overhead and specify the production uniform resource locator (URL) for PayPal. Follow these steps:

1. To disable the debugging functionality, proceed to the directory where the source code was precompiled and then to the Web.config file. Open the Web.config file in Notepad; you will see the following contents:

```
<?xml version="1.0"?>
<!--
    Note: As an alternative to hand editing this file you can use the
    web admin tool to configure settings for your application. Use
    the Website->Asp.Net Configuration option in Visual Studio.
    A full list of settings and comments can be found in
    machine.config.comments usually located in
    \Windows\Microsoft.Net\Framework\v2.x\Config
-->
<configuration>
<appSettings>
<!-- Sandbox PayPal -->
<add key="PayPalAPIUsername" value="psarknas_api1.yahoo.com"/>
<add key="PayPalAPIPassword" value="R97V3NVZUPH92PK8"/>
<add key="PayPalAPIURL" value="https://api-aa.sandbox.paypal.com/2.0/"/>

<add key="CertificatePath" value="~/Certs/LittleItalyVineyards.p12"/>
<add key="CertificatePassword" value="ps5150"/>

<add key="TaxRate" value="7"/>
<add key="SMTPServerName" value="localhost"/>
<add key="ToAddress" value="info@littleitalyvineyards.com"/>
</appSettings>
<connectionStrings>
<add name="SQLCONN"
connectionString="server=Lumberg\SQL2005;uid=sa;
pwd=*****;database=LittleItalyVineyard"/>
</connectionStrings>
<system.web>
<!--
            Set compilation debug="true" to insert debugging
            symbols into the compiled page. Because this
            affects performance, set this value to true only
            during development.
-->
<compilation debug="true">
<assemblies>
<add assembly="System.Security, Version=2.0.0.0,
  Culture=neutral, PublicKeyToken=B03F5F7F11D50A3A"/>
```

```
</assemblies></compilation>
<!--
            The <authentication> section enables configuration
            of the security authentication mode used by
            ASP.NET to identify an incoming user.
        -->
<authentication mode="Forms">
            <forms name="LITTLEITALYUTH" loginUrl="~/Admin/Login.aspx"
protection="All"
timeout="120" path="/">
            </forms>
        </authentication>
        <authorization>
            <allow users="*"/>
        </authorization>
<!--
            The <customErrors> section enables configuration
            of what to do if/when an unhandled error occurs
            during the execution of a request. Specifically,
            it enables developers to configure html error pages
            to be displayed in place of a error stack trace.

        <customErrors mode="On"  defaultRedirect="ErrorPage.aspx">
        </customErrors>
            -->
</system.web>
</configuration>
```

2. Let's focus on the compilation tag that currently has the debugging value set to true:

```
<compilation debug="true">
```

Change the debug attribute to false:

```
<compilation debug="false">
```

3. Now change the PayPal sandbox URL to the live PayPal URL for utilizing the PayPal APIs:

```
<add key="PayPalAPIURL"
value="https://api-aa.paypal.com/2.0/
  "/>
```

Also, do not forget to register for your live account with PayPal and obtain and use a live certificate. You will also need to change the username and password values in the Web.config file too.

4. Finally, save the changes.

In this exercise, you disabled the debugging feature and changed the PayPal URL and are now ready to deploy the finalized code to the production servers, which you'll do in the next chapter.

Summary

This chapter demonstrated how to prepare and precompile the source code with the intent of copying the finalized code to the production environment and servers. In next chapter, you will officially launch the application by configuring the hosting environment along with any other configurations that may be necessary.

■■■

CHAPTER 27

Configuring the Production Environment

In this chapter, you'll address where your application will live in the vast world of the Internet. I will cover the hosting plan along with its necessary configurations and setup. You can choose from many options of hosting plans. Therefore, the goal of this chapter is to explain the options available and provide guidance for configuring the production environment.

More specifically, this chapter will cover the following topics:

- Registering and configuring the domain

- Developing a website hosting plan

- Setting up and configuring IIS and the database

- Installing the SSL certificate

- Deploying the application

Setting Up the Domain

Now that the application is ready for production, you will register a domain name for your application. This process is not overly complicated, especially as a result of the many companies that offer domain registration services. Domains are registered (rented, really) for a period of time, which is usually a minimum of one year, and for a specific fee, which will depend upon the registrar of the domain.

Registering Your Domain

As mentioned, several companies offer domain registration services. The following are a few:

- Yahoo

- GoDaddy

- Web.com

- Register.com

- Network Solutions

You should browse each of these companies' websites and investigate their services and prices so you can pick the best registrar for your situation.

The first step of registering a domain is to determine whether your desired domain is available. All companies that offer registration services will give you the ability to query the database of registered domains maintained by ICANN (http://www.icann.org). You simply enter the domain you want to register, and the query will be made to the registration database. The result of the query will inform you whether the domain is available. If the domain is not available, usually the registrar will suggest similar names or will suggest the same name with alternate suffixes such as .net, .tv, or perhaps .biz.

Going into greater detail about domain names and the registration process is outside the main scope of this book. However, it is important to understand the basics so you can deliver an application on the Internet for your client and in this instance for the case study. For the case study application, I have registered the domain littleitalyvineyards.com. The next step is to update the information regarding the name servers.

Setting Up the DNS Servers

Once you have successfully registered a domain, you need to tell the domain where to find the hosting plan. More specifically, you'll set the DNS servers of the hosting server. Regardless of where you register your domain, in most cases the registration company will supply you with a password-protected account where you can make changes to not only the billing, contact, and technical information but also to the DNS server entries.

At this point, you may not have a hosting plan established. If you do have a hosting plan and environment set up, you can go ahead and make the necessary DNS entries. If you do not, you can move to the next section of the chapter to learn about your hosting options.

Setting Up the Hosting Plan

A major aspect of having an e-commerce application, or any type of website, is to determine where it will be hosted. Hosting is basically where your web application will live, thus allowing the public to access it. Like with domain registrars, a great deal of competition exists, so you're sure to find affordable hosting services. In fact, many of the companies that offer domain registration services also offer hosting.

When shopping for hosting plans, you need to consider a number of aspects prior to making your decision. The case study requires a hosting plan that has the .NET Framework 2.0 installed along with access to a SQL Server 2005 database. Many of the hosting plans will offer this along with other features and component installations. The following are a few hosting companies that are of reputable status:

- MaximASP

- ORCS Web, Inc.

- DiscountASP.net

- 1 and 1 Internet Limited

- ASPWebhosting.com, LLC

These hosting companies are a few of many companies that offer ASP.NET 2.0 hosting. They also offer different types of hosting. More specifically, they offer shared or dedicated hosting. The difference is that with *shared hosting*, other web applications will be using the same web server and database server. The company will have security measures in place to keep your information isolated. This kind of hosting generally costs less and could be a good choice for launching a web application where you do not expect a great deal of traffic initially. You can later scale to meet increased traffic as the application grows. One downside of shared hosting is that you will usually not have full access to the web and database servers.

The other option is *dedicated hosting*, which means only you and your application will be using the hardware, and you will have full control of the operating system. This is generally more expensive but is best if your application is going to have a great deal of traffic from its inception.

Regardless of what type of hosting plan you choose or what company, make sure the company offers adequate customer and technical support, a backup system, redundant power supplies, and network connections. In fact, most companies advertise 99.9 percent uptime. Do not accept anything less for your needs.

Now that I have discussed many of the available options, I will share my preference. I prefer having a dedicated server as a hosting plan because of the control I get over the entire hardware. This option, however, costs more and really is effective only if you have many web applications that you need to host.

Many times when developing an application, a standard shared hosting plan will be more than sufficient to start. When this is the case, you will be provided with an FTP site to deploy your application where most of the configurations will be managed for you. At the same time, some applications will need dedicated hardware, as with the case study; therefore, you'll need to organize the configurations and setup.

Setting Up IIS and the Database

To configure and set up the hosting environment for Little Italy Vineyards, you need to address the database and web server. The web server that you'll use for the case study is Internet Information Services (IIS) 6.0, which is included in Windows Server 2003. You will need to make several configurations prior to uploading any of the compiled source code to the production server, as described in the following exercise.

Exercise: Configuring IIS

This exercise shows how to set up and configure IIS on the production server, Windows Server 2003. Follow these steps:

1. Since the selected hosting plan is a dedicated server that you have full control over, you have the ability to log in remotely to the server. You will use Terminal Server to log in to Windows Server 2003 and then proceed to the main directory of the web root for IIS. Depending on how the Windows installation was set up, this directory's location will vary. When this directory is located, create a directory named LittleItalyVinyards, as shown in Figure 27-1.

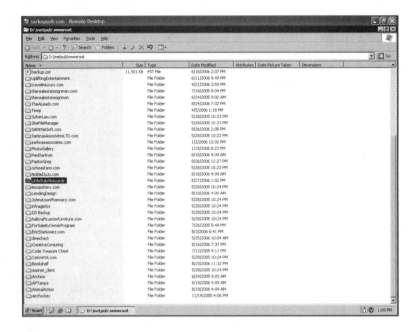

Figure 27-1. *The LittleItalyVineyards directory*

2. Launch IIS Manager. When it's displayed, expand the Web Sites folder, right-click the Web Sites directory, and select New ➤ Web Site, as shown in Figure 27-2.

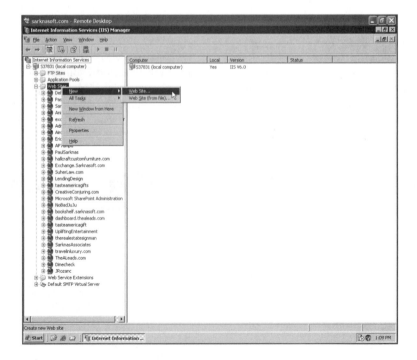

Figure 27-2. *Creating a new website with IIS*

3. Upon making the selection to create a new website, you will see the Welcome to the Web Site Creation Wizard. Click the Next button, and then enter the name of the website so IIS can identify it. You can simply enter **LittleItalyVineyards** for the case study, as shown in Figure 27-3.

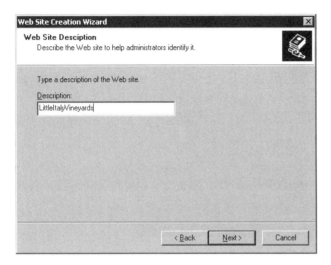

Figure 27-3. *Naming the new website*

4. Click the Next button, and you will be navigated to the next step of the wizard where you need to enter the IP and port settings. As shown in Figure 27-4, choose the All Unassigned option for the IP address; then enter **80** for the port, which is the default; and enter **www.littleitalyvineyards.com** for the host header.

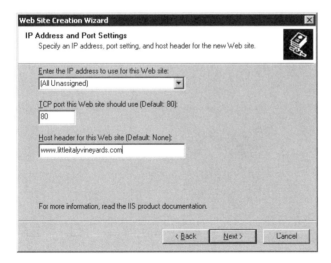

Figure 27-4. *Entering the IP address and port settings*

5. Click the Next button, and you will be navigated to the next wizard step where you should set the path to the main directory that you created in step 1, as shown in Figure 27-5.

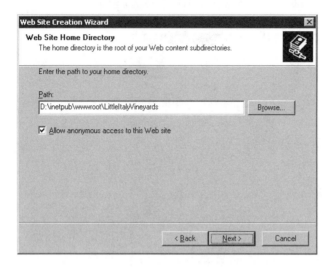

Figure 27-5. *Entering the website home directory*

6. Click the Next button, and then set the permissions for the website home directory. You can leave the selected default, which is Read, as shown in Figure 27-6. You should also choose the Run Scripts (Such As ASP) option.

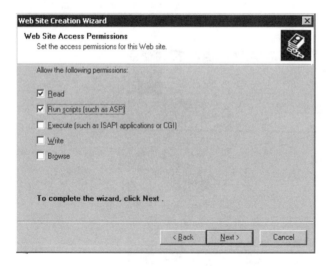

Figure 27-6. *Entering the website access permissions*

7. Click Next, and you will be presented with a notification that the wizard is complete. Click the Finish button, and you will see the new site created in the tree list on the left. Right-click the newly created website, and choose Properties, as shown in Figure 27-7.

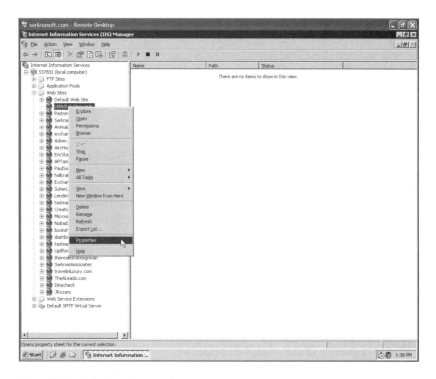

Figure 27-7. *Selecting Properties*

8. The Properties dialog box will be displayed for the website. Click the Advanced button, which will then display another dialog box, Advanced Web Site Identification. In this new dialog box, click the Add button. Then enter **80** for the TCP port, and enter the domain name, without the *www* prefix, as **littleitalyvineyards.com**, as shown in Figure 27-8.

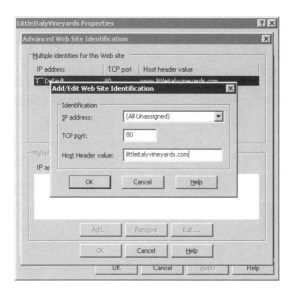

Figure 27-8. *The advanced website identification*

In this final step of the exercise, you enabled the web server to display the website if the user enters www.littleitalyvineyards.com or if they enter only littleitalyvineyards.com in their browser. At this point, you have the IIS web server configured to serve your website when the compiled source code is deployed.

Configuring the SQL Server 2005 Database

The next step is to configure your database. There will be different scenarios based upon what type of hosting plan you chose. If you have a dedicated server and hosting plan with full access to the hardware, your options are open as to how to configure the SQL Server database.

Regarding the case study, imagine that you have direct access to the hardware, so therefore you can run the complete SQL script to create the database. If the hosting plan that you have is a shared plan and you do not have full access to the hardware, many of the hosting companies will provide you with some type of control panel where you can either upload the SQL script or execute it. If you are still unsure as to how to accomplish this, contact the technical support group of the hosting plan you have decided upon, and they will be able to further assist you.

Configuring the SSL Certificate

In the following sections, I'll discuss how and where to obtain a certificate and how to install and configure it in your hosting environment. To refresh your memory as to why you need a certificate, you are not using a third-party shopping cart or credit card–processing server. You have implemented a custom shopping cart, and you will be submitting the customer's credit card information through the PayPal credit card–processing application programming interfaces (APIs). As a result of this action, you will be transmitting sensitive information from the client to server, so you need to do so over a secure channel. Now that you know why you need a certificate, I'll discuss where and how to obtain one and how to install it.

Obtaining the SSL Certificate

As mentioned, when registering a domain and finding a suitable hosting plan, you'll find a great deal of competition in the marketplace. Likewise, many companies provide certificates, and thus the cost is quite affordable. The following are just a few companies that offer certificates:

- GoDaddy

- Network Solutions

- VeriSign

- Thawte

- DigiCert

Examine each of these companies' websites and their associated prices for certificates, and then make a decision about purchasing from the company of your choosing. All the companies will have a slightly different registration and purchase process; however, regardless of what company you choose, you need to perform similar steps prior to receiving your actual certificate. Specifically, you need to generate a certificate-signing request (CSR) and then send it to the certificate provider to generate the actual certificate. The following exercise shows how to generate the CSR.

Exercise: Generating the CSR

This exercise shows how to generate the CSR that will be needed by the company providing the SSL certificate. Follow these steps:

1. Return to IIS Manager in the production server, and find the new website you created in the previous exercise. Right-click the website, choose Properties, and then choose the Directory Security tab, as shown in Figure 27-9.

Figure 27-9. *The Directory Security tab*

2. In the Secure Communications section, click the Server Certificate button. You will be presented with a wizard. Choose the first option, Create a New Certificate, as shown in Figure 27-10.

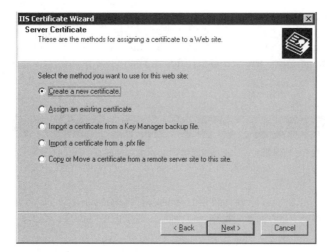

Figure 27-10. *Creating a new certificate*

3. Click Next, and then choose the option Prepare the Request Now, but Send It Later. Click the Next button again, and then enter a friendly name, as shown in Figure 27-11.

Figure 27-11. *Entering a friendly name*

4. Click Next twice. Then, enter the common name that will need to be a fully qualified domain name, **www.LittleItalyVineyards.com**, as shown in Figure 27-12.

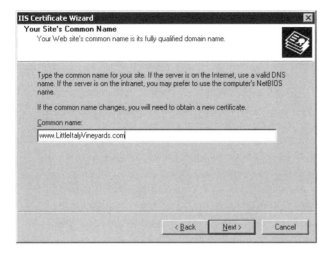

Figure 27-12. *Entering the common name*

5. Click the Next button, enter the geographic information about your company or website, and click Next again. The next step of the wizard is to select the path and filename for the CSR output request. Choose a path that is easy to navigate to, as shown in Figure 27-13, and then click the Next button once again.

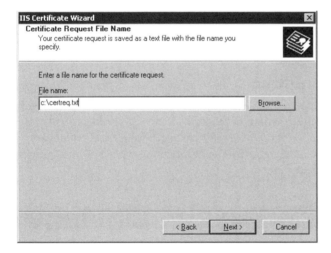

Figure 27-13. *Entering the path*

6. Next, you will see the information you have entered for confirmation. If you find everything satisfactory, finalize the wizard by clicking the Finish button. Then proceed to the where you saved the CSR output file. Open this file in Notepad, and it should look similar to the following:

```
-----BEGIN NEW CERTIFICATE REQUEST-----
MIIDaDCCAtECAQAwgYwxCzAJBgNVBAYTAlVTMQswCQYDVQQIEwJQQTETMBEGA1UE
BxMKUGlOdHNidXJnaDEfMBOGA1UEChMWTGlOdGxlIEloYWx5IFZpbmV5YXJkczET
MBEGA1UsvdANBgsvdbkiG9woBAQEFAAOBjQAwgYkCgYEAvO8pQWTJHmxF
5dhsOi8TD1MAQjlDbjiWjVuyUs1vxlSOOOhH3+Y3bB4FaSSTvbQ7uegJ2pCbheCZ
94gp/p1OsH2hvCYaCpt3Cnt2DueTAnr7VrYZSiEn+tnpcNgPFz+JRwmnyRXzlWJ8
9XX1xdNAGm3sbsFksEUTN5F/SD4LBcCAwEAAaCCAZkwGgYKKwYBBAGCNwOCAzEM
Fgo1LjIuMzc5MC4yMHsGCisGAQQBgjcCAsdvxbf1UdDwEB/wQEAwIE8DBE
BgkqhkiG9woBCQ8ENzA1MA4GCCqGSIb3DQMCAgIAgDAOBggqhkiG9woDBAICAIAw
BwYFKw4DAgcwCgYIKoZIhvcNAwcwEwYDVROlBAwdbYAdAAgAFIAUwBBACAA
UwBDAGgAYQBuAG4AZQBsACAAQwByAHkAcABOAG8AZwByAGEAcABoAGkAYwAgAFAA
cgBvAHYAaQBkAGUAcgOBiQAAAAAAAAAAAAAAAAAAAAAAAAAAAAAAAAAAAAAAAAAAAA
AAAAAAAAAAAAAAAAAAAAAAAAAAAAAAAAAAAAAAAAAAAAAAAAAAAAAAAAAAAAAAAAAA
AAAAAAAAAAAAAAAAAAAAAAAAAAAAAAAAAAAAAAAAAAAAAAAAAAAAAAAAAAAAAAAAAA
AAAAAAAAAAAs8whGItBrbjoIdJuZtxP3/DodS7yaTvjbUNIaPZoDv4vs
ROtgoYYbi6bTQKtM2hZ8b9uYCt1jVnmxJHkhGHj9g9AvQO6iS8yJzVclrxg7R6FL
NAGm3sbsFksEUTN5F/SD4LBcCAwEAAaCCAZkwGgYKKwsidobhswoiaoewianacac
cFG6GLQvNX8k2j9S
-----END NEW CERTIFICATE REQUEST-----
```

Copy this file or the contents of this file. You will need to submit this information to the company or provider from which you purchased the SSL certificate. Typically, when making a purchase for an SSL certificate, you will be able to enter the CSR information displayed here, and then you will be able to generate the finalized SSL certificate, which you will receive via e-mail or via download from the provider.

Installing the SSL Certificate

The next step is to install the finalized SSL certificate that is generated from the provider to which you submitted the CSR information. As mentioned, the SSL certificate will probably be e-mailed to you or will be provided via a link on the provider's website. In either case, when you have the finalized SSL certificate, return to the production server. The next exercise demonstrates how to install the certificate.

Exercise: Installing the SSL Certificate

This exercise shows how to install the purchased SSL certificate on the production server. Follow these steps:

1. Locate the finalized SSL certificate that you received (either via e-mail or via download) from the provider. Once you have located this, copy this file to the production server, and then launch IIS Manager. Select the website you created earlier, and right-click it. Choose the Properties menu item and then the Directory Security tab. Click the Server Certificate button, and proceed to the wizard. Choose the Process the Pending Request and Install the Certificate option, as shown in Figure 27-14.

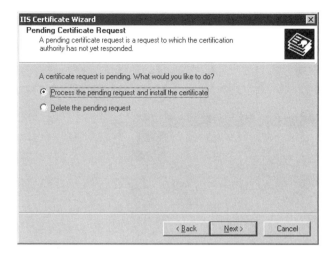

Figure 27-14. *Processing the pending request*

2. Click the Next button, and browse to the location in which you uploaded or saved the SSL certificate. This will have a file extension of *.crt, so you might need to change the File of Type drop-down list in the Open dialog box to view the certificate file, as shown in Figure 27-15.

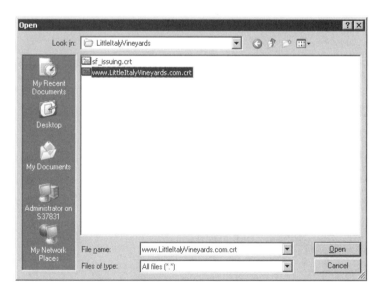

Figure 27-15. *Locating the certificate file*

3. The next step of the wizard will ask which port should be used for SSL transmissions. The default value of 443, as shown in Figure 27-16, will be adequate for your needs.

■**Note** As a result of the hosting environment in this exercise being a name-based hosting environment (or more specifically, allowing you to have multiple websites hosted with one IP address), you can have only one SSL certificate installed and configured.

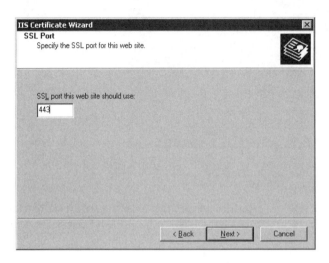

Figure 27-16. *The SSL port*

4. Moving along, you will be prompted to confirm the configuration information, as shown in Figure 27-17. If the information is to your liking, finalize the wizard by clicking the Next button.

Figure 27-17. *Confirming the configuration information*

You have completed the hosting configuration and the SSL certificate installation, so you can now process secure orders.

Deploying the Application

All that remains is to deploy, or copy, the compiled source code to the production environment. To accomplish this final task, you need to remember back to Chapter 26 where you compiled the source code to prepare it for production. If you have made any changes since then, recompile the code.

Copying the Source Code

For the most part, regardless of what hosting plan you have decided upon, you will be able to upload the compiled source code to the production servers via FTP. In some cases, you might have access to a VPN connection where you can connect to the production environment as opposed to an FTP connection. Regardless, connect to the directory that you have configured in this chapter (or what is supplied to you from your hosting plan), and copy the compiled source code to the production server. After copying the source code, you are now ready to perform some additional testing on the production platform and then, with the blessing of your client, take the entire application live to your customers.

Finalizing the Web.config File

Now that you have decided on a hosting plan and are ready to utilize the system in the production environment, you need to address one last issue. Specifically, you need to alter some values in the Web.config file. The section of the Web.config file that you need to change is the connection string to the database from what was being used in the development environment to what will be used in the production environment:

```
<connectionStrings>
    <add name="SQLCONN"
        connectionString="server=production_server_example;uid=sa;
        pwd=production_password;database=LittleItalyVineyard"/>
</connectionStrings>
```

In the connectionStrings tag, the name will remain the same as a result of it being referred to in the source code. However, the connectionStrings element will change since you need to specify a different server name on which the database will reside as well as specify the credentials for this database server. Again, depending on your selected hosting plan, you might need to refer to the documentation or the administrator for this information.

Finally, if you have not done so, you need to change the PayPal API username and password to use the APIs in the live PayPal system.

Summary

Well, it has been a long trip, but you have now completed the next-to-last chapter in the book. After finishing this chapter, you can officially launch your e-commerce application to your customers. The next chapter will discuss some best practices and issues to be aware of as you launch the application, and it will cover what tools you can use to monitor and provide maintenance. See you in the next chapter to wrap up your project!

PART 8

■ ■ ■

Aftercare

The application that you have worked so diligently on is now complete and deployed to the production environment. After some additional testing and feedback from the client, you can officially announce and launch the application to the public and to your customers. After that occurs, most of the hard work is complete—but not all of it. You still need to closely monitor the application and provide maintenance for it. This final part of the book will outline some of the best practices for providing aftercare for your application.

CHAPTER 28

Supporting and Maintaining the Application

Can you believe it? You have finally arrived at the last chapter of your long journey. You have engaged in quite a bit of planning, developing, coding, and configuring, all performed with one goal in mind: delivering the best possible e-commerce application to your client and ultimately to your client's customers.

This final chapter will discuss the following:

- Monitoring the traffic

- Correcting errors

- Optimizing the application

Monitoring the Application

One of the most important tasks after you officially launch your e-commerce application is to monitor it closely. This includes monitoring the overall traffic that the site generates as well as monitoring any errors or exceptions that might arise during the initial duration of the application's life.

Many commercial tools are available that you can use to generate reports of the traffic that your site generates. Many of these tools utilize the log files that are generated from the IIS web server because a wealth of information is available there. You can also implement your own traffic-monitoring device or functionality, but this can end up being quite tedious, especially after you have invested so much time in building the application.

Therefore, I recommend you purchase a third-party tool that will monitor the traffic for you; you will be amazed at the reports you can generate from these tools. Some examples of third-party tools and companies are as follows:

- WebLog Expert

- Alter Wind

- Open Tracker

Depending on your budget and individual needs, simply search for these tools, and follow their instructions for implementing them to gain access to valuable information about your web application's traffic. Some of the tools will be provided as a service with a monthly cost, and others may allow you to purchase the software for a one-time fee.

My favorite is WebLog Expert, which you can find at http://www.weblogexpert.com. The software comes in two versions, the lite version and the expert version. The lite version is actually free but, as you might expect, does not have the same functionality as the expert version. The expert version has the ability to send the compiled reports in different formats via e-mail or FTP. Even with these additional features, though, the cost of the software tool is still quite affordable.

Why This Is Important

It is important to closely monitor the traffic from your e-commerce application for several reasons. For starters, if there is a steady increase of traffic over time, you will need to prepare for this by scaling the hosting plan to accommodate the abundance of traffic. Generating reports about the traffic is a great tool to keep a close eye on everything.

Another valuable reason is that most of the traffic-monitoring tools will provide you with information about where your users or customers originated. Therefore, if you have been advertising on another affiliate website or several websites, you will be able to monitor how successful these advertising campaigns are to your application and business by viewing how many individuals are originating from each source.

Lastly, you will also be able to identify any errors that have been occurring. The next section of the chapter will discuss this in more detail.

Performance

In addition to monitoring the traffic of your web application, it's important to monitor the overall performance. This type of monitoring is important because there is no true test for how the application will perform until you deploy it to the production environment and the users begin utilizing it.

One such tool provided by Microsoft is Performance Monitor. Performance Monitor can give you real-time statistics about an ASP.NET application running on a server. These statistics include the amount of CPU cycles being used, the number of threads being used, and the amount of memory being consumed. To use this tool, click the Windows Start button, and then select Run. Type **perfmon** in the Run dialog box. When you execute this command, the Performance Monitor will launch, as shown in Figure 28-1.

When the Performance Monitor appears, you can use three default counters: pages/sec, average queue disk length, and % processor time. Since you are more concerned with ASP.NET counters, you can add ASP.NET specific counters by right-clicking the main window and choosing Add Counters. After choosing this menu item, the Add Counters dialog box will launch, as shown in Figure 28-2.

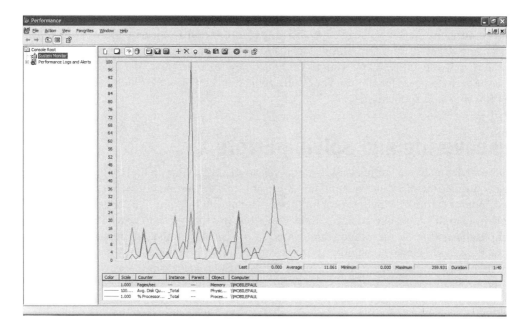

Figure 28-1. *The Performance Monitor*

Figure 28-2. *Adding a performance counter*

When the Add Counters dialog box appears, you'll see a drop-down list of many different performance objects that you can view. Focusing on the ASP.NET objects, choose the ASP.NET object, and select All Counters. This will then add all the performance counters to the monitor that pertain to the ASP.NET applications running on the specified machine. On the top menu, click the various views. Finally, run your web application, and view the different counters to monitor your web application.

Discovering and Solving Errors

Undoubtedly, after you launch your e-commerce application, you will find that some errors are occurring. You might luck out and find these errors in the testing phase, but that is certainly not the norm. The main reason for this is that you can test only to a certain degree to find any complications in your application. Therefore, it is important to watch for any of these complications after the application is launched so you can diagnose them quickly, make the corrections, and redeploy the updated source code.

In the case study, you added some basic logging of any exceptions that occur within the application. However, you will need to check this log frequently so you can determine whether errors have been encountered. An excellent addition is to create an e-mailing feature for the exceptions so that you do not have to check the log manually all the time.

Optimizing the Application

As your application lives longer and expands, the goal is to gain more and more traffic for the e-commerce site. Knowing this, you will probably find some bottlenecks in certain areas that you'll want to address. Or you might come to the conclusion that you need to scale the hosting platform to accommodate the increased volumes of traffic. Although this is a great problem to have because it will potentially mean more sales for the company, it will require some additional work.

As a result, you will need to make some optimizations to your application. Optimizations can take many forms, such as additional caching of data, stress testing of the overall application, or even the introduction of a new feature, such as SQL cache invalidation. You can cache data within the code in the form of retaining information on the server. As the product catalog grows, this is a prime candidate for implementing SQL Server caching.

SQL caching invalidation is a new feature within the .NET Framework 2.0 and SQL Server 2005 where you can have the local machine or client cache information keep displaying the cached data until a value in a specified table occurs. This is a great technique for the product catalog so that if there are no alterations made to the overall catalog, the cached information will be displayed when requested by a customer.

The following exercise shows how to set up the SQL caching invalidation functionality.

Exercise: Implementing SQL Cache Invalidation

This exercise shows the necessary configurations within SQL Server 2005 as well as any web forms that will take advantage of this feature. Follow these steps:

1. You need to configure the LittleItalyVineyards database and the table so you can achieve SQL caching. You do this by using the ASPNET_REGSQL utility. This utility is included when the .NET 2.0 Framework is installed and is in the following directory:

   `%windir%\Microsoft.NET\Framework\FrameworkVersion`

   Be sure that %windir% represents the Windows default directory where the .NET Framework 2.0 is installed along with the version. At the time of this writing, version 2.0.50727 of the .NET Framework 2.0 is being used, so the full file path will look like the following:

   `C:\WINDOWS\Microsoft.NET\Framework\v2.0.50727`

   You'll need to use this path in the command window in the next step.

2. In the previous step, you determined where the ASPNET_REGSQL utility is located. Now you can use the utility by opening a command window. Click the Start button, and then click Run. In the Run window, type **cmd**, and click OK. In the command window, change the directory to the path where the utility is located by using the following command:

   `cd C:\WINDOWS\Microsoft.NET\Framework\v2.0.50727`

   The command prompt will be set in the command window, as shown in Figure 28-3.

Figure 28-3. *The command prompt*

An easier way to run the utility is to launch the Visual Studio 2005 command prompt by clicking the Start button and then selecting Programs ➤ Microsoft Visual Studio 2005 ➤ Visual Studio Tools ➤ Visual Studio 2005 Command Prompt. By launching this tool, a command prompt will be automatically launched with a path that lets you run the ASPNET_REGSQL utility without entering the path manually.

3. From this point, you can focus on the utility. The ASPNET_REGSQL utility needs specific information passed as parameters, including the server name, username, password, database name, and database table name. So, enter the following command all on one line:

```
aspnet_regsql -S <Server> -U <Username> -P <Password>
-ed -d LittleItalyVineyard -et -t [Table Name]
```

How It Works

As mentioned, the ASPNET_REGSQL utility requires a certain number of parameters. You also need to specify two other switches. As shown, you already specified the server name, username, and password. However, after the password, you specify the switch –ed to enable a database for SQL cache dependency. Following the switch is the database name, LittleItalyVineyard, and then the final switch, –et. The –et switch simply instructs the utility to enable a database table for SQL cache dependency followed by the name of the table you want the caching to monitor. Lastly, if your security model for your database is using integrated security, you have the ability to provide a connection string specifying the switch –C.

4. After entering the complete utility command with the specified parameters, press Enter, and if the utility executes without any errors, you'll see a message indicating that the command has finished and the configuration is complete.

Note Administrative access will need to be granted to the database to use the ASPNET_REGSQL utility.

---

5. A few last pieces of functionality remain. You need to make an addition to the root Web.config file, as follows:

```
<caching>
    <sqlCacheDependency enabled="true" pollTime="60000">
        <databases>
            <add name="LittleItalyVineyard" connectionStringName="SQLCONN" />
        </databases>
    </sqlCacheDependency>
</caching>
```

How It Works

In the Web.config file, the SqlCacheDependency is enabled to true, and it references SQLCONN as the connection string to use. Lastly, the pollTime element is set to 60000, which is evaluated in milliseconds; this means that one time per every minute, the application will check the cache table for changes.

6. The last task necessary is within the actual web forms where the SQL caching will take place. You will provide a template for what needs to be added to the web forms. Therefore, add the following page directives to any web form where you want to take advantage of this caching functionality:

```
<%@ OutputCache Duration="3600"
SqlDependency="LittleItalyVineyard:[Table Name]"
VaryByParam="none" %>
```

How It Works

These page directives specify the SqlDependency using the LittleItalyVineyard database and the name of the table. When this is placed in a web form, any data being displayed from the table specified from the LittleItalyVineyard database will be cached until a change or update is made to the specified table. VaryByParam is a required parameter that specifies whether any variables will be cached in separate entries. Lastly, the Duration parameter is also required, which specifies the length of time the cache will remain, also measured in milliseconds.

You have arrived at the end of the final exercise—congratulations! You have the required knowledge to implement caching for your application, which will allow for greater performance.

Summary

At long last, you have completed the entire e-commerce application. You should definitely congratulate yourself because you had quite a lot of information to comprehend. You can view the case study application that was built step by step in this book at http://www.littleitalyvineyards.com, and you can test the functionality as a customer or as an administrator. You can download all the source code for this case study site from the Apress website.

I would sincerely like to thank you for purchasing this book, and I thoroughly hope you enjoyed the challenge and learning opportunity. If at any time you have any questions, do not hesitate to contact me at my company's website, http://www.sarknasoft.com, or at my personal website, http://www.paulsarknas.com. I would love to hear your feedback about your experience.

Lastly, I am available on a consulting basis for any of your technology needs, including building an application from scratch, offering guidance for an existing project, or helping resolve a difficult scenario or business logic question. I hope to hear from you soon!

Index

You Need the Companion eBook

Your purchase of this book entitles you to buy the companion PDF-version eBook for only $10. Take the weightless companion with you anywhere.

We believe this Apress title will prove so indispensable that you'll want to carry it with you everywhere, which is why we are offering the companion eBook (in PDF format) for $10 to customers who purchase this book now. Convenient and fully searchable, the PDF version of any content-rich, page-heavy Apress book makes a valuable addition to your programming library. You can easily find and copy code—or perform examples by quickly toggling between instructions and the application. Even simultaneously tackling a donut, diet soda, and complex code becomes simplified with hands-free eBooks!

Once you purchase your book, getting the $10 companion eBook is simple:

❶ Visit **www.apress.com/promo/tendollars/**.

❷ Complete a basic registration form to receive a randomly generated question about this title.

❸ Answer the question correctly in 60 seconds, and you will receive a promotional code to redeem for the $10.00 eBook.

2560 Ninth Street • Suite 219 • Berkeley, CA 94710

eBookshop

THE EXPERT'S VOICE™

Offer valid through 6/30/07.